The Murder of
Billie-Jo

The Murder of Billie-Jo

Siôn Jenkins and Bob Woffinden

metro

Published by Metro Publishing
an imprint of John Blake Publishing Ltd
3 Bramber Court, 2 Bramber Road,
London W14 9PB, England

www.johnblakepublishing.co.uk

First published in paperback in 2009

ISBN: 978-1-84454-818-7

British Library Cataloguing-in-Publication Data:

A catalogue record for this book is available from the British Library.

Design by www.envydesign.co.uk

Printed in Great Britain by CPI Bookmarque Ltd, Croydon CRO 4TD

1 3 5 7 9 10 8 6 4 2

Papers used by John Blake Publishing are natural, recyclable products made from
wood grown in sustainable forests. The manufacturing processes conform to the
environmental regulations of the country of origin.

Photographs courtesy of Siôn Jenkins, Davinia Close, Rob Brown, PA Photos,
Getty Images and Rex Features

Contents

PART II: THE LAST SIGH

PART III: THE INVARIABLE CLUE

Chronology

13 March	Siôn re-arrested
14 March	Siôn charged with murder and held on remand
17 March	Sussex police visist Dr Arnon Bentovim
20 March	Sussex police 'debrief' the children, telling them their father murdered Billie-Jo
21 March	Bentovim report delivered
26 March	Siôn given bail and returns to Aberystwyth

1998

22 April	Trial (1) due to start; delayed
3 June	Trial (1) begins
2 July	Siôn convicted of murder and sentenced to life imprisonment
21 December	Leave to appeal granted

1999

30 November	Appeal (1) begins
21 December	Appeal (1) dismissed

2000

14 January	Leave to go to House of Lords refused

2002

5 February	Annie and Charlotte re-interviewed

2003

12 May	Case referred back to appeal
23 July	Lois makes crucial third statement, repudiating her daughters' evidence

2004

15 June	At Royal Brompton hospital in London, scientists examining slides of Billie-Jo's lungs realise she had pulmonary interstitial emphysema
30 June	Appeal (2) begins
16 July	Appeal succeeds. Conviction quashed; retrial ordered
2 August	Siôn granted bail and leaves prison
6 August	Mrs Justice Rafferty orders removal of campaign website

2005

7 February	Siôn marries Tina Ferneyhough
8 April	Trial (2) due to start; delayed
22 April	Trial (2) begins
11 July	Trial ends; jury unable to agree
31 October	Trial (3) begins

2006

9 February	Jury unable to agree; Siôn acquitted

Introduction

I am an innocent man.

I was caught up in the justice system for nine years. Altogether, I have had to face: three murder trials, one in the historic No.1 court at the Old Bailey; a magistrates' court committal hearing; and two appeals at the Royal Courts of Justice. Six full hearings in all. There have also been innumerable other interim court appearances, so that in total I've spent more than nine months of my life in the dock in various courtrooms of England while others have decided my fate. Perhaps no one before in English history has ever had to endure such a lengthy ordeal.

My reputation had been systematically undermined from the moment I was charged. For years, many in the media have pursued a campaign of relentless hostility against me. Journalists thought they could write whatever they wanted about me and I became one of the most vilified people in the country. My faith in God was to provide me with the strength and hope I needed at my most desolate moments.

Accordingly, my first reason for wanting to tell my story is so that there can be a proper, enduring public record of exactly what happened. This record will naturally be shaped by my own perceptions; but it will also be informed by many thousands of pages of legal paperwork that have accumulated during the ten years that the case has been going on.

At about 3.30 in the afternoon of 15 February 1997, Annie, Charlotte and I got back from a trip to the DIY store. We'd only been out for about twenty minutes. We walked into the house, straight into this unbelievable, terrible scene. There was a moment when I was living a normal existence, surrounded by all that I knew and was comfortable with; then in the next moment, just as long as it takes to walk through a door, I had entered a world of nightmares.

I have had to look many, many times at photographs of the scene, both to prepare my defence with my lawyers and to assist juries at trials. They in no way represent what it was actually like.

When I found Billie, the scene was brutal, yet the air took on a particular stillness. It left me feeling disconnected from what I was seeing in my own home. The scene resembled a bloodbath in which poor Billie's body was lying on the patio in a place where we as a family had spent many happy times. As I moved towards her, I saw what I saw very clearly; there were, as I now know, brain tissue, shards of skull and blood clots around her face. The scene was frightening and cold. I sensed in that moment that an evil had descended on our home. There was even a different smell. The room that we entered had changed, not simply because Billie's crushed body was there. The atmosphere of a happy family home had gone; it had been replaced by a deathly aura.

The second reason for telling my story is the knowledge that someone killed Billie. I believe I know who murdered my foster daughter and I will not rest until he has been brought to justice. Since my acquittal, the police have made little progress in their inquiries, so it has become necessary for us to re-evaluate all the available evidence.

My third reason for writing this is that I hope it will help to prevent similar catastrophes from happening to others in the future. My case represents a series of blunders by all the agencies involved, either directly or indirectly, in the criminal justice process. If a high-profile case like mine is being handled so misguidedly, then it is reasonable to suppose that other cases, which are not receiving national attention and the same level of public interest, are also being dealt with incompetently.

When I was first convicted in 1998, Bob Woffinden, whom I did not know but who had been writing articles and books about miscarriages of justice during the previous ten years or so, wrote two articles about my case, in the *New Statesman* and the *Daily Mail*, in which he championed my innocence. At the time, I was immensely grateful to know those pieces had been published. They gave me enormous encouragement at one of my lowest points. I felt that someone was listening and it gave me a lot of strength.

The chapters dealing with my own direct experiences will be interwoven with ones written by Bob which relate what was happening in the case during my enforced absence.

My fourth and final reason for wishing to tell the story is more personal. All these years, I have grieved for my daughters, who have lost so much. They lived in a tranquil and happy family setting that was turned completely upside down. They lost all that comforting stability of childhood. In a very short time, they lost a sister, a parent and were separated from their paternal grandparents, aunts, uncles and everyone from my side of the family.

Since my conviction in 1998, I have seen my daughters, in total, for less than two hours, and even that was in a visiting room at Wakefield high security prison. Never since have I seen all of them together. Whilst I was still in prison, their mother, with her new partner and baby son, took them to live in Australia and I have not been able to talk to them since.

Now is the time to explain the horror that descended on us all. My daughters have been told that their father has let them down and disgraced them. They have been told that he is a murderer. They have never been told the real story of what has actually happened over the past ten years.

So this is a father's attempt to explain to his children why our family was torn apart and why they have had to endure so much distress and heartache.

So, to Annie, Charlotte, Esther and Maya, this is my life for the past ten years without you. This is the first opportunity I've had to tell you what it has been like. It is your first opportunity to hear it.

Siôn Jenkins
Lymington
January 2008

Part I
Trial and Vilification

Chapter One

Convicted

When the jury came back into court, there was at first a hush and then a dreadful silence. At that moment, I could not believe I was the person standing in the dock. The clerk of the court asked the foreman if the jurors had reached a verdict. He answered, 'Yes.'

The next word I heard was, 'Guilty'. It just hadn't occurred to me that a jury would convict me. I simply couldn't take it in.

When the verdict was delivered, the court erupted and the whole atmosphere immediately became heated and claustrophobic. In some respects, the court resembled a scene from a Brueghel painting. Men and women leant over the balcony of the public gallery, their faces distorted with anger and rage, shouting 'Murderer', 'Evil bastard', and worse. Bill Jenkins yelled down at me, 'Get out of that!'

Although I do remember the word 'Guilty', much of what was said afterwards simply did not reach me. I went into shock. I seemed to enter a dark tunnel and was not able to take in most of what was happening. In some ways, this was a blessing as a growing number of people appeared to want to rail against me or even do me physical harm.

I can remember the judge saying that he had no alternative but to give me a life sentence. Parole, tariff – I might have heard those words but I had no understanding of their relevance to me. The judge said that I would spend the rest of my life in prison. At that moment, that was certainly what I believed would happen.

Although I had to listen, as the minutes went by I found myself closing down more and more. I was emotionally overwhelmed. My mind raced. I thought about my daughters and what they would be going through; my parents and family; my legal team; my friends; and about how they would all suffer and their lives be irrevocably changed. I thought about why the jury had convicted me. I thought about spending the rest of my life in a prison cell, locked away from those I loved and cared for.

The judge then ordered that I be taken down to the cells. I went into the central corridor below, where court staff appeared shocked and distraught. Two security guards I had got to know looked upset and bewildered; one of the women was sobbing. Another security guard, who had helped me get into court every day, appeared to be doing his utmost to keep tears at bay. There was little that anyone could say. I was dumb.

Approximately five minutes later, I was called up again and emerged back into the court, surprised to find my legs still working. When I was first charged with murder, the police had found out that I had given false information on my curriculum vitae in a job application, so they had also charged me with obtaining a pecuniary advantage by deception. I had to go back up into court so that they could decide what to do about this.

The courtroom was now quiet. As I stood in front of the judge, all I could think was, I'm going to prison for the rest of my life – and now I'm going to have to stand trial, again?

In the event, the Crown said they weren't interested in pursuing the charge, and the judge said he saw the sense of that and ruled that it should be left to lie on file. Then he ordered that I be taken back down again and there was a second eruption of noise. It appeared that those in the public gallery were now free to abuse me further. I realised how medieval our courts still are – with all the various parties engaged in ritualistic behaviour, and those in the public gallery given licence to break out into sporadic bursts of mob uproar.

I was led outside in handcuffs. I could see people on roofs with cameras; the photographers had climbed up so they could see me coming out of the back entrance of the court. For the first time I was put into one of those white prison vans with cubicles that are used to transport prisoners – and that I quickly learned to call a sweatbox – and was taken the short drive to Lewes prison.

When I got there, I went to reception and was led to an open area where I was told to strip naked and squat. Prison officers check that you are concealing nothing anywhere on your person, including in your rectum. Ordinarily, I would have found the strip-search humiliating. I was by now feeling numb, exhausted and beyond caring what they did to me or what happened to me.

I was given prison clothes and told to put mine in a cardboard box.

'You can have those back', one of the warders said to me, 'when you're an old man'.

The comments amused the screws – the prison warders – around me. When I glanced into the box, I saw that one of the prison officers had put a picture of Billie-Jo on the bottom. I was too traumatised to fight back in any way. All my strength had drained away.

I was then taken up on to the wing and locked in a cell on my own. Lewes is an antiquated Victorian prison. The cell was small and airless and very dirty. I was given a blanket and two sheets. The mattress was badly stained and reeked so much of urine I couldn't bring myself to lie on it.

I sat on a chair and put my hands over my face. I didn't sleep that night, not even for five minutes. I stood staring out of the cell window. How had I reached such a point of despair in my life? And yet if I had known then all that my journey in the coming years would entail, I'm not sure that I would have been able to face it.

In the morning, I was released briefly to collect my breakfast. I was told that the newspapers were filled with accounts of my conviction and that there was great hostility towards me. I made a point of not reading them myself, but I felt for my daughters reading such things.

At about 10.30, a prison officer came to my cell to say that I needed to pack my few possessions. A colleague of his joined in the conversation, and said,

'The Governor doesn't want you in his prison, you're too high profile'.

I could not understand what was happening. I was led back to the reception area of the prison. Two officers took my bag. I was searched again and then taken to a waiting vehicle. I asked where I was going, but they refused to tell me. However, as we drove off, I heard a news bulletin on the radio. It said that Siôn Jenkins was being moved to Belmarsh, the maximum security prison in south London.

I was the only one in the sweatbox. As we drove through east London, we passed Kilmore House in Poplar, where I once had a flat. Then we passed within a few metres of a friend's house. Memories flooded through me. This was the area where we used to live. I felt as if my past life was passing before my eyes in slow motion. I was a young man when I had last walked these streets. Now, at the age of thirty-nine, I was going away for ever.

Chapter Two

Glasgow Academy and Nonington College

I was born on the 12 July 1957 in Greenwich, south London. I was the first son of David and Megan Jenkins, and my earliest memories are of life with my brother, David Llewellyn, who was fifteen months younger than me.

My father was a policeman with the Metropolitan Police for the first few years of my life, but then in 1962, when I was five, he joined the Michelin tyre company. As this new job entailed a lot of travelling, my mother took the leading role in bringing up my brother and me. However, even if my father was absent, we communicated a great deal as a family and evening meal times were always an opportunity for us to talk together and share what had happened during the day.

I lived for sport, and also had a real interest in drawing and painting which, in my teenage years, developed into a love of sculpture and sculpting.

The most testing time came when my father's work took him to Scotland. I was anxious about leaving England and going to what seemed to me the other side of the world. My parents bought a house in Brookfield, a peaceful village on the outskirts of Glasgow where everyone knew everyone else. It was a lovely house with a large garden and our time there was idyllic.

After we'd been there about a year, David Llewellyn and I sat entrance examinations for Glasgow Academy, the oldest fully-independent school in the city. It was fee-paying and took in both day-boys and boarders. We gained admission, and so started our secondary schooling.

However, soon after we'd started, my father was offered promotion again, which was to take him and my mother back to London. As children, my brother and I had already been to so many schools that it was decided that, rather than have our secondary education disrupted, possibly for a short period, we would stay at the Academy and become boarders.

I played several sports for the school, and was also captain of the chess club. My life was mainly tennis all summer and rugby all winter. I just have very happy memories of going off on a Saturday morning to play rugby for the school. I loved the camaraderie and that team ethic of playing hard and socialising hard.

On Friday and Saturday nights, I'd go out with friends, possibly enjoying more freedoms than other boys in their early teens might have done if they'd been living at home. The school was in the middle of Glasgow and, as we advanced through the school, we were allowed to go into town to make phone calls or to go to the shops.

Nevertheless, having to be back in at nine o'clock became increasingly irksome. We'd go to the rugby internationals at Murrayfield in Edinburgh and invariably get back very late, having drunk too much. So after a number of run-ins with the housemasters, in the summer of 1974 I was expelled from the Academy.

Although I felt a sense of relief that I was free, my father wasn't impressed. It had cost him a great deal of money, and no doubt he believed that he was providing greater opportunities for me.

Was public school any use to me at all?

The regime is generally strict and regimented. One acquires habits and disciplines – simply, for example, of getting up in the morning and collecting your breakfast. One becomes used to having lots of people around, and to the routines of sharing good and bad times: the camaraderie, the bravado, the dark humour. Fortunately, the public school regime seems an ideal preparation for prison.[1]

When I left school, my love for sport continued. After doing A levels at Windsor and Eton College of Further Education, I was accepted on a course to study P.E. and English at Nonington College of Physical Education near Canterbury in Kent.

Those years were, I admit, directionless. I got my Certificate in Education, but I had no wish to go back for a fourth year (as some people did, in order to convert their certificate into an honours degree). At that time I thought that teaching was the last thing I would end up doing. It was the other interest in my life that was now beckoning: art.

At Nonington I started carving stone. There was a sculptor there who took me under his wing and taught me various techniques. I used to go down to the arts studios in my own time and I would carve. It wasn't part of my curriculum, but the fact that I wasn't having formal training was, for me, an irrelevance.

When I left Nonington, I completed all the works I had started and decided to try to earn a living by sculpting. I spent a year doing tedious factory jobs to pay off college debts and to save towards a deposit.

My father again got a new job, this time working for his friend Tom Farmer, who had started Kwik Fit, the car maintenance company, and so he and my mother moved back to Scotland. I went to London and got a studio at the Metropolitan Wharf in Wapping, and found a flat to rent nearby.

The Wharf was a large complex of studios housing painters, sculptors, fashion designers, film-makers, printers and others. There were open days and exhibitions that would be advertised in *Time Out*.

I had a first-floor studio that looked out over the Thames with a lot of floor space. There were many frustrating episodes. I had to buy all the materials, and then pay for them to be hoisted into the studio, and as I didn't have much money, I sometimes tried to cut corners. Once I bought a piece of limestone cheaply. I'd roughed out the shape of what I was going to do and spent ages preparing it. When I hit it with the chisel, it just sliced right in two. Weeks and weeks of work were totally wasted.

But by my second year there, things were changing around me. Another wharf had been bought by property developers and converted into luxury flats. Other wharves were being sold and suddenly floor space like mine became very valuable. The rent quadrupled and I had to take teaching supply work at the local Stepney Green boys' school. After teaching all day, I would go straight to my studio. I would then sculpt from about 5.00–10.00pm. This routine was back-breaking, especially as carving marble or granite can be such strenuous physical work. By the time I returned home, I was drained, dusty and exhausted.

As I was not selling enough sculpture, and supply teaching was poorly paid, I realised I simply couldn't afford to stay in Wapping. I decided to put my tools into storage until I could find an alternative, cheaper studio, and to teach every day on supply to clear my debts.

I'd arranged to take a flat in Globe Road in Stepney but, on the day I went round prior to moving in, I found it had been vandalised. I explained my predicament to Howard Wynne, a colleague at Stepney Green, and without a moment's thought, he said I could sleep on the sofa in the flat in Poplar that he rented with three other men.

It was through Howard that I met a number of other friends, some of whom were medics. In early December 1981, he and I went to a function at the Royal London Hospital in Whitechapel. Among the doctors and nurses, Lois Ball happened to be there. I didn't really notice her too much and, indeed, didn't speak to her until we all left the hospital bar.

A friend had offered five of us a lift home, Lois included. I was getting into the back of the car with her and this guy who was obviously very drunk. He got in first. As Lois was about to get in, I stopped her and said, 'You'd better let me go next to him'. It was at that point that I had my first conversation with her. One of the doctors was going to have a New Year's Eve party, and she asked if I'd be going. I said, 'Well, are you?' And she said, 'Yes, I'm going'.

I went to the party. I spent time with Lois, and we ended up kissing. From that evening, we were an item. Effectively, we started going out together on 1 January 1982.

Lois interested me. There was something enigmatic about her. Her language, habits, interests and reactions were unfamiliar to me and, because of that, I found her fascinating.

I can remember taking her to the Salisbury, a large Victorian pub in St Martin's Lane. They had photographs on the walls of some of the world's icons of popular entertainment – Marilyn Monroe, Humphrey Bogart and John Lennon. As I talked about each of them, I suddenly realised that Lois didn't have a clue who any of them were.

She then explained that she rarely watched television and had had an unusual childhood.

Chapter Three

Family Life

Lois was the eldest of four children and grew up with her family in Poole, Dorset. She was born on 13 October 1961, so she was twenty when I met her. Her parents, John and Gillian Ball, belonged to the Exclusive Brethren, a rigidly ascetic sect that was an offshoot of the Plymouth Brethren. Going to the cinema or theatre or watching television or mixing in wider society was not encouraged by the Brethren.

Around 1973, Lois's parents left the Exclusive Brethren, which was deeply traumatic for them. Lois's parents then started to foster children. So the four natural children grew up with a permanent foster brother and four other foster children who overlapped at various times.

Lois went to Poole technical college to do A levels, but left without completing the course. Then, in 1980, she embarked on a three-year nursing course at the Royal London which explains how she came to be at the party where we met in December 1981.

For the first few weeks, Lois and I saw each other regularly. When I had finished work, I would collect her from the hospital and we would go into the West End. Our lives at that time were full. We were always doing something – cinemas, galleries, museums. She was new to so many things.

Her family didn't immediately start living differently; this developed over a number of years. Leaving friends and family behind was difficult.

By April or May 1982, we decided that we wanted to get married. Lois came up to Edinburgh with me to meet my parents, and I met her parents. Lois's family were pleased, as were mine. We looked at all the possibilities and chose to marry on Saturday, 18 December, when we'd effectively been going out together for a year.

Our first home was a small flat in Tomlins Grove, Bow, in east London. I was by now working full-time at Stepney Green, initially as a supply teacher, although I was then offered a permanent position teaching art. Then I had a stroke of luck, and found a relatively cheap studio.

The Crown Estates managed a number of properties at the edge of Regent's Park, which sometimes became available at reasonable rents. Among this cluster of properties was the Diorama, which had been built in the mid-nineteenth century to give experimental film shows. Although a building of genuine historical importance, it was by the 1980s in a dilapidated state and was boarded up and unused.

A couple of enterprising artists went in and took it over, effectively as squatters. They tried to establish it as an artists' colony. I finally managed to get a studio there. I had two rooms, with water, electricity, everything. To have that kind of facility, looking out over Regent's Park, was wonderful.

After completing her training, Lois worked for a few months as a nurse at the Royal London Hospital, but then gave up nursing to become a registered childminder after the birth of our first child.

Annie Victoria was born on 12 June 1984 at the Royal London. I can remember the smallest details concerning her arrival into this world. I was mesmerised by her tiny features and her exquisite hands and feet. Holding her in my arms for the first time was one of the most memorable and unbelievable moments of my life.

Three or four of us had the chance to put on a figure exhibition at the Royal Festival Hall, and Lois helped me with that. It lasted two or three weeks. I displayed a few pieces of stone and of wood, and I sold a couple.

However, what I was selling – for relatively small sums – simply wasn't enough. A few years earlier, I had vowed to myself that I would never become a teacher. Now, things were different. Questions about whether I did or didn't want to teach became irrelevant. What became important was that I had a mortgage and a wife and a child, and we needed a regular income so that I could support them. In any event, I was uncomfortable spending time away from home once Annie had been born. So I gave up my studio for the last time.

When I started doing supply teaching at schools in east London, it was a very exacting area to teach in. The schools were rough and hard. But I enjoyed working with difficult teenagers.

You have to find a way of working with them and building trust; young people will respect you for that. I loved the classes that some staff dreaded. The harder the class, the more difficult the pupils, the more I loved it.

The head, Jim Taylor, asked me to take lower-school English. I did it for about six months, and then I took upper-school English up to GCSE level. I was also asked to teach religious education for a year.

Within a couple of years, I'd decided in my own mind what my philosophy of education was, what I thought worked and what didn't work, and how a curriculum should be managed. I became head of year and a curriculum coordinator.

We stayed at our small flat, in Tomlins Grove, for two or three years. Then we moved to another flat nearby, also in Bow, in Ellesmere Road off Roman Road, where Charlotte Mary was born on 19 March 1986. But the area was becoming very expensive and we were still in financial difficulties.

We moved to Newham, where housing was much cheaper, and got a four-bedroomed Victorian terraced house with a garden at 12 Henry Road in East Ham. Esther Louise was born there on 13 February 1988 and Maya Cornelia on 4 November 1989.

Family Life

Our married life was probably like many others – we were worrying about money, trying to clothe and feed the children, arranging holidays, seeing respective parents, and then having worries when the car didn't work. We knew that money was going to be tight, but we were also happy that Lois brought up the children; we didn't want to put them with a childminder.

Lois got a part-time job running a toy library and then became involved in setting up playgroups and toddler groups.

In 1989, I got a new job, and was appointed head of the faculty of communications at McKentee school in Walthamstow. It was a mixed school and was also very deprived, with an indigenous white population. My department embraced English and foreign languages, as well as careers and IT. So by then my role was more of an education manager, looking at the whole curriculum and not just at individual subjects.

These were difficult years, as I left for work at 7.00am, and taught all day. Three or four times a week, I'd finish teaching at four o'clock, stay at school until five attending management meetings, and do my own marking and preparation from 5.00 until 6.00. Then, I started teaching adult education classes for two evenings a week. I didn't leave there until gone nine o'clock, so it was nearly 10.00pm when I was getting home.

There's one incident that I remember well from Henry Road, mainly because it was so painful. I was playing with Esther, she was about three at the time, and she was on the other side of the room. She had these plastic flags, the kind one gets children for carnivals or fairs. I picked them up and stupidly put them in my ears so they were hanging out. Esther saw me and was so happy, and cried, 'Daddy!' She came running over. I panicked, thinking she was going to grab them, so I quickly went to take them out. I got the one in my right ear, but missed the one in my left, and instead ended up punching it right through my eardrum. The blood poured out. I was taken to the Ear, Nose & Throat Hospital. There was a hole in my eardrum, so they had to operate and build the eardrum up. I stayed in hospital for a few days and Lois brought the children to visit me. I would never have expected this to become an evidential issue, but it did.

In two years at McKentee, I had changed the whole faculty around and the headteacher, Len Bannister, gave me a number of other tasks around the school. As I was effectively doing the job of a deputy head, I felt I could now apply for jobs at that level, especially as I was also working my way towards an MSc in education management at the University of East London. I would be awarded the degree in November 1992.

Lois and I felt that leaving London would enable us to buy a larger house for our growing family and give the girls an improved quality of life. Len was generous enough to write me an outstanding reference.

Then a deputy's job came up at William Parker School in Hastings, Sussex, on the south coast. I could see what they wanted and recognised the type of school and its culture. So to make it more likely that I would be called for interview, I invented details on my CV. It seemed an almost insignificant matter at the time. The whole issue, of course, was to have major and dramatic repercussions later on.

The interviewing process took three days. At the end, the governors called me through and offered me the job. It wasn't long before I was on my way back to London to share the good news with Lois and the children: we were moving to Hastings.

Chapter Four

Billie-Jo

It is now necessary to interrupt Siôn's narrative for the first time in order to explain that it was coincidentally at this juncture that he and Lois were again thinking of extending their family. In February 1992, Lois had shown him an advert in a local newspaper about two children who needed a foster home. The two children were Billie-Jo Jenkins and her half-brother. The coincidence of the surnames being the same was just that: a coincidence. However, Lois and Siôn were not given full details of the children's history and, indeed, were not to learn them until several years later.

Billie-Jo was born on 29 March 1983, so she was then eight years old; her half-brother was five years older. Their mother, Debbie, had been born in January 1958. Debbie never knew her own father and, as life was complicated for her mother (who had four children by four different fathers), was brought up by her mother's parents in Dagenham, Essex.

Debbie met Billie-Jo's father, Bill Jenkins, on a kind of blind date in Wandsworth prison. A friend whose partner was inside asked if she would accompany her and visit the partner's friend – make up a foursome, as it were – and the latter turned out to be Bill Jenkins. He had served time for several violent offences, including grievous bodily harm and assaulting a police officer. When he was released, he began seeing Debbie and eventually moved in. Billie-Jo was born in Barking hospital. Debbie married Bill six weeks later.

Writing in the *Independent*, Dea Birkett pointed out that Bill Jenkins had been born into a family that was proud of its East End heritage. 'Each generation is named after the one that went before,' wrote Birkett. 'Bill Jenkins was named after his father, and Billie-Jo was named after him.' Their household included a Burmese python and a pair of ginger cats, Reggie and Ronnie – named after the Kray twins.

When Debbie herself was jailed for a period for credit card fraud, Billie-Jo was temporarily looked after by her grandmother (Debbie's mother). Even by this early stage, the effects of such a turbulent upbringing were beginning to show. As soon as Billie-Jo started primary school, teachers remarked on her verbal and physical aggressiveness. 'I saw how fearless she was for myself', explained Debbie. 'At the age of four, she nearly drowned the little boy next door by forcing his head into a bucket of water. When she was five, she tried to attack a fourteen-year-old with a potato peeler.'

Debbie's relationship with Bill Jenkins finally ended – 'dissolved in arguments, drink and prison spells for both', as Dea Birkett wrote. Struggling to find somewhere to live, Debbie voluntarily – and, as she no doubt believed, temporarily – placed her three children into care. When she succeeded in finding a one-bedroomed flat, however, Newham social services told her that it was too small for the children. The children were then sent briefly to live with their aunt, Bill Jenkins's sister, Margaret Coster. She then agreed to look after the youngest, but could not take on the two older children as well.

The children were placed with temporary foster parents in Ilford, Essex. However, this family couldn't cope with them, particularly as the mother was expecting another child of her own. They pressed Newham social services to remove Billie-Jo and her half-brother. It then looked as though they would have to be placed back into a children's home. However, Newham social services made one last attempt to place them elsewhere, and put an advertisement in the local paper for foster parents. This was the advert to which Lois responded.

Chapter Five

A Normal Teenager

I'd never considered fostering. But Lois was one of four children, and she now had four children of her own; her parents had fostered, and now she wanted to foster too. I had no objections, and indeed gave Lois my full support.

Lois and I were interviewed, both individually and together, a number of times over a number of weeks. Social services also spoke to the older children, and fed back snippets of information to Billie-Jo and her half-brother in order to ascertain their feelings. Billie-Jo was then at Nelson primary school in East Ham, the same school as Annie and Charlotte, and was in the year above Annie. As a result of the social services inquiries, Annie and Billie-Jo, who were friends, were soon able to put two and two together themselves. Consequently, we became aware that Billie was the girl concerned before social services held a formal meeting to introduce her and her half-brother to us.

We anticipated the whole process possibly taking months. But when the children's temporary placement in Ilford suddenly broke down, it seemed that social services had two obvious choices: to send them back to a children's home; or to place them with their own family who lived in Newham. Neither was considered a viable option; the children had been very unhappy in institutions and a place could not be found in Billie's extended family.

We were asked if we would care for Billie and her brother as an emergency placement. We agreed to this primarily because we were already involved and did not want to think of two children being more unsettled than necessary.

So, one Friday afternoon in June 1992, Billie and her brother arrived. When social services originally spoke to us, they had provided only limited information so we had no idea of the details of their family history. The family circumstances and the details of Billie's early life had been skated over; her wildness and violent outbursts were not mentioned. Some parts of the story we found out accidentally, mainly through Annie and Billie being at the same school. For example, we learned that, because of her general behaviour, Billie had been on the point of being excluded from Nelson primary school.

Now, suddenly, here they were in the house. Billie was quite disturbed emotionally. She didn't know how to live in a home.

Billie and her half-brother were put with us on that Friday afternoon. The social workers were not available over the weekend so we were left, initially, without any kind of support. Everything deteriorated so quickly that Lois and I sat down and discussed whether we were going to be able to cope.

I can remember us going to speak with Margaret Coster, the aunt who had had Billie for a brief period. She actually lived just around the corner, and we just wanted to glean some information that might be useful to help us settle Billie. But we left, none the wiser.

After a few days, Billie's brother was taken back to a children's home, although not at our behest. Lois and I complained to social services about this. We felt that his removal, and the manner in which it was done, lacked any sensitivity to the needs of the boy and was cruel. My heart went out to him and I visited him over the following weeks to encourage him.

Social services asked us to keep Billie. She then had to find her feet again in the sense that her brother was no longer around. That gave us time. She'd only been with us a short period, a number of weeks, before we knew we were going to move to Hastings. So we then had that fateful discussion with her: do you want to stay in Newham and possibly go back to your aunt and your sister, with your family close at hand? Or do you want to come with us to Hastings? But if you do that, then, for you, that's going to be quite a distance from your home area.

She was adamant. She didn't want to stay in Newham. She wanted to move away with us – she had no concerns, no anxieties, there were never any doubts in her mind. She saw the move as a chance to start again and find happiness. Certainly, social services were delighted that she now had a real opportunity to make a fresh start.

The move to Hastings was idyllic for her. She lived opposite the park in a seaside town and had her own bedroom. She spent hours of those first weeks by the seaside, enjoying the sea air; I'm not sure if she had ever seen the sea before. Once she was in that environment, she began to thrive.

There were still times when you looked at her face and it appeared distorted with what I can only describe as emotional pain. As she matured, she began to talk about her natural family, sometimes showing anger and resentment. She often said she did not understand why she had been put into care whereas her younger sister had been looked after by the family. During these times, Lois or I spent a great deal of time talking to her and offering reassurance. Billie could respond to her confusion by being hurtful to friends or, sometimes, by bullying younger children.

On one occasion, she attacked Esther, who was about five at the time. I heard screaming coming from Esther's bedroom, and raced up to see what was happening. Esther had a plastic box full of dolls, and Billie had been ripping the heads off and destroying them one by one. As I told Billie to stop, Esther launched herself at her, and Billie reacted by grabbing Esther and pulling her hair, so I had to separate them. Later, Billie recognised that, in attacking Esther, she had hurt her. As she grew older, Billie stopped using violence as a way of reacting to disappointments or testing situations.

From the outset, our overall strategy was both to encourage her to maintain contact with her own family while at the same time playing down the fact that she was fostered and treat her as one of our own.

Even in her appearance, she fitted in. Billie and Annie, who were the closest in age, had the same coloured hair and looked similar. So not only because her name was Jenkins but because of her looks, she seemed like a sister. When she met our daughters' grandparents, she accepted them as her grandparents, both on Lois's and my side of the family. She made a point of calling them 'Grandma' and 'Granddad' and, because of it, I think she felt quite secure.

Billie's social worker, from Newham social services, visited regularly and became a familiar face around our home. He usually arrived in the late afternoon and would then take Billie out – either they'd go off in his car, or they'd go for a walk in the park, so that he could talk to her privately about how she was getting on. As each month passed, so he appeared more and more pleased with how she was responding to her new life. By then, she certainly didn't want to go back to London and was very keen to stay; equally, social services were very keen that we did keep her with us.

Because social services knew that Bill Jenkins had a history of violence to his family, they wouldn't allow him to spend any time with Billie unless he was supervised. But we found it difficult to get him to see her anyway, and often had to chase him for contact. Yet, though the natural family were hardly in a position to raise objections, they deeply resented the whole fostering arrangement. Even before the move to Hastings, Bill Jenkins had made one unorthodox attempt to get her back.

We'd taken Billie for a pre-arranged meeting with him, which social services had insisted must take place at their offices. At about 4.00pm, he arrived and said he wasn't prepared to see his daughter in those circumstances. Lois and I were in the main room, and Billie was by reception. He threatened the women who were on the door, grabbed Billie, dragged her out and threw her into a taxi outside, in which one of

Billie's aunts was waiting. He then took her to a pub the family used, sat Billie down and proceeded to just drink and drink.

After a few hours, Billie was so worried and frightened she managed to speak to the landlord. He then called the police. Billie was rescued and brought back to our house at about 11.00pm at night. From then on, the social services were even more adamant that Bill Jenkins must not be allowed to see her on his own. Naturally, that made him even more aggrieved.

Sometimes, after we'd heard nothing from Bill Jenkins for months, he'd phone out of the blue. The calls, which would sometimes be late at night, were upsetting for Billie. She would be very subdued afterwards. Once, he phoned on Christmas Day, when I happened to take the call, and his tone to me was very loud and intimidating.

After this, Billie's social worker arranged for her to have her own phone line, which social services would pay for, with her own private number for family calls. During those years, her natural family made few attempts to see her.

In September 1994, Billie started at Helenswood, the local girls' secondary school. As the eldest, she was the first of my children to go to secondary school. She quickly found her feet, responded well to the environment and her lessons, and formed close friendships. Holly Prior and Ruth Bristow both became very important to her. She especially enjoyed going round to Ruth's home and meeting her family; I think she saw Ruth as a permanent friend.

Billie would occasionally be naughty, but when reproached could become quite soft, and cried easily. She rarely sulked and knew how to say sorry and get on with things. She could be stroppy and opinionated. It was interesting that she almost never argued with Annie or, despite the dolls incident, Esther. If ever she did argue, it would be with Charlotte or Maya, who could themselves be stubborn and opinionated.

Sharing was something that, initially, was quite foreign to Billie – everything would be 'mine'; it took years for her to learn to share. She remained prone to occasional outbursts of wilfulness, from which even

24

A Normal Teenager

close friends could suffer. 'She lashed out at me once', recalled Ruth, at the third trial. 'She slapped me, I was quite shocked. It was the kind of slap that made me jump and think, that's not right.'

Then there was the much-recounted bottles-of-beer incident. We had come back from a holiday in France in the summer of 1995 and, like virtually every other family, we'd brought back cheap bottles of French beer. A few days after the September term had started, we noticed a large bottle-opener sticking out of her schoolbag. We then found one of the bottles in her bag. So we learned that she had taken some of these bottles into school and distributed them amongst her classmates.

We tried to tackle it calmly. I don't think that's abnormal or worrying behaviour for a teenager. She wasn't shouted at. We just explained to her that giving beer to Year 7 pupils wasn't the brightest idea she'd ever had. That was it; there were no raised voices.

She was confident and she'd let you know what she was thinking. She could be direct and firm and would never be pushed around. In the rough and tumble of school, she knew how to look after herself. In that sense, she was streetwise. But she wasn't out round Hastings at night – she was very happy to have boundaries drawn up for her. She became reliable and independent and a girl whom, in many situations, Lois and I could trust. If you gave her responsibilities, she responded well.

Like many girls of that age, she loved small children. If we went to friends' houses and they had any younger children, she'd spend most of her time there looking after them.

She didn't make any more demands than any of the others, wasn't especially fashion-conscious (after all, she was only thirteen when she died) and would often just be happy in a pair of shorts riding her bike round Alexandra Park with her friend Dan (a boy who went to William Parker School).

Billie wanted to feel a part of the family and there came a point where she came to me and said, although I forget her exact words, that she didn't want Newham social services making decisions about her any longer; 'I want you to do it', she said, 'I want you to adopt me'.

25

I spoke to a solicitor friend, David Collins, who was also a governor at William Parker School. He said that adoption was likely to be a lengthy process and recommended that we go for a halfway-house arrangement. We could take Billie out of care and Lois and I could seek a Residence Order and become her legal guardians. This necessitated protracted discussions with social services, who had to consult everyone involved including, of course, the natural family. Billie constantly asked how things were progressing, as she was eager to be taken out of care.

As she began to achieve more success at school, so she responded with enthusiasm. She was particularly excited about drama; she lived for it. I can remember her announcing, 'We've got drama today', and she just couldn't wait to go to school.

Later on, she played hockey for the school and was her year's representative on the school council. Every Sunday evening, I would take her and Annie to play squash, and afterwards gave them rudimentary driving lessons on a deserted industrial estate.

I remember the last Christmas we all had together, in Aberystwyth in 1996, and my parents had some people round. Billie was with my other daughters. I realised then that she had totally adapted.

Because Billie was doing so well in drama, Lois and I drove her up to London for her to look round a drama school. Later that term she was going to be choosing her options. Did she want to do drama at GCSE and, if she did, did she want to do a GNVQ in performing arts, which the school then offered? The purpose of the trip was to show her the possibilities and to help her decide; it was to say to her – this is what you can have if you knuckle down and work hard, and she was excited by that.

While we were in London, I took her to see her natural family. No one knew it then, but it would be for the last time. We went there for the afternoon and part of the evening.

Despite the continuing frustrations, however, we thought it essential for Billie to maintain links, so when Newham social services ceased funding Billie's phone line in February 1997, we decided to pay for it ourselves, so that she could continue to talk privately to them.

By then, the lengthy process of taking Billie-Jo out of care had reached its end. The hearing was held in December 1996 at the family court in Newham. Bill Jenkins was there, together with his sister and another family relative, though I don't think they played any part. Certainly, they raised no objection and the Residence Order was uncontested.

Lois and I were called in individually to see the judge in his chambers. He asked me just general questions, such as how long had I been considering it, and was I happy with the situation. He also asked whether we would be able to offer a home without any support at all from social services. I replied it was something that Billie wanted, that we loved her, that she was very much part of the family and that we could offer her a home until such time as she wanted to leave.

He then saw Lois and me together.

He had studied all the reports from social services and the education authorities, and was fully satisfied with Billie's progress and the family arrangements made for her. She was taken out of care and Lois and I obtained the Residency Order for her. There were now no social workers or other authorities involved; we were her legal guardians. Billie-Jo was no longer a foster child.

When we returned home, she smiled and walked around the house. She was excited, her shoulders were pushed back. She knew, at last, that she would never again have to go to a children's home. For the first time in her life, she had a secure future to look forward to.

Chapter Six

Living on the South Coast

We moved to our new home in Hastings on 19 August 1992. We arrived just ahead of the removal van. It was 48 Lower Park Road, a spacious, three-storey, six-bedroomed semi-detached house that overlooked Alexandra Park and was also close to the town centre. The girls rushed in and immediately ran upstairs. The race was on to choose bedrooms, though everything was sorted without any problem. It transpired that Annie and Billie wanted to share a bedroom, as did Esther and Maya. Charlotte wanted her own bedroom, and chose the one next to ours.

During a break in unpacking, I walked across to the park and went round the duck pond. The grass was newly mown, the sunlight rippled through the trees and I suddenly felt very optimistic for our family's future.

That first day, however – sadly for us – it was the seedier side of Hastings that made an instant impression. While we were out shopping that afternoon, the house, which we'd only occupied for about three hours, was burgled. The front door was kicked in and the television was stolen.

Nevertheless, our first year there was exciting. We made the house into a home and became part of the community. Our daughters went to local schools, and all the family started attending Halton Baptist Church.

I took up my new post at the start of the school year in September 1992. There was a great deal to be done, but it helped that I got on so well with the headmaster, Roger Mitchell. As I was given more responsibility, I realised that I enjoyed the job; and if you enjoy something, you are more likely to work harder and to do it more successfully. As each year went by, the governors increased my salary over and above the annual staff pay rises.

To begin with, Lois remained at home, organising the children's daily routines. Then she told me that she wanted to return to work, and was going to apply for a post with social services in Sussex. She was successful, and became an inspector of children's services. In order to manage the logistics of getting the girls to and from school, we took in an au pair. Over the years, we had a number, the last of whom, Regine Renac, was still with us when Billie died.

During our years in Hastings, all the most important aspects of my life revolved around our children. The girls continued to grow and to develop their individual personalities; I enjoyed their differences and their samenesses. Annie was a gentle girl. She never felt she needed to be doing things. She was reflective and enjoyed daydreaming, or going for a quiet walk. She never name-called or spoke harshly of people, she was kind and thoughtful and able to empathise quickly with people who were in difficulty. She was the only one who really appreciated what it was like for me – in a household full of girls – and would often interrupt conversations, to say something like, 'Poor Dad, having to listen to all this'.

Charlotte was more vivacious. She was sure of herself and could be abrupt. Where Annie was disorganised, she was very organised; whereas books would be scattered round Annie's room, Charlotte's room would be meticulously tidy. She loved perfumes and make-up and had all her bottles and jars neatly lined up. She was an analytical thinker and enjoyed her own company; but she was also socially confident, and always made friends easily.

Esther's nickname in the family was 'bubby'. She loved being loved and was always wanting cuddles. She was the most girly of them all, she was very soft, and lived in a world of dolls and dolls houses. She had a wonderful imagination. She was frightened of spiders, frightened of flies, frightened of everything. If I told them all a ghost story, Esther would always be the one who'd scream the loudest.

Maya was a strong character. She was intelligent and had an enormous personality. She would often mix with children older than herself but, whomever she was with, she would dominate. She was articulate, she fought for what was hers and stood up for herself. She loved being up and about. I taught her to ride a bike, and of course she fell off a few times. Whereas the other girls might have cried and gone home, Maya would get back on and continue until she'd managed it. She was a delight.

Of all the children, she could be the most naughty, although always in an irreproachable way. If ever the au pair complained about one of the girls, or Annie or Billie complained about one of their sisters, it was always Maya they would be complaining about. But I could never tell her off because she was the baby of the family. I'd always say, 'You wouldn't do that, would you, Maya?', and she'd say, with charming insincerity, 'No, it was nothing to do with me'.

She always worked on the basis that I'd sort everything out for her, and was completely trusting of me. She developed this annoying habit of climbing up on to the kitchen work-surfaces, and throwing herself off when I'd walked by, for me to catch her. I used to say, 'Don't do that – one day I might not turn round quickly enough.' But she wouldn't listen.

Although the fact that Lois was now working placed different demands on us as a family, we all adapted to the new routines. The au pair or Lois would take the younger girls to school, while I would usually drive Annie and Billie either straight to their school, or to my school, which was only a few minutes' walk away, and they would walk from there. Afterwards, Annie and Billie came to William Parker about 4.30. When they arrived, I used to walk to the local shop and buy them both a Marathon bar. I took it back to them, and they did their homework at the computer in my office whilst I attended meetings, until around 5.00–5.30. Then I'd take them home and, the au pair having collected the other girls, we'd all have tea together. Just sitting with the girls chatting while they sat by the fire eating toast – that's one of my most valued memories.

As deputy head, I would meet other professionals and local politicians at meetings. At one of these, two local Conservative councillors asked if I had considered standing as a candidate in the local elections. This was in the spring of 1994, two years after I'd arrived in Hastings. By this time, everything was running smoothly at school. I wondered if I could afford the time to be a councillor, but I was interested. I knew there were aspects of town life that I would like to be involved with.

Although I wasn't thinking at the time of embarking on a career in politics, I did take the view that if I was able to attend council meetings and make a contribution to life in Hastings, I would be happy to do that. So, after discussing it with Lois, I said I'd stand. I duly became Conservative candidate for the local council for the West St Leonard's ward.

I really thought it was just a minor decision. When I'd been at McKentee, one of the deputies there was a Labour councillor, and no one thought anything of it. It was just something he did in his own free time; it was never discussed, it was an irrelevance.

I believed that that would be the line people would take in Sussex. But they didn't. It became a major issue. It was a big talking-point with many staff at school. County Hall, the people who ran the education system in Sussex, were displeased. People I knew in other schools said to me, 'You're treading on ice. Do you realise what you're getting involved with?'

Then there were the difficulties at home. When they sent a photographer around for a campaign leaflet, or when other people from the Conservative party came to the house, although Lois didn't actually say anything, it was clear she wasn't happy.

I was socialising with Conservative local politicians. I can remember John Major, who was prime minister at the time, coming to Sussex, and I met him at a country house with other Conservative officials, and Lois became very uneasy. She hardly spoke to me. She just saw my involvement developing momentum.

By the time I was intensely involved in the campaign, our relationship was suffering. 'If you have any aspirations about going into politics and representing the Conservative party', she told me, 'you won't be doing it with me, you'll be doing it on your own.'

Well, despite my manifesto pledge of, among other things, 'more facilities for young people', I lost. My political career was stillborn. I thought the Conservative association would be quite disenchanted, and say something like, 'Bad luck, but don't call us' – but it wasn't like that. Their attitude was, it really doesn't matter, we've got something else that we'd welcome your involvement in; in time, you could decide whether you would like your name to be put forward to stand as an MP.

In September 1996, Lois decided to take a part-time social work job back in east London. She became a project manager for Tower Hamlets social services, helping to set up a care scheme for adults with learning difficulties. This meant that, on the three days she worked, she would be away from home for longer and would be returning late. She had to write reports at home and had some flexibility with her hours of work but, like many part-time workers in the social services sector, found that the demands of the job increasingly encroached on her own time. She would often get back to Hastings station between 8.30 and 9.30pm. By that time, all the girls would be in their nightclothes and slippers. Occasionally, I would bundle them all into the car and we'd drive down to the station to meet her off the train.

In her new job, Lois started mixing with a new group of people. We seemed to have become strangers, with nothing in common apart from our daughters. None of my interests interested Lois, and she especially disliked my politics. Emotionally, a chasm developed between us.

Lois had met Denise Lancaster who, with her partner Chris Lancaster, lived just a few doors away down Lower Park Road. She and Lois got on exceptionally well. As Charlotte commented in her police interview, 'Denise and my Mum are sort of like best friends, and they just tell each other everything that, like, goes on'.

Then, at the nursery school that Maya attended, Lois met Peter Gaimster, who had a young son there. He and his wife, Julia, lived in St Helen's Road on the opposite side of the park. As Julia lectured in fashion at a college in Croydon, most of the family child-care devolved to Peter. He had a shop in Hastings old town.

Lois got on very well with Peter. Natalie, the Gaimsters' daughter, also became good friends with our children. Interviewed by police, Natalie said that Charlotte and Annie were 'like the friends you don't even consider friends, they were more like family'.

Although Lois was very good friends with Denise and Chris and with Peter and Julia, I wasn't usually around simply because I spent so much time at school. The only time I ever spent a social occasion with Peter without Lois and Julia being present was when he and I went to the Old Golden Cross pub together during Euro '96 to watch the England⁵ Switzerland game on the big screen.

In early 1996, Lois had asked if the Gaimsters could come with us on our annual holidays. I had no objections. Usually we stayed in caravans or *gites* and we went to the south of France, but I don't think the Gaimsters wanted to travel very far, so we ended up in Brittany. Things went reasonably well – as I thought at the time.

Another friend watching football with us during Euro '96 had been Felix Simmons.[2] He also lived nearby in Lower Park Road. Shortly afterwards, he suffered serious mental illness.

I like Felix. Because I didn't understand what it is like to break down, and because I'd never met anybody who'd had a full breakdown, I didn't know what to do. So basically I avoided the situation, and I avoided him. Now I look back at that time when he was having his breakdown and he was struggling, and I wish I'd been more supportive. It was an episode that, for me, represented a personal failure. There are situations in life where you feel you've let yourself down badly, and this was one.

The 1996–7 Academic year at William Parker was to be Roger Mitchell's last; he announced his intention to retire. He encouraged me to apply for the headship. I enjoyed Roger's company; we had a good professional relationship and during my years with him I had learnt a great deal.

Lois was not enthusiastic about my applying. She had started to talk about returning to London, but I didn't want to move the family because the children were now so settled. However, I wasn't sure about the job; I procrastinated. Then some governors asked me to apply and I decided I would go for it.

This created a problem: the CV. If I'd applied for the headship of a different school, it wouldn't have been a problem. I could have just written the truth: I'd been a senior teacher and head of faculty for three years and a deputy for five years. The only question the interviewers would have been interested in was: how has he performed as a deputy? But obviously the CV in this application for headteacher had to be exactly the same as the one for the deputy post back in 1992.

I couldn't remember what I'd put down, but it didn't present any practical problems; all the staff applications and CV details were in the filing cabinet in my office. So, I took out my old CV and simply transferred the details to the new one.

The interviewing process took place over three days from 3–5 December 1996. After completing a range of management exercises, role-play and administrative tasks, I was interviewed by a panel consisting of local education officials, governors, teachers and parents.

On 5 December, whilst cooking dinner for the family at home, I was telephoned by Ken Ashmore, chairman of the governors. He said the school wished to appoint me as the new headteacher. Over the next few days, my appointment as head was announced to the school's staff and pupils, as well as to the parents. Fairly soon afterwards, someone I knew, who was very well-connected in the local area, said to me, 'Siôn, you need to watch your back. There are senior people at County Hall who did not want you to be appointed to this position'.

I think the primary reason why they didn't want me as headteacher of William Parker was because of my involvement, peripheral as it had been, in Conservative party politics. At that time, there was the issue of grant-maintained status. The school had been the old Hastings grammar school and they feared that I would take it back to grant-maintained status and re-establish it along the lines of the old grammar school.

When I got the job, Lois was quiet and said little, but my daughters erupted with delight.

Nevertheless, we decided that we would have to look for a new home in Hastings. The security situation was deteriorating. There had been further break-in attempts at our home, one of which had damaged the patio doors. Our side entrance was often used as a short-cut between, at the front, the park and the road leading from the town, and at the back, the allotments and the housing estate further up.

There was an attempted break-in from the back towards the end of 1994, which was when the French windows were damaged. As a result, we acquired Buster, a Staffordshire bull terrier, albeit one of the less fearsome of that breed; he was not the most effective of guard dogs.

There was frequent damage to our vehicles, and glue had been squirted into the locks. On one occasion, the Renault was vandalised, though we thought that some of these problems could be attributed to Lois's work. Certainly, one local family believed that she had reported them to the local child protection team. This family subsequently made an official complaint to the Director of Social Services, and we had to engage a solicitor to respond for us.

The house next door, which adjoined ours, was a constant problem. After the previous owners left, it had been purchased by Orbit, a housing association that aims to deliver affordable housing in line with community needs. However, the property had stood empty since Orbit had bought it in March 1996.

It attracted the homeless, looking for somewhere to bed down.

'It has been burgled numerous times,' said Lois in her first statement. 'Fireplaces have been stripped out and lead has been taken off the roof. As far as I am aware, people have been considering squatting there and prowlers were often hanging around, which increased the vulnerability of our house.'

After Lois corresponded with Orbit, the house was boarded up but the problems continued.

'People are still getting in there', she asserted. 'I have called the police each time I have heard heavy footsteps inside. Since it has been unoccupied, it has given me the feeling that people have been hanging around our house. It got in such a state that I made several complaints and took some photographs and some workmen did come and tidy the place up.

'Denise and I used to walk the dog in the late evening. One day I returned to see Siôn looking very pale and I understood there had been a prowler at the rear of our house. Sometime around 3 December, the dog started barking and going berserk about 11.00pm every night. When I let him out, he shot up the garden. On one of these occasions, I found that the side gate was open. Siôn and I talked about reporting these prowlers, but I believed that if next door was sorted out, everything would be alright.'[3]

That Christmas, while we were away at my parents' house in Wales, our neighbours did report to police seeing a man staring through the windows of the house. On our return, I saw someone standing in Alexandra Park opposite staring into the house. I went out, taking the dog with me, but the man had disappeared.

Just before the murder occurred, the scary incidents became even more concentrated. 'Towards the end of January, there was a week when we had a lot of problems with the side gate being opened', said Lois. 'It always happened when the dog was out. On Saturday 25 January, I came back from walking the dog to find the side gate open, the same again on the Monday.'

On Tuesday 28 January, I saw someone at the back of the house. I went to the French windows and then flicked on the spotlight and was aware of someone moving across the garden. I went to the kitchen to see if the person was going to go, but by the time I went outside he had gone.

Two days later, we had security lights installed at the rear of the house. They were put up for us by Chris Lancaster. On Tuesday, 4 February, he came back to put up security lights at the front. Unsure whether the incidents were human- or animal-related, Lois took further precautions.

'I bought a padlock on Saturday [8 February] for the side gate', she said, 'but I started putting a bag of compost and a red pole against the gate to establish whether it was a badger or a prowler.'

We had already had the house valued by local estate agents, and had looked at other properties, though all had been too small to accommodate our family. On the very afternoon of the murder, Lois, as she said, 'intended to call into the estate agents opposite the Blue Dolphin chip shop', but had arrived about three minutes after they closed at 4.00pm.

We had also received a number of silent telephone calls, where the caller simply hung up without speaking. 'As far as I'm aware, this happened three times since last November,' said Lois. 'Siôn received two such calls, and Billie said that she had had calls too, although I was not sure if she had. We'd check through 1471. On the occasions where the phone was put down, the number was withheld.'

Lois mentioned one particular call. 'On either the 5 or the 12 January, we returned from church to find a message on our answerphone', she stated. 'It was an American female voice which said something like, "He will come again to be our judge". It sounded like a tape-recording, like a preacher's sermon. It was quite a chilling experience.'

The first half-term week of that year began on 10 February 1997. Usually, we spent these school holidays all together as a family. This time, however, as Lois had her new job, she would be working in London although on the Wednesday she'd arranged to take some of the girls with her. I'd organised my work so that I could look after the children for much of the rest of the week. I can remember that Esther and Maya wanted to cook, Billie wanted to put on a drama production, Charlotte wanted to play tennis with Annie, and they wanted me to umpire. The week would be a good one.

Of course, as the new head, I was also busy planning for the next academic year, and sometimes I had to collect papers from my office. When I went in, I often took the girls with me. They enjoyed revolving in my swivel chair, pretending to be the head.

I had also brought the school's camcorder home with me. William

Parker was seeking special sports status and looking to improve its athletics facilities. I'd intended to make a film of the school's playing fields to illustrate the kind of improvements that were needed.

'Dad, what's this?' the children asked.

They passed it around, recorded each other, put the tape in the video-player and thought it was 'brilliant'. They had a box of dressing-up clothes and performed Billie's little drama. There was only one videotape, but that week they used it over and over.

Billie and Annie were keen to earn some extra pocket money, in order to buy new trainers. Lois and I had just opened Barclay's bank accounts for them all, so I said, you've got some money in your account, I'll pay you a little extra for some chores, put that towards it and you can go and buy them.

So Billie and Annie wanted to be allocated jobs. I suggested that they wait until the end of the week, partly because I was stuck trying to think of jobs for them to do. However, they came up with their own ideas: washing the cars; painting the patio doors; and clearing out the utility room.

Towards the end of the week, Billie-Jo took telephone calls from Bill Jenkins and her aunt, Margaret, and her cousin. This was the first time she had spoken to them for quite a while.

Thursday, 13 February was Esther's ninth birthday. That afternoon, Ruth Bristow was dropped off at our house by her mother. She was surprised to see Billie-Jo, with Buster, the dog, waiting for her outside the house.

I was working at William Parker. Lois had taken the other children to the adventure play area, leaving Billie to wait for Ruth. When Ruth arrived, Billie-Jo told her she had been too scared to remain inside the house on her own because of her fears about a prowler. Of course, we had no idea about this at the time. Indeed, no one at all knew anything about it until nine years later when Ruth gave evidence at the third trial.

That evening, Billie-Jo had a sleep-over at Ruth's house. The following morning, she went swimming with Holly. I picked them up and brought them back home. It must have been before that that I'd been to Do-It-All, the local DIY superstore, to get paint and a brush to paint the French windows.

Living on the South Coast

This was to be the last week I would spend with my daughters. One day, we decided to make a tuna pasta bake. Esther and Maya loved the mess, and getting their arms covered in flour and milk and margarine. Annie and Billie helped them, and Charlotte moved between her two sets of sisters, enjoying her different roles with each.

So the end of the week soon came. In the afternoon, I allowed Billie-Jo to go into Hastings with Holly. As far as I know, they went through the arcades of the Old Town, and into Superdrug and Debenham's, where Billie chose the trainers she wanted to buy the following day.

Denise Lancaster arrived to use the computer, which was in Annie's room at the top of the house. She had an arrangement with us that she could come in at any time to use it, as she didn't have one of her own. (She had keys to the house, as well as to one of our cars.) In her statement, she said:

> It was around 5.00pm, and Siôn was at home with the children. The house was incredibly calm. Siôn had made all the children a meal and quite clearly seemed to be enjoying himself. He brought a cup of tea up to me, and I could hear him chatting to the kids and getting them ready for their baths. The atmosphere was remarkably nice, and I remember thinking that the household was lovely.

I fitted in some school work, and at tea-time telephoned Dr Robert Megit. He was both the school's chemistry teacher and also the senior administration officer. The school was going through a difficult patch, and it looked as though some staff would have to be made redundant. I asked him about the timetabling implications of that. He promised to work out the details for me and said he'd let me have them 'over the weekend'.

Lois returned home from London.

The girls wanted to tell her about their day. I think Lois was just tired, and basically when the girls rushed up and said they'd had a lovely day, it just irritated her. When Billie told her that she had been into town to look at trainers, she turned on me and demanded to know why I had let Billie go into town with Holly. She said that Billie did not deserve a treat, and anyway was too young to go wandering around town.

I didn't know that in the previous week Lois had done exactly the same thing and allowed Billie to go into town with Ruth. More importantly, when she had taken the girls to London for the day earlier in the week, she had taken them to London Zoo in Regent's Park and left them there while she carried on to work. I had no idea she was going to do that, and would never have allowed it.

That evening, when Regine Renac, the au pair, came at about 7.30 to babysit, Lois said she wanted to go for a drink at the Anchor pub in Hastings old town. We'd been there an hour or so, when I looked up to see Peter Gaimster peering through the window. It turned out that the Anchor, which was very near to his shop, was his local.

He and Julia said they were going to a concert, and asked if we would like to join them. Lois said, 'Shall we?' I felt that my Valentine's evening with Lois had been hijacked, but I accepted the situation and said, 'Yes, I'm happy with that'.

However, we'd told Regine we would be back so that she could go out. By this stage, it was almost 10.00pm and when Lois phoned to try to get her to extend the babysitting time, Regine was understandably not open to persuasion. She had made her own arrangements to go out with her boyfriend, Ardie Griffiths.

So, after Julia Gaimster had lent Lois a coat (as it was fairly cold), we went home.

As I went to sleep, I was thinking about what to do over the weekend. The weather forecast was good, and I wanted to do something together as a family before the girls went back to school.

Chapter Seven

Remembering the Day

It is impossible for me to relate the events of that dreadful day myself, because of what might superficially appear to be two irreconcilable reasons. On the one hand, everything that happened remains too horrific for me to contemplate; on the other hand, I have been through it all a thousand times.

I have reflected on the nuances of every action and reaction, however minor. During my prison years, I thought about all this constantly. I had to deal with it all, and the emotions that welled up as the memories were rekindled, on my own. I continue to have flashbacks about what I saw; and, whenever I do, I am overwhelmed.

It was truly a scene no one would ever wish to see. When I pulled Billie towards me, I'd heard what I described at the time as a 'squelching sound' – but in fact it was more of a deep guttural sound coming from within her. I had never heard a noise like it. There was thick blood everywhere. The blood contained clots and dark tissue and smelt of tar. Around her face were pieces of bone and what I now know was brain tissue.

Then my daughters, Annie and Charlotte, were crying and screaming.

I felt I had to spare them the horror of actually seeing her, so I closed the dining room door and tried to keep them in the playroom at the front of the house. That was virtually my last instinctive natural reaction. After that, I think I closed down emotionally and just went into deep shock. For much of the time, I could not respond to or even hear what was being said to me. I can remember Lois, when she arrived, asking who had found Billie. When I said I had, she said, 'You poor thing', and put her arms round me, trying to comfort me.

Nothing in my life had prepared me for such a situation. If it had been a stranger I had found, then perhaps I could have been more rational and better able to cope. But not in those circumstances; not when it was Billie who was fighting for, and then losing, her life.

I was left feeling totally disconnected, and somehow alienated from those who couldn't understand the enormity of the tragedy.

Over the years since, I have been interrogated for days about everything that happened, both in police interviews and in the course of examination and cross-examination during three trials. I seem to have been picked up on every word I have ever used. I have also heard everyone else's evidence in exhaustive detail and pored over their statements hundreds of times. A point comes where you need to ask yourself whether you are remembering events as they happened or as they have finally emerged in the collective consciousness of all those involved.

So, the following account of the day is taken from the statements and recollections of those involved when their memories were at their sharpest and not muddied either (in the immediate aftermath) by utter distress or (in the longer term) by having been influenced by extraneous ideas or the requirement to stick to a received scenario.

Chapter Eight

Saturday, 15 February 1997

Siôn awoke, opened the curtains, and the sun streamed through the first-floor bedroom windows. The bright weather held the promise of a perfect day.

Nevertheless, there were moments of discord almost from the start. Having seen the trainers she wanted, Billie-Jo wanted to go into town with Ruth to buy them. But Lois, who was perhaps still fractious from the evening before, told her there were jobs to be done instead, and Billie-Jo left the room petulantly, muttering under her breath something that could have been, 'You bitch'.

So as Siôn came out of the bathroom, there was tension already. His initial instinct was to confront Billie-Jo but Lois demurred. If she had called Lois a bitch, it would have been for the first time; and Lois wasn't even sure that it had happened anyway. Was that what Billie-Jo had actually said? Lois didn't know. Siôn decided to smooth things over. Apart from anything else, he had a high regard for Ruth, and was keen to encourage Billie-Jo's friendship with her. So he said that Billie-Jo could go out later on, once the jobs had been done. She telephoned Ruth, and they arranged to meet at about 4.00.

Charlotte, with her friend Bobby, was given a lift to the Saturday cinema to see *Toy Story*. Annie had also intended to go but, annoyingly, her friend had cried off. She asked Lois to take her instead, but Lois had refused. In her police interview, Annie commented, 'I was angry with Mum 'cos she wouldn't take me'.

During the morning, Lois cleaned and hoovered, and Billie-Jo walked Buster in the park. Siôn went out to collect his MG from its garage in St Helen's Park Road on the other side of the park, about fifteen minutes' walk away. They were a three-car family. The main vehicle was a Citroen Synergie – they'd always had a people-carrier, just because of the number of children. They also had a gold Opel saloon, a basic family car; if just two or three of the girls needed transporting, they'd probably use that. Then there was Siôn's white MG sports car which, as it wasn't safe to leave a soft-top sports car out on the road, had to be garaged.

Meanwhile, back at home, Regine arrived. She had come over from France six months earlier, for the start of the 1996–7 school year, to work for them, initially as a live-in au pair. She had, however, moved out to her own flat the previous weekend. Now, she was checking on future babysitting assignments, although the main purpose of her visit was to patch things up with Lois after the flare-up between them the evening before.

Regine entered the dining room, where Lois was talking with Annie, Esther and Maya. There was almost immediately friction between Lois and Regine, who then stormed out of the room. Lois went after her and took her upstairs. She told her not to behave like that in front of the children, adding that she had been offended by her conduct the night before. Regine told her that she had ruined her Valentine's evening, and then started crying. So the tension ebbed. 'I told her that I did not like the way she had treated me the night before', explained Regine. 'We apologised to each other and parted on good terms.'

Having returned from collecting the MG, Siôn went into the bedroom where they were talking to ask for the cheque book to pay the milkman. By then, Ardie was waiting outside in his car, and Regine went off with him. Lois then took Annie, Esther and Maya with her on the weekly shopping trip to the local Safeway's supermarket.

Billie-Jo preferred to stay in and play with the camcorder. The dressing-up box lacked some articles of clothing, so she asked Siôn, who was going through some paperwork, for an old tie she could use. He found one, and showed her how to tie it on herself, and she then put it on the dog and filmed him. She also spent time playing with Charlotte and Bobby, who had arrived back from the cinema very soon after Lois had gone out.

The phone rang. It was Annie, ringing from the supermarket. Lois had a mobile phone, the only one in the household, but did not keep it properly charged. As the battery was low, she gave Annie 20p to call Siôn from a pay-phone.

It was a minor emergency. They were at the checkout with a trolley-full of goods, but Lois had forgotten to take her cheque book and had no means of paying. Siôn would have to drive down to Safeway's with it.

As the day was so sunny, just about the first sunny Saturday of the year, he had already folded down the MG's soft top. Now he drove the car down to Safeway's to settle the bill, only to discover that there was a further snag. The cheque book he had grabbed from the bedroom was the wrong one; there were no cheques left in it, only paying-in slips. Lois explained which of her bags the new book was in. So, taking Annie with him, Siôn drove back to Lower Park Road and waited in the car as she dashed in to get Lois's bag. They then drove back to Safeway's so that Lois could pay for the food. Siôn and Annie drove back again, and Lois arrived about ten minutes afterwards with the other girls and the groceries.

Bobby went home, and the Jenkins family had soup for their lunch. By then, already, the day had not been uneventful: there had been domestic flashpoints, with friction between Lois and Billie-Jo, Lois and Regine, and Lois and Annie; and a double muddle at the supermarket. Lois described the family sitting down together to lunch as 'the calm after the storm'.

In view of the fine weather, Siôn raised the possibility of them all going out for the afternoon, but Billie-Jo and Annie had firmly resolved to do the jobs. Although there was some rivalry about who was going to get which job, they had by then resolved it between themselves. Lois had another conversation with Billie-Jo, after the latter confronted her, saying, 'You don't want me to buy the shoes this afternoon'. Lois made it clear to her that she might not be able to get them after all and that in any case she, Lois, wanted some involvement, if only to make sure that Billie-Jo bought the right ones.

Annie and Billie-Jo ran upstairs to change into some old clothes in order to do the jobs. Annie at first came down in an Armani T-shirt, so Lois went with them. She found suitable clothes for Annie and gave Billie-Jo some of her old clothes: a jumper, ski pants and a pair of her old boots. Then Billie-Jo started to sweep the patio while Annie began clearing out the utility room.

No sooner had one domestic muddle been resolved than there was another. Charlotte had a clarinet lesson at 2.00 with her friend, Ellen Carey. There seems to have been an arrangement between their mothers that one family would take them both and the other would pick them up. So Mrs Carey arrived and took Ellen and Charlotte to the music lesson.

Lois had decided to go out. She was going to take Esther and Maya into town so that Esther could spend her birthday money, and then they would walk the dog along the seafront. This meant that Siôn would have to pick up Charlotte. However, he didn't know where Nicola Holt, the music teacher, lived (the lessons were given at her house); and nor did Lois have her address. She did, however, know which house it was. So, together with Esther and Maya, they got in the Citroen and Lois then drove them there so that Siôn could see where it was. They arrived almost straight after Mrs Carey, who could hardly have failed to notice them (whatever merits people-carriers may have, inconspicuousness is not among them).

They drove back to drop off Siôn. Lois then went off with Esther and Maya. She parked the Citroen, and left the dog in the car while they went to Debenham's, where Esther chose a T-shirt and a black skirt. Lois bought the children some sweets, and they went to the seafront. The children had rides on the ghost train and the roundabout and then Lois bought them some chips.

Meanwhile, when Siôn had got back into the house, he found that both girls felt they had completed their initial jobs. Billie-Jo had swept up some twigs and leaves into a black bin-liner bag. Annie had cleared out the utility room, putting some things, including the tent pegs, on top of the coal-bunker. However, as this had a bashed-in top, rainwater collected there, and so the contents of the tool-box – hammers and suchlike – were laid out on the picnic table on the patio at the back of the house to ensure that they stayed dry.

Now, the children were ready to move on to less menial, more responsible tasks. The patio doors had needed painting since an attempted break-in. Although the intruders hadn't succeeded in getting in, they had damaged the wood and broken a pane of glass. This had been replaced, but the putty was still bare. The day before, Siôn had got a tin of paint and a paintbrush. He then began to show Billie-Jo how to paint the patio doors, starting at the top and working downwards. He explained that she was not, of course, to get paint on the window-panes.

Annie was waiting to start cleaning the Opel. Siôn took two cheap buckets, a beige one and a black one, from under the kitchen sink. He filled one with hot water and left it on the table, put detergent in the other and, picking up a sponge, went out to show Annie how to wash the car. He returned to Billie-Jo to find her painting the inside, not the outside, of the doors, and explained again what he wanted her to do. She stuck her tongue out at him in jest. He went back to Annie and helped her for a few minutes.

Siôn continued tidying up. He went to the side gate, which closed the passageway between the front steps, and the garden and patio area at the back of the house. The latch did not work properly. He removed the red broomstick that was used to secure the gate, and put a bag of peat there to keep it open. He swept the area along the side of the house and around the utility room, and then returned to see how Billie-Jo was getting on.

'Billie', he said, 'what are you doing?'

Her painting was a mess. She was getting paint over the windows. He showed her how to do it again. He'd also noticed that she was squatting on her haunches, and looked uncomfortable; so he fetched a blanket, folded it and put it inside a black bin-liner, so making her a cushion to sit on. He demonstrated how to paint, going along the bottom of the door with a brush, which gave Billie-Jo the opportunity to clamber on his back, putting her legs over his shoulders as if he were giving her a piggy-back. She got down, resumed painting and Siôn walked off. He had got paint on his cuff. He had also noticed paint on the patio tiles, and realised he needed white spirit.

'Aren't I doing it properly?' she called after him.

He returned and cuddled her. 'Of course you are', he said.

Annie was tipping out the dirty water so Siôn refilled the bucket with clean and went out with what he described as a 'leather' to dry off the car. Subsequently, he remembered momentarily sitting at the kitchen table and snatching the kind of two-minute respite that parents of growing children learn to be grateful for. However, Annie soon returned for the dustpan and brush in order to clean the inside of the car, and Siôn got the keys and opened it for her.

By then, it was nearing 3.00, and time to fetch Charlotte. In fact, Siôn was by now a little late. Annie wanted to go with him, but Billie-Jo was listening to the radio and said she would continue painting. They arranged that Annie would take over the painting on their return from picking up Charlotte. On his way out, Siôn closed the side gate and used the bag of peat to hold it shut.

When he got to Nicola Holt's house, there were three children outside waiting for him. Charlotte had been trying to contact him, and had rung her mother's mobile to ask where her father was, but Lois now had it switched off. Nicola Holt, who was preparing to go out herself, then suggested that Charlotte and Ellen, with her own daughter for company, should go and wait outside.

Now, there was a further example of faulty communication lines: Siôn was surprised to learn that he was also obliged to take Ellen home. So Annie sat in the front passenger seat, with Charlotte and Ellen on the bench at the back, the girls' long hair streaming out behind as they drove. Ellen had only just moved house; she knew where she lived but not how to get there. So Siôn drove back to Lower Park Road – the idea being that she could phone her mother from there – although, as they arrived on familiar territory, she said she thought she could find her way. After a few false turns, the navigation was successful and Siôn got her home. As her daughter was overdue, Mrs Carey was anxiously looking out of the front window when they arrived; she estimated that Ellen was dropped off between 3.15 and 3.20.

They went back to Lower Park Road. Charlotte quickly dropped her clarinet back into her bedroom, then came back downstairs and opened the dining room door to go into the kitchen to get a bucket of water. The arrangement was that while Annie would take over the painting from Billie-Jo, Charlotte was going to wash the MG. But Siôn told Charlotte to hold on as they had to go out again; if the painting was going to continue, then they would certainly need white spirit. They went out again. As they reached the car, Annie commented to Charlotte that she didn't think the car needed washing, but Charlotte wasn't to be dissuaded; she was looking forward to doing her job.

Siôn always drove off in the direction the car was facing; he considered it too dangerous, especially with children in the car, to do three-point turns on a winding road with free-flowing traffic. So he went round the bottom of Alexandra Park and turned up the other side. It had been a lovely day, but it was now getting late to be bothering about painting, so he decided to return home again. However, as he turned back towards home, he could tell that Annie was upset.

'How desperate are you to paint?' he asked.

'Very desperate', she replied.

Annie's disappointment was not the only factor. He was aware that the little dispute earlier in the day about which of the girls was going to do the painting had been settled by arranging that each of them did some. So, as every parent knows, he had to treat the children fairly and keep his promises. Siôn drove past their house and again took up the temporarily abandoned route to the local DIY store. Just as they reached it, however, Siôn felt in his trouser-pocket and realised he hadn't taken any money with him. He only had a few loose coins in his trouser pocket; he checked in the glove compartment but there was nothing there. The children, of course, didn't have any. 'I think I said to the girls, well, you know, I've tried', Siôn stated feebly. He turned round in the entrance and returned home.

It was then that the girls discovered Billie-Jo.

As they went into the house, the children running in ahead of their father, as children do, there was suddenly a dreadful cry from Charlotte.

'Dad! Billie's hurt!'

She was lying on the patio, facing away from the house and broadly parallel to it, with her legs straight out. Her right shoulder, Siôn noticed as he went to her, was slightly raised and the left side of her face was against the patio concrete. There was blood, thick blood, all around her head. He realised that Annie and Charlotte were moving warily towards him and turned back to usher them out and into the playroom. Both girls were crying, and he tried to say something reassuring: 'Billie's had an accident, but she's going to be OK'.

He was about to call an ambulance, but at that moment the telephone started ringing. Already panicked, and now racked with indecision, he was momentarily in a quandary. He wondered how to disconnect the phone, but then simply picked up the receiver and slammed it down, several times, to prevent it ringing. Eventually, it stopped.

The hiatus, brief as it had been, caused him to vacillate. Had he really seen what he thought he'd seen? He returned to Billie-Jo and pulled her up towards him. Only then did he get an inkling of the extent of her injuries. 'As I pulled her towards me, there was a squelching sound', he said in his statement. 'Her head was limp and she was covered in blood. I thought initially of trying to render mouth-to-mouth, but she was totally covered in blood. I was absolutely horrified, I then released my grip on her shoulder and ran back through the dining room. I was aware that Annie and Charlotte were crying in the playroom. I knew by this time that what had happened to Billie couldn't have been an accident, although I may well have told Annie and Charlotte that she'd had an accident.

'I used the telephone in the hallway, Billie's phone, and rang for an ambulance, I think that the girls and I were only in the house for around two minutes before I actually rang for the ambulance. Everything happened very quickly.'

The call to the emergency services was timed at 3.38. It was recorded, as are all calls to the emergency services. Siôn gave his address, adding, 'And it is an emergency'.

The operator asked what had happened.

'I don't, I really, I don't know', replied Siôn. 'My daughter's fallen, or she's got head injuries, there's blood everywhere, she's lying on the floor.'

The operator asked if she was conscious.

'No, she's not conscious. I've just run. I'm going to go back for her now.'

'You say she's unconscious', continued the operator, 'Is she breathing alright?'

'I don't, I don't know, I haven't looked.'

'Right, OK, and did this happen while you were out of the house then?'

'Yes, it, I've just, I've just this minute got back.'

'Oh, right, so you don't know how long…'

'I don't know how, well, in the next, in the last, I don't know – half-an-hour, three-quarters of an hour.'

The operator told Siôn to lay his daughter on her side in the recovery position and to tilt her head back by lifting up her chin.

'But I need to go to her, can you get the ambulance quickly?'

The operator explained that she was telling Siôn what to do until the ambulance could get there. She added, 'And if she's not breathing, you need to ring us back, okay?'

She then said goodbye. Siôn said, 'So if she doesn't move, do I phone you back?'

The operator repeated her instructions about rolling her on to her side.

The children were screaming that he should phone their mother. As Siôn did not know the number, Charlotte telephoned, again using Billie's phone, but Lois's mobile was still switched off. In any event, she was on the beach. Siôn needed immediate assistance – he had Billie-Jo in one room and two utterly distraught children in another.

He returned to Billie-Jo and said something like, 'It's going to be all right', checked again on Annie and Charlotte, and then telephoned Denise Lancaster. Her six-year-old son answered the phone and, when he passed it over to his mother, Siôn said something like, 'It's Billie, there's been an accident, will you come, I don't know what to do'. Denise reacted straightaway to the urgency in his voice.

As he moved ineffectually between Billie-Jo and the two inconsolable children, Siôn, at that moment in the front playroom with Annie and Charlotte, saw Bob Megit coming up the drive. Of course! He'd asked him to drop off those figures. Megit could scarcely have arrived at a more inopportune time. Siôn simply opened the door, said, 'Thanks, Bob', and went to close it straightaway, however discourteous it seemed. Megit could sense that there was something wrong – 'Normally', he said in his statement, '[Siôn] was very friendly' – and naturally did not wish to intrude on a difficult family situation. It was not a moment for accidental outsiders.

In fact, Megit and Denise Lancaster had arrived almost simultaneously, and just in the few brief seconds that Siôn had opened the door to him, she'd ran through and into the house. Siôn indicated that she should go into the dining room, saying, 'It's Billie, I've called an ambulance'.

Denise looked at Billie and moved her slightly by the shoulder. Billie's head was lying in blood which had collected in a pool on a black bin-liner beneath her. Her right hand, covered in paint, was up towards her face. Denise felt for a pulse; the girl seemed warm. She said she would have put Billie-Jo into what is termed the recovery position, but could immediately see that her injuries were so acute that she was fearful of moving her. Though Siôn had received no first-aid training, she had done a short course. 'One of the things you're told', she explained, 'is that you don't do anything in a situation like that.'

She then went into the playroom to comfort Annie and Charlotte. 'Either he or I would be there [with Billie-Jo]', she explained, 'and the other was with Annie and Lottie, who were pretty hysterical.'

Although she and Siôn were never with Billie-Jo at the same time, they both returned to her separately in those few minutes. 'I got a towel from the downstairs toilet and put it around her head', said Denise. 'It was my intention to stem the flow of blood from her head wound. Then I looked at her more closely and saw that her head was completely shattered – you could see her brain and her skull. It was devastating.'

At this point, she also noticed that one end of the bin-liner on which Billie-Jo had fallen was actually stuffed up the girl's left nostril. She pulled the bin-liner out of the nose, and later remarked, 'I was astonished at how deeply it was in the nose, it was hard to pull out'. When she had pulled it out, blood flowed from Billie-Jo's nose.

'That was the only movement', she said. 'The scene was still, she was still. Her body felt warm.'

While this was going on, they were both encouraging Annie and Charlotte to keep away. The dining room door, leading to where Billie-Jo was lying, was kept closed. 'From where Annie and Lottie were, you could see through to the patio if the door was open', said Mrs Lancaster, 'so the door was closed to obscure her from the children.'

Siôn then crouched down beside Billie-Jo. 'I felt her neck. I moved her hair off the side of her face,' he said in his statement. 'I then became aware that her forehead appeared to be different, it was mis-shapen. I also saw that her eye was swollen, as if someone had punched her. I then noticed a bubble from her nose and I believe that she was alive at that moment. I also noticed that I had blood on my hands – I felt sick. I stood up and tried to shake the blood off my hands, it was actually my left hand that was covered in blood.

'I went into the dining room and started to go back to the girls. My hand still had blood on it so I went to the downstairs toilet and washed it off by running my hand under the tap. I came out of the toilet and went to see Annie and Lottie and told them everything was going to be alright. Denise was still in the playroom with the girls and I then returned to Billie.'

When making this statement a few days later, Siôn said, 'To illustrate the way I felt, probably from the moment that I crouched next to Billie and used my hand to move her hair, I think that an elephant could have been in my house and I wouldn't have noticed it, I was so shocked'.

Although it had initially crossed Denise's mind that Billie-Jo had fallen, she did look at Siôn at one point and say: 'This was no accident'.

She suggested they should phone the emergency services again. 'Everybody was in a state', she said, 'because the ambulance hadn't arrived.'

This second call was timed at 3.46, eight minutes after the previous one. There followed another recorded conversation. Siôn explained that he had already phoned for an ambulance, but it had not arrived. Denise then grabbed the phone and said:

'This is a total, total emergency.'

'Is there any pulse?' asked the operator.

'Very, very, very faint', replied Denise, 'she's slightly warm and yet she may have just lost it by now, she's very, she's just warm, tepid, you know…'

Charlotte then yelled out that the ambulance had, in fact, just gone past the house. Denise continued talking to the operator. 'Have you got paramedics coming?' she enquired. 'Her skull is just smashed. She's fallen over and it's just… '

'She's fallen over and she's got *that* injury?' queried the operator.

Siôn and the girls rushed outside to expedite the arrival of the paramedics. In fact, the ambulance had overshot because there are houses only on one side of the road – Alexandra Park being opposite – and so, unusually, they are numbered consecutively, not in odd or even numbers. The ambulance team had accordingly miscalculated. Siôn saw that it was stationary further down the road. He ran down to it and rapped on the front passenger side-window and the driver started to reverse. The two-man crew said they were aware of Siôn, Denise, and one of the girls on the path all beckoning them in.

As Annie diverted another accidental outsider away from the house ('Lottie's friend was outside the door and I had to tell him to go home, 'cos he was, like, coming to see Lottie'), Gerry Radford, who'd worked for the local ambulance service for twenty-four years, grabbed a portable defibrillator and followed Siôn into the house. Christopher Burton, the ambulance driver, finished reversing back and then grabbed more equipment and quickly went inside.

Already, by the time Burton got there, Radford had carried out basic checks and recognised that Billie-Jo's injuries were clearly fatal. A police car arrived at 3.55, straight after the ambulance. As police constables Christopher Bruce and David Morgan watched, the ambulancemen turned Billie-Jo over and on to her back and, in doing so, exposed the full extent of her injuries for the first time. A large part of her skull had been shattered; in the centre of the wound, a piece of skull was sticking out at a right angle. On the adjacent bin-liner, Burton noticed blood, fragments of bone and pieces of brain tissue. He also saw two large and almost complete footprints, of both a left and a right sole, on Billie's legs, one on the right-hand side and one on her left upper thigh. 'I had the impression', he said, 'that someone had stood on Billie-Jo's legs.'

There was no sign of a pulse and Billie's pupils were fixed and dilated. She was cold and turning blue. A pair of glasses, her own, were on the ground, close by. They had been neatly folded. Then, on top of the second black bin-liner, lay a bloodied metal bar.

At some point, meanwhile, Siôn seems to have got into the MG. 'Although I don't physically remember getting into the MG', he explained, 'I do recall actually finding myself sat in it.'

The instant he realised where he was, however, he understood that it was 'a stupid thing to do… I remember thinking, "What the bloody hell am I doing here?" Literally the minute my bottom hit the seat I was up and out… The impulse of getting in to the MG was immediately followed by my getting out of it'.

He then went into the house. 'I can remember standing in the hallway', he said, 'and I felt alone. I didn't know where Denise was. I just felt like I was in a nightmare.'

He walked back towards the dining room. Seeing him approaching, PC Bruce ushered him out and suggested he wait upstairs, saying, 'You can't go in there, the ambulance crew are doing all they can'. Siôn went to his bedroom, where Denise was trying to comfort Annie and Charlotte.

'Is it the prowler that's done this?' asked Charlotte. 'When we left, the side gate was shut. When we got back, the side gate was open.'

'Are you sure, Lottie?' asked Siôn.

'Yes, I am sure.'

Siôn then phoned Lois again, after Charlotte had told him the number, but again there was no answer. He left a message: 'Hurry up and get home, something dreadful's happened'.

Billie's friend, Ruth, then phoned. Of course, Billie had arranged to go to Debenham's with her.

'Is Billie coming round?' asked Ruth.

'No', Siôn said, 'she isn't going to meet you.'

'Why?'

'No, Ruth, too much going on.'

While the ambulancemen and the two police officers were attending to Billie-Jo, members of the family were not allowed through. In his statement, Siôn continued, 'I can remember one of the girls saying to me, "Why aren't they taking her to hospital?" and I can actually remember thinking that myself, though I told the girls that they've got everything they needed here already.'

The ambulance crew told the police officers that Billie-Jo had died. At 4.07, a police car containing two plain-clothes officers, Detective Sergeant Anne Capon and Detective Constable Paul Hilton drew up, and Capon took charge of the situation. Seeing Siôn coming downstairs, she briefly spoke to him, and suggested that he go into the lounge. PC Bruce went in with him, asking, 'Can I have a brief word with you?' Siôn recalled, 'I sat down on the sofa. He didn't actually tell me that Billie was dead, he said to me that they did everything they could to save her'. According to Bruce's notebook entry, Siôn was 'stunned'.

Siôn went to tell Denise. They thought about telling the children, but he acquiesced with Denise's feeling that Lois must be told first.

Lois did then telephone. It was about 4.20, and she had decided to take Esther and Maya to the children's room at the Pump House pub, and thought it would be a good idea for Siôn to bring the other children to join them. So, she switched on her mobile and phoned home. Siôn, who had been expecting her back between 3.00 and 4.00, answered immediately and told her that Billie-Jo had had an accident. She naturally started to ask questions, but Siôn interrupted, telling her to 'Get home quickly'.

Denise then took Annie and Charlotte along the road to her flat, as she didn't want Lois to be straightaway confronted by them 'being as hysterical as they were at that point'. Nor did the scenes-of-crimes personnel who were already assembling want to put on their white suits until Lois had arrived and been told.

But she didn't need to be told. When she drove in, past Sergeant Smith who had already been posted at the bottom of the steps to monitor movements, and past the police cars and the ambulance with its back doors ominously wide open, Lois perceived 'a certain hush which, having been a nurse, I associate with death'.

She rushed up the steps, with Capon trailing in her wake (though Capon at least managed to detain Esther and Maya outside). As she entered the house, Lois glimpsed 'a police officer with tears in his eyes at the top of the steps'. She was shown into the front living room where she found Siôn who was, she said, 'white, gaunt and… crying'. He told her that Billie-Jo had died, and they embraced, trying to console each other. Lois asked to see the dead child but Capon wouldn't let her into the dining room. Already, their house was no longer their own.

Capon asked them to leave, and sealed the crime scene for the scenes-of-crime officers (SOCOs, as they are known) to deal with. She walked with Siôn and Lois, and Esther and Maya, as well as the dog, up to Denise's flat. A lot of people were already there. As well as Denise and her husband and their son, Denise's brother Peter was also there with his wife Michelle and their two young children. It was there that Siôn told everyone that the ambulance men had not been able to revive Billie-Jo and she had died. Either Annie or Charlotte said, 'I knew it'. Lois stated, 'The children howled'.

At 4.50pm, the police surgeon, Dr Joseph Ludwig, pronounced Billie-Jo dead. 'Her skull was split in two directions and the brain matter was protruding', he commented. 'I have twenty-six years' experience as a police surgeon, and this was without doubt the saddest and most brutal murder I have ever attended.'

One of the immediate practical problems facing the Jenkins family was where they were going to stay. Denise's flat was far too small. So Siôn telephoned the Gaimsters, as they lived in a four-bedroomed house on the other side of the park. Julia answered the phone. Siôn asked her and Peter to come, but told them not to bring the children.

Julia had assumed that Peter was in the house, but it transpired that he had gone out, so she drove to Denise's on her own. As she drew up, Siôn was outside, at the roadside, waiting for her. He told her what had happened. She went back to her house in order to get someone to look after her two children temporarily and then found Peter at the Anchor pub. The two of them drove back to Denise's, where they straightaway agreed that the Jenkins family could stay at their house for the time being.

Others, too, had arrived at Denise's, including Lisa Franklin, Denise's sister. Capon, who had gone back to No.48, then returned. Capon also introduced them to two new police officers, DC Steve Hutt and WDC Tracy Christmas. While Christmas spoke to Lois in one room, Hutt was with Siôn in another.

Lois found people she knew from church who were willing to give Buster a temporary home. Wanting to make himself useful, Peter Gaimster offered to take him. All the others were congregated together in the open-plan living-area of the flat. As the hours passed, the children found the atmosphere increasingly oppressive, so Charlotte asked if they could leave. Julia offered to take them on to her house. Denise's brother, Peter, kindly offered to drive them all there. Joseph, Denise's son, went for the ride, so there were seven of them in the car.

WDS Capon then returned to deliver officially the news that Billie had died in suspicious circumstances, and that it was now a murder investigation. She asked questions about a crow-bar. The bloodied metal bar next to the body was 18" in length, ½" in diameter, and weighed 1½lbs. There was no possible doubt: it was the murder weapon. She could not afterwards recall whether it was Siôn or Lois who told her that it was probably one of the tent pegs. Siôn then explained about Annie clearing out the utility room and laying out the tools.

It was after nine o'clock when Hutt and Christmas were ready to drive Siôn and Lois to the Gaimsters'. The first stage of the car journey was merely a few yards, back to No. 48. They drew up and Hutt got out. Lois then saw Felix Simmons approaching the police car.

'I can remember Lois saying to me, "Felix is coming over"', stated Siôn. 'I can then remember WDC Christmas turning and saying, "Do you want to see him?" and Lois saying emphatically, "No". Tracy Christmas then got out of the car. I remember feeling very relieved when she went to deal with him.'

The purpose of stopping at their house was to enable Siôn and Lois to collect a few things. The police had cordoned off the house and were bringing in equipment to conduct forensic searches. Siôn and Lois noticed the scenes-of-crime personnel: 'lots of men walking around in white suits, snowmen suits'. An officer came over to the car to ask what the family needed. They began to tell him and he then asked if anyone had a pen and paper. 'I can remember thinking', said Siôn, 'they have all this equipment and yet nobody has got a pen and paper.'

Lois took an old envelope out of her bag, and made a list on the back: pyjamas, toothbrushes, books of telephone contact numbers, etc. A little while later, the man returned, saying he couldn't find several items, and that they weren't allowed the books containing the telephone numbers – were there any numbers they specifically needed? Siôn asked for the contact details for Roger Mitchell, the headteacher at William Parker.

Eventually, the officer returned with a brown paper bag containing the household items and, at about 10.30, Siôn and Lois arrived at the Gaimsters' house. By then, all the children had been put to bed.

Peter Gaimster, in the first of what would become a series of statements, said that there was a lot of activity, and that Lois had a lot of 'nervous energy'; Siôn, on the other hand, 'just sat there staring'; he 'wanted to be on his own', added Gaimster, 'and went up to bed at about 11.00pm'. Gaimster said that he and Julia and Lois stayed up talking until about one o'clock in the morning.

It had been a terrible, tragic day. Even so, none of the Jenkins family

could possibly have envisaged that the tragedy would envelop them for
years and years and destroy their family life.

Chapter Nine

Man on a Bench

The murder inquiry was led by the newly-promoted Detective Superintendent Jeremy Paine. 'This is a ferocious attack on a young girl in her home', he said. 'Jenkins and his two young daughters were confronted with a dreadful scene. You cannot begin to imagine what must have gone through their minds.

'It would have been easy for the killer to pick the tent peg up. Whoever was responsible for this vicious and evil attack must have been stained by blood, and probably by white paint on their clothing as well.'

Sussex police carried out immediate house-to-house inquiries in Lower Park Road. As forensic experts examined the murder weapon and the crime scene, police divers searched for clues in the park's ponds. Detective Superintendent Paine added that the family had been concerned about prowlers since Christmas. The police noted that the next-door house was run-down and unoccupied and thought it possible that the murderer could have hidden behind a hedge in the garden there, watching Billie-Jo painting the patio doors and laying in wait until the family went out before striking. 'It's the closest he could have got to her unseen so that he could have pounced without warning', said a police spokesman.

The story was extensively covered in all national newspapers. All the reports highlighted the immense tragedy of the murder. Jenny Blackburn, headmistress at Helenswood school, told the *Evening Standard* that Billie-Jo was 'lively, popular and caring' and added that 'she was full of character, and especially interested in acting'. The *Daily Telegraph* reported one neighbour as having described the Jenkins family as 'absolutely brilliant'; another, according to the *Express*, had pointed out that, 'You wouldn't [have known] Billie-Jo was a foster daughter. She was just one of the family. They all got on so well.'

Straightaway, the murder was linked to other crimes. 'Has the murder maniac struck before?" asked the *Express* in a front-page headline. Most papers instantly linked it to the high-profile and still-unsolved murders of Lin Russell and her daughter Megan in Chillenden, Kent, the previous year.[4]

However, there was one local incident that was of particular interest. Just a few months earlier, on 21 August 1996, a twelve-year-old girl was abducted at knifepoint as she wheeled her bike through a park in nearby St Leonard's. The attack took place in broad daylight, between 2.00 and 3.00pm, during the school summer holidays. The attacker forced the girl into nearby woodland, where he sexually assaulted her. A plastic bag was placed over her head and she was left for dead. Fortunately, she survived and was able to tell police, among other things, that her attacker had a scarred face.

'This is one of the most serious sex offences I have known in my career', said Detective Inspector Dick Barton, the man leading that investigation. 'This man is definitely unstable and we need to find him as soon as possible.'

Highly significant evidence about the Billie-Jo murder was provided by Denise Lancaster who was (leaving aside the Jenkins family) the sole independent witness. She was so concerned about one aspect of the murder – the plastic bag that she had pulled from 'deep' inside Billie-Jo's nose – that, with everyone gathered in her flat straight after the murder, she drew WDS Capon aside to impress it upon her.

'I told her about the plastic bin-liner in Billie's nostril', she said, 'I actually showed her what I was talking about by laying on the ground and demonstrating with one of my own bin-liners.'

The notion that someone might have carried out a brutal murder in broad daylight and then, rather then fleeing the scene straightaway, have lingered in order to feed a corner of a plastic bin-liner up through the victim's nose, was utterly extraordinary.

Reports began to emerge of a man with obvious mental difficulties wandering in the vicinity of the Jenkins home around the time of the murder. He was easily recognisable because, as one witness said, 'he had a prominent scar on his face. It was pink and vivid, not a new scar, and went from his forehead down towards his left cheek.'

On 17 February, therefore, there was some unanimity in the press about who the main suspect was. In its first report about Billie-Jo's murder, the *Daily Mirror*'s front-page report proclaimed:

FIND THE SCARFACE KILLER OF BILLIE-JO

The *Daily Mail*'s front-page headline was:

BILLIE-JO MURDER: HUNT FOR SCARFACE

The public did all that the police asked of them and supplied an abundance of information. The movements that day of the man with a scar on his face were easily established. In the morning, he had gone into the main NatWest bank in Hastings, claiming to have lost some cheques. The assistant there found him 'weird' and somewhat threatening. He then went into Safeway's, about an hour after Lois Jenkins had been there with three of her children. He told the checkout assistant that he'd been poisoned by milk he'd bought there. He nevertheless paid 39p for a French-style stick of bread, though he asked, 'Is it poisoned too?' The assistant thought he was 'probably suffering some form of mental complaint.'

He then headed away from the town centre towards Alexandra Park.

One witness who was working on his car said the man 'gave the impression that he had a mental condition'. This witness couldn't remember the scar particularly, although he said the man was 'quite red in the face'. He added, 'I think he had too much clothing on'.

Several people were disconcerted by the mere appearance of this man. One young mother, walking her young son in his buggy, commented, 'I thought this man looked a bit strange, and checked behind me to see if there was anyone else about.'

At about 3.00pm, he knocked on the door of 59 Lower Park Road, where for sixteen years Brian Kent had run a well-respected guest-house. The man asked about accommodation. 'I wouldn't have considered accepting him', said Kent, 'he was quite obviously suffering from mental health problems'.

Kent advised him to go back towards town, and was so anxious about him that he looked out of his window to ensure that he was leaving the property. Because of hedges and shrubs, Kent could not follow his progress down the road, but did know that he had turned right, in the direction of No.48.

In the middle of the afternoon, there were many sightings of this man, again in the park. One witness, whose young son was happily riding his bicycle, saw him on her way through the park down to the café. This first time, which was, she thought, towards 3.00, she said merely that, 'for some reason he made me feel uneasy'. However, her reaction was very different when she saw again on the way back: 'He was now leaning forward and was blowing his nose in a disgusting manner on to the ground. It made me feel awful and I wanted to go past him as soon as possible. I would say that the time then was about 3.55-4.00.'

A project manager said that his attention was drawn to this man as 'he had his finger poked up his nose'. Another witness, walking through the park with her fiancé, noticed him and commented, 'He appeared odd... I saw this man rubbing his nose and making sniffing noises and snorting through his nose... A short while, literally a few minutes after seeing this man, my attention was drawn to an ambulance speeding down Lower Park Road'.

Since virtually all of these witnesses had noticed this man's prominent facial scar, many locals began to ask whether these sightings had any connection with the assault on the twelve-year-old girl a few months earlier, the one that had been carried out by the man with 'a scarred face'.

Foremost among them was the girl's mother, who said, 'My little girl still wakes up screaming because of what happened to her. I can't begin to imagine what Billie-Jo's family is going through tonight. This man must be caught.'

There must be many hundreds of murder cases in which police have an immediate suspect but no means of identifying him. This case was an exception. The man was identified almost instantly. Two witnesses actually knew him. The first of these witnesses, a psychiatric nurse, saw him at about 2.30 by the junction with Dordrecht Way. Towards 4.00pm, a nursing assistant, out walking for the afternoon with her boyfriend and his two children, saw him coming towards them. She had been employed for eighteen months at a local hospital (although by then she had moved on to a different job). 'I immediately recognised him', she explained, 'and felt scared and nervous… '

The man was Mark Lynam.[5] He was in his forties and had a long history of mental illness. The previous day, an attempt had been made to section him. Social workers – a so-called rapid response team – had gone to his flat. Lynam was not at home. The team gave up and, their mission unfulfilled, left it for the weekend.

When he was seen for the last time on the Saturday, at about 5.30, he was walking along the seafront in the direction of St Leonard's, where he lived.

On Sunday morning, someone described as having 'red scarring on forehead and down nose' was seen at Chailey in Sussex, thumbing a lift northwards on the road from Lewes to Newick. That would appear to have been very unpropitious territory and a very unpropitious time for anyone thumbing a lift anywhere.

He was back at home the next day when police called at lunchtime to arrest him for the murder of Billie-Jo Jenkins.

As the police continued to knock, neighbours congregated and said they hadn't seen him all weekend. Another resident then produced a spare key to Lynam's flat (which he held at the request of Lynam's father). WDC Briggs then found they couldn't open the door as it was deadlocked from the inside. So he was in after all. Pyle and Law went to see if they could climb the fence at the back and get through the garden to the back entrance.

They'd been gone about ten minutes when Briggs heard them knocking at the back. Then, with just the two women there, the front door was suddenly opened and Lynam rushed out. Slamming the door behind him, he bolted for the front steps. Briggs tried to stand in his way. 'Lynam appeared very frantic and would not stop', she explained. 'He grabbed me with... his right hand around my throat and with one arm lifted me from the floor and threw me against the wall'.

As he ran down the steps outside, she succeeded in grabbing hold of the back of his belt. Lynam held on to railings outside and kept kicking her in the shins as he tried to pull himself away from her. He was deaf to Knowles' entreaties to calm down and, as Briggs bravely continued to hold on to him, he again grabbed her. 'I felt pain in my throat', she said, 'as he squeezed round my larynx'. Knowles ran back to alert Pyle and Law and, as Lynam tried to push Briggs backwards, a passing member of the public came to her assistance. 'Lynam then again became very violent', she reported, 'and began thrashing about with his arms and legs. We were having great difficulty holding him.'

At some point the three of them ended up on the ground, but Briggs was able to radio for urgent assistance. Then, having succeeded in entering the flat from the back only to discover that their man had flown, Pyle and Law arrived. The five of them finally managed to pin Lynam down.

The passer-by with a sense of civic responsibility modestly failed to leave his name and exited the scene anonymously. Sergeant Alan Gates and PC Christopher Kentdicks, who had been patrolling nearby and answered the call for assistance, put Lynam in handcuffs and took him to Hastings police station. 'He continued to make aggressive remarks', said

Man on a Bench

Law, who sat with him, 'and kept saying, "Check with the Victoria Hotel, I have a room there"'.

Lynam remained 'very violent and uncooperative', and, even as he was taken into the station, was, according to the custody officer, still 'struggling violently'. He was searched and told to empty his pockets. A list was made of the items taken from him. These included:

Belt
Seiko watch
Black empty wallet
Used tissues
A spoon
Biro (no nib)
Black pen (no nib)
Torn blue plastic bag
One small piece of blue plastic
One small piece of white plastic
One small piece of transparent plastic

Lynam then had his jacket and shoes removed and was placed in a cell. Shortly afterwards, Law, checking through the wicket-gate in the door, noticed him take something from his sock and hold it up to his mouth and nose. Worried that he was about to swallow something, Law urgently called back the custody officer (who had the key to the cell) and other colleagues. They rushed into the cell. Law said, 'Lynam was curled up in what I would describe as the foetal position with his knees up... and had both hands at his face'.

They prised his fingers open and saw that he was grasping a small piece of blue plastic. They then strip-searched him thoroughly and the officer examining the inside of his underpants found that he had secreted two more pieces of blue plastic there, one at the front and one at the back.

As a result, they took away all his clothes apart from his underpants and issued him with a white body-suit. Lynam refused to wear it. He took off his pants and lay there naked. At 3.48, he was formally told that he had been arrested on suspicion of murder and he was cautioned.

At about 4.00, Dr Joseph Ludwig arrived. He examined Lynam and recorded fresh multiple abrasions to his face, the top of his head, his hands and right knee. After being examined, Lynam put his white suit on. Ludwig also looked at Dawn Briggs' injuries and saw that she had a reddening of the throat – she found it difficult to swallow for the next twenty-four hours – and also bruises to her right leg.

Offered a hot meal and a drink, Lynam responded, 'I must be released'. He told the police custody officer that he wanted an international lawyer.

While he was being held, at seven o'clock, his flat was searched. There was not a great deal there. Police retrieved a Safeway's bread wrapper, and also took what few items of clothing there were.

With Lynam in the cell, a duty solicitor, a consultant psychiatrist and a social worker had all arrived; each was statutorily charged with safeguarding a different aspect of his well-being. The social worker was acting as the responsible adult whom police must contact when they are holding a vulnerable person. Why they had not contacted Lynam's parents, who were close at hand, is not clear; at that juncture, Lynam might well have felt only antipathy towards social workers, as he knew they had been trying to section him.

While all these people were in his cell, along with the police custody officer, Lynam took his suit off again and put his underpants back on.

At 9.30 that evening, Brian Kent arrived at the police station and was taken down to the cells for what is termed a confrontation identification. Kent confirmed that Lynam was the man who had called at his guest-house at about 3.00 on Saturday afternoon. He stated, 'There is absolutely no doubt that this is the same man'.

The consultant psychiatrist at the police station reported as follows:

This man is well known to our service and suffers from chronic paranoid schizophrenia. There is no previous history of violence. He needs to be eliminated positively or negatively from the current enquiry. He has a set of grandiose delusions about his station in life. He is not fit to be interviewed for the inquiry. We also feel that he is not fit to be released on bail and is a potential danger to the public. Dr [Gregory] Weppner, consultant forensic psychiatrist, will assess him tomorrow.

By 7.30 the next morning, Lynam was again naked and was given a blanket to wrap himself in. He was examined at 11.00pm by Dr Weppner, Dr Ludwig and Peggy Knowles. As a result, at five minutes to one that Tuesday, he was taken away from the police station. He was detained under the Mental Health Act, and released into the care of Eastbourne and County NHS Trust. He was sent to the Ashen Hill secure psychiatric unit, just outside the village of Hailsham.

So events had moved very swiftly after the murder – not that Siôn and his family were aware of any of this.

Chapter Ten

The Next Morning

So much of that Sunday remains blurred in my memory.

When I awoke – or, came to, since I couldn't say I'd slept – initially I could not understand why I wasn't in my own bed. Then there was a knock on the door, and Julia Gaimster came in with the *News of the World*, with a photograph and a report about Billie. Until that moment, I think I'd been deluding myself that it was all a nightmare.

None of us wanted to speak. We wouldn't have known what to say. We just couldn't comprehend what had happened.

We knew we needed to make phone calls to family and friends to give them the awful news. Lois phoned Margaret Coster, and their response, from Bill Jenkins's side, was, we want her buried in east London. I phoned Debbie Woods, Billie's mother. It had to be me who made that call because she refused to speak to Lois. As far as I was concerned, I was delivering the awful news to her; she reacted as if she was hearing it for the first time.[6]

I called my parents and found my voice faltering. They were completely supportive and said they would contact the rest of the family and then come down to Hastings on Tuesday. Lois, too, phoned her parents. The girls needed comfort and cuddles and stayed close to us.

DC Hutt arrived with WDC Christmas. I remember thinking that although Hutt looked familiar, I couldn't place where I'd seen him before. He said that he and Christmas had been designated as the family liaison officers, and this meant that they were there to support us and provide any information we required.

Later in the morning, Lois and I tentatively started to discuss things we never thought we would need to discuss. We knew we'd have to arrange a funeral. We also thought we wouldn't be able to go back to the house, and in fact we didn't want to go back into the house.

Julia Gaimster took the children to Clambers, the local adventure play centre, to give them a brief respite. During the rest of the morning, we just braced ourselves for whatever was going to happen.

Hutt told me that the police wanted to do video interviews with Annie and Charlotte while the events were fresh in their minds. I found it difficult to make any decisions and just went along with whatever I was told. So we were all taken by police car to the Old Courthouse in Battle.

Chapter Eleven

The Daughters'
Evidence

That Sunday afternoon, twenty-four hours after the murder and the discovery of Billie-Jo's body, police officers conducted video interviews with Siôn Jenkins' two eldest daughters, Annie and Charlotte, both of whom had been with him throughout the previous afternoon.

A male officer took the lead in the questioning of Charlotte, and a female officer was the lead for Annie's interviews (of which there would be two). Realising that the interviews could be used as actual courtroom evidence, the officers emphasised to the children that it was important for them to tell the truth. Each girl confirmed that she understood and would tell the truth. Despite the tragedy that had just overtaken them, neither girl looked in any distress or in any way incapable of undertaking the interview.

Charlotte went first. The start was timed at 3.50. After the introductions and preamble were out of the way, the interview proper began as follows:

Q: Right, so, well thanks for coming up here and do you understand why you have come up today? Right. Why do you think that is?

A: Cos, I, um, saw Billie and I saw the gate open, open and it was closed before.

Q: OK. The things you started to talk about, when did they happen?

A: What happen?

Q: When did those things happen?

A: The gate?

Q: The things you have mentioned – when was that?

A: Yesterday.

Q: What I want you to do is to think very, very carefully and I would like you to take me through what happened yesterday.

A:... We went to Do-It-All, we forgot the money so we had to come back again and, but before we went to Do-It-All, I just noticed that the gate was shut and when I came back, we came back, the gate was open.

The evidence the children would need to give related to all that happened between approximately 3.00 and 4.00pm: the trip to pick up Charlotte from her clarinet lesson; the first return home; the abortive trip to Do-It-All to purchase white spirit; and the second return home whereupon they found Billie-Jo. The utmost significance of the gate being shut when they left for Do-It-All and open when they returned home had not escaped this ten-year-old child. She thought the information so important that she was determined to get it across straightaway. As the interviewer did not appear to be paying attention, she even reiterated the point:

A:... I ran upstairs to put my clarinet back and when I came down, I just noticed that, um, the gate was closed...

Then, during the interview, Charlotte gave her account of exactly what had happened, starting at the point when they reached Do-It-All:

A:... we realised we had forgot the money... and Dad said it was, like, too far to go back, get the money and then come back again, so we just went back, and my Dad said it would be OK if, like, Annie

73

just did the MG with me and if Billie was careful she could just carry on with the painting…

Q: OK, what happened next?

A: We turned round and came back home and we all got out of the car, we all went into the house. I, I just noticed that the gate was open 'cos normally you just see a blank gate, but I just saw the rabbit hutch and so I just noticed that it was open and I went into the dining room and I just saw Billie laying on the floor with blood all over her…

The interviewer asked for further details:

Q: Could you see Billie from the dining room?

A: The dining room. Well, you just go into the door and all I could see, you, I couldn't actually see her head, I could just see her body and her clothes covered in blood.

Q: Where were you standing when you could see that?

A: Um, a few steps into the dining room.

Q: OK. What did you do?

A: I started to cry.

Charlotte's account went on:

… he [Dad] called the ambulance and it probably seemed longer than it was because you're actually waiting for it and it, my Dad called again and he needed, he had to keep on running back to me and Annie, and then back to Billie so he phoned up Denise and asked Denise to come over, and Denise took about two minutes to run over and Denise came to sit with me and Annie, and my Dad sat with Billie and then the ambulance hadn't come yet so, oh no, my Dad had phoned once and then Denise came round and then it hadn't come yet so my Dad phoned again and Denise said that she needed paramedics, so my Dad told them that and he went back to Billie… Denise took me and Annie down to Denise's house and we stayed there and then about half-an-hour later my Mum brought round my other two little sisters… and while my Mum was like talking to the police and everyone, because me and Annie told the policeman that, um, that the gate was open…

The interviewer finally went back and asked Charlotte to repeat her 'gate' evidence.

Q: Tell me about the gate, where is the gate?
A: You go up the stairs and if you just walk straight and there's a gate, there's the door on the side, the right-hand side and about a metre ahead of that there's the gate.
Q: Now you said the gate was open, so what made you notice that?
A: Um, I don't know really, normally you just see a brown gate and that time I saw a rabbit hutch, I just caught the rabbit hutch.
Q: Is the gate normally shut or open?
A: Shut.
Q: Is there a reason for that?
A: So when my dog goes out in the garden, sometimes he just needs to go outside for a little while so he doesn't… run out – so people can't get up, up there. It's not actually locked, if you're a tall person you can actually put your hand over and open it… Children can't reach to open it from the out- , from the side, because if you shut the gate, then you might like think it's padlocked or something.
Q: OK.
A: We just shut it so. If we shut it we… might think that… we get less burglars or something if we shut the gate, so they won't go up the garden or something.
Q: Alright, so you noticed that the gate was open.

At 5.19, Charlotte's interview finished. Annie's commenced sixteen minutes later, at 5.35. As it happened, Charlotte's key point about the gate has not been noticed at all by Annie:

Q: What do you think happened to the side gate?

A: I think Dad closed it… when we were going out.

Q: Later, when you came back from Do-It-All, did you notice anything about the gate then?

A: No.

Since timing in this period was going to become a critical factor, several seemingly minor aspects of the statements are of significance. Both Charlotte and Annie separately confirmed that Siôn was unable to take Ellen directly home because she had recently moved, and did not know how to get to her new home from the clarinet teacher's house.

The prosecution were later to argue that one of the suspicious features of Siôn's movements was the fact that he had set off to Do-It-All the long way, round the park, and had driven round not once, but twice. Annie, who could have had no idea of the significance that would later be attached to this, dealt with this point in a straightforward way:

A: What happened was, we drove round once, round the house and, um, Dad, I think Dad asked us if we minded going to Do-It-All and… we, our house, we have to go, like, round that way to get to our house, round the park bit and, um, we had, like, turned off already and Dad was expecting me to say that I didn't mind not doing any painting, I think, but I said No, so we had to go round again and like we went past the house and that's when we went back again, we had to go back again to Do-It-All again to get some white spirit.

So, firstly, Siôn did not do three-point turns outside his house because it was near a bend on a busy section of road. Annie confirmed this ('we have to go, like, round that way to get to our house, round the park'). Secondly, having embarked on the journey, Siôn almost immediately changed his mind and turned to go back home again. He resumed the trip at Annie's insistence. So, at the outset of the investigation, an allegedly suspect element of Siôn's movements was unambiguously explained.

Two other features that would, at various stages, be held to be suspicious conduct on Siôn's part were also explained here. The interviewer asked if it had been usual to leave Billie-Jo on her own.

Q: Has Billie ever been in the house on her own before?
A: Yep.
Q: So she wouldn't have been, it wasn't the first time, she wouldn't have worries like it being the first time.
A: No, it wasn't the first time.
Q: OK, that's fine.
A: She stays in there sometimes when my Mum and Dad need to just pop out for five minutes and go and get something.

Siôn had closed the dining room door on the dying Billie-Jo. To some, this may have seemed strange and even callous behaviour. Charlotte said:

and so my Dad took me and Annie into the playroom and shut the door... I don't think he wanted me and Annie to see Billie like that...

He had tried to shield his two daughters from the full horror of what had happened to their sister.

Just as Charlotte's interview contained what should have been a vital piece of evidence, so did Annie's. As they were all leaving, she herself had spoken to Billie-Jo:

A: I waited in the hall and I think Dad was with me as well and I looked into the dining room and Billie was sitting on the floor near the doors painting, like, the bottom bit... And she said 'Hello' to me and I said 'Hello' back and then we all just walked out. I went out with Lottie.
Q: And when you were saying hello to Billie and she was saying hello, where was Dad then?

77

A: I'm not sure. I think he was with me as well, but I don't know.

A natural interpretation of this, because of the odd way in which it is phrased, is that in her response to the interviewer Annie meant to say something different. Perhaps what the children had said to each other was not "hello" but 'goodbye'. After all, you don't say 'hello' to somebody and then 'just walk out'. However, she mis-stated it and the interviewer compounded the problem by going on to refer to the 'hello' exchange between Annie and Billie-Jo.

If the officer had been on the ball and perceived that '... she said "Hello" to me and I said "Hello" back and then we all just walked out... ' doesn't really make sense, and accordingly probed at this critical juncture to ascertain precisely what they did say to each other, it may well be that this case would never have taken the direction that it did.

Annie's interview then concluded at 6.14 which means that Charlotte's, at eighty-nine minutes as opposed to thirty-nine, is much the longer (although her time includes a refreshment break).

One begins to understand from these interviews that, barely twenty-four hours after the murder, the police were already ensnared in their preliminary view that Siôn himself must have been involved in what had happened. Both girls were asked about prowlers and other possible suspects and whether, in general, they had noticed anything suspicious. Yet there seems scant interest in the answers. For example, Charlotte was asked:

Q: You mentioned about having your gate shut... do you ever get anybody coming round your house that sort of shouldn't be there?
A: Well, we've lately had silent phone calls with people breathing down the phone... That's on the... normal phone... and late at night my Dad opened the door and a man ran away. There was a man hanging around our house and when he opened the door he ran away... he just ran away. That's what my Dad said... Last Wednesday, I went to London with my Mum because she was going

to work and it was my day off, so I went to London with her and we were talking about it in the car.

The children try to open up avenues of questioning about other suspects, but the interviewers tend to turn all these into cul-de-sacs; and these potential lines of enquiry are rapidly abandoned. The questions keep coming back to Siôn. Naturally, the children were not so naïve that they didn't notice.

Someone at police headquarters already seems to have put together a scenario: Siôn had murdered Billie-Jo while the children were outside, at the front of the house; and then quickly thought up the ruse of going to Do-It-All for white spirit as a means of distancing himself from the scene. Charlotte was asked:

Q: At what point did you know you were going to go to Do-It-All?
A: Um, my Dad went down, down the stairs and he had the leather cloth to wipe the car with, but he didn't bring down the bucket and when we got down the stairs he said, 'Jump in', so he must have not got the bucket because he remembered the white spirit.
Q: Were you surprised 'cos what did you think you were going to do at that point? What did you think?
A: What, when I didn't see the bucket?
Q: Yeah, what did you, because after you dropped your clarinet off, what did you think you were going to be doing next?
A: Cleaning the MG.
Q: Right, yes. So you didn't know you were going to be going to Do-It-All at that time?
A: No.

If there were embryonic suspicions, then these answers may well have reinforced them. Elsewhere, however, Charlotte's replies reveal just how brief the first return to the house had been:

A: Yeah, we went home and my Dad said, 'Run in and put your clarinet back'... and when I came back down the stairs, my Dad said, 'Just jump in' and... he said, 'We need some white spirit' because Annie wanted to paint and Billie was already painting but in case she got it anywhere.

The interviewing officer continued with this line of questioning:

Q: When you went into the house... did only you get out of the car?
A: I think we all got out of the car, but Annie and Dad were waiting for me to come down so we could go and get the white spirit.
Q: What I am trying to ask you is, how many of you went to the front door and whether... all of you went into the house or not?
A: My Dad opened the door, I think I can remember my Dad putting the keys on the mantelpiece. I can't remember where Annie was though. I ran and put my clarinet in my room and came back down and then my Dad realised that we needed the white spirit, so then we went to get the white spirit...

Another passage in Charlotte's interview is interesting. She has already said:

A: We got to Sainsbury's and we realised that we had forgot the money.

(Although this answer seems awry, it is perfectly accurate as Sainsbury's and Do-It-All were on the same site.)

The interviewer decides to find out more about this:

Q: Does Dad normally have a wallet, or does he just keep his money in his trouser pocket...
Q: When Dad is at home, do you know where he keeps his wallet?

In the context both of this fledgling inquiry, and of this particular interview – in which Charlotte has already provided gold-plated evidence about the overwhelming likelihood of an intruder having entered the house during their absence from it – these are surprising questions. The interviewers were focusing on one issue: when the girls and their father left to go to Do-It-All, did they all leave simultaneously? This issue was explored with Charlotte, in a final question:

Q: Before you go, there is just one question I wanted to ask.
There's then an interruption, and the officer monitoring the session outside suggests that the interview is ended.
Q: I promise it will be just one, OK?... Just one question. When you left to go to get the white spirit... Who left the house first?
A: I think it was me... I think Annie was waiting down by the MG... I think I went out first and then my Dad shut the door behind with his door keys, because you can't shut the door... without putting the key in.
Q: Was there any time between when you left the house and when your Dad left the house?
A: No. I, like, came out and he came out just after me and then shut the door.

When Annie is interviewed, she too is asked about a possible interval between her and Charlotte leaving the house, and their father doing so:

Q: Right. And then when you had said hello and Lottie had put her clarinet back, you and Lottie came down to the MG like you told me, and how long was it before Dad came out?
A: A few minutes – about two minutes, one minute.

The entire case teeters precariously on top of this response. It is of incalculable importance. Almost nine years later, it would be mentioned again and again throughout the Crown's case at the third trial. So examine the question-and-answer exchange again:

Q:... how long was it before Dad came out?
A: A few minutes – about two minutes, one minute.

The question presupposes a time interval. It is a leading question, and Annie was being led. The way a question is framed can induce a particular response. Here, Annie is asked, 'How long was it?...' She goes with the flow of the question, before instantly realising that her answer wasn't accurate. So she closes down the time period (two minutes, one minute).

So the question, like all questions in criminal investigations, should have been put neutrally. The problem with leading questions is that they produce misleading answers.

In this instance, moreover, the interview immediately went from bad to worse. Having obtained this response, the interviewer compounded her error by completely failing to grasp its significance. She didn't seek confirmation or elaboration and instead moved straight on to something else:

Q: Right, and then you went off to Do-It-All in the MG?
A: MG.
Q: Right, OK, do you know who was ringing on the phone? Did anybody answer the phone?

It was not until right at the end of Annie's interview that the male officer returns to the point to try to clarify it:

Q: Now just before you went to Do-It-All – I know [the female officer] has already asked you this one – I just wanted to ask it slightly differently – just before you went to Do-It-All... You were standing by the MG with Lottie, is that right?
A: Yeah.
Q: Where was Dad then?
A: I think he was next to Opel, next to our other car, but I'm not sure. I don't know.

Q: And where was…

A: I think he was outside as well.

Q: And where was he just before that?

A: With me, just, don't know, just…

Q: OK. Was he in the house with Billie at any time?

A: No. I was in the house and I saw her…

The evidence on this one point that can be extracted from the interview is this. On the one hand Annie, in response to a leading question, said that her father was in the house alone for 'a few minutes'. On the other hand, in answer to other questions, she had answered at different points as follows:

'… we all just walked out'

'… I think he was with me as well, but I don't know'

'… Then Dad said, 'Come on, so I just went with him'

'… I think he might have been behind me'

'… I think he was with me as well, but I don't know, I can't remember'

'… we went outside and Dad, I think Dad was outside with us as well'

Each time, Annie is indicating that they were together, their exits having been more or less simultaneous. So, finally, the officer asks what has now become the million-pound question:

Q: Was he [Siôn] in the house with Billie at any time?

A: No. I was in the house and I saw her.

The question – not a leading question, but an appropriate one – has been put, and the answer has been given. The answer is No.

To all this, of course, should be added Charlotte's evidence:

Q: Was there any time between when you left the house and when your Dad left the house?

A: No.

One response suggested that Siôn may have had the opportunity to murder Billie-Jo; eight responses suggested that he had no opportunity at all.

During their interviews, each girl has provided vital information: Annie has spoken to Billie-Jo directly before leaving the house; and both of them have said that their father was not in the house alone with Billie. The interviews must be examined carefully, in their entirety and not selectively. Despite the hazards posed by the clumsy and sometimes calamitous questioning, they convey a picture of the afternoon's events that is clear enough.

For all the horror of the previous day, the girls are natural and straightforward; neither appears emotionally unable to cope with the questioning. Charlotte's recollections include details like 'paramedics' and the 'faint pulse' phrase from Denise Lancaster's conversation with the ambulance service operator – which are examples of those minor but telling features of an account that help to bear out its veracity.

The slight inconsistencies in the two accounts are not hard to resolve. What matters is the overall cumulative force of the evidence. In this instance, each account buttresses the other and also provides, as it were, advance corroboration of what Siôn would say in his statement over the next few days.

Nevertheless, the critical point with which Charlotte started the interview session – that the side gate was closed when they went out, and open when they returned, plainly suggesting that there had been an intruder on the premises in their absence – was ignored virtually from the moment it was uttered.

Chapter Twelve

The Mortuary

I sat outside, not speaking to anyone, while Annie and Charlotte were being interviewed. I was just thinking about Billie. I could not accept that she was dead; I kept wanting to go home to her.

A social worker came up and introduced himself and said he'd been assigned to provide support for the family. At that stage, you are in so much of a daze that when someone says they're there to support you, you just find it very welcome. As it happened, though, I wasn't to see him again for almost four weeks.

The police had told us that the clothing we had been wearing would have to be sent to the laboratory for forensic examination. This presented a practical difficulty: as the police wouldn't let us back into the house, none of us had a change of clothing.

So, after the girls' interviews were concluded, we were driven back to the Gaimsters'. While Hutt then went back to the station, another officer took Lois back to Lower Park Road, where she sorted out fresh clothes for us. Hutt returned at about 8.15pm. So then, more than twenty-four hours after the murder, he bagged up the clothing and put it into his car.

We were told that we would need to identify Billie at the mortuary the next day. Hutt also mentioned that Lois and I should do a television appeal, asking the public to come forward with information about the murder. From the start, I'd been finding it difficult to make decisions and just went along with what I was told. However, in this one instance, I did feel strongly. I was sure I had no desire to go on television, least of all at this juncture, and Lois was equally adamant. So we declined.

That Sunday evening our daughters were full of questions. They wanted to know when they were going back to school; they asked if Billie was going to have a funeral. I can also remember Charlotte saying, Are we ever going to live in our house again? I didn't know how to answer.

We decided not to send the girls to school the next day. Of course, I was also due back at work, but Roger Mitchell had heard the news on the radio and, indeed, had brought flowers round. I didn't see him, but he left a very sympathetic message, saying that I was to take as long as I needed.

Towards the end of the day, Lois and I went for a walk. We walked past our house. The lights were on and a policeman was standing outside, as if on sentry duty. Flowers were starting to accumulate on the wall and the pavement. I read some of the poignant messages before we carried on back to the Gaimsters'.

It was to be another endless night.

On Monday, the day began in silence. At some point, I remember, Esther came in and nestled into me. She talked a little, very softly. Someone had bought several of the morning's papers. In almost all of them, whether tabloid or broadsheet, Billie's murder was the main story. Throughout the day, it was also reported on most radio and television channels. From that morning, the press seemed to descend on Hastings.

DC Hutt arrived. He reminded us about going to the mortuary. However, there was now further pressure on us to do the television appeal. We were grieving – we certainly didn't feel any need to see our faces all over the television and the newspapers. The murder was being reported absolutely everywhere anyway, and I didn't want to be part of any media circus.

However, Hutt told us that senior officers believed that it was very important. Their argument was: we need you to do this if we're going to have a hope of catching the killer. So what can you say? You don't want to feel unhelpful and even obstructive by saying you're not contributing. Finally, with the utmost reluctance, we agreed. Hutt promised that the police would draw up a statement for Lois or me to read at the appeal. By that stage, all the willpower had drained from me. I went along with this; I should not have done.

The post-mortem on Billie was conducted that morning by Dr Ian Hill, a Home Office pathologist who was based at Guy's Hospital in south London. It took two hours, from 10.00am to midday.

Then, at 2.00pm, we were driven there. We arrived at a nondescript redbrick building. I'd envisaged walking through long corridors so that, as we did, I'd be able to prepare myself. But it wasn't like that. We just went in through this back entrance and were shown straight into a small room. Billie was lying there.

She was laid on a table with a white sheet covering the top part of her head so that all we could see was her face. That image has remained with me ever since. Her face was like marble. She appeared asleep and at peace; though whether that was the skill of the mortician or simply what I wanted to believe, I'm not sure. Nevertheless, I could not bear what I was seeing, and somehow refused to accept it.

We identified Billie to the police.

We were at the mortuary for twenty minutes. As we left, my stomach felt as though someone was tying knots in it. I was again unable to speak.

I have no memory of the rest of the day. I was told I sat in a chair staring out of the window. At some point I went to bed. Already I was functioning like an automaton. Life had lost all direction. Billie, my home and everyday family life had been taken from me.

On Tuesday morning Lois and I were collected in a police car and taken to Hastings Police Station. I knew I looked terrible. I was crushed emotionally. I was hypoglycaemic due to not having eaten. Before we had left the house, I had to change my trousers; I'd lost so much weight in the last three days, they were falling down.

We entered a side door and were taken to a room close to the conference area. I asked an officer for the statement I was to read. He went off, and returned with a pen and paper. I asked what it was for.

'To write your statement', he replied.

I tried to explain that the police were writing it and I was reading it. He ignored me. Another officer then came up to me.

'You'll be on soon', he said, 'just write a short statement'.

I felt tired, subdued and bamboozled. I did as I was told and waited.

I noticed policemen queuing up at the mirrors to comb their hair, prettying themselves up for their TV appearance. Then, I felt a stabbing pain at the back of my head. I looked round to see a middle-aged officer walking away with a clump of my hair. I have no recollection of being asked for or granting permission for the officer to take hair samples.

We were led into the conference room and seated at a long table, flanked by police officers. I looked up and saw a wall of journalists and cameras. I froze and thought I would not be able to speak.

Somehow, I retreated into professional mode; I was, after all, a senior teacher who was used to addressing large gatherings. But I was living entirely on my nerves. I cannot remember speaking, although I know what I did say, as I have since had to watch the video many times. I was gaunt and strained. I had nothing left to give emotionally.

Chapter Thirteen
The Witness Statement

We were driven back to the Gaimsters' after the press conference. In the interim, my parents had arrived. We embraced and talked about what had been happening. The girls were excited to see their grandparents. My parents responded to their warm smiles, but I could see how concerned they were about everything – from Billie's death to how much weight I had lost and where we were now going to live.

In no time at all, it seemed, Hutt re-appeared. He'd said that he'd collect me after lunch to take me to the station to make my formal statement. My parents had decided to stay close by at the Beauport Park Hotel, so we agreed that I would join them there when I had finished.

Hutt drove to Battle police station, and took me into a small room on the ground floor.

'So what happened?' he asked.

I was startled by the abruptness of the question and didn't know how to answer or where to start. I asked him at what point on the Saturday he wanted me to begin. He said that he wanted me to tell him about the Friday. At the time I couldn't see the relevance of beginning there.

During the afternoon and evening, he asked detailed questions about every five-minute period of time. Again, I couldn't understand why such domestic minutiae were considered relevant to the investigation. If I'd been told then that the police thought that I was the murderer, I'd have been incredulous. Also, I would obviously not have spoken to them in this way, without the interview being tape-recorded and without a solicitor being present.

As soon as I began, I realised that I was having real difficulty in remembering, probably because I was over-tired and was only functioning on autopilot. By the evening I was beyond rational thought. I had had nothing to eat that day, only cans of fizzy drinks.

I told Hutt that parts of the day were vague or confused. I said I was having difficulty remembering all that happened in the correct chronological order, and that my memory of the day just seemed to be a series of disconnected flashes. Hutt suggested that I should make notes about what I could recall as an *aide-mémoire* and then bring them with me. Each day, accordingly, I'd arrive with two or three pages of notes.

That first evening, Hutt said he would take me back to the Gaimsters'. I asked him to drop me off at the Beauport Park. I had dinner with my parents that evening but was too tired to eat much. I can remember my father's surprise at how late it was and that we hadn't finished the statement.

I returned to the Gaimsters' to find that my daughters were already asleep. I was disappointed because I had had very little opportunity of seeing them during the day. I went upstairs, got out some paper and started to jot down bullet-points whilst trying to stay awake, though in the event I did not sleep that night.

On the Wednesday morning, Hutt arrived early and we went off again to Battle. I showed him my notes and used them as prompts. I still found the exact sequences confusing and I was not sure that some of the details were anything other than educated guesses. I explained this to Hutt and he told me not to worry.

The Witness Statement

I described picking up Charlotte and Ellen and taking Ellen home:
Obviously we had the MG soft top folded down. During the journey,
I can remember Lottie kissing my cheek as she leant over towards me,
and I can recall saying to Lottie and Ellen, 'What a brilliant day it is'.

Then we returned to the house.

... We were probably only in the house for around two minutes...
I would state without a shadow of a doubt that the side gate was
closed... We then all got into the MG, Lottie was in the back and
Annie was in the front.

There followed the abortive trip to Do-It-All, the return home when we
found Billie-Jo and what happened then. We continued until lunchtime.
Hutt left the room and returned with two packets of crisps and a can of
the same unpleasant drink. I asked if I could phone home as I was worried
about my family. He told me I couldn't.

I felt I was being pressed for more detail than I knew. Hutt emphasised
that the investigating team needed more detail and encouraged me to fill
in any spaces I could not remember. I realise, with hindsight, that such
requests for speculative guesses should be turned down, but I felt under
real pressure to complete my account.

Again, we continued until late in the evening and Hutt took me back to
the hotel. I walked up to my parents' room and collapsed into an
armchair. This time, I was too tired even to sit at a dining-table; my father
had sandwiches sent up.

As I related the day's events, he became increasingly concerned. Why
was I being asked to provide a witness statement whilst obviously in
shock? Why hadn't I had a solicitor? I realised that he was worried.

'You're in a vulnerable position, Siôn', he said. 'You shouldn't be making
such long statements without any support or witnesses. Even when you
talk to us, you say things that are confusing because you're so tired and
emotionally drained.'

91

But I was too worn-out to challenge the police.

The children were in bed again when I returned to the Gaimsters'. Hutt wanted notes for the next day and this time he wanted diagrams of the routes I had taken in the car. I believed that he wanted them for timings, so that the window of opportunity for the killer could be narrowed down.

On the Thursday, once again, Hutt arrived early. I followed him down the outside steps to the car and off we went. I cannot remember much about this day. I had nothing left to give and know that I had difficulty speaking.

Later in the day, Hutt left to take a phone call. I decided to stretch my legs and walked down the corridor. I heard Hutt's voice coming from a nearby room.

'No, he hasn't signed it yet'.

Then, someone asked him a question, and I heard him respond:

'… but I don't think I can get him to sign it tonight'.

Why was it so important that I had to sign it then?

Hutt then came back smiling, saying nothing. We continued for about an hour and then I could take no more. As it was, I was uncertain about the accuracy of much that I had said that day. More importantly, I wanted to see my family. Hutt then asked me to sign the statement. I said it would take me at least an hour to read it and it would be better if I did that when I was rested. Hutt pressed me, saying, 'But the investigating team are waiting for it'.

In fact, this would already be my fourth version of what had happened at the time of the murder. Police officers had already taken three initial reports of what I recalled about the afternoon. These were the first, by Hutt, of all that I'd said to him over a three-hour period from 6.00–9.00pm at Denise Lancaster's on the day of the murder; the second, again by Hutt, of comments I'd made on the Sunday evening; and the third, by PC Darren Bruce, the first officer to arrive at 48 Lower Park Road, of what I had said immediately after the discovery of the body. The latter should have been the first account chronologically, but it is in fact the third documented account as Bruce did not put it into a statement until Wednesday, 19 February.

Small variations within these three accounts would haunt me for years.

On Thursday evening, I signed my forty-two-page statement. I had not read what Hutt had written.

I had been speaking to him for nearly three days. I had pushed myself physically and emotionally to give the police everything they wanted. I had signed it in the belief that it was safe to do so.

It hurts me to write that now, but six days of utter emotional and physical exhaustion had taken their toll. At the moment that I signed it, all I was thinking of was getting away so that I could see my daughters. I did not know what they had been doing or how they were feeling. I was feeling very guilty about having been away from them for so long at such a critical time.

Meanwhile, entirely unbeknown to me, there had been a lot happening in the investigation that week. Two suspects for Billie's murder had now been arrested.

Chapter Fourteen

The Second Arrest

Earlier that week, on Monday evening, Mark Lynam, the first man arrested in connection with the murder, was positively identified by the guest-house owner Brian Kent as the man who had been wandering near to the Jenkins home around the time of the murder. He was detained under the Mental Health Act and, the following day, was sent to the Ashen Hill secure psychiatric unit.

On Wednesday, 19 February, Lynam's father gave the impression to police that he regretted that his son may have been 'responsible' for the murder.

By that point, however, police attentions had shifted elsewhere, as they had now arrested a second suspect: Felix Simmons. Three factors led to his arrest.

The first was that Lois Jenkins and Peter Gaimster considered him a likely suspect, and had pointed the police in his direction. Lois, indeed, had thought of him from the start. As they were all leaving Denise Lancaster's house on Saturday evening, she had whispered to Denise, 'I hope it's not Felix'.

Secondly, he had suffered a mental breakdown the previous summer.

Police had been called out a number of times due to what Lois described as 'Felix's violent behaviour'. Then, a complaint from Peter Gaimster had led to his arrest on charges of kidnapping and criminal damage.

Simmons and Suzanne[7], his wife, who was a solicitor, were spoken to separately as part of the initial house-to-house inquiries. Within hours of the murder, Suzanne answered preliminary inquiries by saying that she and her husband had been talking in the kitchen during the afternoon. The following day, Simmons himself said he had been at home all day until about 8.30pm when he and his wife went out.

On the Monday, the police paid a further visit and found him decorating the kitchen. The third reason for his arrest was that the officers noticed that he had splashes of white paint on his clothing, whereas he was actually painting the kitchen yellow.

While Siôn was composing his witness statement at Battle police station with DC Hutt, Lois and Gaimster spoke to the police about Simmons.[8]

At 9.00pm on Friday, 26 July, Gaimster said that he was kidnapped from his home by Simmons and driven round Hastings for four hours. 'At one point he made me kneel and said words about God, punishment and evil', reported Gaimster to the police. 'I thought I was going to die.'

About twenty calls regarding Simmons were then made to police. He was sectioned straightaway and was diagnosed as suffering a hypomanic episode. He was released after a few days.

On 14 August, the day of the Hastings carnival, at the insistence of Lois, police checked our front garden in Lower Park Road to check whether Simmons was hiding there. The police checked, but couldn't find anyone.

Officers went round again to Simmons's address. His wife said he was out at work, so they asked her to make sure that on his return home he reported to Hastings police station. He arrived there on his own at 9.00pm, and was then arrested on suspicion of the murder of Billie-Jo. His clothing was taken from him and sent to the laboratory. Senior officers decided that he could not be interviewed until both a psychiatric nurse and the duty solicitor could be present, so Simmons was taken down to the cells to await their arrival. Meanwhile, WDS Capon went to his house with a search warrant and took away other articles of his clothing for forensic examination.

It was twenty minutes past midnight when officers finally began interviewing Simmons. He gave an account of his movements for the day of the murder. He reiterated that he had only been out of the house for about forty-five minutes around lunchtime.

He said that, when they heard the sirens and activity that followed the discovery of Billie-Jo, Suzanne went outside to see if she could assist in any way. At that stage, no one understood why the emergency services had been called. Simmons said his initial thought was that Siôn had caught a prowler at the house; his wife had mentioned to him about two weeks earlier that Lois had told her the Jenkins family were worried about prowlers.

At 8.30pm, he and Suzanne went out for the evening, his in-laws having arrived to babysit. They returned soon after 10.00pm and he then walked his in-laws to their car. That was when he spotted Siôn and Lois in the police car and walked over to speak to them, only to be intercepted by WDC Christmas. As he walked back to his house, a neighbour told him that Billie-Jo had 'fallen through some glass' and been killed.

Having provided this account, Simmons was taken back to his cell for the night.

Suzanne Simmons spent much of the following morning on the phone to the police station. She complained about the fact that they'd held her husband in a cell overnight, and also emphasised that she did not want him represented by the duty solicitor. She had arranged for a different solicitor to attend.

The second interview took place that afternoon. This time, things were different. The new solicitor told police that his client had already provided a full account of the movements on the day of the murder and advised Simmons to give no-comment responses to questions.

Meanwhile, other officers took a statement from Suzanne Simmons. This made it clear that she could provide a firm alibi for her husband; he was with her throughout the afternoon.

It had also by now been established that the white splashes that officers thought they had discerned on his clothing were in fact yellow, the colour he was using to decorate the kitchen.

That evening, the taxi-driver who'd spotted someone walking briskly down the path away from 48 Lower Park Road arrived at the police station. At 6.47pm, Simmons was put on an identity parade. The taxi-driver did not pick him out. Simmons' fingerprints were taken, as were intimate samples for DNA profiling, and he was then released at 8.25pm. He had been held for just thirty-five minutes short of twenty-four hours.

In view of how this case was to unfold, the next development was of particular interest. According to reports to the police, that same evening, Peter Gaimster arrived at Hastings police station with two friends to complain about the anticipated release of Simmons. (They were not informed that Simmons had in fact already been released.) They insisted that, were he indeed to be released, they would need police protection.

They said they had all been victims of what they described as Simmons's 'terror tactics', and then put forward a number of very damaging allegations about his behaviour. These included the assertion that among the things that could trigger Simmons' mental instability were football, sunny days and tall men. (Gaimster himself was over six foot tall.) The officer who dealt with them commented that 'the three men were in an agitated state and had clearly been drinking'.

Nevertheless, in view of Lois's and Gaimster's concerns, police went to the Gaimsters' house the following day to install a security warning system linked directly to the police station.

DC Paul Hilton spent the following weekend (22/23 February) with Gaimster, taking his statement.

'Over the two days that I was with Gaimster', he reported afterwards, 'Simmons was the main area of concern.'

Chapter Fifteen

The End of the First Week

What I remember most is that the grieving just intensified. I began to think of all the various alternatives. You find yourself thinking, maybe if I'd done this, or that, it wouldn't have happened.

My parents had to return to Wales on the Friday, though they indicated they would soon be back. They had offered to get us into furnished rented accommodation for the short term so that we could leave the Gaimsters'. One evening, when I got back late from giving my statement, Lois and I went out to look at the outside of a house we knew was available for rent, just to see if it was a possibility.

Then there was the evening when I read some of Roald Dahl's *Charlie and the Chocolate Factory* to Annie. She was in our bed when I went upstairs and, rather than moving her straightaway, I read to her for a while before she went back to her own bed. This was another trivial incident which would be blown out of all proportion to become a significant – according to the prosecution – piece of evidence. No one, myself included, has ever been able to say when it occurred. It certainly happened that week, possibly on the Friday.

Once I'd signed my statement, the police officers' attitude towards me changed. At the start of the week, Hutt's attitude towards me had been almost obsequious. He acted as though he wanted to be my friend, and had the annoying habit of winking at me. By the end of the week, his smiles and winks had gone.

Officers brought round Lois's statement to the Gaimsters' house on Sunday morning for her to approve and sign. That morning, Denise Lancaster had taken Lottie, Esther and Maya swimming. Annie at the last moment decided that she didn't want to go and so I said I'd take her out to the park. Of course, the press were still around, all the trees and posts had police notices with pictures of Billie-Jo on them, and Lois was immediately concerned.

'Don't take her there', she said, 'she'll be spotted and they'll want to talk to her. Take her out of Hastings, take her to Bexhill.'

So, at Lois's suggestion, I took her to Bexhill, five miles west of Hastings. We were soon walking along the seafront. Annie noticed a brightly painted café and we went in. I had a coffee and Annie had an ice cream. In fact, as a special treat, I bought her a large knickerbocker glory. It was lovely to get out of Hastings. For a few fleeting but precious moments, I felt I could let the terrible events in Hastings go and simply enjoy the tranquillity of being there with Annie.

The children had been off school all week while they were coming to terms with their sister's death. We had desperately wanted to bring some stability to our family; in a sense, we were pulling up the drawbridge so that we could look after them. We were also aware, of course, that there were reporters outside both the girls' schools.

We hadn't been able to give the children the time that we'd envisaged. It wasn't a week in which we could support each other. As a family, we never had times to ourselves. We couldn't come together to discuss and reflect on what had happened because we were never all there together; there were always other people around, and certainly there were always police there. Lois and I were rarely there at the same time, and sometimes neither of us was there; the time I was engaged on the statement overlapped with when she was making hers.

The Murder of Billie-Jo

We decided that we needed to get our lives back on track, and get the girls back into their normal routines. Because all this had directly followed half-term week, they'd now had two weeks off. They knew all their friends were together at school. Lois and I jointly decided that it was time for them to return.

So that night they went to bed a little earlier. It was the first time Lois and I had sat down together for nine days. I think we just both felt that our family had been through a seriously traumatic time, and that it was going to continue; and that it was important that we stayed close and helped the girls pull through it.

Of course, I had no idea then what the next day would bring.

Chapter Sixteen

Taken in for Questioning

Police arrived at the house at 7.46am. The girls were dressed in their school uniforms and looking forward to going back to school. I had just put on a pair of jeans when a police officer in a suit walked in to the bedroom.

I didn't quite take it all in. He said that he was arresting me for Billie's murder and that I should put a shirt on and come with him. I only took in some of what he was saying and although I'm sure he read me my rights, I didn't hear them.

'Can I have a wash and a shave?' I asked.

'No, you can't', he responded.

Two officers, whom I now know as DI Moore and WDC Birnie, led me downstairs. My children were in the lounge and watching me through the open door. Though the police wanted to take me straight out of the door, I insisted on going to have a word with Lois, who was crying at the kitchen table.

'Listen', I said, 'everything will be alright'.

'It won't, though', she replied.

I was then handcuffed and bundled into a police car. As I was being pushed in, I happened to notice all the people, including a number of children on their way to school, waiting at the bus-stop opposite. Understandably, they were all following events with a keen interest.

This played a part in prejudicing the community against me. If I was a dangerous murderer, why hadn't they arrested me over the weekend? Now, I was being arrested in a way which was bound to stir up emotions against me locally. All the people at the bus-stop would know what they had witnessed, and would be certain to tell their family, friends and colleagues about it. Of course, the timing also meant that my arrest would receive blanket coverage on news reports throughout the day. The symbiotic relationship between the police and the media was beginning to become clear.

As the car drove away, I looked back and could see my daughters' faces at the window. I knew what was happening but could not accept the reality of it; it was like being in a film. 'What's going to happen to my wife?' I asked during the journey to Hastings police station.

DI Moore replied that she and the children would be looked after by a child protection team and taken away from the house 'for their own best interests'. I turned to one of the officers and said, 'Are you arresting me because you want more information or because you think I'm responsible?'

When we arrived at the custody area of the station, Birnie asked me to sign her notes of the morning's events. She had written down my question as, 'Are you arresting me because you want to find out more things? Or because I've done it?' She's always maintained that she wrote down my exact words; I've always firmly disagreed.

At the station I was taken to a reception area, asked various questions and told to empty my pockets. My shoes were removed and then I was taken to a cell. The door was slammed and the noise echoed down the corridor. Over the next hour a series of little events took place including seeing a doctor, having my fingerprints taken and being photographed.

'Do you want a solicitor?' they asked.

'Do I need one?' I replied.

'Well, we suggest you do. We'll get you the duty solicitor.'

So, twenty minutes later, Brendan Salsbury walked in. He was a partner in the local practice of Funnell & Perring. Far more importantly, from my point of view, he was clerk to the governors of William Parker School. I'd known him for about three years. It was good to see a friendly face. Brendan sat down and took out a fat purple fountain pen. At moments of crisis, it's interesting what trivial details impress themselves on one's memory.

The first time the issue of my possible guilt had arisen was at the Gaimsters' on the previous Tuesday. Julia was flicking through the BBC's Ceefax pages. She reached the report of our press conference, the last sentence of which was, 'Siôn Jenkins is not considered a suspect'.

'Oh, look, Siôn', she said, 'you're not a suspect'.

Naturally, few things are more alarming. Does that mean I ever was a suspect? So that was really the first trigger.

Then, members of my family wondered about the statement-taking. They asked why I was being questioned so intensively. Then, there were the comments I'd overheard by Hutt, about getting me to sign my statement. Then there was the change in his demeanour after I had signed it.

Although in hindsight one can see all the warning signs, at the time, I think possibly to protect yourself, you can't actually bring yourself to face what might be happening. So, when they did come to arrest me, I was completely unprepared.

That was why I had that exchange in the car. I really needed that clarification (even though my question wasn't answered) – were they arresting me just to pump me for more information, or did they actually think I'd done it?

Later that day I was taken to an interview room. I sat at a small table with Brendan. Opposite were WDS Capon and DC Michael Groombridge. A tape recorder was switched on and the interview began. As the day wore on, the questioning became more aggressive and the interviewers more unpleasant. I tried to answer the questions, but I was constantly interrupted and my answers rephrased. If only I knew then what I know now.

During the day I regularly asked how Lois was and if she was waiting to see me. The police refused to comment. I spent most of the night wondering about her and the children. I believed that, when morning came, the police would realise their terrible mistake.

Those two days were absolutely horrendous. Then, at one point, the police took Brendan out of the interview room. This, I now know, was to tell him about the forensic science evidence.

Adrian Wain, at the forensic science laboratory in Lambeth, south London, and the senior investigating officer, Jeremy Paine, had a telephone conversation about the progress of the tests. Wain told him that bloodstains had been found on my clothing. At that point, the scientists were awaiting confirmation that it was Billie-Jo's blood. By the next day, they had it. So Wain faxed a brief letter to Paine at Hastings police station the next day, Friday, 21 February. He wrote:

A preliminary examination of Siôn Jenkins' trousers and jacket has shown that there are many tiny spots of blood on the lower left leg of the trousers and the lower left sleeve of the jacket.

These spots are typical of those which I would expect to find following an impact onto a surface wet with blood. The size of the spots also indicate that the force of the impact was considerable and that the wearer was close to it.

Wain confirmed that the blood had been tested at the laboratory in Wetherby, Yorkshire, and it had proved to be Billie-Jo's. The letter had obviously been composed in haste for it contained a significant inaccuracy; the spots were actually on the right, not the left, trouser leg.

So, even though the letter clearly stated that this was a preliminary examination; even though it added that further tests were continuing; and even though it was couched in superficially restrained language, it was saying one thing and one thing only: that I was the killer.

This was the evidence which they then put to me on Tuesday lunchtime. It was their ace card, and, looking back on it, I think they expected me to crack, to break down and confess. Nothing like that happened. I explained again how I had tended to Billie. If there were spots of blood on me, then they got onto me when I crouched down and touched her. I reiterated my innocence just as vehemently.

When Brendan managed to speak to me privately, he said that he had got a barrister, Anthony Scrivener QC. He eulogised Scrivener and expected me to be impressed. However, I thought it was all irrelevant and interjected: 'Brendan, the police are not going to charge me. I haven't committed a crime and I'm sure they will soon release me'.

Brendan then became more focused and said that he did anticipate that the police would charge me. Gerald Funnell, one of the senior partners from Funnell and Perring, arrived. Both he and Brendan then began to speak about the inevitability of me being charged. Time went by.

Brendan left and returned to report that there was an enormous argument going on between the police and lawyers from the Crown Prosecution Service as to whether they could charge me.

By 6:00pm I had no idea what was happening and was becoming frantic for news of my family. Finally, Brendan then came into the cell to tell me that the police were releasing me without charge.

We were told to leave the police station by the back exit, as there was a large crowd of reporters and photographers at the front.

I went out into the night. The night sky was clear and full of stars. I can still remember the exhilaration of feeling fresh cool air on my face again. Brendan drove me part of the way back, then dropped me off, so that I walked towards the Gaimsters' on my own.

I expected everyone to be waiting for me.

Chapter Seventeen
Feed into Mum

The interviews may have been difficult for Siôn; they were also difficult for those interviewing him, essentially because the investigators had dealt their interviewing officers such a poor hand. The forensic science evidence was their solitary card. They'd played it. That was it; there was nothing else.

The senior officers in charge of the case were watching the interviews in another room at the police station. They had seen what scant evidence they had being put to the suspect. The interviewers were making no headway. In what must have been something close to desperation, senior officers hit on an alternative plan. They wanted the same evidence to be put to the suspect's wife. They told WDC Christmas to tell DC Hutt and WDC Gregory to 'feed into Mum'.

'Feed into Mum' are the three most important words in the Billie-Jo murder case. The phrase is critical not just for the case itself but for the lives of all those who were unhappily caught up in it; its importance is such that it will now become a key phrase in British criminal justice history.

Feed into Mum

On Sunday, 23 February Siôn and Lois discussed at length whether it was right to send the children back to school. Whatever inner tensions there may have been, there were very few outward signs of disharmony in their relationship. In just a few hours on Tuesday, 25 February, all that changed. Once the police had fed into Mum, Siôn and Lois's fifteen-year relationship was broken and their entire family life shattered.

As the impact of the instruction was to prove so devastating, it might seem axiomatic that we would know who had issued it. However, we do not know. The officer's identity has remained a mystery. The person has never voluntarily come forward; and WDC Christmas was to give sworn evidence at two trials that she could not recall who had issued it. Someone has blacked out the name in her notebook.

DC Hutt and WDC Gregory had by this time been appointed as family liaison officers. In expecting them to implement the instruction, however, the senior officer (whoever he or she was) had overlooked two matters of cardinal importance. Firstly, whereas the ostensible role of FLOs is to offer support and reassurance to victims and the bereaved, these FLOs were now being required to undertake the exact opposite. At this time of continuing emotional stress for the family, they were being instructed not to provide succour but instead to exacerbate the grief by opening up fresh wounds. Secondly, there are strict legal guidelines that dictate the way in which evidential material is placed before the suspect; there are none whatever to guide the police in how it is transmitted to the suspect's wife.

Having received their instructions, DC Steve Hutt and WDC Julie Gregory returned to the Gaimsters' house at about 11.00am. They said they needed to speak to Lois. She was asked if she would like anyone with her, and she said that she wanted Denise Lancaster to be there. The officers then spoke to them in one of the upstairs bedrooms. According to their records:

> We informed her [Lois] of the scientists findings. She was distressed and we spoke at length… Once Lois had been informed of the scientists findings and had accepted the fact that there could be little

or no other explanation, it became apparent that there was further information she could offer relating to Siôn.

Although there are no apostrophes in these records, we know that Lois could only have been informed about the *scientist's* findings, not the *scientists'* findings, because the only evidence in the police's possession at this stage was the view of Adrian Wain.

Two points must be made here. Firstly, Wain himself emphasised that his view was a preliminary one. Secondly, this initial opinion was based on information that he had been given by the police. This information was at best incomplete but was more probably wrong. He seems to have been told that Siôn arrived home to find Billie-Jo's body. As he was to acknowledge at the second trial, he had no idea at that stage that she might have been still alive and, more importantly, of Siôn's account, as given to police and in his witness statement, that he had touched Billie-Jo.

Nor was this all that Lois was told. The police records continue: 'the differences in the accounts of Lottie and Annie compared with Siôn's were disclosed to her'. Yet the children's accounts were highly supportive of Siôn's and buttressed his in essential respects. Given what they had so recently experienced, and the unskilled questioning, any slight differences were minor and understandable. Moreover, Charlotte's evidence about the gate – suggesting that there had been an intruder – was particularly clear.

So what were the police actually feeding into Mum? They were giving her the preliminary opinion of a solitary forensic scientist – an opinion, moreover, that was founded on incomplete and even inaccurate information; and an edited version of what her children had said in their witness interviews. It was on this basis that she was told – 'without a shadow of a doubt', as she understood it – that Siôn was the murderer of Billie-Jo.

Lois responded to what must have been this devastating news by acquiescing with the views of the police and presenting a damaging portrayal of Siôn. This is what the police report records:

Feed into Mum

She said she knew very little about his background and history other than he was a public schoolboy sent to boarding school... She has always felt uncomfortable with his family, they tried to persuade him not to marry her, so much so that the day before their wedding they took Siôn out for a meal to try and persuade him to change his mind. She stated that he has an injury to his left knee and has a pin in it. He has never told her how he came to have this. She has been concerned that there are things in his past that she has been kept in the dark about. Siôn's parents have always been supportive to him throughout everything, yet there has been a distinct lack of support from his parents since his arrest. She felt it was as if they were expecting something.

She then went on to tell us he has a violent temper and has hit her in the past. She has also expressed concern re his heavy-handed smacking of his natural children. (At no point is she aware that he has ever hit Billie, he was very aware of where the boundary was with her being a foster child.)

She said he has hit her throughout their marriage and that she has come to accept this as the norm, believing this is usual in a relationship. She has considered leaving him and discussed it with Annie who is aware that her Mum is frightened of Siôn. However, she does not know if Annie has actually seen Siôn hit her. She said he does not need much of a trigger to lose his temper but can just snap for no apparent reason and after losing his temper cannot recall the event. It is as if it did not happen... She commented that she always thought it would be her, and found it difficult to believe not that Siôn had done this but that he had done it to Billie...

On the night of the murder Lois recalls that Siôn had taken his blue fleece off. As they left Denise's house, Lois saw that Siôn was not going to put it on. She told him to put it on because it was cold, but he said he didn't want to and Denise went after him with it and gave it to him. Denise was with Lois while we were talking about this and recalls it too. In hindsight, Lois thought this was odd. She also mentioned that when they returned to the Gaimsters', Lois tried to wipe what she thought was bird's mess off Siôn's trousers. In fact, it was white paint and Siôn got very cross with her when she tried to do this.

It is our opinion that Lois has suffered physically and emotionally at the hands of Siôn for the last 15 years. She has been unhappy and frightened and although not wanting to believe he has committed this murder has had her suspicions all along. This has been reflected in her comments re the press conference when an appeal for Billie's killer was put out, and Lois said that she knew the killer was not out there.

It appears that Lois has reacted to what she has been told about Siôn by revealing disturbing details about their relationship. Yet precisely because this police report contains not only evidence that bears on the Billie-Jo murder case, but also other allegations, it needed to be very carefully studied. The very last reaction of anyone – least of all a police officer – should have been naively to accept it all at face value.

Is there a way of testing the veracity of such a document? Yes, there is. There are parts of all this that can be objectively analysed. That first paragraph, for example; what is the strength of that?

Lois said that Siôn's family took him out to dinner the night before their wedding to try to persuade him to call it off. However, on the night before the wedding, Siôn was staying with Dr Dent and his wife, friends of Lois's parents. There was no family dinner to try to persuade him to change his mind. Lois's suggestion is untrue. It is not even likely to have been true. The wedding was a big, well-planned occasion in Bournemouth and all sorts of arrangements had been made. Family and friends had bought new clothes and wedding presents and booked hotel rooms. There was never any suggestion from his side of the family that they were unhappy with his choice of Lois as a wife until the police information changed their relationship.

Secondly, Lois states that Siôn had a strange injury to his left leg about which he was very reticent. She uses this as the platform from which to float suggestions that he may have had much more to be secretive about in his history. Again, however, it is entirely untrue that Siôn has a pin in his left knee or any other kind of sports injury.

Lois's third point is perhaps the most staggering of all. She says that Siôn has suffered 'a distinct lack of support from his parents since his arrest'. Siôn's family learned of Billie-Jo's murder on the Sunday morning. By Tuesday, his parents, David and Megan, were staying in Hastings at the Beauport Park hotel where Siôn saw them, usually for dinner, in the evenings.

David Jenkins agreed to finance alternative accommodation for his son's family and as a first step had already given Lois £1,000 in cash, should they need to make an immediate deposit. Siôn and Lois had been to view one house. When David and Megan had to return to their home in Aberystwyth at the weekend, David Llewellyn, Siôn's brother, made immediate arrangements to go down to Hastings. When Siôn was arrested on the Monday, David Llewellyn had arrived. Indeed, Lois herself would see him later that day in the police station. So, in the aftermath of the murder, Siôn's family had provided rapid and unqualified support.

Indeed, DS Hutt himself, the officer who was actually feeding into Mum, knew that Siôn's parents had been in Hastings. The previous week, after spending all day with him working on his witness statement, he had dropped Siôn off at the hotel so that he could dine with his parents. One evening, Hutt had remarked that it was after 10.00pm and they'd be lucky to get a meal at the hotel at that time.

So, in that first paragraph of this vital report, Lois makes three separate assertions. All are demonstrably untrue.

Lois is recorded as having said 'there are things in his past that she has been kept in the dark about' and that she has 'always felt uncomfortable with his family'. The fourth paragraph of this police report is also hugely important. At this point, Lois has just been told that the blue fleece jacket is the most vital piece of evidence in the entire case. Either she or Denise, or both of them together, recall a fleeting incident from the Saturday. As they were leaving the Lancasters' house, Siôn refused to put his jacket on. The implication was that he avoided wearing it because he knew it was spattered with Billie-Jo's blood.

A logical explanation of Siôn's refusal to take it immediately was that it was an almost instinctive aversion to being fussed over. In any event, the idea that he was in some way panicked by the thought of wearing the jacket because he knew it was stained with Billie-Jo's blood doesn't make any sense. Siôn had continued to wear the fleece jacket after the murder. When he left his home to go to Denise's, and was then being accompanied by WDS Capon, he was wearing it. Moreover, when the incident outside Denise's happened, police officers were accompanying Siôn and Lois and were leaving the house with them. They were professional observers who should have been particularly vigilant in the immediate aftermath of the murder, yet they noticed nothing untoward. Subsequently, Siôn made no attempt to destroy or hide or even change his clothing.

The fact that Siôn had paint on his trousers is hardly surprising – after all, he'd been helping Billie-Jo with her painting.

According to the police report, Lois says that Siôn 'has hit her throughout their marriage and that she has come to accept this as the norm, believing this is usual in a relationship'. Siôn is not a violent man and certainly not prone to domestic violence. It is hard to imagine Lois making the allegations reflected in the police report.

Lois was a social worker with left-leaning political views who'd been unhappy – indeed, virtually distraught – to learn that her husband was going to stand as a Conservative candidate. In studying for an MA in social work studies, she was undertaking research into the 'institutional abuse' of children by predatory men in care homes. The idea that a woman making an academic study into institutional abuse would have done nothing about it when it was happening to her and her children was completely bewildering.

This is, then, the context in which the very first allegations of domestic violence in the case emerge. The police should have been wary from the outset about all these allegations.

Feed into Mum

Regine Renac was the au pair employed by Siôn and Lois, who had been a live-in au pair from September until just the weekend before the murder. As she was the one outsider who was inside that house, it was essential to gain her views. The police did so. She told them: 'The Jenkins family gives the appearance of being a nice family... I never saw any violence in the family.'

It seems inconceivable that another woman would have been brought into, and remained in, a house of violence.

The process of taking Billie-Jo into the Jenkins' home started in 1992 and continued virtually up to the moment of her death in 1997. Just weeks earlier, a residency order had been obtained for her. 'This was something that the whole family wanted', explained Lois in an early statement to police, 'so that Billie would no longer be a foster child'.

Consequently, throughout this entire period, there was regular contact between the girl herself, and social services (with many opportunities for her to speak to them in private), and the Jenkins family and the family courts.

In fact, however, until Lois reacted to 'feed into Mum', there was never any suggestion from anyone, including Billie-Jo herself, that the Jenkins's household provided anything other than an entirely suitable home for the girl.

Such doubts concerning the reliability of the information contained in this report should have multiplied significantly when it was assessed alongside the one made immediately afterwards. At 2.00pm the following day, WDC Christmas, who had passed the order to feed into Mum, went to see Lois.

According to WDC Christmas's report:

Lois stated that on arrival home last evening she was hallucinating with all the information she had been given throughout the day. From when Steve and Julia spoke to her upstairs, Lois then said: 'by the time they had finished Steve had to spend two hours convincing me that my husband had murdered my child.

I wasn't convinced but I was beginning to move into paranoia. I don't remember everything I said, also conscious of my trying to cope with Annie's distress, which was evident, Lottie, who was screaming, and the household. I lost control of myself and the household and every little thing became a mountain I wasn't coping with at all.

When I got home I heard on the news that the press had filmed me going into the police station and said I was returning voluntarily for further questioning.

In fact I was taken to the police station in a mist of an emotional hype that I have never experienced before. It was a nightmare. I was OK until Steve and Julia spoke to me for about an hour and anything I said or did after that I am not prepared to take any responsibility for. I was not in a fit mental state or not prepared – Steve was sat with his face three feet away from me for about 25 minutes looking me in the eye just convincing me that Siôn had committed this crime without a shadow of a doubt and that he would be charged.

I was faced with the situation where I had to protect myself and my children and my mental state was not appropriate at the time.

I am conscious I broke down with Julia and Steve and I am not conscious of everything I said... I am conscious I did not sign consent for Annie's interview last night... The other thing I would like you to know is that when I was at the police station I was faced with sitting in the room with Siôn's brother who I haven't seen since the beginning of this trauma. Listening and watching him being told that his brother had almost certainly killed his daughter. I am afraid that also freaked me as well.

The final thing is when I went to bed in the room with the six children. It was a room of distress, they were all having nightmares, they thought I was being taken away, they were seeing people being killed...

Feed into Mum

So these were the circumstances in which this information, which was completely traumatising and was delivered with absolute authority, was given to her. A police officer 'sat with his face three feet away from me for about twenty-five minutes looking me in the eye just convincing me that Siôn had committed this crime without a shadow of a doubt'. The effect of this on Lois seems to have been metaphorically, if not literally, hypnotic. It straightaway seems to have produced something close to mental collapse in her. She had been 'freaked'. She was 'hallucinating'. She was 'not conscious of everything I said'. Most importantly, *anything I said or did* after having been told that Siôn had murdered Billie-Jo, *'I am not prepared to take any responsibility for'*.

Accordingly, nothing in all this should have been relied on in any way. This is not what happened, however. Instead, the reverse happened. The 'fleece refusal' would become a key component in the prosecution case – both in the courtroom and, because it featured in just about every media report of the case, outside, in the court of public opinion.

Far more importantly, the suggestions that Siôn had been violent towards Lois and his natural daughters (although not, at any stage, to Billie-Jo) became part of the superstructure of the prosecution case, even though none of this would be used at trial.

Two other points about this aspect of the police investigation need to be underlined. The first is that when Lois was being told this, she was not on her own. Denise Lancaster was with her. They were close confidantes. Charlotte, remember, had already told police that 'Denise and my mum are sort of, like, best friends... they just tell each other everything that, like, goes on.'

Lois had not been at 48 Lower Park Road immediately after the attack on Billie-Jo; but Mrs Lancaster had been there. So the calamitous instruction to 'feed into Mum' did not merely affect Lois, but inevitably must also have affected Mrs Lancaster, who was an actual and important witness to events.

Secondly, it is striking that even at this very early stage, Lois is on Christian-name terms with the police officers ('Julia' and 'Steve'). When investigations of this kind are getting under way, some police officers will have an investigative role and some will have a counselling role. The one can be informal; the other should be more formal. It is accordingly very important that these roles should not become confused. If a familiarity or friendship develops between investigators and witnesses, then another route to potentially contaminated evidence is opened up. For example, there will be a risk that witnesses will tailor their evidence to suit what they believe their new friends would like to hear.

Instead of examining the implications of all this evidence carefully, and retaining a proper scepticism while they did so, police officers appear to have immediately set off in the direction now indicated by Lois.

After the press conference, it seems, Lois had 'said that she knew the killer was not out there' – the unambiguous implication being that she knew that the killer was Siôn. Again, it is important for pieces of evidence not to be passively accepted, but for them to be considered both on their own merits and in conjunction with other pieces of evidence. According to the police report Lois said at the time of the press conference that she knew the killer was not out there. There is no record of Lois having said this at the time of the press conference.

It is not surprising that there isn't, because the statement as reported does not fit with the events. *The day after the press conference, Lois encouraged Sussex police to go and arrest someone else:* Felix Simmons. So he was arrested and held in custody.

Once the decision had been made to 'feed into Mum' the evidence became distorted. Once the well of evidence is polluted with distorted information, then everything in it is polluted. No one can subsequently separate the molecules that are pure from those that are impure.

Chapter Eighteen

Annie's Second Interview

At one point during the second afternoon of Siôn's interrogation, his solicitor Brendan Salsbury left the interview room to go upstairs to the incident room.

When he returned, he told Siôn that there was a furious argument in progress between the police and the Crown Prosecution Service. He believed that Sussex police were ready to press ahead and charge Siôn. However, CPS lawyers demurred. They were quite rightly concerned about the absence of viable evidence implicating him and – even more seriously, from their point of view – the presence of eye-witness evidence tending to exonerate him. His daughters had effectively provided him with an alibi.

The impasse was resolved in this way: Annie would be re-interviewed immediately. If, on this occasion, the girls' alibi for their father was undermined in any way, then Siôn would be charged.

So, after school, Annie was driven back to the Old Courthouse in Battle. Her three sisters went with her. They were accompanied by their mother and Peter Gaimster. Annie's second interview then began at 6.03pm. Like

117

the previous interviews, it was video-recorded. Her mother sat beside her. The lead interviewer, a woman police officer, was the same as for the first interview, nine days earlier. Annie was told that 'a few questions have come up' and then, after the usual preliminaries, the interview got under way. She was asked about the dispute between her and Billie-Jo over which of them was to get the plum job of painting the patio doors:

Q: You told me last time, there was this thing about the painting, wasn't there?
A: Yeah.
Q: Can you tell me about that?
A: Well, I wanted, we were both meant to be sharing the painting.
Q: Hmm.
A: And Billie got to do it first and she was like winding me up about it, when I was clearing out the utility room and stuff and, um, I did the car thing and when we were leaving to go to Do-It-All to get white spirit… she said 'bye to me but, like, horrible to wind me up, 'cos she was doing the painting.

Another officer present then asked a question:

Q: When you just said… that Billie had been winding you up and she said goodbye to you, what happened then?
A: We all walked outside, Lottie and Dad and me and Lottie like walked down, Dad closed the door and then we all walked down together and got into the car.
Q: Alright, OK. You said that Billie winds you all up, is that sort of, used to wind you all up, does that, did that used to happen a lot?
A: Quite a lot.
Q: Yeah.
A: We all wound each other up sometimes. Not all the time.
Q: And what about you all winding your Mum and Dad up? Did that used to happen?

Annie's Second Interview

A: Sometimes.

Q [lead interviewer]: How about that day, Annie?

A: No, didn't wind each other up. Not Mum and Dad.

Q: Not Mum and Dad. And how about Billie? I mean, did she wind Mum and Dad up that day?

A: No.

Q: Was there any arguing going on? Did you hear any arguing?

A: No. I was angry with Mum 'cos she wouldn't take me to the cinema in the morning.

Already it is clear that the standard of interviewing, which had been poor originally, had now deteriorated significantly. This is presumably because the police were now under real pressure; they needed to get something from Annie in order to be able to proceed with their case.[9]

One exchange in the passage above is particularly striking:

Q: [Billie] said goodbye to you, what happened then?

Annie replies:

A: We all walked outside, Lottie and Dad and me and Lottie like walked down, Dad closed the door and then we all walked down together and got into the car.

At this point, the embryonic case against Siôn should dissolve. That simple answer establishes his innocence. There really is nothing more to be said. His alibi is secure, copper-bottomed. The nascent police argument is that Siôn murdered Billie-Jo in the house before joining his daughters outside. This evidence, contained in just three lines of transcript, destroys it.

At this juncture, the interviewer must probe the response carefully. The information is so critical that it is vital to show whether or not Annie means exactly what she is saying. Instead of doing this, however, the

119

interviewer does precisely the opposite. She ignores the answer altogether and steers the interview in a different direction, asking about Billie 'winding up' the others, and whether there was friction in the family.

This passage contains a clear leading question:

Q: And what about you all winding your Mum and Dad up? Did that used to happen?

Annie answers, 'Sometimes', and again there is a feeling that the compliant twelve-year-old is being led by the question. The lead interviewer then comes back in to push the conversation further along that track:

Q: How about that day, Annie?... And how about Billie? I mean, did she wind Mum and Dad up that day?

The interviewers are cutting to the chase. They know the answers they need. Yet, this time, Annie responds firmly; there were no simmering clashes or arguments between Billie-Jo, and Siôn and Lois. There had, of course, been a clash at the start of the day between Billie-Jo and Lois, though Annie may not have been aware of that. All she is aware of was her own unhappiness with her mother.

The officers continue probing:

Q: What did you think about Dad locking the door?
A: I thought we were going downstairs to... I didn't know we were, we were going to...
Q: So would the door need to be locked if you were going to go and wash the MG?
A: I didn't know Dad was locking the door, I just, like, he had shut the door.
Q: Right, but you don't need to shut the door with the key? Your door.

A: Yeah, I didn't know, I don't know, but he did. I think he just shut it or something

Q: I mean normally I would think that if you are going to go down and wash the MG or the Opel you would leave the front door open, wouldn't you? You must use your front door.

A: Hmm.

Q: Mostly in your house because it is on the side, isn't it?

A: I didn't think about it. I just thought we were, I didn't know what we were doing, we just walked down, it was just, we just went...

Q: Right, but you said to me that Dad locked the door, so were you aware that he locked the door?

A: No.

Q: Right, you just...

A: Just, I just, I don't know, I just thought he did because it was, like, he was just behind us and he just followed on.

This scarcely qualifies as a normal interview where questions are asked and answers are sought. The child has already given the answers at her original interview; but the answers didn't fit the prosecution schema so they appear to have been rejected. Now it seems that the interviewers hope that by going over the same areas again and again, they will obtain answers that fit in with their presumptions. Annie resists the pressure:

Q: Do you think there is a chance you didn't go back into the house and you are getting it muddled up with another time?

A: No, I definitely went into the house.

So they move on to another area:

Q: Right, this bit where Ellen has been dropped off and you have come back to the house. Now, as I say, I spoke to you last time and I have watched the tape... And this time and it has been different three times. Now that's not a criticism... You tell me, from imagining yourself in the MG, just imagine what you did and tell me what you see yourself doing. And I want it to be what you remember.

A: I think Lottie was moaning about Dad collecting her late.

The criticism – and it certainly seems like criticism – is entirely misplaced. An objective analysis of her first interview would have shown that in all key respects, Annie's answers were free of ambiguity. What should have been apparent is that her sometimes uncertain recollections do not impinge on the crucial areas. They concern the minutiae – who put the dustpan where, and what happened to the car-washing bucket – the small details of minor tasks that are frequently forgotten as soon as they're done.

This is a final passage from the interview:

WDC Gregory: So the sweeping thing was, was there and the cloth was there and you went up to the house.

A: Hmm.

Q: Do you think? What do you think happened to it? Do you think it stayed in the car or do you think it came with you or... ?

A: I think I might have taken up the cloth. I think Dad got the dustpan and brush out of the boot of the Opel Fruit car and then he took it up and when he went into the kitchen I think he put it back into the kitchen, the dustpan thingy back into the kitchen.

Q: Right. Annie, did you at any time notice any blood on your Dad's hands, or clothes?

A: No.

Q: At any time?

A: I wasn't really looking.

Q: No, I just wondered whether you saw anything?

A: No.

A point of total exasperation seems to have been reached: *Right. Annie, did you at any time notice any blood on your Dad's hands, or clothes?* Leading questions don't come any more leading.

Annie's Second Interview

Note, however, how Annie deals with it. When the question is put, she gives her answer: No.

So the question is, in effect, put again. Annie now says, 'I wasn't really looking' – a response which is sadly absurd in these circumstances. It becomes clear that the child is seeking to be as accommodating as possible, and not to reject outright the suggestions of the interviewer. As such, this small exchange provides further evidence of the dangers of leading questions.

Interviewing is a difficult art to master, and Annie was not an easy interviewee. In the original interviews, Charlotte went first and gave a far more clear-headed account of what had occurred. Her interview lasted much longer than Annie's. It was almost as though Charlotte had said everything that needed to be said. However, Charlotte's answers had provided secure evidential backing for Siôn. It was Annie whose answer in the first interview (that it was 'a few minutes – about two minutes, one minute' before her father followed her and Charlotte outside) provided the platform on which the prosecution case was now being erected. The only way the investigators could take their case forward was by eliciting extra detail from Annie about this supposed time gap.

However, all they had established was that there was no time gap at all. The passage quoted above, which begins with the question, 'What did you think about Dad locking the door?', finishes with Annie re-stating, 'He was just behind us and he just followed on'. There are five other passages in this interview – making six altogether, just as there were six in the previous interview – in which Annie reiterates that she and Lottie and her father all left the house at just about the same time.

Lawyers for the Crown Prosecution Service had been watching and listening to Annie's interview, which finished at 6.50.

Ten minutes later, her father was released.

123

Chapter Nineteen

Homeless in Hastings

The short walk back to the Gaimsters' house took longer than I expected. As I approached, there was no sign of life.

I needed to speak with Lois about the next few days as the police had told me to leave Sussex. In fact, I now know from the statements in the case precisely what happened when the custody sergeant, Kevin French, released me:

> I made it clear… that the investigation was ongoing and that I considered his daughters Annie and Lottie to be witnesses. I warned him that if he discussed the case with them, then he would be in charge of contempt and perversion of justice.… I also advised that I considered it inappropriate to reside at the same house as his wife and children in view of the investigation and asked him to consider alternative arrangements.

At the time, the full impact of this hadn't sunk in and I was then assuming we would all go as a family to my parents' house in Wales.

I rang the bell at the Gaimsters' house. The door was answered by a young girl (their temporary au pair) who told me no one else was there and made it clear that I was not being invited in.

I walked the streets in a daze. I had a plastic carrier bag filled with dirty clothes. I hadn't been permitted to shave so I looked dishevelled and unkempt, which only increased my feelings of wretchedness. I was homeless. I had nowhere to go.

I then remembered some friends from my church who lived nearby. I walked to their house, just hoping they would be in. I rang the doorbell but there was no answer. I was wondering where else I could go when I stepped back from the porch and saw them hiding behind their curtains. When they realised I had seen them, they closed the curtains.

Then I thought of Roger Mitchell, the school headmaster. I walked all the way up St Helen's Road to his house. Very tentatively, I walked up the drive. I did not know what kind of reception I would receive, if any. I trusted Roger, but then I had trusted others who were now turning their backs on me.

I was feeling utterly forsaken when I pressed the doorbell. Margaret, his wife, answered the door. Without any hesitation, and any words being spoken, she held out her arms and put them round me. Then she said, 'You're very welcome'. I cried. I had tried to keep myself strong, but her warmth and kindness melted my resolve. I will forever be indebted to them for their kindness. At last, I was safe with them. I had found sanctuary.

After a much-needed hot drink, I asked Roger if I could use his phone. My first call was to my parents, who were delighted that I had been released.

'Do you know where Lois and the girls are?' I asked.

They didn't know. My father told me that David Llewellyn, my brother, was in Hastings. This news cheered me. I then phoned Lois's parents and spoke to her father, John Ball. He, too, said that he was thrilled that I had been released but, like my own father, had no idea where Lois or the girls were. He commented that he was surprised she wasn't with me.

My brother arrived within an hour. When I saw him I felt a sense of relief. We embraced and then discussed what was happening. David said

125

that he had been at Hastings police station in the late afternoon. He told me the police believed they were going to charge me. Indeed, someone had briefed the media to that effect. He had heard the reporters practising, running through what they were going to be saying: 'Tonight, Siôn Jenkins has been charged with the murder... '

I phoned my parents again and explained that I had no money, no clothes and had been told by the police to leave Hastings. I was unable to do planning of any complexity as I was too bewildered. (Although I now realise that I was in shock, at the time I was still unaware of this.) From that moment, my father went into overdrive. He arranged that at 10.30 the following morning I would be picked up at Lydd airport in Kent by Kwik Fit's private Beechcraft jet, and flown to a small airport just outside Aberystwyth.

Later that evening, I was informed that Lois would be coming to see me the next morning before I left.

I didn't sleep at all that night.

When my daughters ran into the Mitchells' house the following morning, all my sadness evaporated in an instant. I hugged and kissed them. At school the previous day, Charlotte had drawn me a picture which she proudly gave me. It has become one of my most treasured possessions.

After fussing my daughters I realised that Lois and I had not spoken. She was with a friend of ours whom I had known for many years, Dave Mann. I had often invited him for meals in London. He had become a lay minister for a small Baptist church in Newham. It seems he had renewed contact with Lois after Billie's death. Until that moment I had thought that he was a friend of both of us.

When I looked at Lois, she appeared disconnected from the meeting. She did not explain her sudden disappearance, or where she and the children had spent the night. Dave Mann appeared on edge. Although I didn't say anything, I objected to his presence. He was an intruder into what was an intensely private family meeting.

The meeting was over almost as soon as it had begun. Lois, it appeared, was not coming with me. How does a father say goodbye to his children at a moment like this? I had never been apart from them before. It took all my powers of self-control not to cry in front of them.

When the children had left, I was briefly alone with Lois and Dave Mann. He stood close to Lois and stared at me. I asked him to leave so that Lois and I could say goodbye and discuss the girls. He refused to leave. I was by now very irritated. The fact that he was there at all made it an unsatisfactory meeting. It was almost as though he was there as a minder, a self-appointed police support officer, making sure we didn't discuss the case – which, of course, we didn't. Lois left with him.

I was soon on my way to Lydd and was met at the airport by Bob, the company pilot.

'I'll have you away from here in minutes', he said.

My journey was peppered with reflections on the morning meeting. Why had Lois not spoken to me? Where did Dave Mann fit in? What had happened to my friendship with him? What about Billie's funeral?

My parents were there to meet me when we arrived. As I walked towards them, I could feel my trousers falling down. I would never have believed one could lose so much weight in so short a time.

I can't remember that first evening in Aberystwyth, yet I do remember the sense of isolation because Lois and my daughters were still in Hastings.

During that week, my grandmother, Mary Jenkins, came to see me regularly. She lived about fifteen miles outside Aberystwyth, in the small house in Ystrad Meurig which I had often visited since childhood. She gave me tremendous support during those first bleak days back in Wales.

After two days I still hadn't heard from Lois and I also wanted to speak to my daughters, so I phoned the Gaimsters' home. Julia Gaimster answered.

'You shouldn't be phoning', she said. 'Lois doesn't want to speak to you'.

'But I'm allowed to speak to my family', I replied, 'the police said nothing about not contacting them.'

Julia firmly ended the conversation, saying, 'Do not phone again'.

After this call I was in despair. I was completely shaken by Lois's sudden and unexplained remoteness. I convinced myself that Lois was either being prevented from supporting me or was unable to cope with the pressure. If I had made a list of all those people I could be sure would stand by me, at the very top would have been Lois.

At the end of that first week, Dave Mann suddenly turned up in Aberystwyth. He was accompanied by Howard Wynne, whom I hadn't seen for some years. They came into the house.

Mann said, 'I need to speak to you alone'; and so, we went for a walk; I was expecting to hear news of Lois and my daughters. I was wrong. He said to me, 'You would make it a lot easier on everyone if you admitted guilt'. He actually tried to persuade me, for the sake of Lois and the children, to say I was guilty. He cited the story of David and Uriah the Hittite: David arranged for the husband of Bathsheba, with whom he was having an affair, to be put in the front line of battle so that he would be killed. Then the prophet Nathan appeared, and exposed David, saying, 'You are the man'.

'I've been reading the Bible', Mann said, 'and I'm Nathan, I've come to tell you that you're guilty, and you need to confess.'

I told him that I just couldn't believe what he was saying. I emphasised that I was innocent and was going to fight to clear my name. So he and Howard went back to London. They'd driven all the way up to see me, but they'd been there less than an hour. Howard apologised to my parents and looked sheepish and embarrassed by the whole thing.

Then, Mann went back to Hastings and – as I later found out from reading the case papers – started telling the police everything I had said to him privately.

I was over 200 miles from my family, and Lois wasn't taking my telephone calls. So I did the only thing I could. That Sunday, 2 March, I wrote her a lengthy letter:

My dearest Lois,
I'm writing this letter and giving it to you through our respective solicitors as I want to do nothing that could be used against you and our children...

Above: Siôn Jenkins aged 13 (second from left, middle row), in the Glasgow Academy Rugby team.

Below: Siôn and Lois' wedding, 18 December 1982.

Above left: Christmas day 1991.

Above right: Billie-Jo in the summer of 1996, sitting in the dining room, happy and settled.

Below: All five of the Jenkins' daughters together, enjoying a family holiday in France in 1995.

Above: The Jenkins family (with Siôn's mother Megan) in happier times, summer 1995.

Below: Billie-Jo and Annie, autumn 1996. This is one of the last photographs of Billie.

The back and front
of the Jenkins
family home, No.
48 Lower Park
Road, in Hastings.

Above: The side passage, showing the back gate.

Below: The back patio, with the doors Billie-Jo was painting at the time of the murder.

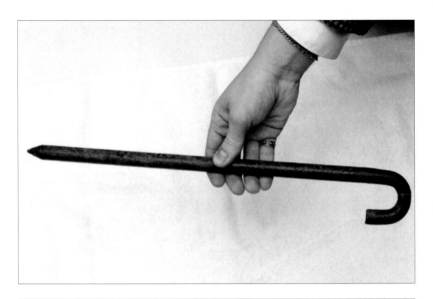

Above: The murder weapon – an 18" metal tent peg.

Below: Siôn Jenkins' fleece jacket, following preparation by the prosecution for exhibition at trial.

Above: Siôn and Lois at a police press conference, four days after Billie-Jo's murder.

Left: Siôn leaves Lewes Crown Court after his second day of questioning in the witness box.

Inside Wakefield prison, where Siôn spent six years.

You and our children will always be my first priority... I am convinced that a time will come when we will be reunited as a family...

The strain of this is beyond what is humanly possible for one to cope with. But I believe it will come to an end and that we will be together again. I know, Lois, how difficult it must be for you to be surrounded by the police and social workers, all giving a view on this case. I'm sure that most of Hastings probably has an opinion by now. Yet the only person who has been removed from the scene and is unable to defend himself is me.

I was appalled that pressure has been applied to you Lois, and further that Annie and Lottie have also been pressured... I do not want our girls being put through emotional torture to appease the misguided whims of a small corps of people...

I did not murder Billie-Jo. I did not hit her, push her, or in any way harm our daughter. I know the police believe I committed this crime but they are wrong. I am angry that the police refuse to hear what I am saying. You must believe in me Lois – don't be worn down by the gossip and gentle bullying of those around you. One of the most upsetting aspects of this affair is that her killer still walks free whilst my character is being systematically destroyed by the police force.

Two days ago I was so depressed that all I wanted to do was to curl up and die. Today, I am beginning to recover. I refuse to accept the injustice that is being perpetrated against me and my family...

Over the next few weeks, Lois, it will be essential that we talk. We are still responsible for our four girls who need us and will be relying on us. Despite having gone through what must be the worst few days of our lives, we have not talked or communicated at all. The wedge that some have tried to drive between us is evil and sinister. We must talk and communicate, otherwise the pressure and strain will be too much for our family to bear...

I want to see you very soon, Lois. I love you dearly and know that I will not be able to come through this without you. Continue to pray for me as I do for you.

My love to you as always,
Siôn.

My letter appeared to have no effect at all.

At my second trial, a juror would ask how it was that an intensely private letter from a husband to his wife could have become part of the documentary record of the case. The answer was very simple. Despite the fact that I had taken the precaution of sending it through confidential legal channels, Lois had quickly passed it to the police.

Chapter Twenty
The Innuendo Increases

It would be many months before Siôn found out exactly where Lois and the children were the night he was released from custody in Hastings. In fact, they themselves were also at the police station, together with Peter Gaimster. When Siôn was taken out through the back, he and Brendan Salsbury, his solicitor, were told this was in order to shield him from the reporters congregated outside. In fact, the real reason had been to keep him apart from his own family. Then, while he was out looking for them, they were driven away by officers to spend the night in a local hotel.

The police had told Lois that Siôn had committed the murder. She then watched as they also told David Llewellyn, Siôn's brother (and, she commented, 'That had freaked me as well'). She herself would naturally have informed Peter Gaimster, who was with her as these events unfolded. He said in a statement that, 'Whilst Siôn was under arrest and in custody at Hastings police station, we, that's me and Lois, talked a lot'.

So it was hardly surprising that it was not only Lois's attitude towards Siôn that changed completely; so did Gaimster's. Six days earlier, he and Lois had set police on the trail of Felix Simmons. Five days earlier, when

Simmons had been released, Gaimster had gone to Hastings police station with two friends to protest that his release had put their lives in such danger that they would need special police protection.

Now, at about 8.00pm on that critical Tuesday, Gaimster told police that the release of Siôn had endangered Rita, the student whom he employed as a kind of au pair. He was alarmed to learn that she had been alone in the house when Siôn had called there about an hour earlier. So WDS Capon drove him home from the station so that together they could check on her well-being.

On that very short journey, Gaimster started providing Capon with some explosive information, which included the 'fact' that Siôn had 'kicked the living daylights out of Billie' when the families had been on holiday together in France. On her return to the station, Capon immediately informed Detective Superintendent Paine, the man leading the investigation. He would not have known that, only forty-eight hours earlier, Gaimster had signed a statement in which he described that holiday in France as 'wonderful'.

The next day, Gaimster again spoke to Capon, hinting that Siôn may have been abusing his foster daughter, and adding that Lois 'in her heart knows' that he committed the murder. He suggested that Siôn was now going to flee the country.

During the next week, DC Hutt and WDC Gregory were in constant attendance at 48 Lower Park Road. (The scenes-of-crimes team having completed its work at the house, Lois and the children had moved back in.) Hutt and Gregory's ostensible role, as family liaison officers, was to support the family in the immediate aftermath of bereavement. Their actual role, however, extended far beyond this. They had already played the key part in the case – by feeding into mum – and they now understood their function to be to gather information to assist the inquiry. Since all those central to the investigation now unreservedly believed that Siôn was the culprit, this meant gathering information either that further incriminated him or that undermined his putative defence.

Siôn had been released because of the evidence contained in the children's video interviews, and at this stage that block of evidence was the main obstacle to any successful prosecution of him. What the police needed, therefore, was some variation in the children's accounts.

Very soon, they had it – not from the children, but from their mother and from Peter Gaimster. On the afternoon of Monday 3 March, Lois began to intimate that her daughters' evidence was changing. She told Gregory that Annie had told her that her father had been trying to stop her seeing Billie because he was embarrassed that Billie was doing the painting and not her. She said she couldn't remember whether she had waved to Billie when she had said at the interview (that is, when they were leaving on the white spirit trip) or whether it would have been earlier. Annie is reported as having told Lois that she couldn't understand why her father needed white spirit as he had bought some the day before. She had thought it odd that he had run down the steps and told them to get into the car quickly. Lois said she asked her daughter, 'What mood was he in?' and Annie had replied, 'A bit of a funny mood'. Both Annie and Lottie, so Lois reported, had been puzzled that Siôn drove round the park twice.

Even if the police had had reservations about the new thrust of Lois's evidence – although, in fact, there are no signs that they had any at all – those doubts must have been removed that same day once they'd taken Gaimster's second statement. This chimed exactly with what Lois was now telling the police. The affable tone of Gaimster's first statement had gone and he was now clearly antipathetic to Siôn. He stated that Siôn 'has in fact taken [Annie] out alone on a number of occasions' and said bluntly that Siôn 'could prime Annie into what he wanted her to say'. He personally, said Gaimster, remembered Annie saying to Lois in the lounge of his house: 'You know, I think I was outside with Lottie when Dad came out'.

WDC Gregory filed a report of her conversation with Lois. It was to become the first of a series in which Lois relayed purported conversations with her daughters, the invariable effect of which was to bring into question the accounts they had already given – the accounts that exculpated their father. Lois's fresh snippets of information were cumulatively disastrous for her husband because they pierced the heart of what would be his defence. It is, though, important to emphasise that all of these are reports of what the children are supposedly saying. Nothing is first-hand; none of these reports originates from the girls themselves.

When DC Hutt spent Tuesday evening at the house, Lois volunteered further thoughts. She said she thought that as pressure continued to build on Siôn, he would try to snatch the children and flee the country. She said she felt totally unsafe knowing that he could return and was 'absolutely terrified' of the prospect of him suddenly turning up at the house. She would, she said, like to discuss this with Detective Superintendent Paine.

Lois also remarked that whereas originally David Mann had asked local churches to pray for Siôn's speedy release, he was now asking congregations to pray that the truth should be established.

She passed on further points about the day itself. She said that Annie had said she went in and out of the house a number of times and could remember Billie screaming at her. Annie said that Siôn saw this and was cross with Billie. She then went on to say that, after leaving the house to continue washing the car, she attempted to get back in, but Siôn wouldn't let her. Annie formed the impression that he was trying to keep her and Billie apart. Lois stated that Annie told her that she couldn't actually remember putting the tent pegs out.

To Hutt, Lois expressed concern for Annie's emotional well-being and the way that she was coping, and also stated that Annie would like to talk to him, although she wouldn't do this on video. A significant final comment was written on the report. Hutt said that Lois had been advised *again* to time and note any comments made by Annie. He added that the point would be reiterated *again* tomorrow.

As these reports were being made, the officers were taking a second major statement from Lois. It was completed and signed on Friday, 7 March. Her original statement had been merely an account of what she herself did on the day of the murder. The second was very different. It explained her family background in some detail – her upbringing as a member of the Exclusive Brethren, and then how she met Siôn, their marriage and family life together. She explained the circumstances in

134

which they had fostered Billie-Jo (and, initially, her brother); the difficulties they had in raising her; the various issues presented by Billie-Jo's natural family, and the problems of living in Hastings, such as the prowlers and nuisance telephone callers.

Significantly, the statement contained a number of allegations that Siôn had used physical violence against her and the children. She accused him of having hit her several times and also of having used corporal punishment on the children. One incident of alleged violence against her occurred when, she said, Siôn lost his temper while trying to fix a toilet-roll holder. He hit her across the head and as a result she sustained a perforated eardrum. She said that she had meekly told friends and her doctor that she had hit her head on a kitchen cupboard.

Yet the point when the marital disharmony reached what she described as 'an all-time high' occurred not as a result of any domestic violence but over another matter entirely – Siôn's embryonic political career:

In 1995, Siôn announced that he would be standing as the Conservative candidate in the by-elections for the West St Leonard's ward. I was surprised and upset... I thought we were of a like mind as far as politics were concerned... To stand as a Conservative went against everything I thought we believed in. It caused friction between us and drew the two of us further apart... Siôn was invited to functions which I refused to attend, and consequently Siôn formed a different circle of friends. Siôn and I rowed during this period.... It introduced a distance between us which has not recovered. I am disappointed with myself that I allowed this situation to develop. I wish I had been more flexible.

Nevertheless, her marriage to Siôn had lasted for fifteen years and, at this time, the memories were not all bad. The police quoted her as saying that despite the problems, 'we were happy together and had some very enjoyable times as a family'. Lois studied the police account, crossed out the word 'some' and inserted instead, 'many'.

Several times, also, she stated that the relationship between Siôn and Billie-Jo had been entirely normal:

> Siôn would discipline Billie by sitting her down and talking to her. There was never any animosity between Siôn and me over Billie. I always felt we were united in our approach to her. In the past Siôn had worked in some deprived inner-city schools and was able to develop a good rapport with socially deprived children. During that time he gave a lot socially as well as academically. Billie brought out the more gentle, humane side of Siôn. I felt that having Billie come to live with us made up for the fact that Siôn was no longer involved with children from his previous schools.

The statement was prepared; but Lois demurred. The police stated that she was 'reluctant' to sign it and had used 'delaying tactics'. In fact, before signing it, she actually went through the typed-up version of this new statement very carefully, and made scores of alterations. She crossed out some bits and added others, changed words and sentence construction and even moved paragraphs about. Only then did she sign it.

No sooner had she signed it, however, than she was dropping heavy hints that she had been less than frank. So on the one hand, the police were taking a very lengthy second statement from this key witness; on the other, they were excitedly making internal reports that this was not a completely true and accurate account. According to the internal police reports that were being drawn up even as the statement was being signed, Lois 'has stated that we (the police) are on the right tracks but refuses to expand at this moment in time'. She also told them that 'when Siôn is charged and convicted, then she would tell us why he actually committed this offence'.

Among the other comments that Lois made not in her statement but in conversation to officers, she said that 'Siôn really loved Billie'. The police noted that this 'was said in such a way that it appeared that Lois may have been jealous of the relationship between Billie-Jo and Siôn. Lois posed a specific question to WDC Gregory, as to what actually constituted child abuse – a peculiar question for a woman in her position to ask'.

Peculiar? It certainly is. Yet it becomes even more extraordinary when one takes into account that on the very same day that she was hinting that the relationship may have been an abusive one, she was signing a statement in which she said that 'Things were fine between Siôn and Billie'.

Even as they took a signed statement from Lois, the police were informing each other that it did not represent a full and accurate account but was instead 'a watered-down version'. Then, over the coming days, weeks and months, they allowed Lois to say whatever she wanted – irrespective of whether it contradicted points in her signed statement.

That weekend, Lois had clearly worked herself up into a state of panic. She was so alarmed at the possibility of Siôn's return home that she asked the entire Lancaster family to sleep over with them on the Sunday night; Lois and the children were, according to police records, 'terrified'. Throughout the night, officers constantly checked the house. Lois said to Denise (again, according to police records), 'Why did he kill Billie and not me?'

On the Monday evening, the police returned. According to their notes of what Lois told them that evening:

On Saturday, [Siôn] had insisted Lois go out with the younger two [children], which was unusual. She mulled over whether the murder could have been premeditated, but dismissed it almost immediately, thinking it more likely that he just could not cope.

BILLIE AND SIÔN'S RELATIONSHIP
Lois was certainly not aware of anything of a sexual nature taking place... Re [Billie] taking Siôn's boxer shorts to Ruth's [on] Thursday night. Billie took them from Siôn's drawer, then told him she had done so. Siôn told Lois. Lois felt it was not alright, she was aware of what Ruth and her parents might think. Lois does not know what Billie actually wore in bed at Ruth's, she presumed the boxers

and some sort of top. On the previous Wednesday, Billie had had a conversation with Regine about wearing boxers in bed. All the French girls do, so Lois was not surprised Billie did this.

Lois does not think Siôn has had any affairs because she always knows where he is. He rarely goes out without her. And she does not think he has had the opportunity.

The officer taking the notes, WDC Gregory, concluded her report by saying, 'I will be going over some of the above points in more detail with Lois'.

Denise Lancaster slept overnight at the house again on the Monday evening.

Judging by her conversations with police the following day, Lois seemed to have given fresh thought to the whole concept of a 'prowler'. As the police put it in their report:

Lois seems to have picked up on the fact that it is only Siôn and Billie that have actually had any experiences with regard to prowlers. She herself has never seen anything and her only reasons for being anxious are that both Siôn and Billie fuelled her fears. She also mentioned that these prowler incidents only happened when Siôn and/or Billie were in the house. She never saw or was aware of anything all the times that she was in the house alone. None of the other four children nor the au pair Regine saw or heard anything either. Lois feels this is somewhat strange and makes her wonder whether in fact there was a prowler at all.

On the Wednesday, Lois again confided in WDC Gregory. She told her that Annie had said that if Dad has done it (murdered Billie), it would have been because Billie was painting and being horrible to Annie, who really wanted to paint. On two occasions while Annie was washing the Opel, she went up to the house to get clean water. Both times Siôn prevented her from going in. He shut the door and got the water for her.

Annie thinks Dad was stopping her seeing Billie. Lois added that, when Dad drove round the park prior to driving to Do-It-All, he seemed in Annie's words, 'disorientated'. There was another important point: Annie, according to Lois, had said that 'Dad didn't phone the ambulance for a long time'.

By now, the police had decided to charge Siôn with the murder. They received a fresh report from the forensic scientist Adrian Wain, to the effect that the blood staining on Siôn's clothing was consistent with his being the killer. The only obstacle to charging him – the alibi evidence of his two children – had been demolished by Lois, both in her conversations with the family liaison officers and her reports purporting to suggest that the children were re-thinking their evidence.

The plan was that he was going to be lured back to Sussex by the opportunity of meeting his children, whom he hadn't seen for a fortnight, on Thursday, 13 March. He would be arrested at the end of that family get-together. Lois wanted the Baptist minister David Mann to accompany her to the meeting, so he arrived back in Hastings on the Tuesday to stay with her and the children for a few days.

Chapter Twenty-One

Charged with Murder

It was very difficult for me being in Wales, away from everything. I still believed that the day would come when the police would tell me they had arrested Billie's murderer.

I had no contact with Lois whatsoever. She would not take my phone calls and she had not responded to my letter. I was missing the girls desperately. By the second week, I was missing them so much that I phoned Brendan and asked if he could make arrangements for me to see them. His request was flatly rejected.

Then, Brendan phoned to say that Lois's solicitor had contacted him to set up a meeting for me with my daughters. Although I had still not heard from Lois herself, this did not spoil my delight at the thought of seeing the girls. The visit was scheduled to take place at a social services safe house – a term I was not familiar with at the time – in Hailsham, which was just north of Eastbourne. I had no choice other than to accept the arrangements.

My father anticipated that I might find the visit emotionally overwhelming so he suggested that he should fly down with me. On the morning of Thursday, 13 March, we flew back down to Lydd airport and I then took a taxi to the meeting-place.

It was just an ordinary, small semi-detached house. When I walked up the pathway, I saw the girls peeping from behind the curtains. My heart leapt. I saw Esther smiling broadly, quickly followed by her sisters as they pulled back the curtain. The girls clustered in the middle of the lounge. They surrounded me and wanted to be held. Charlotte, especially, was very, very emotional and held me tightly. I sat down with them all and listened to their stories. I explained that their grandfather would be coming to pick me up.

As I looked around, there were a surprisingly large number of police officers in the room, and I was doubly surprised to discover that there were even more in the back room. Why were they all here at a private family meeting?

Also present, in this very crowded room, was the social worker. He was the man whom I had not set eyes on since he had introduced himself to me almost a month earlier, saying that his role was to support us all in the aftermath of the murder. He sat silently in the corner.

Lois was sitting in a straight-backed chair pushed up against the wall. Her body was rigid and she sat bolt upright as if something was about to happen. Her face was ashen and her expression fixed. Her eyes gazed out at nothing. She appeared totally different from the person I had known for fifteen years. She just looked as if she had been battered emotionally. I tried to initiate eye contact with her, but it was impossible and, despite repeated attempts on my part, she would not be drawn into conversation.

I needed so much to discuss things with her. Time was passing. It became imperative that I spoke to her. Then, to my surprise, she suddenly said she'd like to talk to me privately. She took me to a side-room and, looking as if she had walked onto the stage in a play, sat down. I momentarily thought that I was alone with her and there were no police or social workers around. However, my attempts at offering words of comfort were constantly interrupted by a police officer putting his face round the door and asking if she was OK.

I tried to say that I loved her, and that everything would be all right, she musn't worry, I was going to do my best to get this cleared up. Lois appeared as if she was drugged or hypnotised; she struggled to make a simple response. She then stood up and a police officer walked into the room. Lois and the officer left the room together.

It was a good job I'd said what I had. The room was bugged, although I hadn't realised that at the time. The police had been listening to everything I said to her.

Before I rejoined the others I went upstairs to the toilet. A plain-clothes police officer followed me up. When I came out, there was a policeman standing outside the door. I thought, why are they following me around?

On returning to Lois and my daughters in the lounge, I was told by the police to say goodbye to my children. I hugged each of them, telling them that I would not be away for much longer. Annie, Charlotte and Esther went outside.

Lois then left with the social worker. She did not say goodbye. I heard him saying to her, 'Shall I drive the car?' The car he was referring to was my car. It reinforced the feeling of hopelessness, that my life was being completely taken over – who was this man who was driving my car to take my wife and daughters home?

Maya didn't want to leave. She lingered; she went towards the door, but then took some steps back. So before she had left the house, while she could still see me, they arrested me and put my hands behind my back and handcuffed me. The cruel realisation hit me that my girls had been used as bait to get me back into Sussex. From my point of view, it had been worth it just to see them; but I thought it had been immoral to use my daughters to trap me. What about the effect it could have on seven-year-old Maya to see her father arrested like that?

They pushed me into a police car and, like a scene from the movies, the car accelerated away at speed. We arrived back at Hastings police station and I was put in the same cell I'd been in before. Brendan arrived and told me to prepare for more questioning.

Meanwhile, at Lydd airport, my father and two pilots were waiting.

When my father found out what had happened, he went to Hastings police station and asked how long I was going to be kept for. He was told he couldn't see me and that I was being charged. Of course, he had to fly back to Aberystwyth on his own.

The questioning now was more aggressive than before. The police continued, as I saw it, to twist words and phrases from my witness statement. It was also during this session that the police first suggested I had been violent towards Lois. I thought they were making it up just to try to unsettle me.

WDS Capon then said that they now had a statement from Lois, according to which I had been violent toward her over the fifteen years of our marriage. The situation I was in was already extreme; this new development was shocking.

On the second day, the officer leading the investigation came into the interviewing room and charged me both with murder and also with obtaining a pecuniary advantage by deception.

This latter charge, relating to the CV I had provided when applying to William Parker School, seemed particularly to amuse the police. At the time I thought it was insignificant compared to the murder charge; I didn't appreciate its long-term implications for my defence. The charge helped the prosecution to portray me as a man of bad character. Like everyone else, I have good and bad points; but only the bad would be fed to the media machine.

Brendan said I would be taken to Lewes prison and that I could spend up to a year on remand there.

Lewes is an old Victorian prison and the architecture reflected its Dickensian past. I was led to the reception area and asked several questions. I can remember specifically being asked, 'Do you have any identifying tattoos?' But before I could reply, the prison officer looked up and answered for me, 'No, you wouldn't, would you?'

I had woken up that morning in Aberystwyth. From leaving Wales, to seeing my children in Hailsham, to being taken to Hastings police station and then to Lewes prison – it hadn't been a pleasurable day, but it had certainly been an extraordinary one. That first night was a mixed blessing. When my door was slammed shut, the echo had a kind of finality about it. My cell was dirty and I did not know what to expect, yet the solitude of that moment finally gave me peace.

The next day, Friday, 14 March, I appeared in court. After being formally charged, I was taken back to prison and moved into a dormitory with five other prisoners.

On Saturday afternoon, I was called out for a legal visit and saw Brendan there with my father, who had come straight back down from Wales, and my brother. I was so pleased to see them. As I walked in I felt ashamed that I was dressed in dirty prison clothing. My father tried to encourage me and focus on what needed to be done. My legal team, including Anthony Scrivener QC, had decided to seek bail. I found this perplexing as I assumed the chances of success were remote.

The first week there was a time of familiarising myself with the routines of prison life. The hardest part was getting through every day expecting Lois to visit me. She had made no contact in any way, but I couldn't accept that she had decided to live her life without me. I still believed that she would come.

It was during my second week that I was told I did have a social visit. I didn't know who it was and was not expecting anybody. I sat in the visiting room and waited. I was shocked when Dave Mann appeared. I momentarily thought Lois might have been with him, but she wasn't. If I'd known who it was, I wouldn't have seen him. He sat opposite me and appeared in a strange mood. He asked how I was coping and what the food was like. I hardly spoke as I was wondering what he really wanted. Then he said I needed to confess so that everyone could move on. I asked him to leave. As he was going, I asked how Lois was and whether he knew if she was coming to visit. I remember his words.

'If she does come', he said, 'she only wants to talk to you about money.'

I returned to my dormitory. I needed to be alone with my sadness.

I do know, from the case records, that after seeing me Mann reported straight back to Lois and the police.

During this week Brendan approached me about my position as headteacher-designate of William Parker School. All this time, of course, he'd been wearing two hats: he was my solicitor but he was also clerk to the governors of the school. I was unsure what to do and wanted to discuss it with Lois; but she never did come to see me.

I resigned.

Most of the prisoners were naturally concerned with their own situations and weren't interested in mine. However, one prisoner – he was a large man with a ponytail – started to behave aggressively towards me. One afternoon, whilst the rest of the wing was on association – when men are permitted to leave cells for recreational purposes – I returned to the dormitory to collect a book. I sat down on the bed but then became aware of this man moving towards me. He had a pencil in his hand and quickly lashed out with its sharp point. I pushed him away but he again attempted to strike my eyes, using the pencil as a spike. The rumpus alerted the screws, who came running in. Apparently this man wanted to get his name in the papers. After the incident, he remained in isolation until I left. However, he did get his wish; the attack was duly leaked and reported in the press.

Two days later, on Tuesday, 25 March, I was taking a shower. The dormitory was quiet. Suddenly, one of the men ran in shouting that he'd just heard on the radio that I'd been given bail. I stopped showering and called to one of the officers asking whether it was true. He said that he'd have to go and find out. Finally, a senior officer confirmed that I had been granted bail. For me, that was one of the more defining moments in the last ten years. It was too late to leave that day, but tomorrow morning I would be gone.

I went back to the dorm and offered a prayer of thanks. I didn't know what the conditions of my bail were or what Tony Scrivener had told the judge, but I was getting out. I immediately wanted to call my daughters and was glad they had been spared visiting me in prison.

The next morning I had a legal visit. Brendan's clerk came to explain that I had been given bail at a hearing in chambers by the judge, Brian

Smedley. I was to reside with my retired parents at their house in Aberystwyth. I was not to enter Sussex.

Bail was set at a quarter-of-a-million pounds. My parents put up £100,000 of the surety, with my uncle John and his wife Iona agreeing to £50,000 of it. In the face of considerable advice, because of the high profile of the case, Sir Tom Farmer[10] had also agreed to put up £100,000, for which my family have always been very grateful. Tony Scrivener had gone to a lot of trouble to make sure that all the arrangements were in place and all the arguments were properly presented. Even so, some judges would have refused the bail application; to Mr Justice Brian Smedley, I am eternally grateful.[11]

A small gate within the main gates was opened and I was allowed to walk out. Brendan was waiting. I had eaten little during the two weeks inside and so had lunch with my parents in Brighton before we departed for Wales. Brendan was planning my defence and said he would phone me at the weekend as there was much to be done.

All I could think was that I had been in prison and now I was free. The tentacles of the state had released their grip, if only temporarily.

Chapter Twenty-Two

The Bentovims' Report

After Siôn's re-arrest on 13 March, Lois's dialogue with the police continued. She passed on to them a stream of increasingly damaging material about her husband, which they recorded in a series of regular reports. She was, or so they may have thought to themselves, spilling the beans.

By now, the police had carried out basic checks on Siôn's background. They had discovered that, in his applications for the posts to which he had been successively appointed at William Parker School (deputy headteacher in 1992; headteacher in 1996), Siôn had given himself an academic record which he did not possess; he had significantly exaggerated his educational qualifications. He had also stated that he had been educated not at the Glasgow Academy (for all that it was one of the more reputable schools in Scotland), but at Gordonstoun (the school attended by both Prince Phillip and Prince Charles).

The family liaison officers immediately conveyed this to Lois who, according to Hutt, 'was not surprised to hear that Siôn was not particularly well-qualified. In fact, she was quite chuffed with the thought that she was actually better qualified than him.' (As it happened, Siôn was better qualified than Lois. Lois, who actually knew all the details of Siôn's academic history, seems to be reflecting the police misconception.)

Lois told the police that Siôn had got a criminal record for damage to and theft of a vehicle.

Much more disturbingly, Lois began to provide more information about Siôn and Billie-Jo. Hutt reported that, 'over the last 3–6 months [Lois] had been concerned over the relationship between Siôn and Billie-Jo, though she did not actually specify the reason behind that.' Whereas, at the beginning of the week, she had told police that with regard to the relationship, she was 'certainly not aware of anything of a sexual nature taking place'.

Hutt added in his report, 'I am quite convinced that Lois is merely supplying the bare minimum when it comes to issues she has mentioned in her statement and I believe that there is the potential for a lot more useful "evidence" to be gleaned from her.' (Those intriguing quotes round 'evidence' actually do appear in his report.)

By Friday, 14 March, a mere twenty-four hours after Siôn's arrest and as he was being arraigned in court, Lois had taken on board the idea that he had been having an affair with the seventeen-year-old girlfriend of a colleague's son. Yet only a few days earlier, at the beginning of the week, she had firmly ruled out such a possibility because she 'always knows where he is'; he 'rarely goes out without her'; and 'does not think he has had the opportunity'.

Lois's growing belief that he'd had an improper relationship with Billie-Jo were at odds with the other evidence: the medical evidence; the evidence of the au pair and Billie-Jo's best friend; the evidence contained in the social services records; and even by the previous evidence of Lois herself. However, it is the uniquely insidious nature of sexual allegations that they do not require corroborative evidence to germinate; once the seed of innuendo has been planted, however barren the soil, it tends to thrive. People tend to be so tantalised by the idea that there is a secret story to be told (something improper was going on) that they reject the mundane reality (nothing was happening).

It is also instructive that what Lois is passing on is information only in the loosest sense; it is actually surmise and hearsay. Nothing is documented in any way. This is despite the fact that the police specifically requested her to make a documentary record, and to time and date her snatches of conversation with the children; this request, Hutt recorded, would be *reiterated again*. Yet it was never complied with. When she was asking for Annie to be interviewed again, she added the condition: but not on video.

Accordingly, the allegations both of physical violence against her and of cruelty towards the children should be carefully examined against the background that nothing else that she was saying at this period was borne out by any available evidence; and, moreover, that she positively resisted the gathering of properly documented evidence.

The only physical injury she said she incurred was a perforated eardrum. Lois qualifies this by stating: 'I cannot be sure that my eardrum wasn't perforated previously by an infection or something similar.' This was exactly the same injury as Siôn himself had suffered when playing with the three-year-old Esther. Whereas Siôn had an operation at a London hospital, Lois never received or was treated for such an injury.

If the police had checked the details Lois was reporting they would easily have discovered that Siôn did not have a criminal record for the theft of a vehicle. Nor was he going to snatch the children and flee the country; and he was not going to break his bail conditions and return to Hastings.

However, the police tended to cherry-pick the bits of Lois's reports that they could use to support the case they were preparing against Siôn.

She had suffered the profound psychological shock of being told that her husband had murdered her foster daughter. Having become fully persuaded of this herself, this belief also affected her friends Peter Gaimster and David Mann. It was now suggested that the children needed to be spoken to.

After the weekend, on Monday, 17 March, Hutt and Gregory paid a visit to Dr Arnon Bentovim, the leading child and adolescent psychiatrist, and his wife Marianne Bentovim, the social work consultant and family therapist. By the end of the week, on Friday, 21 March, the Bentovims had jointly produced a report on the family background to the Billie-Jo case. They recommended a course of action and submitted their report to Sussex police.

Arnon and Marianne Bentovim began by explaining that they had discussed the case with Gregory and 'her D.I. colleague'. Apparently, the Bentovims had not ascertained Hutt's name. What was remarkable, however, was their mis-perception that he was a Detective Inspector. By the time of the third trial, in November 2005, he had reached the rank of Detective Sergeant; at this time in 1997, when the Bentovims thought he was a D.I., he was a mere Detective Constable.

Their report, in which Billie-Jo's name is mis-spelled throughout, is of the utmost significance. These are extracts:

[Siôn Jenkins] is articulate and very middle-class in his way of speaking and manner, and there is some contrast with his wife in this respect... Although he was due to take up a deputy headship of a school, it has been revealed, through investigation, that he has no relevant qualifications... in fact, he achieved poorly and, given the somewhat Victorian high level of discipline in his own family, it seems likely that he has received a good deal of negative feedback from his own family at his lack of achievements...

It seems that he has been violent with Mrs Jenkins for some time... It also appears that his capacity to care adequate care [*sic*] to the children was limited...

[Billie-Jo] has matured physically and sexually and was quite an exhibitionist. It appears that this has been fostered by Mr Jenkins, for instance, buying her clothes that are inappropriately grown up for her...

[Annie] appears to have become very confused through the process of Mr Jenkins frequently talking to her in an intimate and physically close way. There was a significant change in her evidence between the first and second occasion when she was interviewed... So that the process of grooming and inappropriate closeness which may well have been developing between Mr Jenkins and Billie-Jo was then transferred to his natural daughter. There is no evidence of actual sexual abuse of Billie-Jo, but this would not preclude an inappropriate breaching of boundaries... as a possible preliminary for later abusive actions.

A further issue was that Mr Jenkins had an affair with a 17-year-old girlfriend of one of his friend's sons...

It appears from [Mr Jenkins's] own account that Billie-Jo was extremely provocative to him... There is a hypothesis that a rage attack may have been triggered. If Billie-Jo was on a level with Mr Jenkins, through some sort of partnership with him, whether sexualised or not, then she may well have felt empowered to be very provocative to him. This could have triggered his rage when his grandiose false self was punctured...

Given that Annie has made two statements which are contradictory, to carry out further interviews may very well confuse her even more... It would be important for Annie to know that her statements... were not responsible for the prosecution of her father, and she needs the opportunity to understand something of the process which led her to make very different statements...

It would seem unhelpful to interview the younger children, given that they have given brief statements, and they were not present in the home on the day of Billie-Jo's death...

[Lois] is collaborating with the investigation and appears to be aware that her husband is responsible for Billie-Jo's death...

(Report of Dr Arnon and Mrs Marianne Bentovim, 21 March 1997)

One is amazed by this report. As far as I am aware, the Bentovims had neither spoken to nor even seen any member of the Jenkins family; they had neither met nor spoken to any of the social workers who'd been responsible for Billie-Jo's care until just a few weeks before her murder; nor had the Bentovims been supplied with reports or any documentation at all about the family. In fact, they had not seen a scrap of genuine evidence. As a result, many fundamental errors appear in this report.

Some of the more egregious errors stand out like pylons: Siôn Jenkins was not due to take up a deputy headship; he was due to take up a headship. He had, of course, fabricated some of his CV, but that is not the same thing as saying that he had 'no relevant qualifications'. Far from it; he had a master's degree, an M.Sc, in education management (and the reason the school had appointed him as head was as a result of his five years' successful work as a deputy – perhaps the most relevant qualification of all). The idea that he 'has received negative feedback from his own family at his lack of achievements' is absurd.

The Bentovims wrote that 'his capacity to [give] adequate care to the children was limited'; what was the basis for this conclusion? There had been no suggestions that Siôn had neglected the care of his children. (For example, just the day before the murder, Denise Lancaster had commented that 'Siôn has been wonderful with the children today.')

As a rule, fathers probably do not buy clothes for their teenage daughters; in most families, that would be regarded as the mother's prerogative. In this regard, Siôn Jenkins was no different to other fathers; he may have bought the children trainers, but he certainly did not buy their clothes. (On the day of the murder, Lois had taken Esther and Maya shopping for clothes.) What is the evidence for the assertion that he bought 'clothes that are inappropriately grown up' for Billie? He hadn't bought any clothes at all for her, appropriate or not.

The report asserts that the absence of evidence of abuse 'would not preclude an inappropriate breaching of boundaries'. This concept – just because there's no evidence, that doesn't mean he's not guilty of it – means that anyone can be burdened with the presumption of guilt. (If the context is changed, one can immediately appreciate how bizarre the concept is: there is no evidence that Mr Jones has committed a bank robbery; however, that does not rule out either the possibility that he may have committed one, or his potential for committing robberies in the future.)

With regard to Annie, the Bentovims start off by alluding to 'a significant change in her evidence between the first and second occasion when she was interviewed.' What is this change?[12] Referring back to it subsequently, however, they allude to 'two statements which are contradictory' and to 'very different statements'. (Annie, of course, didn't make any statements at all.)

Elsewhere, the report states that Siôn conducted an affair with a seventeen-year-old girl. Where is the evidence for this? There was no affair with a seventeen-year-old.[13] 'It appears from [his] own account that Billie-Jo was extremely provocative'? What is the evidence for this? As far as I am concerned, it doesn't. The violence towards Lois Jenkins? There was only one source for this, and that was Lois Jenkins herself.

The most extraordinary feature of this report, however, is that someone is missing from it. Charlotte is missing. It seems that the Bentovims were under the misapprehension that at the relevant time of the afternoon, when Billie-Jo was being murdered, Siôn was with Annie only. Charlotte is not referred to at any stage and is merely grouped with 'the younger children'. The vital considerations – that Siôn's alibi witnesses were *both* his elder daughters and that their evidence was mutually corroborative, and therefore doubly supportive of their father's account – are completely absent from the report.

What does emerge from the report, however, is that there was already in place a number of misguided theories about the case, with the lesser misconceptions (that Siôn was a violent man; that he had had an affair with a teenager, etc.) underpinning the major one (that he had murdered Billie-Jo).

On the day that she and Hutt saw the Bentovims, Julie Gregory wrote up a report of the meeting in which she said:

Annie has had her own thoughts reconstructed by Siôn and now needs to have them deconstructed to allow what she knows to be true to be evident. This should be done in a therapeutic rather than an evidential mode. It was felt that the children need a debrief.

The so-called debrief then took place on Thursday 20 March, at 7.00pm. One of those expected to be present at the meeting was the social worker whom Siôn had met twice – when he said that he had been deputed to support the family; and when Siôn was re-arrested. However, for whatever reason, the social worker did not attend.

Accordingly, this hugely important meeting with the four children went ahead with just two police officers, WDS Capon and WDC Gregory. Lois, of course, was there as well.

The police told the children that Annie and Charlotte's interviews had been helpful, but that their father had not been arrested because of anything they had said. He'd been arrested because of other evidence – the tests that had been carried out on his clothing.

'You're talking about blood on his clothes, aren't you?' asked Charlotte.

This remark came as a complete surprise to the officers. It turned out that, although Lois had clearly and repeatedly told them that she had not been discussing the case with the children, she had indeed mentioned this important forensic evidence to Charlotte. As Gregory put it in her report, 'Faced with this, there was little option but to explain that there had been blood on his clothes'. The children then talked between themselves about the implications of this, and raised the possibility that Siôn had got blood on his clothes in tending to Billie-Jo.

The officers continued by telling the children that Siôn had been dishonest about his qualifications and so was not entitled to the post of headteacher. The children then tried to suggest that perhaps he had made a mistake, as they were sure he would not have been untruthful on purpose.

The police then told them that Siôn had been violent towards their mother.

'That's not true', Charlotte shouted out.

Gregory assured her that it was, and Lois confirmed it herself. Charlotte then stormed out of the room in tears, her mother following.

In essence, that was the debrief of the children.

Perhaps only three points need to be made at this stage. Firstly, the purpose of the meeting was supposed to have been therapeutic; yet it seems to have been far from therapeutic, and actually to have left the children even more distressed.

Secondly, it was supposedly also the purpose of the meeting to deconstruct Annie's thoughts to return them to what the police believed was their natural state. Again, this does not appear to have been accomplished – and, indeed, it was a futile exercise since the premise itself bore no relation to reality.

Thirdly, the whole purpose of going to see the Bentovims was to seek high-level professional guidance about how to proceed regarding the children. Therefore, one feels compelled to ask how it was that the meeting with the children took place *before* the Bentovims had completed and delivered their report.

The debriefing of the children in effect completed the process begun on 25 February. On that day, the police 'fed into Mum', giving both Lois and Denise Lancaster, one of the key witnesses, significant inside information about the case. According to a police report, Lois stated she had begun 'hallucinating' and then in turn provided the police with increasingly damaging reports about her husband's character and conduct, which seems to have had the effect of confirming the police view of the case.

Once the police, acting on the advice of the Bentovims, attempted to debrief the children, the evidence became hopelessly muddled; and it would be almost ten years before the truth could come to the surface.[14]

Chapter Twenty-Three

Lois's Reports

It felt to Siôn that Lois, who was by now convinced that he had killed Billie-Jo, together with those who were essentially acting on her behalf (her mother, for example, and David Mann), began to exert emotional pressure on him to try to persuade him to confess. These attempts having failed, Lois tried herself, in a letter written on 30 April:

I know that the only relief in all of this for those involved will be when an admission of guilt is made by the perpetrator of the crime. The girls would, I know, be relieved of enormous burdens if they felt that human beings had the capacity to own up to things and to enable both themselves and others to move forward in life. Denial simply generates mistrust in the human nature...

I am living in constant awareness of the need for the children and others to experience again the reality of honesty and confession. I do hope that they are able to experience this, otherwise the damage to these small girls will be very difficult to heal.

Near the time of Siôn's birthday, in mid-July, his mother-in-law, Gill Ball, wrote to him:

> Our lives have been just shattered this year, but tragedy seems to bring out the best in people and we have been surrounded with Christian love… Our earnest prayer is that the person who killed Billie will have the capacity and the courage to own up to it – most of us have been forgiven everything by God and I am sure we would have the capacity to forgive this person.

On 3 September, Lois herself returned to the theme:

> The only answer to this turmoil is for the children to receive a full and honest confession from Billie's murderer. Then, and only then, will we be able to confidently tackle the future… Only when Billie's murderer confesses to their actions will we be able to face the tragedy.

What an extraordinary watershed 'feed into Mum' had been. Prior to that episode, Siôn and Lois had been together for fifteen years and had scarcely spent a day apart. After 'feed into Mum', Lois straightaway cut herself off from him, almost completely. She refused to take his telephone calls and, other than writing a total of four letters, had no further direct contact with him whatever. She had been told that he had committed the murder and that was what she now believed.

This perception by necessity affected those around her and through them to the wider community. A tide of gossip engulfed Hastings, with Siôn hundreds of miles away. Lois told him that 'the community is angry and saddened about Billie and the death of a child provokes strong feelings'.

The scarcely-veiled thrust of the three letters that she wrote that summer was that she accepted that Siôn had murdered Billie-Jo – although, at the time, the fact that she could have believed that was so far beyond Siôn's comprehension that he never really took it in. What was unquestionably more real was that it quickly became clear that Lois wanted to end the marriage:

> I am concerned Siôn by your constant references to the time when we will live together again... We cannot pretend that life will carry on unchanged – I wouldn't want that... Whatever the outcome of the trial, my faith has been shattered and I do not believe we will be able to live together as a family afterwards.

On 1 July, she informed him that, in his absence, the small social network that he had never particularly felt part of was thriving. She wrote that she and the children spend 'most of our time with Chris and Denise and Peter and Julia. It's much easier to be with people who have been involved and it's easier for the children too'. Lois said that they had been camping several times, had been on holiday to Greece, and that she and Julia had taken all the children to Paris.

On 3 September, she made direct contact with him for the penultimate time (with the exception of a solitary letter concerning financial arrangements, it was afterwards always through lawyers). She bluntly told him, 'I now know that I will never be able to live with you again. I am therefore filing for a judicial separation'.

All this was distressing enough. However, what Siôn was not to realise for many months was that something even more serious was happening. Lois was continuing to pass to the police details of purported conversations that she had had with Annie and Lottie about their father and what had happened on the day of the murder. The initial indications from Lois that the children might be changing their evidence had led to Siôn's arrest. Now, even as he and his lawyers prepared for trial, her continuing reports to the police were fatally compromising the defence case.

On 16 July, Siôn travelled down to Bexhill, to a social services house, for a meeting ('contact session', in social services terminology) with his children. Later that evening, after Siôn had returned to Wales, Lois claimed to have had a conversation with Annie. The next day she passed on the details to DC Hutt. According to Lois, Annie was now saying that, on the holiday in France with the Gaimsters in August 1996, she had 'actually witnessed Siôn kick Billie-Jo'.

Hutt's report, in which he reported what Lois had told him, went on:

Annie stated that... Siôn felt guilty about allowing Billie-Jo to do the painting on the patio in preference to herself. She stated that Billie-Jo had manipulated Siôn in this matter... She was using the chamois to clean the MG... Siôn came running down the steps and told both her and Lottie to get into the car. She stated that she then told Siôn that she would put the chamois leather inside the house.... Annie stated that Siôn appeared to be 'peculiar'. She said his eyes were funny and he looked disorientated...

He then drove off towards Do-It-All, put his hand on his pocket and said that he had no money. He did a u-turn and returned to the house...

Annie stated that when they got to the door, the door was open. She thinks this was because Siôn left in such a hurry he didn't have time to close it properly...

Siôn told them that Billie-Jo had had an accident, this was without even going over to her... Siôn didn't do anything else other than pace up and down everywhere....

Later on in the evening that Saturday, whilst at the Gaimsters', Siôn took Annie to the rear of the dining room and said, 'We'll be alright, we were together, weren't we, Annie?' She stated that Siôn kept taking her away from the others and talked to her about the case. One evening, he told her he wanted to read *Charlie and the Chocolate Factory* to her, but put the book away and kept going over her story...

She discussed the fact with Lois that Siôn preferred Billie-Jo to herself and the fact that Billie-Jo flirted with Siôn.

Some months later, towards the end of November, there was the first hearing proper in Siôn's case – the committal hearing at Hastings magistrates' court. This seemingly triggered further discussion about the case in Lower Park Road. Once again, Lois immediately contacted the police. This time, it was DS Capon who recorded what Lois said:

[Annie] mentioned one time when he [Siôn] punched her in the stomach, winding her so much that she had to lay down on her back in order to recover. She also told Lois about an incident when Siôn dragged the youngest daughter, Maya, up two flights of stairs by her ears...

Annie also made mention of the holiday in France when Peter Gaimster saw Siôn kicking Billie-Jo. Annie said that all of the children were together as they walked upstairs to the first floor where Siôn and Lois's room was. She said that at the time Siôn was following them up and when they got level with the room he pushed Billie-Jo into the bedroom and on to the floor before closing the door. Having seen this, she then ran downstairs and that was when Peter Gaimster then ran up to the room and saw the incident between Siôn and Billie...

She stated that she was not allowed back into the house once she had been sent outside to clean the car and she attempted to come in on a number of occasions but Siôn always refused to allow her... Annie told Lois that by this time she was getting quite concerned with matters, so she crept into the house to make sure there was not a problem with Billie. She stated that she got into the hallway and looked through the dining room and that's when she saw Billie-Jo painting and that Billie looked at her and said in quite a quiet voice, 'Hello Annie'. Siôn, in the kitchen at the time, obviously heard this, came out and pushed Annie back out...

Annie said that when they went off together to collect Lottie, she asked Siôn whether or not Billie was coming and he told her that No, she was staying here. Obviously, Annie felt that this was quite unusual as Billie was never normally left in the house on her own...

It was while she and Lottie were waiting downstairs by the MG that Siôn suddenly came running down with a peculiar look in his eyes and then drove the girls off on the trip to Do-It-All after driving round the park in a state of disorientation...

Annie told Lois that [if she had been in Siôn's position] she would have spent her time with Billie, making sure she was all right, that she would have got the two children... to call an ambulance and to call other help and she could not understand why Siôn was not doing this...

Siôn told her that she was with him the whole time and she replied, I am waiting downstairs when you came out. He then told her again that she was with him the whole time. She was pressured so much by him that basically she was unsure what to say at any stage after that...

Annie also mentioned to Lois that there is apparently an entry in Billie-Jo's Forever Friends diary stating that Siôn had hit her.

The next development in the case, so far as Lois was concerned, occurred on Friday, 19 December when Siôn met the children at a pre-Christmas meeting in Bexhill. Early in the morning of Monday, 22 December, WDS Capon was about to leave Hastings police station to catch a train to attend a conference in London when she was surprised by the sudden arrival of Lois Jenkins.

Lois explained that she needed to pass on details of a conversation she'd had with, this time, Charlotte. She filled in the background for Capon, explaining that the children had been having nightmares and sleepless nights and these disturbances appeared to follow visits with their father.

According to Lois, a fresh conversation about Billie-Jo's murder had been initiated by Esther, who started questioning her sisters while Lois was driving:

Esther started asking more questions but Annie stopped Lottie saying anything further. Annie apparently doesn't agree totally with

Lottie's recollection of events. However, Lois cannot understand how Annie is aware of Lottie's version because to her knowledge Annie and Lottie have never discussed it together and she [Lois] has made a point of never discussing it with the children but allowing them to talk to her if they wished...

That evening [Sunday 21 December] Lottie asked her mother, What if she were called to give evidence... what if she were to say something that would incriminate her father or what if her dad didn't like her for the rest of her life...

Lottie said, 'Her dad kept slowing down at Dordrecht Way and he kept saying, "Shall we get white spirit or not?" They then got near to Do-It-All and her dad felt his pocket and said, "Oh, I haven't got any money"'. Lottie then said to her Mum, 'Then I just knew'. Lois did not ask her what she knew.[15]

Lottie then said she could recall that when the policeman called to collect their clothes, her dad had tried not to give the policeman his jumper. Lottie told her Mum that she [Lois] had had to go and ask him for the jumper...

Lottie ended by saying that she knew her Dad had killed Billie but knows he didn't do it on purpose.

Capon concluded her report by saying that she had had very little time to go into any of these points with Lois as she, Capon, had been rushing to catch her train.

Lois had reported to police a series of alleged conversations with her daughters that took place during March and on 16 July, 27 November and 22 December. The initial reports encouraged the police to charge Siôn with murder, and the rest were to have devastating consequences for him. In years to come, the defence team would refer to these collectively as 'the false reports'. At the time, however, they didn't call them this. In fact, at the time, they didn't know what to make of them.

Chapter Twenty-Four

Exile

I was to remain on bail in Aberystwyth for fifteen months, from March 1997 up until my trial in June 1998. I had to sign on at Aberystwyth police station every day at 6.00pm. I couldn't sign on earlier than that – if I arrived early, I had to wait until six o'clock; on the other hand, had I once been a minute late, I could have been taken back into custody.

This apparently simple, but absolutely vital, routine became a source of constant anxiety. All through the day, I would be worried lest for some reason I was unable to sign on or simply forgot. Some days about 7.00pm, I'd have sudden rushes of concern and think to myself, did I forget to sign on? Within minutes, I'd convince myself that I'd forgotten and be sweating with anxiety.

Nor was the dead-on six o'clock appointment the only pressure I faced. Dyfed-Powys police, apparently acting on instructions from Sussex police, would often arrive at the house unexpectedly, sometimes in the early morning, ostensibly to verify that I was actually living where I was supposed to be living. I began to see these continual visits as a form of harassment. The Dyfed-Powys officers were often at pains to explain that they too thought the visits unnecessary. At that time I had a growing perception that Sussex police were intent on destroying what little remained of my family life.

In the first month of my exile in mid-Wales, another development further crushed my already depleted spirits. Brendan told me that the funeral of Billie was to take place on Wednesday, 23 April. No sooner had I learned this, however, than I was informed that Sussex police would not allow me to attend. Indeed, I was prevented from playing any part, whether direct or indirect; I was not even allowed to send flowers. I had become a non-person in her life story.

This was a period of intense, inescapable anxiety, and yet through it all my mother kept house and home together wonderfully; she was stoical in her defiance of the authorities who were trying to take away my freedom and deprive her of her son and grandchildren.

For almost half my lifetime, I had attended church regularly. I'd noticed an imposing church looking out over the sea in the middle of Aberystwyth. After a few weeks, I went to a Sunday service there and sat discreetly at the back.

I returned the following week and decided that I would like to attend on a regular basis. However, in view of the circumstances in which I had become an Aberystwyth resident, I felt I should first introduce myself properly to the vicar, the Rev. Canon Stuart Bell. I phoned him up and he agreed to see me.

While Stuart listened intently, I related all that had happened to me over the previous three or four months. It took me about an hour. When I had finished, he asked a series of questions. He then welcomed me to St Michael's. He could tell immediately that I was in need of spiritual and emotional support on a regular basis; so we went on to meet every week, outside of services, to talk and pray. He and his wife Prudence, a local magistrate, were to become friends not only of myself and my family but also of several of those involved in my campaign.

Arrangements were made between the police, social services and my solicitor so that I could again have a meeting in Bexhill with my daughters. It was, as before, very emotional; Charlotte cried and clung to me, refusing to let go.

However, these visits became increasingly fraught and ill-natured – not because of the children, but because of the adults accompanying them. At this first meeting, Lois did not speak to me but sat and occasionally exchanged smiles and small talk with the social worker, the same one whom I had seen previously. At one point, when Maya was sitting happily on my knee, this man offered her a sweet. She went over to him to get it and he then picked her up and sat her on his knee. I was incensed and complained – but, of course, everyone ignored me.

When I arrived in Bexhill for the second visit about six weeks later, the girls were not there initially. Instead, I was met by a new social worker.

'If I want to offer the girls a sweet, I will', he said. 'If you object, I'll end the session'.

He proceeded to tell me that if I objected to anything at all, he would end the meeting. I did not react.

We waited for twenty minutes. When the children arrived, they ran in and were so excited. The chairs were spread around the room, so I gathered five together and arranged them in a circle. The children sat down, with Esther and Maya on my lap. Then I looked over at Lois. She was laughing and joking with the social worker, but it was something else that caught my attention. I noticed that she had removed her wedding ring. It was such a shock, such a devastating emotional blow. Matters, however, were to get even worse. The police arrived. Capon brought in a tray of cups of tea and soon got into conversation with Lois about the children. I asked Maya if she knew who the woman was.

'Auntie Anne', replied Maya.

At that moment, I realised the extent to which the police had insinuated themselves into my family. I was powerless to do anything about it. The girls were so young and so vulnerable. Capon then left the room and called out to Esther and Maya. They went out to her. When they didn't return, I went to find them. Capon was playing a game with them; she had Esther and Maya photocopying their hands. There was a stack of photocopied sheets around them. I was infuriated. This was my contact visit, a rare opportunity for me to meet my daughters; Capon was an investigating police officer who was play-acting at being a family aunt and depriving me of precious moments with them. Yet it was clear that none of the adults there cared in any way about my feelings.

During this visit, Lois's manner and body language were different from previous occasions. She engaged in chit-chat with the police officers and the social worker.

The girls had all been told not to speak to me unless the social worker could hear what they were saying. There were to be no private asides. When we stood up to say our goodbyes, Maya smiled at me, ran up and held out her arms, and pushed her little hand into my pocket. I hugged her and the others and then they all left.

As I went outside to meet my father who had driven us down from Wales, I reached into my pocket. There was a scrap of paper. Maya had written, 'I Love You', something she had not been able to whisper to me because she knew it would have contravened the social worker's instructions. The seven-year-old had outwitted him. Well done, Maya! Today, I treasure that piece of paper and look at it often.

The knowledge that Lois had removed her wedding ring left me numb. Shortly afterwards, she made her position totally clear as she told me she wanted a divorce. My lawyers tried to emphasise to her that, if she just waited, she would easily have been able to divorce me on the grounds that we had been living apart for two years. However, she instructed lawyers actively to file for divorce and kept forcing the issue. My parents begged her to hold back, arguing that 'Now is not the time to make such a big decision'. She, however, was determined. She ignored my parents, saying, 'It's time for me to move on'.

I wrote to Lois giving her sole possession of the house and all the monies in our joint accounts. Yet she soon began requesting additional sums from my parents. My father always wrote out cheques, a number of which were for significant sums, as she requested them. Since she always suggested that the funds were required to accommodate his granddaughters' needs, he found it impossible to refuse her.

Exile

My solicitor, Brendan Salsbury, was a very affable man. Everyone liked him. He had a taste for highly coloured shirts and was, by the ridiculously conservative standards of the legal profession, an eccentric dresser. A big fan of the music of Genesis and Pink Floyd, he was incredibly laid-back. His favourite saying – at times when my case would be in a state of virtually complete chaos – was 'No problem'.

I remember meeting him one morning when I was due to make an appearance at Hastings magistrates' court. I asked Brendan if all the arrangements had been made and he assured me that they had.

So we set off in his Mini and drove to the court. As we approached, we could at first hear and then see the hostile crowd.

'No problem', said Brendan.

He said we could simply drive down the side road leading to the underground car park. When we got to the car-park barrier, however, nothing happened. The barrier stayed firmly in place. Brendan had forgotten to organise our entry arrangements with court security.

So we could not go forwards. Nor could we go backwards; I saw a group of men, one of them brandishing a baseball bat, running towards us. At such times, a Mini isn't the most secure vehicle to be travelling in. I got out and made a dash for a side-door underneath the car park. Thank God someone opened it for me, and immediately slammed it shut when I was through. I looked back and could see angry faces pressed up against the glass panels of the door. They were shouting obscenities and abuse. My trial was still months away yet, according to the rule of mob law, I had already been proclaimed guilty.

At the hearing itself, the Crown raised the issue of bail. Thankfully, the magistrate said that, although he could not understand why I had been given bail, he was not prepared to challenge a High Court Judge.

I was, of course, desperately missing my daughters. Part of the routine I devised to keep myself sane was to spend a long time each week choosing a particular card for each of them. Then I would spend ages writing the cards, choosing the most appropriate words. Apart from the occasional and highly-regulated contact sessions, they were my only

167

means of communicating with them. They replied regularly. Lois, however, remained captious and, through her solicitor, told me that I was writing to them too frequently. I carried on sending the cards.

By the end of the summer, the amount of legal papers arriving in Aberystwyth for me to read had reached staggering proportions. Brendan decided that he needed to come up to Wales for three days to discuss everything with me.

The next day I got up early, keen to get started. Brendan came to our house and we had coffee. Then he explained that, before he could continue with my case preparation, he had a matter of some importance to attend to. He had to go into town to buy a cricket bat.

There had already been many times over previous months when I'd thought that, if I wrote it all down as fiction, everyone would say it was far-fetched and not credible. This was another of those moments.

Whatever else Brendan had done or not done, he had recruited Anthony Scrivener QC to be my counsel. Funnell and Perring, the practice for which Brendan worked, had given Scrivener his very first brief as a barrister, and ever since Scrivener had returned the favour by doing their major cases. A former chairman of the Bar, Scrivener is one of the most senior, respected and engaging of criminal defence barristers.

After Brendan's visit to Wales, a conference was arranged at Scrivener's chambers in Gray's Inn in London. So Brendan put in a formal request that my bail conditions be altered to allow me to spend the night at my uncle's house in Bromley, south London. Astonishingly, Sussex police objected. It seemed that they felt that I should travel down from Aberystwyth and back in the same day, knowing that, realistically, this would leave little time for legal discussions. Did they want me to be able to plan a defence at all, I wondered?

Fortunately, this was one legal argument that went our way. We not only won it, but in doing so, we set a precedent and I was able to stay over in London for all future legal conferences.

At the chambers, I was met by Brendan and the junior counsel, John

Haines – although Haines, who works a lot with Scrivener, is one of those so-called 'juniors' who is actually rather senior. Scrivener's room manages to be both large and cosy, and has the backdrop of Gray's Inn's lawns. Scrivener is a tall man, with an imposing personality. Once he'd arrived, he seemed to fill the room. I noticed that Brendan always addressed him as 'Sir'.

In years gone by, defence lawyers in criminal cases had produced what the prosecution termed 'ambush alibis'. Since the Criminal Justice Act 1967, therefore, if a defence intends to put forward alibi evidence, it must provide the prosecution in advance with full details, including the names of the witnesses on whom it intends to rely. Scrivener filled out a Notice of Alibi for the Crown Prosecution Service, with my daughters, Annie and Charlotte, listed as my alibi witnesses.

Meanwhile, one event took place in which I had been due to be centrally involved but which, in the circumstances, I wasn't conscious of at the time. William Parker School held its annual speech day on 1 December. In view of the difficulties created by my situation, Roger Mitchell had agreed to assist the smooth running of the school by postponing his retirement for a year. At the ceremony, his speech included these remarks:

For nearly five years Siôn Jenkins and I had worked closely together, creatively and harmoniously. His talents had brought new energy and vision as my deputy, leading to many of the developments which enabled the school last year to achieve such a good report from Ofsted [the government's schools inspection service]. Once the governors had selected him as my successor, we were working towards a smooth transfer of responsibilities with confidence and purpose.

All that collapsed with the tragedy of Billie-Jo's murder last February. The impact of those events on the school were as nothing compared to the misery and devastation experienced by Billie-Jo's family and friends. Nonetheless, the loss of an able deputy and headteacher-designate is not without its consequences and all of us at school have struggled to adapt to the disaster and changed circumstances.

In view of the depths of hostility that had been generated against me in Hastings since my arrest in March, these remarks of Roger's were extremely courageous. Although I did not become aware of them until later, it was the second time since Billie's murder that I had particular reason to be very grateful to him.

I was to see the girls just twice more before my trial. When I arrived for the third visit, I realised that the social worker's apparent antipathy towards me had intensified. He refused to shake my hand. He then issued fresh directives. Firstly, I was not to move the chairs (as I had done on the previous occasion). Far more disconcerting, however, was the other newly-invented rule.

It seemed that, after the previous visit, Lois had complained about my father parking outside the social services house and waiting there for me. Lois didn't want the children to see their paternal grandfather. So I was told that he had to park out of sight, round the corner. I objected strongly. It meant that my father, who had driven down from Wales and who was dying to see his grandchildren, would not only be allowed no contact whatever with them, but would not even be allowed to glimpse them. Once again, the restrictions imposed by social services seemed inhuman to me. However, I was told that those were the rules; if I didn't accede to them all, then the visit would not take place.

During one of the visits, I happened to say to Annie that I had spoken to one of Brendan's sons the previous day. Clearly, she mentioned this to Lois who, assuming I had been to Brendan's house in Sussex and had therefore breached my bail conditions, quickly passed the information on to the police. The next day, officers arrived on Brendan's doorstep to question him about this. Of course, he explained I hadn't been there and it had just been a telephone conversation. Lois had jumped to the wrong conclusion, and in doing so had caused more police time to be wasted; but I then began to appreciate the true extent of her feelings towards me.

I continued to write every week to my daughters. That particular Christmas, my first apart from them, was heartbreaking. I posted their presents early and woke on Christmas Day, full of memories of previous Christmases. We had spent our last family Christmas together in this same house. Now, a year on, most of the day passed in a joyless silence.

The first anniversary of Billie's death came and passed in a similar fashion. I spent the day with my parents and brother, searching for some relief from all the accumulated distress. There was none.

As the trial got closer, Brendan would phone me every evening to report on the day's events. One day he didn't phone. I was slightly troubled, so I phoned him. He said it wasn't convenient to talk and asked me to call back at 11.00pm. I thought that oddly late, but I did call back then. He explained that he hadn't been able to talk earlier, as he had had friends to dinner. During the ensuing conversation it emerged that the friends he had entertained to dinner were DC Mick Groombridge and his wife. I was flabbergasted and very scared. What was one of the investigating police officers, indeed one of the two who had questioned me so tenaciously during my interviews, doing at my solicitor's house for dinner – within weeks of the start of my trial?

Brendan, rather abashed, explained that his wife and Groombridge were old friends; they had been to school together. I was hardly reassured; in fact, I was so choked I could hardly speak. I had always known that, as a duty solicitor for Sussex police, he had many friendships with the local force; just as I'd always known that Hastings was a small town. But it seemed to me that there were times when there did need to be a strict demarcation between business and pleasure.

The time now was racing by. My trial was scheduled to begin in April. As it got nearer, so my room filled with legal papers. I chose not to read everything in order to protect myself. It was an impossible strain. It was so emotionally wearing to read hostile statements from those whom one had previously believed to be friends.

Throughout these months the strain on my parents, too, was immense. Both my mother and father took different but complementary roles in supporting me.

I can remember when my father drove me to attend a pre-trial hearing at Lewes Crown Court. Afterwards, we were advised to leave by a side entrance. But the photographers were everywhere; they were around us like wolves. They were aggressive and determined to get their pictures. My father was in the middle of it all and as we struggled to reach the safety of the car through the melee, I could see how difficult he was finding it. But, in that as in every other aspect of the case, he didn't allow anything or anybody to stop him from doing what he believed to be right.

During this time, I also had great support from my brother, David, who would drive from his home in Norfolk to see me. We would walk along the seafront and he would listen to the latest news of my struggles with the criminal justice system. Never, in all those months, could we forget, even momentarily, the case that now hung over all of us.

During our final conference Scrivener outlined our defence against the Crown's scientific evidence. It seemed watertight to me, and I was left wondering why there was going to be a trial. However, it was at this conference that Scrivener said he had to discuss with me fully the evidence of my daughters. As we had named Annie and Charlotte as my alibi witnesses, Scrivener needed to speak to them. However, he was unable to do so; Lois had refused permission.

Scrivener then showed me some of the police reports detailing what Lois had told them that my daughters had said. For the first time, I saw it all set down in black-and-white. I had had no idea of the extent of all this. It was too much to bear. I asked to be excused. In the toilets in Scrivener's chambers, I wept inconsolably.

On my return, Scrivener told me that he had kept much of it from me, believing me to be too fragile. I now knew just how Lois had been acting. I entered a valley of such sadness that for days afterwards I had difficulty in even speaking.

Nevertheless, the trial date, Wednesday, 22 April, was upon us. I told myself that I was ready. I'd spoken at length with my parents and said goodbye to my friends.

I walked along the Aberystwyth shore, possibly for the last time.

Chapter Twenty-Five

Abuse of Process

Siôn's trial, however, did not begin on 22 April. Just one of the many frustrations of being entangled in the criminal justice net is that things rarely run to schedule.

The defence had served expert reports from two forensic scientists, Duncan MacKirdy and Mark Webster on 9 April. These suggested that the blood on Siôn's clothing had been exhaled by Billie-Jo as a dying gasp. More importantly, however, the defence also produced fresh evidence in the form of a statement from John Sinar, a consultant neurosurgeon at Middlesbrough General Hospital, who argued that it was 'probable' that Billie would have been 'still alive' when Siôn went to her. So, after all the parties assembled in Lewes on 22 April, the prosecution asked for time to find and brief a neurosurgeon who could deliver a report for them. On that first day, the judge adjourned the case and set a new trial start date two months hence.

Everyone then re-assembled in Lewes on Wednesday, 3 June. Before the jury was sworn in, there was pre-trial legal argument. There was nothing unusual about that (in a major case, there often is), but in this instance the issue was particularly significant.

In the Notice of Alibi, Annie and Charlotte were named as defence witnesses. At a plea and directions hearing in December 1997, John Haines, junior defence counsel, had said that a television line would have to be available in Lewes in order to enable the girls to give evidence by video link. Annie and Charlotte had been with Siôn at the critical time and so, in normal circumstances, would automatically have been called.

These circumstances, however, were by no means normal. On 10 February 1998, a CPS lawyer, in the process of passing across case material to the defence lawyer, Brendan Salsbury, drew his attention specifically to:

> ... the officers' reports which do contain some very important information and it is only fair that I should draw this to your attention.

The material to which he referred was Lois's reports – the police reports of conversations with her in which she indicated that her daughters were changing their evidence.

Having read the material, Salsbury wrote in some alarm to John Haines:

> It is perfectly obvious now that the girls cannot be called to give evidence... Counsel will see that there are great discrepancies between what [the girls] originally said and what they are now saying and there is obviously a danger about them giving evidence.

Anthony Scrivener QC and the defence team were clearly unhappy not only with the content of the material but also with the fact that the prosecution had fulfilled its formal duty of disclosure so tardily (after all, some of these reports went back almost twelve months, to March 1997).[16] As he prepared for trial, Scrivener's greatest dilemma was this: what to do about the children? Had their evidence really changed? If it had, there were two absolutely vital questions: why had it changed; and, secondly, what exactly were the girls now saying?

The obvious course of action was to ask them. However, neither Scrivener himself nor anyone else from the defence team was able to speak to Annie and Charlotte; Lois refused permission. Siôn, of course, had no inkling of their current state of mind.

What the defence did know was that two of the investigating police officers, DC Hutt and WDC Gregory, had visited Dr Arnon and Marianne Bentovim. Then, ostensibly on the basis of the Bentovims' report, two police officers, WDS Capon and WDC Gregory had 'debriefed' the children on 20 March. The children were then told of the 'strong evidence' that their father had murdered their sister. They were also told that there was other evidence incriminating him, including the fact that he had fabricated his CV and been violent towards Lois.

So Scrivener asked the leading clinical psychologist, Dr Valerie Mellor, one of whose many briefs was to act as consultant to Greater Manchester Police, to prepare a report for the defence. She too was prevented from seeing the children. However, she prepared her report on the basis of the documentary material available to her (which was, essentially, the children's interviews, the Bentovims' report and the accompanying police reports).

Her opinion was that it was 'wholly inappropriate' that the so-called debriefing of the children by investigating police officers had taken place. She viewed it as 'tarnishing the evidence of a witness'. She pointed out that although she considered that the Bentovims' advice to hold a debriefing at all was wrong (unless it had been conducted strictly within the terms of the 1992 Memorandum of Good Practice), nevertheless, what had actually occurred had gone beyond what the Bentovims had envisaged. 'Whatever [Dr Bentovim] meant by "debriefing"', wrote Mellor, 'he did not advise that the children be told of matters extraneous to the investigation'.

Altogether, Mellor criticised Sussex police in four respects: firstly, even though the purpose of the debriefing was – at least, ostensibly – partly therapeutic, the investigating police officers had carried out the debriefing themselves rather than bringing in trained therapists or counsellors; secondly, that if the daughters were going to be told anything, then it should have been kept to a bare minimum, but what they were actually told went far beyond that. This was 'wholly inappropriate', commented Mellor. As a result, the children could be led to change their accounts 'to please their mother, or the police, or to fall in line with other information'.

Thirdly, Mellor continued, if the meeting was being held at all, it should have been properly recorded. In fact, there was no attempt to make any kind of contemporaneous records. Fourthly, even though the 1992 Memorandum of Good Practice did not strictly apply to meetings of this kind, clearly its guidelines would be equally important in respect of other discussions with child witnesses; and so, she concluded, the Code of Conduct accompanying the memorandum had been breached in a number of respects.

In conclusion, she felt that 'the children may well have been influenced to think in a negative way about their father or they may have reacted by feeling over-protective towards him'. Whichever it was, it was going to affect the reliability of their recollections. The police actions had encouraged them to think *differently* about their father; as a result, any evidence they could give was now going to be tarnished.

Armed with Mellor's report, the defence submitted that the trial could not now take place. Scrivener said that it must have been obvious to the police from the video interviews that Annie and Charlotte were crucial defence witnesses.

Of course, the video interviews remained. Properly analysed, they provided conclusive proof of Siôn's innocence; yet, if defence lawyers put forward the video evidence as part of its case and then risked calling the children blind, they were understandably worried that, in view of Lois's series of reports, the children's evidence may have changed and could now be very damaging.

Moreover, the prosecution would then be able to cross-examine the girls in the knowledge that police actions had adversely influenced them against their father. In other words, emphasised Scrivener, the prosecution would be able to benefit from its own misconduct.

Where the inevitable result of conduct on the part of police is to undermine the evidence of a crucial alibi witness, he concluded, then the conduct is so seriously wrong that it amounts to an interference with the administration of justice. It is also, he pointed out, a contempt of court. A fair trial was now impossible.

The judge, Mr Justice Gage, heard the abuse of process arguments from both sides on that first day, 3 June. He then considered them overnight, in conjunction with the available documentation, including the Bentovims' report. The next day, he delivered a written judgment.

'The fact is that the children were asking questions which required some answers', he said. He pointed out that the police then '*sought advice* [italics added] about what to do and although that advice may not have been completely followed, there is no evidence that what they did was done in bad faith'.

The suggestion that it was the children's questions which had led to the visit to the Bentovims could be found in WDC Gregory's report:

> During our time spent with Lois Jenkins, it became apparent that the four Jenkins children needed answers to some of their numerous questions. They were hearing rumours at school and *were being shut out of conversations D.C.Hutt and I were having with Lois.*
>
> [italics added]

Two points, however, need to be made about this. Firstly, when the judge said, 'The fact is that the children were asking questions… ', it was not a direct fact in any way at all. The police officers themselves were not speaking to the children; all their information came through Lois. The judge himself recognised this, saying, 'there is no direct evidence from either of the girls about what they said [to Lois]'. No one should have simply assumed that any reports were accurate, prima facie.

Secondly, if it is correct that the children felt 'shut out of conversations DC Hutt and I were having with Lois', then this was merely another defect of the family liaison officer scheme – whereby family liaison officers and investigating officers were one and the same. The officers were simultaneously doing their duty as family liaison officers (by informing the bereaved, Lois and the children, about the progress of the case) and that of investigating officers. Of course, this was not their fault. They were in an impossible position; they were being asked to fulfil conflicting roles.[17]

The key issue was whether Annie had changed her evidence; and the judge, who had had little time to prepare his judgment, was remarkably muddled on this point. He did reflect the true position (which was that no one had any idea whether Annie's evidence had changed or not). However, he then appeared to disregard his own point, and to conclude that Annie's evidence had changed. He further decided that, 'I am not satisfied, on the balance of probabilities, that it was the [debriefing] session on 20 March which caused [her] to do so. The [reports] show that Annie was changing her evidence by adding to it before 20 March 1997.'

He also cites the argument of the Bentovims, who favoured a debrief on the grounds that Annie 'needs the opportunity to understand something of the process which led her to make very differing statements'.

So in these respects, the judge appears satisfied that Annie's evidence had changed – yet, as he accepted elsewhere in his judgment, that is not what the evidence showed. He said he did not know what Annie's evidence was or what it would have been: 'at present, it is speculation as to what evidence they may give'. This is indeed the core point: it should have been plain from their original interviews what evidence the girls would give; it wasn't, it was now speculation, and that was because of the way in which the prosecution had contaminated the witnesses. It would continue to be speculation until the question was properly resolved – which was not to be for another four years.

Mr Justice Gage acknowledged that, 'It might have been better if the police officers [WDS Capon and WDC Gregory] had not themselves conducted that debriefing', though he added that 'the Memorandum of Good Practice does not specifically deal with the situation which faced the police officers'. The judge didn't take on board the logic of Mellor's point, which was that the core guidelines of the Memorandum could have been presumed to apply also in these circumstances.

He ruled that there had been no abuse of process and concluded that nothing in Scrivener's arguments persuaded him that Siôn would be unable to have a fair trial:

> Even allowing for the full force of the criticisms of Dr Mellor, in my judgment the conduct of the police came nowhere near the sort of conduct which for this reason alone should cause the court to stay this prosecution.

He accepted the prosecution's argument that the debriefing was 'done in good faith' and 'on the advice of professional advisers' (i.e. the Bentovims).

But what had actually happened? Two junior police officers, who themselves were acting on a combination of hearsay and mistakes, went to see the Bentovims and passed this on to them. The Bentovims then produced a report reflecting this combination of hearsay and mistakes which the police in turn acted upon to debrief the children.

As it happened, what the police did went beyond the scope of what the Bentovims recommended. Indeed, the police could not even have known the scope of what the Bentovims recommended because they went ahead with the debriefing session before the report that they were supposedly acting upon had been delivered.

Astonishingly, the Bentovims' evidence had been used both by the police to create the abuse of process and by the judge to rule that there had been no abuse of process.[18]

The circular process of injustice was gripping this case ever tighter.

Chapter Twenty-Six

Brighton

With the trial approaching, a number of practical decisions had to be made. Firstly, where were we going to stay? The trial would be held in Lewes, the county town of Sussex, but I was only too aware of the antipathy that had been generated against me. It would be asking for trouble to stay in Lewes itself. It would also be too far to travel every day from my uncle's home in Bromley. One of my father's friends suggested renting a flat in Brighton marina, so that's what we did.

We arrived in Brighton two days before the scheduled start of the trial, only to learn from Brendan that the Crown were now seeking an adjournment. So that hearing was quickly over and we now didn't need the flat. Fortunately, we were able to re-book it for June.

Having steeled ourselves for the trial to begin, we all trekked back to Wales feeling very disheartened. In some ways, those next eight weeks were the most miserable of all. They passed like cold syrup dripping from a spoon. We could not do anything except wait, and wait.

Then, it was early June, so we went back to Brighton again, and settled into our flat.

Brighton

We knew that the atmosphere in Lewes was going to be very hostile, and therefore had to make two further decisions, neither of which was easy.

The first was that I had to hire two bodyguards, merely to get me safely into court each day. The second was that, because of the physical difficulties combined with the stress, my parents would not travel into court with me, or indeed attend the trial at all, but would wait for me, with my brother looking after them, in Brighton.

These decisions were forced upon us because of the anticipated hostility of the local crowd and the refusal of the police to guarantee my protection. As far as they were concerned, if I wanted them to protect me, then I'd have to be taken back into custody.

However, in public relations terms, both decisions worked against us. It appeared as though I no longer had the support of my family; and it appeared as if I was already such a publicly-reviled figure that I needed special protection merely to be able to walk into court. In retrospect, these decisions, taken in conjunction with my lawyers, were seriously mistaken, as both made me appear guilty from the outset.

That first day we parked the car some five minutes' walk away. As we approached the court, we could see the photographers and cameramen, and also members of the public, clustered round the main entrance. They refused to budge or move aside to let me pass. So my security men had to part these waters of hostile humanity to force a way through for me. As I went in with all the cameras whirring, all I could hear was the jeering and the taunts of 'murderer' and 'child-killer'.

Once inside, security officials appeared. I was taken down a narrow staircase to the cells below and locked up. I was shaken by the sudden noise of the door slamming shut. Even though I'd had two weeks in Lewes prison, all this was still an alien experience for me.

About forty-five minutes later, I was told to climb the stairway which led into the dock. I emerged into the courtroom. All eyes were upon me. I saw the judge in his red robes, and the legal teams to the right and left. The press benches, to my right, were full. I looked at the jury, on my left.

There were police everywhere. Finally, there was the public gallery, which was behind me and which seemed full to bursting point.

I gave my name. Asked how I pleaded, I replied, 'Not guilty'. I was told to sit down.

I wore a navy blue suit and a shirt and tie. That was what I wore through the entire trial. In fact, I hadn't made a conscious decision to dress like that. I just did so automatically, because that was what I wore each day to work. But the Crown used this to their advantage. They presented me as authoritarian and middle-class, and as someone who was always organised and in control. They were able to create a sinister picture from my dress code. Unfortunately, I realised this too late in the day. Now, I would advise any defendant facing trial: don't look too formal by wearing a suit.[19]

With that first day over, I looked out of the window and could see even more photographers and cameramen than there had been in the morning. Although, again, I didn't realise it at the time, that's inevitable. The case was being reported on bulletins throughout the day, and media interest just leads to more media interest. We were told that newspapers and television companies had taken rooms in the hotel opposite the court to get better vantage-points for their pictures.

The daily routine was to continue for another four weeks, though every day was a little more wearing than the one before. I did a lot of jury-gazing and tried to work out what each of them was thinking.

At the weekends, I had to sign on at Brighton police station. At these and other times, when I would walk around the town or along the beach, I wore sunglasses and a baseball cap. What was happening to me outside the courtroom seemed surreal; though it was as nothing compared to what was happening inside the courtroom.

Chapter Twenty-Seven

An 'Impossible' Defence

On Wednesday, 3 June 1998, Siôn Jenkins stood trial at Lewes crown court for the murder of Billie-Jo. The cause of death at the post-mortem was given as head injury caused by repeated blows to the head with a blunt instrument (the tent peg, obviously). There were twenty main injuries altogether with seven large areas of laceration to the head. The skull had been fractured and brain tissue was exposed.

In other respects, the post-mortem confirmed that Billie-Jo had been a virgin at her death. Her hymen was intact and there was no evidence of any sexual activity.

The prosecution argued that Siôn had had a fit of anger, picked up the tent peg and bludgeoned Billie-Jo to death. The many peevish problems of the day had cumulatively rankled with him: there was Billie-Jo's rudeness to Lois; the dispute between Annie and Billie-Jo about who would get which job; Lois's forgetfulness in not taking any means of payment with her to the supermarket, compounded by her failure to explain where her current cheque book was – thereby causing Siôn to have to make a special journey to Safeway's not once but twice; and the unexpected chore of having to take Charlotte's friend home from the clarinet class.

All these factors, the prosecution suggested, had combined to create a day of mounting frustration for Siôn. By the time Billie-Jo exasperated him still more – with her wilfulness, her insolence, her provocative behaviour, her careless painting and, the last straw, her playing of loud music – he could stand no more and cracked. It was therefore a crime carried out at a moment of raw, red rage. The prosecution could not suggest a motive; but they did not need to.

The trip to Do-It-All had been a desperate ruse by Siôn to provide an alibi and buy himself time to concoct a story. You could tell that because he didn't need white spirit anyway; there was a half-full bottle in a downstairs cupboard. In any event, he hadn't taken any money with him. Then there was the suspiciously circuitous route he took to get there – setting off in the wrong direction, before going round the park twice. Finally, the notion of buying white spirit, the solitary reason for this journey, was simply abandoned.

When he arrived back at the house with Annie and Lottie, he deliberately held back, thereby allowing the children to 'find' Billie-Jo. He then behaved as though he had no interest in her welfare. It seemed he hadn't acted on anything the operator had told him. He didn't tend to her effectively in any way – he didn't check for a pulse, or whether she was breathing, didn't put her in the recovery position, and didn't remove (or apparently even notice) the plastic bin-liner that was protruding from her nostril and thus obstructing her breathing. Rather than trying to minister to her, he had actually shut the dining room door, as if she were some kind of dirty secret he needed to close off.

Then there was the very peculiar moment when he got into the MG – ostensibly to put the roof back up because it looked like rain, although he didn't actually put the roof back and just got out again. But had this small incident happened at all? No one had actually seen Siôn get into the car. Irrespective of whether it had actually happened, argued the prosecution, it was inexplicable except in the following terms: Siôn was worried that, in laying his false alibi trail after the murder, he may have left incriminating scientific evidence in the car; consequently, he had to have said he got into the car after tending to Billie-Jo in order to provide an explanation for any evidence there may have been.

He had also, according to the prosecution, told a number of important lies. For example, in the first call to the emergency services he told the operator that he had been away from the house for '... half-an-hour, three-quarters of an hour'. In the second call, in response to the operator asking if he had put Billie-Jo on her side, he said he had – although it seems that he hadn't. He told PC Bruce that, on the return from the clarinet class, he and Annie had waited in the car while Charlotte dashed in to put her clarinet away. This was a clear attempt, said the prosecution, to distance himself from the murder.

Siôn had even said that he had never seen the tent pegs before. There were further examples, in his statements, of inconsistencies and confusion. He had also, remarkably, made a series of jottings, in which he carefully annotated the events of the day, putting everything into chronological order and referring to himself in the third person as 'SJ'. The prosecution asserted that this was evidence of a guilty man trying to get his story straight.

All this was circumstantial, however. The really critical evidence was scientific. Those present at the scene handed over the items of clothing they had been wearing at the time. These were then examined by Adrian Wain, who was employed by the Forensic Science Service and had worked at its laboratory in Lambeth, central London, since 1983. Using a microscope, Wain detected a total of 158 bloodspots on Siôn's clothing. There were 76 spots on the trousers: 70 on the lower right leg, four higher up and two small spots on the left leg. On Siôn's blue fleece jacket, there were 72 spots: 48 in the chest area, 21 on the left sleeve and three on the right sleeve. There were 10 more on his left shoe. Almost all of these were invisible to the naked eye. Areas of the bloodstained clothing were then sent to the forensic science laboratory at Wetherby in Yorkshire, where DNA-matching was carried out and it was quickly confirmed that all this was Billie-Jo's blood.

Wain went on to make a number of other significant points. Whereas the spots were of approximately the same size as those on Billie-Jo's leggings (her top was completely saturated with blood, and so it was impossible to distinguish patches of staining or individual spots), there was no blood on the clothes of Denise Lancaster or of either of the paramedics who had attended the scene. (In fact there were a few spots on one paramedic's left shoe – as there were on Siôn's left shoe – but the evidential value of these was nil.) Nor was there a broad area of bloodstaining on Siôn's clothing – as there might have been if he had, say, cradled the dying Billie-Jo in his arms. Moreover, asserted Wain, there was nothing at all in Siôn's statement or the various accounts he had given that could explain the bloodspots. In Wain's view, that was because there was only one explanation: Siôn had killed Billie-Jo.

Wain said that Billie-Jo had been bludgeoned at close range; the force of the blows was considerable. He said that using the weapon would cause larger blood drops to shoot forward, and also create a fine spray of smaller droplets which would go upwards and backwards towards the assailant. The smaller spots would not travel far, indicating that the wearer was very close. Wain emphasised that the range and distribution of the spots on the jacket and trousers were 'typical of what I would expect to find' had Siôn been the assailant – leaning forward and attacking Billie-Jo and, as he put it, 'impacting a surface wet with blood'. In other words, the first blow will not produce a spray, because at that moment there is no exposed blood; subsequent blows, if aimed at the same area – where blood is now pooling – obviously will.

Russell Stockdale, who had set up a successful independent forensic science company, helped to coordinate the prosecution's scientific evidence and also gave evidence himself. On 8 May 1997, at the Chepstow forensic science laboratory, he and Wain conducted a series of experiments with a leg of pork and a pig's head.

Readers who are intimidated by science, who imagine that scientific disciplines have progressed to such an intensely erudite level that those of us of more humble mental capacities have no hope of comprehending them, may be surprised to learn what happened in these Chepstow experiments: Wain and Stockdale attempted to replicate the conditions of the assault on Billie-Jo by bashing a pig's head round a laboratory with a broom handle. They then carried out a parallel assault on a leg of pork, giving it a fresh coating of blood between each strike with the broom handle.

Wain and Stockdale claimed that the tests bore out their thesis. As it happens, the tests did yield one highly suggestive result. In all of them, the majority of bloodspots were clustered on the striking arm of the assailant. (Although Siôn was right-handed, Wain's examination of Siôn's clothing had revealed significantly more bloodspots on the left sleeve of the fleece jacket.) When this point was put to him in court, Wain replied that it was 'not significant'.

There was also a further point. In cases of this kind, when an assailant wields a weapon over and over in a frenzied attack, one of the tell-tale pieces of evidence that forensic scientists can look for is 'cast-off' blood – that is, blood from the victim that has been transferred to the weapon and then dripped off on to the shoulders or back of the assailant. There were no cast-off drips on Siôn's clothing. Although this could have been a weighty point in the defence's favour, Wain simply asserted that cast-off bloodstains 'do not always occur'.

At some stage, as he had leant over Billie-Jo, Siôn noticed what he described as a 'bubble of blood' at her nose. This 'bubble of blood' now became a key feature of the defence case at trial, albeit a misunderstood one. According to the post-mortem, there was blood in Billie-Jo's airways, and her lungs were hyperinflated (i.e. they were fully extended and air was trapped within them). With these conditions, the defence believed that she may at some point have exhaled a fine blood-mist over Siôn as he leant over her. The 'bubble of blood' gave an indication of how this may have happened. The defence argument was not that this specifically had caused the spray, but the more general one that some form of exhalation by the dying Billie-Jo had caused it.

All the arguments in this case, all the hundreds of pages of scientific analysis that have accumulated over the years, have been concentrated on this one simple but utterly key point – was the blood on Siôn's clothing caused by impact spatter or an exhalation spray?

The prosecution appeared not even to have considered the possibility that the blood on the clothing was caused by an expiration spray until the defence had served the reports from MacKirdy and Webster at the start of April. They then further served the report from the neurosurgeon John Sinar.

An expert in head injuries, Sinar explained there was a difference between a closed head wound, where death can be swift because the intercranial pressure cannot be released, and an open head wound, where the victim may well live longer. He said that the amount of blood indicated that Billie-Jo's heart must still have been pumping blood; so she must have been alive for some time after the attack. It was difficult to say when death occurred. Even after head injuries, breathing can continue relatively normally; and the desire to cling on to life, even for an unconscious person, is considerable. Asked how long Billie-Jo might have survived the attack upon her, Sinar replied that a 'reasonable' guess would be fifteen to twenty minutes. He also explained that respiration could be produced by movement of the body.

At trial, Stockdale said that he could not imagine a situation in which the pattern produced on Siôn's clothes could have been produced by exhalation, and he supported Wain in affirming that the nature and distribution of the bloodspots was 'entirely consistent' with the wearer of the clothing having delivered several blows into blood. Under cross-examination, however, one concession he did make was to acknowledge that impact spatter would generally result in 'bigger spots' than those found on Siôn's clothing.

Duncan MacKirdy, for the defence, made a parallel point, saying that he would not have expected – were the bloodspots to have been produced by impact spatter – all the blood droplets to be of a similar size. He and Mark Webster, a second defence scientist, believed that a pattern of staining similar to that on Siôn's clothing could be produced by exhalation. They conducted their own tests, with Webster exhaling two drops of blood to try to produce a pattern on a close-at-hand target. These appeared to suggest that a similar pattern could be replicated.

The prosecution criticised the validity of the tests, first of all on the basis that Webster, in exhaling the blood, had been face up; whereas Billie-Jo had been lying on her side, so that any blood exhaled by her would not have been projected in an upwards arc. Even if there had been a shower of droplets, argued the prosecution, they would have been at a low trajectory and would not have travelled any distance.

The prosecution also maintained that it would have been necessary for the dying girl to have inhaled a large amount of air in order for her to have been able to have expirated the blood droplets. In performing his test, Webster measured that he had exhaled 2.3 litres of air over 1–2 seconds. Dr Ian Hill, the home office pathologist who had conducted the post-mortem, expressed the view that this was a 'huge amount', which 'bore no relation to reality'.

Hill said that Billie-Jo would not have been able to make 'vigorous breathing movements' as she lay dying, and emphasised that in any case there was scarcely time for her to have done so: 'I do not think she would have hovered between life and death for any great time'. He also made the point that, had she expelled blood in the way suggested by the defence, then someone in close proximity, like Siôn, would have noticed her breathing. Siôn did not. In conclusion, Hill considered the entire defence theory 'so remote a possibility that it can be discounted'.

Stockdale recruited John McAughey for the prosecution. An aerosol expert concerned with the measurement of air-flow, McAughey worked in Abingdon, Oxfordshire, for the Aerosol Science Centre, a sub-division of AEA Technology (the privatised company that had emerged from the former Atomic Energy Authority). He, too, had conducted his own experiments, in the first of which, using a pipette to project blood bubbles, he demonstrated that the bloodspots would simply fall downwards. In the second experiment, he asked a volunteer to blow blood bubbles. The volunteer was a forty-two-year-old woman, though McAughey asserted that her lung capacity was comparable to Billie-Jo's.

He recorded that for her to expel blood droplets with sufficient force to create a spray would need 2.7 litres of air, and that this represented a peak air flow of 50–55 litres per minute, or roughly 80 per cent of Billie-Jo's lung capacity. The flow is the rate at which air comes out of the body, and it is measured in litres of air per minute. Peak flow is the fastest rate of respiration without undue effort. Normal breathing occurs at a rate of about 30 litres a minute, and maximum air flow requires about 70 litres per minute.

The prosecution then called upon David Southall, professor of paediatrics at Keele University, to support this line of evidence. The judge described Southall as 'a very experienced paediatrician [who has been] concerned with respiratory physiological research for many years', but what he was doing in the trial at all was something of a mystery. The prosecution had been granted a six-week adjournment in order to find a neurosurgeon who could deal with Sinar's evidence for the defence; they had not been granted a six-week adjournment so that they could bring in a paediatrician.[20]

Southall told the court that he had long experience in putting children on ventilators. He said that coughing or sneezing, for example, were 'complicated activities which occur only when the brain is working well', so that those possibilities could be ruled out. He dismissed the defence theory by saying that in view of Billie-Jo's severe injuries, it was 'impossible' that she could have expelled even 2.3 litres of air.

Overall, the thrust of the prosecution evidence, in countering the defence exhalation theory, was that Billie-Jo would have needed the lung capacity and fitness levels of a track-and-field athlete in order to generate the air-flow required to produce the kind of blood-spray discovered on Siôn's blue fleece jacket.

The defence brought forward other experts. Professor Douglas argued that both the 2.3 and the 2.7 figures were irrelevant. What caused the 55 litres per minute was not the amount of air but the speed of flow. He said that 55 litres, albeit close to twice the normal level, would be a relatively low peak flow.

In order for the prosecution theory (that Siôn killed Billie-Jo) to hold, they had to be able to demonstrate conclusively that it was not possible for Billie-Jo still to have been alive when Siôn found her; that it was not possible for her to have expirated blood on to Siôn's clothing; and, indeed, that the only possible explanation of the blood on the clothing was that it had been caused by impact spatter.

The judge, Mr Justice Gage, commented that all the various scientific experiments that had been conducted were necessarily unsatisfactory because there were so many variables and it was impossible to reproduce the exact situation.

However, one of the crucial prosecution points, a point that underpinned the scientific evidence, was Siôn's momentary unwillingness to put on his fleece jacket as he and Lois were leaving Denise Lancaster's house. 'I was passing coats to everyone', explained Mrs Lancaster, 'I passed the fleece via Lois. He said he didn't want it. She was insisting because it was very, very cold and she had on a sheepskin coat. He was adamant that he didn't want it.'

The prosecution argued that here was a man who now felt uncomfortable wearing his jacket because he knew that it was contaminated with the blood of the young girl he had just murdered.

The defence case boiled down to the argument that someone else was responsible; the crime had not been investigated properly and vital leads had been ignored. It was 'a murder inquiry which had lost its way', according to the defence barrister, Anthony Scrivener QC. With regard to Siôn's reaction to the attack on Billie-Jo, and what seemed to be his abject inability to deal adequately with the situation, Scrivener called Professor Michael Trimble who gave evidence of the extent to which, in the immediate aftermath of traumatic events, all of us are susceptible to shock. 'You may not be able to cope with instructions', he said, 'you may be disorganised, your response to others may be inappropriate.'[21]

Giving his first interview to the police afterwards, Siôn had clearly explained his predicament:

I have been asked a number of questions and I have said to the police officer that I can remember images of things that have happened and I have attempted to put them in some kind of chronological order but I cannot. I have said that… on a number of occasions. I cannot guarantee the order. There are some sights and some flashbacks that are stronger than others but… clear information was required and there are various points when I am totally blank.

Trimble felt that the otherwise inexplicable aspects of Siôn's conduct – his alleged failure to tend to Billie-Jo satisfactorily, or to act on the routine instructions of the ambulance operator; his action in suddenly getting into the MG car to put the roof up; and his inability afterwards to recollect with any precision the sequence of events – could all be straightforwardly explained by the fact that he was in shock. The prosecution argued that the notes Siôn had made were 'intricate and detailed', and showed that there was no question of shock having affected his memory.

The defence case will normally begin with the defence QC putting his client on the stand, and this is what happened here. Siôn went into the witness-box. There are three stages to a witness's evidence at trial: examination-in-chief, when the witness is gently led through his account by the barrister from his own side. Obviously, this will give the witness the opportunity to overcome his 'stage fright' and get used to the atmosphere. Then there is cross-examination, when he is questioned by the opposing barrister; and finally re-examination, when his own lawyer will have the chance to clarify any issues that have emerged from the cross-examination (or, on occasion, to try to repair the damage it has caused).

Sometimes, defendants will either prefer, or be advised, not to take the stand. This is a high-risk strategy, but the defence QC will point out that it is not for the defence to prove its case; on the contrary, it is for the police and prosecution to prove theirs.

Siôn was anxious to give his own evidence; he was more than prepared to answer any questions put to him. Scrivener, however, asked him just one question.

An 'Impossible' Defence

'Did you murder Billie-Jo?'

'No', replied Siôn.

Scrivener then sat down again. It became known, as far as the media were concerned, as the 'seven-second defence'. It was intended as a *coup de théâtre* and, in some circumstances, it could have wrong-footed the Crown. In this instance, it failed. As an opponent, Richard Camden Pratt, the prosecution barrister, is dour and colourless, but nevertheless dogged and hard-working. He already had his line of questioning worked out and so was not handicapped by the fact that he had to begin about a day earlier than he'd anticipated.

The line of questioning was a low one. Indeed, it was below the belt. The cross-examination began like this:

Q [Camden Pratt]: How old was she when she died?

A [Siôn Jenkins]: She was thirteen...

Q: And had become quite fashion conscious?

A: I would say so...

Q: And interested in her appearance?

A: I would say so...

Q: Were you often alone with Billie-Jo?

A: [pause] Yes...

Q: We have heard that she was menstruating at the time of her death. When did her periods begin?

It was a disgraceful question. Siôn said he didn't know but there was no answer he could give that would undo the damage. The idea that there might have been some kind of sexual dimension in relations between him and Billie-Jo was, as one of those in court put it, 'uppermost in everyone's minds – it was the most obvious suggestion for a possible motive'.

All this was based on no evidence whatever (indeed, it was contrary to the available evidence), but that did not deter the prosecution from subsequently referring to Siôn's relationship with Billie-Jo as 'complex'.

Siôn was doubly handicapped. The 'seven-second defence' had allowed him no opportunity to bring in many salient points in his favour. Now, he appeared increasingly flustered and uncomfortable as, in cross-examination, the prosecution wound its web of scurrilous suggestions around him.

Chapter Twenty-Eight

Unanimous Verdict

In one respect, all the evidence the jurors heard at the trial was irrelevant; what must have been of overwhelming importance was the evidence they didn't hear. This was, of course, the evidence of Annie and Charlotte. Even as the trial was proceeding, an even more gripping drama concerning the children was unfolding off-stage.

Immediately after the failure of the abuse of process application on 4 June, Siôn's defence lawyers wrote to Lois's solicitors asking for permission to talk to Annie and Charlotte in order to ascertain whether their purported comments, as reported by their mother, were accurate. There was an almost instantaneous response: Lois would not consent to the children being spoken to by anyone.

On 7 June, Brendan Salsbury wrote again, emphasising that it was the view of the defence counsel that the children's evidence would assist the defence case and pointing out that they were entitled to issue witness summonses.

In the absence of any immediate reply, Siôn's lawyers fired off a third letter the next day. This did elicit a response. Lois Jenkins said that she wanted advice as to the advisability of her daughters giving evidence and added that she had written to the trial judge to seek his views.

In her letter to Mr Justice Gage, Lois explained that she wanted an independent medical assessment of the likely psychological impact on her daughters, although she added that any examination that was conducted *must preclude any inquiry into the events themselves*. She concluded by saying that she did not wish to do anything that would prejudice a fair trial.

On behalf of the judge, the clerk of the court then responded to Lois's solicitor:

In [Mr Justice Gage's] view, the interests of justice in this trial are such that your client ought to make the children available to be interviewed as sympathetically as possible by the defence... His Lordship hopes that your client will cooperate... and asks that it be stressed that a very considerable degree of urgency attaches to this matter.

At that point, Lois gave her 'cautious approval' for the girls to be seen by Dr Valerie Mellor on behalf of the defence. However, she imposed a number of conditions. She said that she wanted the opportunity to talk to Dr Mellor beforehand; that she, Lois, was to be present throughout the interviews; and that the girls were not to be questioned about the events of the day or their video interviews.

Dr Mellor then saw the girls on 10 June (not, in fact, in Lois's presence). As a result, she felt that they might suffer further emotional difficulties, hardly surprisingly, if they were required to give evidence. Having heard this, Lois refused to allow any further questioning of the girls by anyone.

There was then some further friction between Lois and the defence team, arising from a conflict of views about whether Lois could see a copy of Dr Mellor's report. According to her, that had been a precondition of Dr Mellor seeing the girls at all; according to the defence, no such undertaking had been given. Defence lawyers then wrote again, making it clear that, notwithstanding Dr Mellor's views, they were still holding out some hope that they might be able to interview the girls.

On 17 June, Lois's solicitor replied to these points:

Our client... instructs us that she has the clearest of recollections about this. She only gave her consent [for an examination by Dr Mellor] on condition that she would be provided with a copy of Dr Mellor's report...

If the consequence of our client's decision [not to allow any further interviewing of the children] is that you... apply for witness summonses, then our client will apply... to strike out that summons on the grounds that it would be wrong for the children to be subjected to the risk of harm by giving evidence.

Siôn himself had not been kept in touch with these almost daily developments; obviously, he was fully focused on the trial itself. Once he had been made aware, and taken stock, of the situation regarding the girls, he reacted straightaway. The notion that there could be any conceivable risk to his daughters' emotional welfare arising from their giving evidence on his behalf was, he believed, far too high a price to pay. He instructed his lawyers to call off their pursuit of Annie and Charlotte.

At this juncture, Siôn and his lawyers had very differing perspectives. Siôn believed he would be acquitted anyway; his lawyers understood how damaging this void in the defence case would be. The complete absence from proceedings not merely of Annie and Charlotte but also of Lois (not merely as witnesses; nor did any of them ever attend court) must have not only bewildered the jury, but actually fostered an impression of guilt.

In the summing-up, the judge dealt with the issue in this way:

There is no evidence from them [Annie and Lottie] and that is an end of it. I can tell you this, that under our law no one side had the exclusive right to call a particular witness, either side may call a witness. Mr Scrivener is, of course, right to point out that the burden of proof lies upon the prosecution but equally it is right that

I tell you that the defence as well as the prosecution have a right to call a witness.

Here, the sole criticism of Mr Justice Gage's handling of the case – that he had not understood the abuse of process issue – is amply reinforced. These remarks to the jury completely misrepresented the situation. It was wrong to suggest that it was an open question for the defence of whether or not to call the girls; obviously, the defence stance was that the actions of the prosecution had made it impossible to call the girls.

After the jurors retired, they returned to ask for a full list of witnesses. This was a wholly unanticipated request and, not surprisingly, a list wasn't in existence at that time. Naturally, one was quickly drawn up for them. Why they required this is, of course, not known. (The thoughts and deliberations of a jury are kept entirely secret.) One suspects, however, that they really needed to see for themselves, in black and white, just who gave evidence and, no doubt more importantly, who did not.

Elsewhere in his summing-up, Mr Justice Gage compressed the case for the jury into a series of questions:

What was Billie-Jo's state when the defendant returned to the house? Was she dead or may she have been alive? If so, in what state?... Was she capable of breathing at all?... What did he see and do in relation to Billie-Jo when he got back to the house?... Are you sure that the spots of blood on his clothes must have resulted from a fine spray generated by his striking the blood-wet surface of Billie-Jo's head with the tent peg; or may it have been caused by exhalation of breath, causing those blood droplets when he discovered her?

The twelve members of the jury were sent out to consider their verdict at ten minutes before midday on Wednesday, 1 July. Towards the end of the afternoon, at about 4.15, the jury returned to court with a second request: could they see the crime scene video again?

What was remarkable about this request was that the video in question was already highly controversial. Instead of being just a routine examination of the crime scene, the shots had been edited to pack a visceral punch, with a last, lingering shot of Billie-Jo. The photograph that was used was not, as might have been assumed, the most recent picture of her, in which she wore glasses and appeared rather studious; but an earlier one where she appeared more attractive. There was a flagrant hypocrisy here: on the one hand, the prosecution was endeavouring to imply (albeit without any supporting evidence) that Siôn's relationship with Billie-Jo had been improper; and on the other hand, they themselves were striving to use Billie-Jo's incipient sexual appeal to make a highly emotive point.

Nevertheless, the request was granted. The jury came back into court and did see the video again.

The jury then returned on Thursday afternoon at 3.30pm with their verdict: guilty. Although the jury had by then been told that a majority verdict would be acceptable, it was a unanimous verdict. Two female jurors, reporters said, were weeping.

The judge had anticipated that the court could be in uproar at this point. 'I do understand that feelings in the case on all sides have been running high and will continue to do so,' he had said the day before. He had asked those in court nevertheless to refrain from 'any kind of outburst or disturbance' when the verdict was returned. Almost inevitably, however, there were instant, fired-up reactions to the guilty verdict. There was an unruly commotion, with cheers and angry gestures from members of Billie-Jo's natural family, who punched the air, shouting abuse and calling him 'bastard' and 'monster'. Siôn was instantly bundled downstairs to the cells, while Mr Justice Gage threatened to clear the court.

Once Siôn had returned, he was sentenced to life imprisonment. The judge described the crime as 'horrendous' and Siôn himself as 'a very considerable danger to the community'. The police officer in charge of the investigation, Detective Superintendent Paine, told reporters that the murder was 'a brutal act carried out in a moment of incomprehensible rage and violence'.

Immediately afterwards, Lois put out a statement, through her solicitor, in which she appeared to make it clear that she accepted the jury's verdict:

Sixteen months ago I returned, with two of my children, from a quiet Saturday afternoon walk on the beach to a tragedy more horrific than any person ever expects to encounter in a lifetime.

The loss of Billie, especially in such awful circumstances, has been almost too much to bear. It has been hard to take time to grieve in the midst of a major murder inquiry with all the media and public attention that such an investigation attracts. It has been hard to wait for so many months for a trial, but the need to see justice done generates a strength to carry on.

It is a terrible thing to realise that the man with whom you have lived for 14 years, the father of your children, is capable of murdering your child. There is no reason, no explanation for such a pointless waste of a young life.

Now that the trial is over, the girls and I need peace and quiet to come to terms with all that has happened. Above all we need time to grieve properly for Billie and to learn to remember her as the happy, vibrant daughter and sister whom we knew.

We want to thank all our family and friends not least the community of Hastings for the support and encouragement which has enabled us to continue to live at home and for the girls to continue at their schools. We would also like to thank the many hundreds of people who have written to us sharing our sadness in the loss of Billie and offering their encouragement.

Just now, in the immediate aftermath of the trial, we would appreciate privacy and quiet for both ourselves, our family and our friends.

Having been manhandled down to the cells as a result of the clamour in the courtroom when the verdict was announced, Siôn was then brought back again to be sentenced, then taken back down below, and then brought back up to face the full glare of the public spotlight again. This time, it was for him to be told that he faced a second charge, of obtaining a pecuniary advantage by deception. The judge ordered that this charge should lie on file.

It was a peculiarity of this case that, though irrelevant in the context of the murder trial, this additional charge dictated the tenor of the post-trial coverage. Only in the most extenuating circumstances is someone newly convicted of murder going to receive other than hostile publicity; and there was nothing extenuating about these circumstances. Nevertheless, after his conviction Siôn was struck by a torrent of publicity that far exceeded in anger and acrimony what the average murderer (assuming there is such a creature) has to contend with.

At the bottom of all the bile lay perceptions of class. Someone born into penury or difficult family circumstances may not have too many choices about how to live their life. Coming from a working-class-made-good family, Siôn had not only had a host of advantages, but had taken up most of them. A regular church-goer, someone who had stood for the local council as a Conservative candidate, he had smoothly climbed the ladder of professional success – though with, we now learned, the help of calculated dishonesty. He was the more evil, it seemed, for having been the more successfully camouflaged in the ranks of the respectable middle-classes.

In effect, the lies on his CV became as great a crime as the murder itself. He had utterly betrayed the values of decent society, the very values that the media like to persuade themselves they cherish and uphold. A man without scruples, he was also, now, a man bereft of family or friends, abandoned by all who had once loved him. The man deserved not a shred of sympathy. The newspapers reached for their least savoury adjectives.

The *Times* told its readers that Siôn had obtained his position at William Parker School with 'a false curriculum vitae in which 85% of his "qualifications" were faked'.

The *Guardian* said that Siôn was 'a philandering conman with a volcanic temper who would punch his wife in moments of fury'.

Virtually all the newspapers reported that Siôn was a 'control freak'. One of the investigating police officers told the *Guardian*:

He is delusional and an absolute control freak. We don't really know why he murdered Billie-Jo, except that he had a temper that didn't show itself very often – but when it did, it was extreme.

Jenkins controlled everything about his life and the life of his family, but occasionally lost it. He lost control on 15 February, but from the moment he dropped that tent spike he was in control again.

The papers reported an affair with a seventeen-year-old girl. This level of scandal clearly wasn't adequate for the *Times*, which instead reported 'a string of affairs with younger women' and dubbed him 'a serial adulterer'. While most of the papers indicated that some sexual tension in the relationship between Siôn and Billie-Jo could perhaps explain the murder, the *Times* again went further than the rest:

It was his obsession with his foster daughter, who looked older than her 13 years, which concerned members of her natural family, although there was no medical evidence of sexual abuse.

'The way he loved her was not right', said Maggie Coster, the girl's aunt. 'I thought it was an unhealthy obsession. She was as tall as Lois and she used to wear Lois's shoes. It was like she was his trophy. I think he tried to reinvent her like he had reinvented himself with all his lies. I think he was in love with Billie-Jo. Lois told me he adored Billie-Jo more than his own children. She said she wouldn't leave her alone with him.'

So much for the sex. Then there was the violence – assertions, for example, that Siôn regularly chastised his own children. Lois, said the

Guardian, was 'well-acquainted with his capacity for violence', as she had suffered abuse for fifteen years. On one occasion, he had perforated her eardrum; on another, he had hurt her so badly that she was taken to hospital. 'Even the dog, Buster, was kicked', added the *Independent*.

One particular incident was cited in all the papers as an example of his treatment of Billie-Jo herself. While the Jenkins family had been on holiday in France in 1996 with another family – the Gaimsters – Siôn was, reported the *Guardian*, 'seen hurling' Billie-Jo across a room.

This allegation, made by Peter Gaimster, had not previously been publicly heard as the judge had ruled that it was too prejudicial to be used in court. Now, the *Times* carried full details of Gaimster's inadmissible account. 'I saw Siôn throw her violently', he was reported as saying. 'She landed on the bed, crying. I then saw Siôn violently kick her, using his right leg with full force. The kick caught Billie-Jo against her injured leg. She became hysterical. Siôn then looked around and saw me standing there. He walked over to the door and calmly closed it. The subject was never mentioned again.'

The article in the *Times* about Siôn's character was memorably headlined:

LIAR, WIFE-BEATER, ADULTERER AND KILLER

Siôn Jenkins was convicted, condemned and publicly vilified. As the prison van took him away to start his long incarceration, the valedictory wish of the British people might simply have been that he could be imprisoned forever.

Those who like to read between the lines of the newspaper accounts, however, may have been intrigued by some aspects of the reports. For a start, there was the case itself. The *Daily Telegraph* reported that, 'In perhaps the most telling and damning piece of behaviour, he closed the dining room door to block out the sight of the daughter who lay dead or dying on the patio'. Superficially, this may have suggested an unusual callousness; even so, if this really was 'the most telling and damning piece of behaviour', then could the case be as overwhelming as was being suggested?

There were also a number of indications that the evidence on which the very negative portraits of Siôn were based perhaps wasn't altogether clear-cut. For all those heavy hints about his relationship with Billie-Jo, we learned that 'there was no medical evidence of sexual abuse' (the *Times*); 'no suggestion that he was interfering with Billie-Jo in any way' (the *Guardian*); and nothing to suggest that he was ever violent towards her (*Daily Telegraph*). One neighbour, Carol Crispin, was reported as saying, 'Her foster parents had brought her up as one of their own. They were an absolutely brilliant family.'

Moreover, if his abuse of Lois had continued for fifteen years – as the *Guardian* had clearly reported – then why hadn't she, herself a social worker, not mentioned any of this during the family's entire dealings with social services over their fostering of Billie-Jo?

In fact, 'no evidence of any previous violence' was put before the jury (*Daily Telegraph*). In his professional capacity as a school-teacher, 'there was no suggestion of losses of temper or violence' (*Telegraph*, again). This information was also carried in the *Guardian*, though oddly phrased as 'he was careful never to hit the boys he taught'. One of his former pupils, Kevin Coley, told the *Independent*, 'He was one of the mildest teachers you're going to get... None of us believe he did it'.

The seventeen-year-old with whom he was reported to have had an affair sold her tale to the *Daily Mirror*. She told them that Siôn had 'paraded her like a trophy on their secret dates'.

It seems reasonable to observe that if someone is being 'paraded like a trophy', then it can only be done publicly, not on secret dates. (It also seemed at least plausible that the 'trophy' idea had been suggested by Margaret Coster's comments with regard to Billie-Jo in the earlier report in the *Times*.) More surprisingly, the seventeen-year-old girl added that Siôn had 'weirdly' refused to have sex with her even though, as she frankly admitted, 'he had the opportunity'. (So: damned if you do, damned if you don't.)

A neighbour, Peter Webb, was reported as saying, 'He's a lovely bloke, so even-tempered'; his wife, Ann, added , 'I have never heard him raise his voice' (the *Guardian*). The Rev. Roger Gray, the minister at Siôn's local church, stated, 'Siôn, I would say, was a good and trustworthy man, a strong character. They were a strong and very together family.' (*Daily Telegraph*). With some positive things being reported about Siôn, it was perhaps understandable that the *Telegraph* chose to describe this as 'one of the most complex and inexplicable cases of child murder for decades'.

Yet those readers who do pick up the caveats buried deep in the news reports are a tiny minority. The vast bulk of the populace, with probably no opportunity to study the material carefully, are persuaded by the overall tone and tenor of the reporting. In no time at all, misreported rumours have become established fact. A correspondent to the *Guardian* was 'alarmed' that Siôn had 'fabricated entirely his academic background when applying for teaching posts'. One correspondent to the *Hastings & St Leonard's Observer*, the local paper, asked:

> I wonder how many parents like me with children at local schools were shocked to discover that Siôn Jenkins used an almost entirely false set of educational qualifications to gain his job as deputy head of William Parker. It seems beyond belief that an applicant for such a responsible position should be able to get away with this kind of massive deception... How is it that [council officials] could fail to spot this wholesale lying?

Another correspondent to the local paper was concerned that Siôn had been allowed bail while awaiting trial, and attributed this to the differing approach within the legal system to 'those who have money and those who don't'. He believed that 'because Mr Jenkins comes from a wealthy family, money speaks'.

Crucially, it is often those who write for the papers who are most easily persuaded by what's in them. In the *Birmingham Evening Mail*, Maureen Messent wrote:

> [Siôn Jenkins] ruled his family with a rod of iron because he was an inadequate who couldn't get a teaching job without false

references… I want to know how [Lois Jenkins] allowed her daughters to remain within this brute's orbit… If she had had no children and was content to become a lying tyrant's punch-bag, that would have been her affair… but by allowing children to become her husband's victims, she engaged in a whole new ball-game.

Melanie Reid, a columnist with the *Sunday Mail*, had her own theory about what had happened, and what it said about the nature of men and the class struggle in our society:

He probably murdered Billie-Jo when she rejected his lustful advances. Prepared to commit the ultimate act of brutality to protect his own reputation. Jenkins, in other words, is the kind of middle-class brute we read about but can never quite believe exists…

The pillar of the community is just as likely to beat up his wife as the local good-for-nothing… but he's much less likely to get caught. Middle-class abusers fool a lot of people. They have the money and the confidence to construct a plausible web of lies. They use worthy causes as a cover for their evil… In a tragic way, poor Billie-Jo did us all a favour. She exposed the reek of middle-class hypocrisy.

However, the most bizarre piece of post-trial journalism was written by Dr Theodore Dalrymple for the *Sunday Telegraph*. Although Dr Dalrymple clearly belonged at the opposite end of the political spectrum to Melanie Reid, his condemnation of Siôn was as forthright as hers. Without apparently attending the trial, or reading any of the evidence or seeing any of the legal documentation, Dalrymple, it seems, suggested he knew all about the case and Siôn himself. Indeed, he had *personally*, as he wrote, 'encountered thousands of men like him'. He went on:

Jenkins was a domestic tyrant. At the slightest infringement of his arbitrary and no doubt constantly changing rules, he would lash out at his wife... He would become violent not only to [her] but to his children if anything were out of its ordained place at home.

Men who behave in this fashion assuage their deep feeling of personal insignificance by achieving all-importance in the lives of the few people in intimate contact with them, who they rule with a metaphorical and sometimes literal rod of iron... This feeling of insignificance, which can only be inflamed in a media-soaked society in which celebrity is the only virtue, is what connects Siôn Jenkins's domestic violence with his inflation of his scholastic record and academic qualifications... That there should be a suggestion of illicit sexual activity in Jenkins's case is not at all surprising – it would be surprising if there were not. And his case, far from being unusual, is thus absolutely banal.

He diverted to take a sideswipe at the girl's natural parents...

The insouciance of child-rearing in this country is a national disgrace and Billie-Jo (even her name is a giveaway to those whose ear is attuned to the routine depravity of the English population) was ultimately a victim of that insouciance.

... before returning to Siôn himself:

The *Sun* newspaper called him 'evil' and 'a fiend'; and if ever those words had application, then it is to him.

Part II
The Last Sigh

Chapter Twenty-Nine
Hellmarsh

After a few days in Belmarsh – or, as the inmates routinely referred to it, Hellmarsh – I received a visit from one of the prison probation officers. He spoke kindly and told me that I would shortly be leaving the hospital wing to join one of the main wings. He explained that I would find it difficult and would need to stand up for myself. My notoriety would just encourage other prisoners to attack me.

So, two hours later, I was carrying my prison bags to a wing on the other side of the prison. It was an eerie experience. There was no one around. Because I was coming on to the wing, they'd locked everybody up during their association time. That made me really popular!

They opened the door, pushed me in, and I was in a cell with two others. Prison overcrowding is routine, and this was a single cell, designed for one prisoner, which was actually housing three.

Of course, the following weeks were difficult. The emotional pain was almost too much to bear. I found prison culture alien and complex. I was given a number. I became Jenkins AW4265. I was told I had to quote it on all paperwork, including my letters. Whenever possible, I would 'forget' to use it.

I was still losing weight and the food at Belmarsh was just like slops. When I collected my meal on that first evening I had to pick off the cooked fly. I was undeterred. If I was going to survive, I would have to eat everything that was put in front of me.

What I remember most about those early weeks are two violent attacks. I witnessed one, and was the victim of the other.

During association, prisoners have to decide what their priorities are for that limited period of time (probably, about sixty to ninety minutes): do they want to play pool? make phone calls, and perhaps call their family or lawyer? organise visiting orders (VOs) and other administrative matters? play snooker or chess? take a bath or shower? just meet other prisoners?

I had spent too much time in an overcrowded cell and was feeling dirty and clammy. So I decided to go for a bath.

I lay in the bath and closed my eyes. I listened to the arguments that had already started up around the pool table on the landing below. Two men came in very quickly and, gripping my throat and holding down my shoulders, forced my head under the water. It's difficult to describe my thoughts at the time. For perhaps a few brief micro-moments, thinking it a malicious prank but no more, I expected them to release their grip.

Then, almost instantly, I knew that it was serious and that I had to fight for my life. I couldn't cry out because my face was under water. I grabbed the soft skin of one of the men's necks and pulled him down towards me. I then kicked out to get some leverage to push my body upwards and out of the water and hit and grabbed at the legs of one of the men. He ran off. When the other realised he could not hold me under the water on his own, he also left. But as I came up, I saw there had been a third person there with them.

When I had kicked, I had caught my foot against the taps and damaged it. I got out of the water and saw that the foot was bloodied and already swollen. I still have a damaged foot.

The other incident occurred shortly afterwards. Following 'bang-up' (when all prisoners are locked in the cells for the night), I heard a young black man in the cell opposite me crying. He started to bang on his door requesting to see a senior officer. I looked across. Because Belmarsh is a modern prison, there's a gap in the hinge-side of the door which you can see through.

It seemed that the staff hadn't given him a VO that he needed to organise a visit from his family and he was very distressed about it. He banged on the door and kept repeating, 'I need my application'. He asked them to put it under the door. One officer arrived and told him to keep quiet. He continued to bang on his door. Then a small group of prison officers – two male and one female – walked on to the wing.

They opened his door, grabbed him and threw him to the floor. The male officers proceeded to kick him viciously over all parts of his body, whilst the female officer watched with her arms folded. His cries stopped. When they had given him a thorough beating, the officers left, overturning the furniture on their way out.

About an hour later other prison officers came and opened his door again and took him away. The following morning I looked through his door flap. He wasn't there, and everything to indicate that he had ever been there had gone. No one saw this young black man again or had any idea what had happened to him.

The attack on me changed my attitudes. I didn't say anything to the prison authorities because I instinctively knew that one shouldn't tell tales. Other prisoners continued to shout and pass messages that they were going to harm me. But the attack had given me a kind of strength. I had looked after myself and was alive. I knew that one of the men who'd attacked me was nicknamed Panda, on account of his dark eye sockets. I also knew who the others were. They probably expected me to make complaints and involve the screws. When they saw that I didn't, and that I just got on with it, they stayed away from me.

But I never took a bath again; I always showered.

The first time I walked out to the exercise yard was a shock. Other prisoners had lined up by a perimeter fence. I wondered what they were doing and then I realised they were waiting for me. I then got a tirade of threats. Prisoners in other wings leaned out of their windows to join in the verbal abuse. The prison officers asked me if I wanted to go back inside, but I knew not to show weakness, so I refused.

So, as terrible as Belmarsh was, it toughened me up very quickly.

Within days of my conviction, Bob Woffinden had contacted my legal team and written two articles about my case, one for the *New Statesman* and one for the *Daily Mail*. The former was the cover story. It read: 'Siôn Jenkins is innocent: Bob Woffinden on how British justice failed again.'

When the original piece appeared, I didn't actually see it. The prison wouldn't let me have it. Nobody was allowed to have it; they basically buried it. It wasn't until there was the subsequent piece in the *Daily Mail* that I could get hold of it. I was greatly encouraged by this. Later on, I did receive the *New Statesman* and I put that front page up on the wall – it caused me a lot of grief, because I wasn't allowed to have it up and frequently prison officers would take it down.

As those early weeks in prison passed, the attempts, whether by prisoners or prison staff, to intimidate me began to recede and I learnt how to respond to situations in a way that made my life less uncomfortable. I found out which prisoners influenced wing decisions and politics, and which prisoners could get you what you needed.

One of my priorities was to get a pillow. When I'd very first been in prison, I had foolishly asked for a pillow, only to realise that such a request was merely a source of great amusement for prison officers. So now I taught a particular prisoner how to play chess, and the following day three pillows were delivered to my cell.[22]

The first letter I received after being convicted – it came about four days after I'd arrived in Belmarsh – was from Sue May. I didn't know who she was. She introduced herself and said she was aware of my case and believed I was innocent; she said she saw a number of similarities between my case and her own.[23]

She advised me to stay strong, to make sure I took exercise and got fresh air and kept myself healthy. She said she'd write to me again to tell me about the appeal process, but that in the meantime if there was any information that I needed, and any questions I wanted to ask, then I should do so and she'd share her experiences with me. She said she'd already lost her appeal and didn't want me to make the mistakes that she'd made with hers.

After that, we corresponded regularly. If I wanted to try out new ideas or initiatives, I did it through letters to her and by asking her views. She was just a wonderfully encouraging and supportive friend to have. She said she wanted justice in her own case and that she'd never stop fighting, and she never has.

Another probation officer came to see me and said, 'You've been convicted, we now want you to sign these forms'.

I refused.

'You've got to sign them', he said, 'I'm the prison's internal probation officer and I'll be liaising with the external probation team to work with you over the course of your sentence.'

'I'm not working with anyone', I replied. 'I don't want anything to do with the probation service because I'm not guilty.'

At this point, no one seemed to know what to do; there didn't seem to be a script. A senior prison officer called me into his office and said he wouldn't let me leave until I'd signed the forms.

'I need your signature on this', he insisted. 'You have to sign, you've been convicted.'

'I'm not signing anything', I said firmly.

So, to my surprise, that was that. I never signed them and heard nothing more about it.

Another chain of events made me realise how corrupt was the system in which I was now ensnared. I was put into another cell, a slightly better cell. It accommodated three, but I was alone. The only other person there was moved out early in the day because staff said that they'd found morphine tablets in his shoes; he said it was a fit-up and I was inclined to believe him.

That night, my door was locked at bang-up. That's a big thing in a maximum security jail; cell doors aren't opened again until the morning under almost any circumstances. So it was completely unexpected when my cell door was opened. Andy Veysi was standing there with his prison bags.

'I'm staying here tonight', he said.

I already knew all about Veysi. He was an unpleasant, disreputable character – a habitual criminal who spent his time ingratiating himself with prison officers. I'd already been warned about him. The strange circumstances were made doubly so because I knew that he already had his own single cell and was being released the following day.

He hadn't washed his feet for months. He absolutely stank. I had no wish to associate with him, and no need to.

'I don't have any clothes', Veysi said, 'and I'm going tomorrow'.

'Right', I said, reluctantly answering him.

'You've got some track suits. Can I have them?'

'No. I won't have anything myself then.'

'But you can get something sent in. I don't have anything. Can I have them?'

'No.'

There were maybe a couple of more very brief exchanges, but that was basically the extent of the conversation that passed between us. I settled down and went to sleep. He didn't ask me anything, and I certainly wouldn't have said anything to him if he had.

In the next couple of days, I received renewed warnings about him. I was told that he'd been looking to make some money prior to his release.

That Sunday, there was a double-page spread in the *News of the World*.

I DID KILL BILLIE-JO

Jailed foster dad in shock prison cell confession

Jailed child-killer Siôn Jenkins has confessed that he DID murder his pretty schoolgirl foster daughter Billie-Jo – after sexually abusing her.

The evil deputy headmaster admitted to cellmates that he bludgeoned the 13-year-old to death because she was going to tell his wife Lois the sick truth about him.

Ice-cool Jenkins has always maintained his innocence – and has even instructed lawyers to appeal against his conviction.

But the *News of the World* can reveal that the two-faced fiend BRAGGED behind bars of his lust for Billie-Jo while preparing to waste public time and money on a phoney bid for freedom.

Jenkins sat on his cell bed and asked prisoner Andrew Veysi, 'Would you like me to tell you the truth?'

(*News of the World*, 9 August 1998)

Inevitably the piece would counteract the more favourable publicity I had been getting as a result of Bob Woffinden's articles.

I was not upset when I saw it; as a result of all that had already happened, I was now feeling stronger and full of resolve. I straightaway said I wanted to speak to someone senior, and was taken along to a governor's office.

'What are you playing at?' I asked angrily.

'There's a story here that you confessed', said the governor.

'No, what are *you* playing at?' I said again. 'Your officers put that man into my cell the evening before his release. For that very purpose.'

To my surprise he did not deny anything. Instead he asked me what actions I proposed to take.

'I'm contacting my legal team – not just with regard to Veysi, but also to the machinations that led up to it.'

When I left the room, I was escorted back to my cell. I then went to the phones but I couldn't make a call because they were all down. I wrote about five or six letters, to my solicitor and to friends and family, explaining what had happened and how unscrupulous the prison service had been in putting Veysi into my cell.

Later in the day, I was standing on the wing when I noticed a screw about six feet away from me. I didn't want to be near him, so I walked over to the other side. He followed me. So then I went downstairs, and again he was there. I was literally being followed on the wing.

Evening came. The phones hadn't been fixed so I still hadn't phoned anyone. I didn't sleep particularly well and was wide awake by 4:30am. I knew I had a couple of hours before the cell doors were opened. Within the hour, however, my door was opened and an officer whom I didn't know was telling me to pack my bags. He refused to say where I was going and ordered me to take my pictures off the wall. There was to be no trace of me in the cell.

I knew I would not be coming back. I was then taken to the segregation unit or, as it is known in prison parlance, 'the Block'. That is where prisoners are punished or are removed to if the prison does not want them on the wing. Over the years, I've come to learn that the worst excesses of the prison regime take place while men are on the Block. They are alone and their cries cannot be heard.

I was put in a cell, though it was more of a dungeon. My bags were to be left outside so that they could be searched. When they were returned, all the letters I had just written were gone.

'Where are my letters?' I asked.

'What letters?' came the response.

'I only wrote them yesterday, I put them all there in that small bag this morning.'

'There were no letters.'

The following days were harrowing. You're given your breakfast at six o'clock the evening before. It's a carton of milk and a bread roll, so if you kept it until the following morning the milk is off and the roll is hard. So you have to eat it straightaway. You get food every day, but it's just slops. It's bad in the prison anyway, but in the Block it's awful – you never know whether people are spitting in it, it was very nasty.

My cell was disgusting, I asked for a broom and a mop to clean it; but when you smelt the mop, it stank of urine – that's your mop. No, I didn't want to mop my floor with that. I just had to live in it.

I asked to make phone calls; I was refused. I asked to have writing paper to write fresh letters; I was refused. I asked to speak to a governor; I was refused. I said I wanted exercise, thinking if they won't allow me to make a phone call, I can at least speak to someone then.

So I went for exercise. It was taken in a quadrangle, with a wall that must have been 50 foot high. If you wanted to see the sky, you had to bend over backwards. There were five or six screws, they were the only people I ever saw. I never saw other prisoners. It dawned on me that they can do anything to anybody when you're in the Block, and of course they do. In solitary confinement, there is no way of making contact with the outside world. I was worried for my family. The days spent there just brought it home to me how vulnerable I was.

Later, I realised that the people who get the beatings are usually young men who don't have family or friends, who struggle to get a visit, and who don't have a proper legal team. The prison service will know who they can push around. I realise now that they wouldn't have beaten me because I was articulate and had family and friends and the support of a campaign group and journalists; it would have been too difficult to lose me in the system. But for men whom nobody knows, who could just be ghosted out to another prison and kept there on the Block while all their injuries heal – those are the ones who are really helpless.

Then one morning, there was a knock on my door: Jenkins, pack, you're going. Most of my stuff was already packed because I had nowhere to put anything; I didn't have a cupboard and the floor was very dirty. I was taken out not through the wings, but through the back entrance of the segregation unit. There was a sweatbox there and they put me inside. I asked where we were going, but they refused to tell me and closed the sides so that I couldn't see out of the windows.

At the beginning of my second week on the Block, a governor had come to see me. He told me I would be leaving Belmarsh, and asked which prison I would like to go to. Even then I knew this was a bogus exercise (governors don't ask those sort of questions, and it wasn't his decision anyway). From my discussions with other inmates, I already knew the prison to be avoided at all costs was Wakefield in west Yorkshire. I also needed to stay in reasonable travelling distance for my family and legal team. So I replied, anywhere in the south of England.

I was in the prison van for five hours. When I got out, the first thing I noticed was the sign: HMP Wakefield.

Chapter Thirty

The Road to
Appeal

Wakefield operated what is known as a mixed regime. All men, regardless of their crimes, are housed together on the wings. Other prisons have VP (vulnerable prisoner) wings, for those who are deemed to be at risk from other prisoners. In Wakefield, this didn't apply; so many men have been convicted of emotive and horrendous crimes that the VPs would outnumber the rest. If a man did seek VP status, he'd perhaps be given a short period in the health care centre or simply be put down the Block.

I was in a cell on the top landing. I put my bag on the bed, walked out on to the landing and looked out down the wing. Wakefield, though its history can be traced back to Tudor times, is essentially a nineteenth-century prison.

That evening, I was the object mainly of curiosity. The drive up to Wakefield had taken so long that I missed the evening meal. The prison service makes no special arrangements for prisoners who are inconvenienced in this way, so I knew I would have nothing to eat until the following day. However, before the cell door was locked for the night,

David Collins, a young prisoner whose cell was two doors from mine, came to wish me well. Realising I'd had a difficult time, he returned to his cell and brought me a jar of honey; his only one. I was very grateful for his generosity.

I got to know him. He had a broad smile, and often told me how much he missed his mother. I never knew why he was in prison. One evening, he realised that his water flask had been stolen from his cell. That meant he would have no hot water for tea or coffee until the following morning. Alone, and deprived of the hot drink that would be his lifeline during the long night's bang-up, he cut his wrists and hanged himself. The following morning, a few prisoners, the small circle who had known him, were quiet and reflective. For everyone else in the prison, it was just another suicide.

I soon learned that there were food-boats in various stages of planning and preparation. There was a small kitchen on the wing for prisoners to use during evening recreation. Belmarsh had not had this facility, but men in Wakefield were serving very long sentences and the prison needed them to settle down and occupy themselves. So a group of men join together to plan and cook a large meal, with each of them contributing ingredients. A few prisoners straightaway said they weren't prepared to let me have any of their food-boat. But then two of the men kicked up an enormous fuss and said, 'If he can't eat, we're not eating'. Because of their stand, when the meal was eventually cooked, I was able to have some. This was just one of those small situations that illustrated the intensity of feeling against me when I first went there.

In those early days, however, one prisoner, Peter Seale, came up to me.

'I recognise you', he said. 'You've been stitched up by the system. Are you eating properly?'

'I don't particularly like the food', I replied.

'No problem', said Seale. 'I run the biggest food-boat. Come down to the kitchen on Monday, Wednesday and Friday and I'll have some curry waiting for you.'

So, for some weeks, I had a number of curries. Seale, who'd spent much of his life in prison, was widely respected. He knew the score and could see that I was finding things difficult. Once again, the meanness of some prisoners was offset by these acts of spontaneous kindness.

Whenever you left the wing for labour, you had to follow other men on a 'line route', walking through an outside area with prison officers with guard dogs on either side. In doing so, we would pass a mulberry tree. This is reputed to be the famous 'mulberry bush' of the old English nursery rhyme, Here We Go Round The Mulberry Bush, which started as a song or chant improvised by prisoners as they exercised round this tree in the prison grounds.

Turning right at the mulberry tree, men entered the various workshops. Initially, I was put into No.1, the metal workshop. I was to weld and construct prison gates and doors. The work was oppressive, not because I minded hard labour but because I minded making the means of keeping other men locked up.

Most prisoners were in cells for two, but I was in a cell on my own – the reason I was there at all was because of the alleged cell confession, which prison officers themselves had set up, so the prison service now didn't want to risk further controversy. Most prisoners understood that, so there was no resentment.

However, although many men did not believe the *News of the World* story there were also those that did. I can remember I left the cell for a while and when I returned, there was a puddle of urine on the floor. I told one of the screws. He just laughed.

I went to one of the recesses where the prison mops are kept. There were two prison mops for that whole wing and you can probably imagine (although you may not want to) what they were like. I was on my hands and knees with a small, disgusting mop and I had to clean the floor by hand. It was a very low point for me. I felt wretched anyway, but having to do that cut at the core of my pride and self-esteem. It was a case of taking a deep breath and getting on with it. I had to say to myself: I will do this, and when I've done it the cell will be clean and then I will get on with prison and my life and I will fight my case.

Over the eighteen months or so since my case had started, many so-called friends had deserted me – some at the time of my arrest; others when I was charged, and others on my conviction. Some, however, had remained loyal. There was one particular friend who was both dismayed by my conviction and at a loss about what could be done. Within a week of my conviction, she wrote to Angela and Tim Devlin, who had successfully campaigned together on behalf of Sheila Bowler, someone else who had been wrongly imprisoned in a high-profile Sussex police case. They played a significant part in getting her conviction quashed. Sheila was then acquitted at a retrial, and Angela and Tim wrote *Anybody's Nightmare*, an account of the case.[24]

As it happened, they were good friends with Bob Woffinden and so put him in touch with my friend. By this time, Bob had already met my father and they had discussed ways of taking the case forward. Now, he and my father met my friend, who then took on responsibility for developing the ideas that had been discussed. The upshot was that she organised a team of people to set up a support group on my behalf. Some of these I knew well; others I knew less well or even not at all.

Running the support group involved a lot of work, with regular mailings to all those throughout the country (and overseas) who had expressed concern about my conviction. The primary aim was to provide regular and accurate information about what was happening in my case. The mere existence of this support group also ensured, in the event of any new developments (as there frequently were), that there was a press release on my behalf so that the media was – for the first time – obliged to incorporate at least some comment from my side.

In setting up the support group, they had created a database, so with this already in existence it was then a logical progression to set up a website. This allowed everyone who was interested to keep in touch with the case and its progress. It also provided a straightforward means whereby those with information to impart could contact the defence. In this way, we picked up several small but significant pieces of evidence about the case from correspondents. A number of forensic scientists contacted the website to contradict the Crown's scientific experts. Other people wrote just to say, in effect, We are with you. During my time in prison, I received very little hate mail, but I did receive thousands of letters in support.

However, only a couple of months after arriving at Wakefield, the prison service started applying psychological pressure to persuade me to confess. I can remember the preparations for my first sentence planning board. The staff involved approached me to begin 'offending behaviour' courses. A pre-requisite for attending these courses is to admit guilt. I politely set out my position. I was unable to attend the course as I was unable to admit guilt; I was being held in prison for something I had not done.

Prisoners are allocated to a specific regime: 'enhanced' for those whom the prison decides are 'doing well'; 'standard' for the majority; and 'basic' for those whom they want to punish. So the psychology and prison probation services use the carrot and stick. The carrot is the series of bribes, in the form of better prison conditions, for admitting guilt. The stick is being denied these privileges and remaining on standard regime if you don't. In the case of life prisoners such as myself, staff have no compunction about telling those who do not accept guilt that they will die in prison.

The psychologists warned me that I would never be 'enhanced' if I did not do an 'offending behaviour' course. They also regularly tried to persuade me to attend courses on being 'in denial'. I patiently explained that I couldn't attend these courses either. They had misunderstood. I was not in denial; it was simply that I hadn't committed the crime.

It was 21 December 1998. I was back in the cell in my lunchbreak, listening to BBC Radio 4. I heard on the news bulletin that the Siôn Jenkins case had been sent back to appeal. I was overcome. I believed that my time of waiting and fighting was coming to an end. There would be justice for Billie. My daughters would get their father back.

From the moment it became known that I had been given leave to appeal and was now officially an appellant, the prison psychologists became particularly active in trying to wear me down. The entire prison staff treated me with a renewed vindictiveness. The cell was regularly being searched – 'spun' in prison jargon. Screws would go through the room with deliberate carelessness, lifting the mattress, emptying the cupboards and turning everything over on the pretext of looking for possessions I was not allowed to have. Now, with leave to appeal having been granted, they came again. They turned everything upside down and, of course, didn't find anything.

'Keep your cell tidy and put everything back', they said on the way out.

'No, this isn't my cell', I called after them angrily. 'This has got nothing to do with me. This is *your* cell – don't ever call it *my* cell.'

Just before Christmas, I was attacked again. As I walked down the spiral stairway from the top to the ground floor, a prisoner coming up the stairs demanded I get out of his way. It was a show of strength. I refused to move and he attacked me.

He tried to gouge out one of my eyes. I had nowhere to go and he was intent on inflicting serious harm. The fight seemed to last a long time. I stumbled back to my cell, with a bloodied face, hand and neck scratches and bruising all over. I was shaking from fear and the knowledge that someone had been intent upon taking out one of my eyes. In the long-term, most of the wounds cleared up, but I was left with a shoulder injury.

That first Christmas in prison was devastating. The entire Christmas and New Year period was utterly desolate. The loneliness lacerated the core of my being. I was the father of a family. What was I doing in a prison cell, hundreds of miles away from them? I imagined every second of how my children were spending their day.

After I was granted leave to appeal, the weeks turned to months and, despite my initial optimism, I began to feel drained.

I wrote continuously to my daughters and in return received heart-warming letters from them. Sometimes they enclosed photographs of themselves which I pinned to my wall. Very quickly, however, I had to take them down again. It was just too painful to look at them. I could just about handle desperation, the violence on the wing, bullying staff, and the prospect of spending many years trying to prove my innocence; but Annie, Charlotte, Esther and Maya were my Achilles' heel.

Thanks to newspaper articles and the campaign group and website, the disquiet concerning my conviction gradually increased. During this time, I was contacted by the production team of *Trial and Error*, the now-discontinued Channel 4 television series about potential miscarriages of justice.

The team (which included David Jessel, who subsequently became a commissioner at the Criminal Cases Review Commission) didn't intend merely to relate the story but also wanted, if possible, to make further headway with the case. So they contacted Professor David Denison, one of the world's leading respiratory experts, who was based in west London at the Royal Brompton Hospital. He proved an inspired choice. He became passionately interested in the case. Denison, who was greatly respected by all who knew him, would go on to play a pivotal role in my defence.

I often sent Lois postal orders from my wages, but she never replied. She had never telephoned me, or acknowledged my correspondence or ever visited me in prison. However, I only realised for myself how implacable her animosity was when she tried to prevent the *Trial and Error* documentary from being televised. She complained strenuously to the top executives of Channel 4 about its planned transmission in July 1999.

She suggested that the screening of the programme would distress the children just prior to their long summer holiday. Obviously, I had the opposite view; I thought that seeing a programme which made a strong case for their father's innocence would only hearten them enormously. However, Lois's complaint prevailed – though I'm sure that Channel 4 must have found it bewildering – and the transmission of the programme was delayed until September.

This may seem a matter of little significance, but I felt that Lois's continual sniping was a key factor in undermining the credibility of my case. In this instance, the fact that the programme had a scheduled transmission date, and that Channel 4 then had to announce its postponement, meant that, even before it was aired, some members of the public may have felt that it was flawed or unsatisfactory in some way.[25]

When it was finally transmitted on Wednesday, 15 September, I saw the programme whilst I was in the education department. Despite the scheduling dispute, my support group did view it as an important step forward in the public perception of the case. The programme analysed the scientific evidence – the blood on my jacket – that had led to my conviction, and also highlighted that I was not the only suspect who had been arrested.

Nevertheless, Lois remained intransigent. At the time I simply did not understand her; I still felt that if I could establish my innocence, then that would free our daughters of a terrible stigma, and I could not understand why she would not wish that to happen.

In the wake of the transmission, she did two things. First of all, she publicly attacked the programme. She claimed it had not been 'objective' and said it would have had a 'devastating' effect on our daughters. She argued that there should have been a declaration of interest because the defence barrister, Anthony Scrivener, was on the advisory board of Just Television, the company that had made the programme.

Her remarks, made straight after the programme's transmission, were reported in most national newspapers.

Secondly, she and Peter Gaimster then proceeded to submit written complaints about the programme to the Broadcasting Standards Commission. Each complained on their own behalf; and Lois also complained on behalf of the children. These official complaints would be adjudicated upon the following summer.

In August, our divorce had become final. Then, two days before the *Trial and Error* transmission, I was sewing sweatshirts in the workshop when a prison officer placed an opened copy of the *Daily Mail* on the bench in front of me. It displayed photographs of my wife with another man, Vince Ives. I read the accompanying report, which described him as:

… a handsome martial arts expert 11 years her junior with shaven head and silver nose stud. The contrast with Jenkins, the immaculately-groomed deputy headmaster, could hardly be more marked... Ives worked as a postman but harboured dreams of becoming a rock star... It is not known if he is working.

It was perhaps even more disconcerting to read that Lois had already brought him into the household:

He has taken on many of the duties of a father, helping with the school run, walking the dog and looking after the girls when their mother is at work... He helps her get the four girls ready for school... he sometimes picks up the girls in the family people-carrier.

It naturally came as shock, and I worried about the effect this might have on the girls. The prison officer took obvious pleasure in my discomfiture.

Despite the continuing stress and the emotional turmoil, I was determined to keep healthy and stay focused. I was now using the small kitchen on the wing during evening recreation. I started to buy my own food from my wages, especially pasta, tinned tuna and sardines. I exercised every day. At weekends, I ran round the prison's synthetic football pitch.

It had been a long time to wait but, finally, almost a year after I had been granted leave to appeal, my appeal was due to be heard in London. On 28 November 1999, I collected two plastic bags from the wing office and packed my things. All night, I lay on the top of my bed waiting for the morning. When I heard my name called, I carried my bags along the wing. I passed the men with whom I now shared my life. Some wished me well; others just stared blankly. At reception my bags were searched and sealed. I left Wakefield prison with hope in my heart. I did not intend to return.

After an uncomfortable journey, the van pulled into the central courtyard of Pentonville prison in North London. I was informed by a governor there that, because of the public interest in my case, I was to be kept in solitary confinement. The logic of this escaped me, but I did not care. I was permitted nothing at all in my cell, but I did not care about that either. I dreamt of holding my daughters again.

By 11:00 that night, the segregation unit was quiet, although I could still hear the occasional scream and one man crying. I was full of optimism, confidence and excitement. I prayed to God that my suffering would end.

Chapter Thirty-One

Conflict of Interest

The appeal took place at the Royal Courts of Justice in the Strand in central London. It lasted from 30 November until 13 December 1999, and was heard by Lord Justice Paul Kennedy, Mr Justice Dyson and Mr Justice Penry-Davey.

Lord Justice Kennedy, who would retire in 2005, is also attached to the Devlin family, though in his case it is as a son-in-law, as he married one of Lord Devlin's daughters. His reputation, however, was almost the opposite of that enjoyed by his late father-in-law; he was known as one of the most implacable of appeal court judges.

Scrivener put forward a number of grounds of appeal on Siôn's behalf. Among these were his reactivated point that there had been an abuse of process when the police 'debriefed' the children and that, accordingly, Mr Justice Gage had been wrong not to allow Scrivener's original pre-trial application and stop the trial.

Another ground referred to what the lawyers dubbed 'the confusion issue'. There had been arguments at trial about the volume of air that Billie-Jo would have needed in her lungs to expel the blood spray. There were then misunderstandings about the evidence concerning lung capacity and air flow. There was a particular confusion between 'minute volume' (the amount of air passing through the lungs in a minute when the lungs are not exerted) and 'peak flow' (the amount passing through when the lungs are fully exerted).

Scrivener also asked the court to receive the new evidence of Professor Denison, which had been obtained through the *Trial and Error* television programme. It took several hours altogether for Scrivener to put forward his arguments for why the new evidence should be accepted; and for the prosecution barrister, Richard Camden Pratt, to put forward counter-arguments for why it should not be accepted; and, finally, for the judges to decide that they would hear the new evidence, but might not necessarily receive it. Not for the first time, observers couldn't help wondering why the appeal process could not be streamlined.

At trial, the paediatrician David Southall said that from his experiments with children on ventilators, he knew that it would require the force of an athlete for anyone to have breathed out the blood-spray seen on Siôn, and that a young dying girl simply could not have managed it. The pathologist Dr Ian Hill had argued that 2–3 litres of air (the amount necessary, it had been argued at trial, to cause the expiration of the blood spray) would have been a huge amount for anyone to exhale. He said that in this case it bore no relation to reality; and that in any event, anyone would have been bound to observe breathing movements.

David Denison, on the other hand, now reported that if Billie-Jo's airways contained blood, as in all likelihood they would after trauma, and she had breathed out, that could result in the kind of spray seen on Siôn's clothing. He argued that a single exhalation could have produced all the bloodspots found on Siôn's clothing; and, moreover, that the exhalation could well have been brief, passive, inaudible and invisible, and could even have taken place after death.

Denison, however, posited that there must have been a blockage in Billie-Jo's upper airways. He suggested that when the blockage was eased, the built-up air trapped in the lungs would have been released under pressure, resulting in the exhalation spray. Dr Hill then told the appeal court that this couldn't have happened, as there had been no blockage in Billie-Jo's upper airways, and that any blockage must have been lower down in the bronchioles (the small airways that go into the lungs).

The new evidence from Denison provoked renewed activity from the scientific experts involved in the case, and the appeal had to be halted halfway through while further tests were conducted.

At the end of the appeal, Kennedy reserved judgment. It was on 21 December (exactly a year after leave to appeal had been granted) that Siôn learnt his fate.

Firstly, the judges rejected Scrivener's argument that there had been an abuse of process:

> The good faith of the police has not been challenged, and their conduct was not unlawful. There was nothing unworthy or shameful about the conduct of the police. *The decision to have a debriefing session has not been criticised.*
>
> We have no hesitation in rejecting the suggestion that the police embarked on a deliberate campaign to influence the children and taint their evidence so as to damage the defence of [Siôn Jenkins]. They were *entitled to seek to persuade* Mrs Jenkins that her husband was the killer. On the basis of the finding of Billie-Jo's blood on his clothing, the case reasonably appeared to them to be overwhelming... We can find nothing to criticise in the manner in which the police conducted their inquiries...
>
> The reason for the debriefing was to carry into effect the advice of Dr and Mrs Bentovim. As we have already said, *there is no criticism of the decision to have a debriefing session itself.*
>
> (Court of Appeal judgment, 21 December 1999)
> [italics added]

So the key point in the entire case was swept aside, with Kennedy blithely saying that the police 'were entitled to seek to persuade' Lois that Siôn was the murderer. Whatever view one takes of this, the fact is that this judgment was based on misapprehensions and misconceptions about the evidence. For example, Kennedy's repeated assertion that there had been no criticism of the decision to debrief the children was untrue. This was what Dr Mellor had written:

> It would, in my view, be wholly inappropriate for a debriefing session of that kind to take place... I would regard it as tarnishing the evidence of a witness... If Dr Bentovim advised... a debriefing of that sort, then in my view that advice was wrong.
>
> (Report of Dr Valerie Mellor, 16 April 1998)

Kennedy could not see anything wrong with the fact that the girls had not been called as witnesses:

> The prosecutor was entitled to regard the accounts given by the children in video evidence as confused or wrong, and therefore unbelievable in so far as they supported the appellant's [Siôn Jenkins'] alibi. It is worth recalling that it was Dr and Mrs Bentovim who advised the police that there should be a debriefing because Annie had had her own thoughts reconstructed by the appellant... The subsequent shifts in the accounts of the girls did nothing to make them any more credible as witnesses in the eyes of the prosecution.

Shifts in the girls' accounts? What shifts? There hadn't been any. There had only been indirect evidence to that effect from Lois Jenkins and Peter Gaimster. In alluding to this in the judgment, therefore, Lord Justice Kennedy was relying entirely on their creditworthiness as witnesses.

Another point that needs to be made here is that the Bentovims themselves never wrote that Annie 'had had her own thoughts reconstructed by the appellant'. It was the police who wrote that and implied that that was what the Bentovims had said. In other words, this is a further part of the case which is inaccurate but which, once the appeal court has given it its stamp of approval, wrongly becomes part of the received record of the case.

In relation to the girls' evidence, Kennedy said:

> Of particular significance is the statement on 4 March that Annie tried to get into the house when cleaning, and the appellant would not let her in.

This has never been Annie's evidence; it is her mother's evidence. What sort of appeal system is it that rejects first-hand witness evidence in favour of purported second-hand evidence from someone else – moreover, someone who (as a direct result of the police 'seeking to persuade' her) has a strong animus against the appellant?

The possibility of an alternative suspect for the murder had barely figured in the appeal, and Kennedy gave it short shrift:

> If anyone else killed her... then [he] disappeared quickly and virtually without trace... There was a suggestion that a gate at the side of the house, which was shut when they left for Do-It-All was open when they returned, but that was all.

This is an astonishing misunderstanding of the available evidence. One major suspect in the case was seen by a score of people near to the scene. The 'suggestion' about the gate, as Kennedy put it, was evidence that was firm and uncontaminated and uncontradicted and utterly unambiguous, and it came from Charlotte, who was a particularly impressive witness.

The appeal court judges next decided that the confusion over the scientific evidence didn't really matter. They acknowledged that the evidence of the expert witnesses 'may have misled the jury, as it misled the judge'. However, they concluded that 'it is at least possible that the mistakes made by the experts did not have any real effect at all'.

They turned to Professor Denison's fresh evidence which they agreed, with reluctance, to accept. Having allowed it into the case, they rejected it. Kennedy argued:

> Professor Denison's model necessarily postulates a blockage... no evidence of any blockage was found.

On this basis, accordingly, they accepted the alternative evidence of Dr Hill, who had found no obstruction of the upper airways, and nothing to suggest a sudden removal of a blockage. He attributed the hyper-inflation of Billie-Jo's lungs to the fact that the small lower airways were obstructed by blood.

The judges obviously thought it highly incriminating that Siôn had made what they considered an inexplicable journey to the local DIY store ('he went without money by a circuitous route to buy an item that he did not need'); and so, they rejected the appeal.

The *Mirror* reported the outcome:

GET BACK TO JAIL
Joy as Billie-Jo killer 'dad' loses battle for freedom[26]

The *Sun* was equally delighted:

HELL IS WAITING
The aunt of murdered Billie-Jo Jenkins wept with joy yesterday as the schoolgirl's killer lost his High Court appeal, and said, 'He's going straight to hell'.[27]

In January 2000, a little more than three weeks later, Anthony Scrivener put forward two questions which he asked these same judges to certify as points of law that should be heard by the House of Lords. (This necessitated a further public hearing at the appeal courts, although this time Siôn was not allowed to attend.) The first of these concerned whether, in a situation where it was acknowledged that expert witnesses had both confused themselves and misled the judge, the conviction could be regarded as safe. Kennedy thought this point not significant enough to warrant consideration by the law lords. Scrivener's other point was much more controversial. It concerned one of the other members of the bench, Mr Justice Penry-Davey.

Friends and colleagues of Siôn from Hastings who attended the appeal became somewhat agitated when they saw Mr Justice Penry-Davey, the judge sitting on Lord Justice Kennedy's left. This was because they recognised him. David Penry-Davey was an old Hastonian – that is, an old boy of the William Parker School in Hastings, which had been Hastings Grammar School when Penry-Davey was a pupil there.

He was a well-regarded old boy and, indeed, had been guest of honour at the school's annual speech day in 1997. This was the speech day at which the school's newly-appointed headmaster was due to have presided. He had not done so, of course, because he had been arrested for murder. The speech day was instead taken by Roger Mitchell, whose comments about Siôn would naturally have interested Penry-Davey, who was on the platform with him at the time.[28]

The school, of course, was not an irrelevant issue in Siôn's case, as one of the charges against him related to how he had obtained the position of headmaster.

So what was someone with these connections doing hearing Siôn's appeal?

Anthony Scrivener raised this point with the judges who had heard the Jenkins appeal. He pointed out that Penry-Davey – who said nothing throughout, and looked as though he wished he could be someone else, anywhere else – was someone who clearly had a close association with Siôn's former school and a continuing interest in its welfare. As such, he was bound to have had preconceptions about the case, and may have shared the known view of some of the governors, which was that Siôn's conduct had badly let down the school.

Scrivener accordingly argued that the matter should now go

before the House of Lords on the basis of Penry-Davey's perceived conflict of interest.[29]

No one had expected Lord Justice Kennedy to take this application lightly. For Kennedy, someone steeped in the country's elite judicial traditions, Scrivener's application struck at the heart of all he believed about the much-vaunted independence of the judiciary. In turning it down, he almost exploded with outrage. Scrivener is no sapling, more a sturdy oak, but even so it seemed close to miraculous that he could remain upright in the full hurricane force of Lord Justice Kennedy's wrath.

So the appeal was lost and the opportunity of taking the case to the House of Lords was also lost.

The ineffectual judicial response to this case was quickly complemented by a seriously misleading journalistic one. In the immediate wake of the failed appeal, the BBC transmitted *Trail of Guilt – Under Suspicion*. The *raison d'etre* of this series was to explain to the viewer the key evidence in a case, in order to show how forensic science techniques had led to the arrest and conviction of the guilty. The programme used real-life interviews with investigating police officers and forensic scientists and blended them with dramatised reconstructions of what was purported to have happened.

There were a number of ways in which this programme about the Billie-Jo case seriously deceived the watching public. Firstly, the programme contained a dramatised reconstruction of the alleged 'fleece jacket' incident. It showed Lois and Siôn at home:

Police officer: Would you like me to run you down to your friends' now?
Lois (to officer): Yes, thank you.
Lois (to Siôn): Do you want your coat?
Siôn: No.
Lois: But it's cold out.
Siôn: I don't want it.

However, this filmed sequence was totally misleading because the location had been changed. The actual incident, when Siôn momentarily declined to put his jacket on, happened not at 48 Lower Park Road, but as he and Lois were leaving Denise Lancaster's small ground-floor flat with police officers.

Had the BBC presented this accurately, then viewers would have found the idea that this fleeting episode was indicative of Siôn's guilt puzzling, to say the least. Siôn had already been outside since the murder. He and Lois walked from their own house to Denise's with WDS Capon (as it was just a few houses up the road, they obviously weren't driven there). He was then wearing his jacket. When the momentary 'refusal' incident happened, police officers were present yet they noticed nothing surprising. So in order for this part of the prosecution case even to appear plausible, the evidence had to be distorted.

Secondly, the programme featured police officers saying, with reference to his educational qualifications:

DC Hutt character: The only thing he's got is a general certificate of education from Nonington College of physical education – the guy's a PE teacher.
DS Capon character: Why didn't the school think to check him out?
DC Hutt character: Just glad that we did.

In the context of criticising Siôn for giving inaccurate information about his educational qualifications (but saying that the police have since 'checked him out'), the BBC was giving viewers inaccurate information about Siôn's educational qualifications. Obviously the police, who advised the BBC on the programme, would have known that Siôn had an MSc in education management, just as they also knew that he had never been a PE teacher.

Thirdly, according to the programme commentary:

Before dialling 999, Siôn had called a neighbour [Denise Lancaster] for help.

238

This was untrue. Siôn called the ambulance, then called Denise to assist him, and then called the ambulance again – a natural and logical sequence of events.

Fourthly, Detective Superintendent Paine, being interviewed in the programme as himself, described how, in his view, Siôn committed the murder:

He sees red. He picks up the nearest weapon to hand – the tent spike.

Had this happened, then it may have been a good point for the prosecution. Once again, that is not what happened. The tent spike was by no means the nearest weapon to hand. Again, the evidence had to be misrepresented in order to make plausible the idea of Siôn's guilt.

Fifthly, when dealing with the bloodspots on the jacket, Adrian Wain himself said:

On the jacket we found approximately 48 tiny bloodspots on the upper chest area.
(To lab assistant): OK, so, um, spots, lower right leg, mid-chest, and both sleeves.

Viewers paying less than full attention may have thought from this that there were 48 bloodspots on Siôn's jacket. There weren't; there were 72. These were distributed as follows: 48 in the upper chest area, 21 spots on the left sleeve and 3 on the right sleeve. Once more, had the accurate information been given, then alert viewers may have wondered how Siôn, a right-handed man, could have committed the murder while getting only three spots on his right sleeve but 21 on his left sleeve. Again, this was a strong point for the defence which tended to undermine the prosecution case; again, *Trail of Guilt* failed to present the available information.

Sixthly, the programme showed DS Paine reacting with anger to Siôn's release on bail by Mr Justice Brian Smedley:

Det Supt Paine: He's a danger to the public.

The BBC knew full well that Siôn had spent fifteen months on bail without being any danger to anyone.

Seventhly, the programme put forward misinformation about hairs found in Billie-Jo's hands.

Det Supt Paine: They found a couple of blonde hairs clenched in her hand.

In fact, the hairs were described by Wain not as 'blonde' but as 'light brown'. He identified them as Billie-Jo's own.

Trail of Guilt: Under Suspicion, broadcast on 18 January 2000, in my view represented an extraordinary abrogation of the BBC's journalistic responsibilities. David and Megan Jenkins put in a complaint about it to the Broadcasting Standards Commission. This was not upheld, which was disappointing, but not too surprising in view of the fact that Siôn had been convicted of a brutal murder and had just lost his appeal. The BSC could hardly have been expected to appear to contradict or even challenge the appeal court's findings.

The Broadcasting Standards Commission also held a hearing attended by Lois Jenkins and Peter Gaimster in order to allow them to put forward their complaints about Channel 4's *Trial and Error* programme. The BSC found that neither had been treated unfairly and that "the infringement of the family's privacy on the programme was justified given the overriding public interest in the matters under investigation".

What was strikingly clear, however, was that Lois had objected strenuously, partly on the grounds of invasion of the children's privacy, when a programme was made in Siôn's favour; when a hostile programme about him was made, one that was equally invasive of her family's privacy, she raised not a word of protest.

Chapter Thirty-Two

Breaches of Confidence

I was in a sweatbox and on my way back to Wakefield prison. The appeal had failed. The pre-Christmas traffic in London was heavy and we made slow progress. On the radio, I could hear of the outcome of my appeal being reported. Bob Woffinden was being interviewed. He was saying that first appeals invariably failed but that the lawyers would now take my case to the CCRC – the Criminal Cases Review Commission. It was the first time I'd heard of the CCRC.

At the time, as the van rattled back up the motorway to Yorkshire, I was numb and beyond caring what happened to me. I knew I'd been given a life sentence, but I'd spent my time in prison so far assuming that the conviction would be overturned on appeal. I now knew that years of imprisonment lay ahead.

I had often been told by prison officers that I must accept my guilt and co-operate with the system. Even at this point, I knew I would never do that. I remembered the famous quotation: all that is necessary for the triumph of evil is that good men do nothing. I was determined not to let evil triumph. For the sake of my daughters, if for no other reason, doing nothing – and acquiescing with evil – was never an option.

When we reached Wakefield, the men were already locked up in the cells for the night. The screw on late duty who was waiting for me was enormously pleased with the result of my appeal.

'I've won fifty quid on you today,' he told me, 'so thanks for that.'

He had had a bet on the outcome.

I did not unpack my bags and spent the night wrestling with demons. For all I knew, I was now going to be locked up for the next fifteen, twenty or even thirty years.

On 12 January 2000, two days before the application to go to the House of Lords was heard, there was some movement in the case behind the scenes. Bob Woffinden arranged new solicitors for me. He took my father to Bindman and Partners in King's Cross, central London, and introduced him to Geoffrey Bindman and Neil O'May. Geoffrey had founded the firm in 1974, since when it had developed into one of the leading criminal defence practices in the country; Neil was head of the criminal division. As a result of their meeting, Bindman's agreed to take over the case, and Neil became my solicitor.

I can remember my very first meeting with him, when he came up to Wakefield to see me. I was surprised at how quickly he had grasped both the key issues and also many of the incidental details of the case. He talked about how to move the case forward, and he explained the role of the CCRC. This was an independent review body that had been set up in 1997 in the wake of a number of well-publicised miscarriages of justice. The CCRC's role was to examine cases and, if it uncovered further grounds for appeal, to refer them back to the appeal court. It was now my only avenue of hope.

Neil said we would have to decide carefully what we should focus on for the Commission. He told me that there was a long waiting list and warned that the entire process could take up to seven years. Seven years! Another seven years of me being needlessly plucked out of my daughters' childhoods! I hadn't wanted them to see me in prison but, now that it seemed I was going to be inside for years, then I wanted to arrange to see them as soon as possible.

One day, I collected my mail and walked back to my cell. I saw that there was a letter from Bindman's so I opened that first. Neil informed me that Lois had telephoned the prison and spoken about me to the head of the psychology department. The psychology head, a woman, had told Lois that I had not admitted guilt and therefore was refusing to attend 'offending behaviour' courses.

I was dumbstruck. Lois had divorced me the previous year; she was no longer my wife. Much more importantly, the prison psychology service had always told prisoners that it was bound by rigorous confidentiality rules and unfailingly abided by them. Yet here was the head of the department passing out confidential information to someone on the other end of a telephone line claiming to be my wife. Neil had only discovered this because the psychology head had then written to Lois confirming their telephone conversation. Lois had then sent a copy of this letter to her (Lois's) solicitor who had then – just to complete this incredible chain – passed it on to Neil.

When I went to make a formal complaint to the governor, he initially denied that anything untoward had happened.

'I don't want the head of the psychology department speaking to my ex-wife about what is happening in prison', I told him. 'The prison psychology service is supposed to be confidential.'

'Yes, indeed it is', replied the governor, 'and I can assure you this would never have happened.'

'Well, it did.'

'I know', he insisted, 'that the head of the psychology department would never have spoken to your ex-wife like that'.

'So what's this, then?'

I then took out the solicitor's letter and placed it in front of him. As he read it, he turned white. He did not say anything.

'How did she know it was Lois on the other end?' I asked.

'Well, she said she was your wife', he responded lamely.

'Oh, right, so it couldn't have been a tabloid then?'

Eventually, he asked if I was going to take legal action. Of course, I wasn't. I already knew that one of the problems for many appellants was that they can't keep their eye on the bigger picture. They get side-tracked into taking legal action about comparatively paltry issues like the condition of the showers or about their mail being interfered with. All that does is to expend emotional energy and take away their focus. I did not want my focus deflected from the CCRC application and overturning my conviction.

'What has been done is wrong', I said, 'but I will be happy with your assurance that it will never happen again.'

He gave me his assurance.

Shortly afterwards, I was interviewed by a woman who was collating reports for my next Sentence planning board. While I was there, she let it slip that she, too, had spoken to Lois. I did not react outwardly and merely asked a bland question about it. Unbelievably, she then told me that she had had a long conversation with Lois about my sentence and various family matters including ones concerning the children. So I simply asked how she knew it was Lois she had been speaking to. She reddened, realised she'd been caught out and quickly left.

I told the governor I wanted another meeting. This time, he made no attempt to deny what had happened. He promised that a directive would be sent to all staff instructing them that under no circumstances should they speak to Lois.

My main concern continued to be for the well-being of the children.

As I was staying in prison I applied to move into the kitchens. That's the best job in prison. You earn more money because you do more hours, including one day at weekends. Also, the quality of food in prison is very poor, so it's obviously going to be far better if you can prepare your own. However, the kitchens are like a closed shop; it reminded me of the old Fleet Street print unions, when you could only get in if your father or uncle worked there.

Fortunately, I knew Tony Ignacio. He's a good man, a very straight family man who's very savvy. I used to go to his cell, he'd make me a cup of coffee, we'd talk through the day. He is one of the men whom I trusted.

We could have a proper conversation. By 'proper', I just mean an ordinary conversation that you could have anywhere, whether in or outside prison. It took me a while to find men like that.

He was highly respected by the staff. He put in a word for me and got me a job in the kitchens. Paddy and Little Ian then taught me how to prepare basic meals. Little Ian was a chef who worked for the prison service. Paddy was a prison officer who'd worked for the service all his life. He once said to me, 'The kitchen is the best place for your bird to go quickly'.

Paddy was old school; he had a heart of gold and was much-respected. He wasn't in any way judgmental – it didn't matter what a person was in prison for. I'm happy to say that, while I was at Wakefield, he received an MBE from the Queen for services to the nation. It was richly deserved.

It was also Tony Ignacio who informed me more about blood spatter.

'I know you're innocent', he once said to me, 'because you didn't have any blood on your back, did you?'

As the attacker wields the weapon over his shoulder repeatedly, so telltale 'cast-off' bloodspots fall off on the back of his clothing. There were no 'cast-off' bloodspots on my clothing. My defence had raised the point at trial, but the prosecution had dismissed it.

I found out that there were a number of men who were diligently following my case. I went into one man's cell and he had a stack of cuttings from the papers about my case. You realise that there are many men there who know your case as well as you do. Tony wasn't of that ilk, but he did recommend me to get hold of a book on blood at crime scenes by Hugh MacDonald, the American forensic scientist. After some indecision, the prison agreed to let me have it, but only on condition that I did not show it to anyone else (on the grounds that the book contained graphic photographs of bodies and crime scenes).

Neil came to visit me again. He was still working on the submission to the CCRC. He was confident that the Crown's forensic science evidence was fundamentally flawed. However, the much more important aspect of the case concerned Annie and Charlotte. Neil had studied the reports that Lois had given the police, and advised that in his view we could argue that I had been prevented from having a fair trial. Did these actually represent what the children had said to their mother? Or if not, what did they represent?

As time had gone by, we knew two things for certain. Firstly, there was no supporting documentary evidence. Although the police had time and again asked Lois to record these remarks in writing and date them, she never had. Secondly, there was no supporting witness evidence. Nobody else had ever heard Annie or Charlotte say what, according to Lois, they had been saying. For much of their lives since the murder, the girls had been surrounded by police officers and social workers, professionals whose antagonism towards me seemed boundless, and who would have been only too delighted to be able to report comments of this kind – had they been made. Yet no one ever heard them except Lois and, in respect of a few remarks, Peter Gaimster. So should we get the girls interviewed again to find out for ourselves what the girls were saying?

Neil, ever the cautious lawyer, said that we had to think very carefully about this. Did we want to risk doing this? After all, we had no idea what the children would say. They might say something, albeit perhaps ambiguously, that could be construed to my disadvantage.

'I'm not saying you'd never get out of prison', said Neil, 'but it would be a major blow'.

Therefore, would it be more sensible to set the children aside and just focus on the science? It was a decision I had to make myself. No one could help me.

I decided that we should go ahead; we must know what the girls' actual evidence was.

OK, said Neil. Lois, however, refused permission for Bindman's to conduct interviews with Annie and Charlotte. She did, however, say that, if the Criminal Cases Review Commission felt it necessary, she would allow them to interview the girls.

I then received a letter that completely devastated me. Lois and her partner Vince were to take my daughters to live in Tasmania. I read the letter, which was from Lois's solicitor, over and over again. My feelings of helplessness reached new depths. I fell apart. I had to tell my parents but as all phone calls were recorded and monitored we could say little. I was frightened that I might never see my daughters again.

At the time, however, Lois's plans had immediate implications for my as-yet unsubmitted CCRC application and the re-interviewing of Annie and Charlotte. So the case became even more complicated. We now needed another partner at Bindman's, Katherine Gieve, a specialist in family law, to act in the case.

There were two areas of difficulty that needed sorting out: the conditions under which the children should be allowed to go to Tasmania; and, secondly, the re-interviews with Annie and Charlotte. In response to letters from Bindman's concerning the latter point, Lois replied:

> Under no circumstances will I give my permission for the children to be re-interviewed. They have sought my assurance that I will not let this happen.

She added that Annie and Charlotte were

> ... more than aware of the implications of their comments, particularly in respect of Siôn Jenkins's extensive questioning, discussion and note-taking with Annie prior to her first interview.

She then reiterated that she would not consent to any further interviews as these would be 'immeasurably detrimental' to the children's welfare.

While the legal wrangling about many issues continued, I was eventually able to arrange a visit from my daughters. All sorts of obstacles seemed to be placed in my path. Obviously, the case was not to be discussed with them in any way, although I completely understood that and, indeed, would myself have made it a precondition for the visit.

Eventually a guardian ad litem from CAFCASS[30] was appointed to find out what the girls' wishes were. This man also came up to Wakefield to see me. He was very tough. Eventually, I had to say to him, 'Why are you treating me so badly?' He replied, 'Because you've been convicted of murder.' As though that justified everything, and he could be as objectionable as he liked.

However, having made his enquiries, he did have to say, 'Well, I'm quite surprised – they all want to see you'.

At last, in December 2000, the day finally came. I walked into the visiting room to see them sitting at a far table. Charlotte saw me at once and came running into my arms. She then dissolved into floods of tears and I held her tightly. I then cuddled Annie and Esther and held them close. I was looking round for Maya and when I asked for her I was given no answer. I did not press it in front of the others.

The visit was truly wonderful. They giggled and smiled and soon Charlotte's tears abated as she kept close to me. Soon we were talking as if they were all sitting on my knee back in Hastings. The time flew past and then we had to say goodbye. I hugged each of them. I was full of a father's love and wish to protect them and choked with sadness that many of their normal freedoms were now being curtailed by police and social workers. We had not been able to have the visit just to ourselves; a social worker was with them as a chaperone.

In view of Lois's attitude regarding both re-interviews with Annie and Charlotte, and my being able to retain any paternal rights at all, it soon became clear that there was no alternative to going before a judge again. So once again (this time without any publicity) I found myself sitting in a London court – this time, the family court in Holborn.

The courtroom was very small. Lois was with Vince Ives. They were sitting directly behind me. I could hear their repartee as they sat and joked together; they could have been a young couple flirting on a park bench. I was in front, chained to security officers, one each side of me. I was dressed in dirty prison clothing and was unshaven; at Pentonville prison, where I had been put overnight, they had as usual put me in the Block and hadn't allowed me to shave or to change.

I was at court because I wanted to establish my rights to have contact with my children. For me to be there in that state, and to have Lois and Ives laughing behind me, was difficult and upsetting. Until then, I'd always tried to avoid being even privately critical of Lois, but I felt her actions that day were immature and cruel.

The hearing went in my favour. My barrister made a few specific requests: that the girls should visit me once a year; that I should be kept up to date about their schooling and receive regular school reports; that I should receive regular photographs of them; and that I should also have an up-to-date address so that I could write to them. The judge, saying that all these were perfectly reasonable, acceded to everything. Lois agreed to everything and promised to comply. It was on that basis that she was allowed to take the children out of the country to Tasmania.

As it turned out, after they went to Tasmania, I never received a single school report or school photograph. I did have their first address, but they soon moved and Lois never provided the new one. She just ignored all the undertakings she gave to the family court.

The submission for the CCRC was ready. Neil came to see me again and we had a final conversation about our strategy. Naturally, he wrote to me setting out and confirming all the details of our conversation. The re-interviewing of the girls would be the central point of the CCRC application.

Although all personal letters in and out of prison are censored, prisoners' correspondence to and from the courts and with their own lawyers is confidential and is protected by prison Rule 39. Lawyers mark their correspondence accordingly so that it reaches their clients directly.

From early on in my prison term, I had become aware that legal letters to me had been opened and resealed. The prison staff were monitoring my correspondence; and, in doing so, were acting in contravention of supposedly strict Home Office regulations. Sometimes, so confident were the staff that they could act with impunity, they didn't even bother to reseal them and try to pretend that there had been no interference. When I queried this, I was told that it was a mistake, and that it wouldn't happen again.

On one occasion, an officer had handed me Rule 39 correspondence and insisted that I open the envelope in front of him. I refused. This officer just ranted at me and refused to let me have it. Finally, I told him that I wouldn't take it.

'You keep it then', I said to him. 'This is legal correspondence and I am not opening it in front of you. My understanding is that only one man here can insist that that letter is opened, and that is the governor, and even then he has to give me good reasons.'

The officer then made a phone call and I was given it. But these very minor victories had to be set alongside the continuing heavy defeats, because this problem persisted throughout my imprisonment.

It was now to take a dramatic and sinister turn. No sooner had Neil and I worked out our strategy for the CCRC, and the submission been sent to them, than a story appeared in the *Sun*:

Exclusive

MY GIRLS CAN CLEAR ME OF BILLIE-JO RAP

Killer foster dad's latest claim

Murderer Siôn Jenkins wants two of his daughters to help his bid to be cleared of killing foster child Billie-Jo.

Jenkins has asked Annie, 16 and Charlotte, 15, to give evidence on video about what happened on the day Billie-Jo was bludgeoned to death.

The ex-deputy head, who has already lost one appeal, is hoping their testimony will persuade the Criminal Cases Review Commission to examine the case.

An insider at Wakefield prison, where Jenkins is held, said, 'The girls made statements and Jenkins claims what they said means he could not have committed the murder.

'He is consumed by trying to prove his innocence.'

(The *Sun*, 16 April 2001)

Although the *Sun* had not grasped the essential issues, the overall thrust of its story was obviously correct. Equally obviously, the publication of material like this in the national press was potentially disastrous.[31]

In fact, the whole issue was so sensitive that Neil and I had discussed it only between ourselves, and I had certainly not mentioned it to anyone else. Now, confidential correspondence between me and my lawyers was being passed by corrupt prison staff directly to the *Sun*. As we well knew, this was the police and prison officers' paper of choice for leaked information, as they paid more than their rivals. Clearly, no one involved in this had had the slightest interest in whether it would harm my chances of proving my innocence. (Indeed, at one stage it looked as though this might, because Lois was to put it forward as an additional reason why the girls should not be re-interviewed.)

When the submission arrived, the CCRC assigned a caseworker to my case. She was Dawn Butler. Although I was never to meet her, I had received uniformly favourable reports from all those who had met her. Neil informed her as soon as he heard of Lois's decision to leave the country, and Dawn then quickly made sure that the CCRC prioritised my case (which enabled me to jump the queue, although I doubt whether this was Lois's intention.) The Commission then asked Lois for permission to interview the children. She refused.

The case went back to the courts. Lois then agreed again to allow the interviews to take place. Once the hearing was out of the way, she changed her mind and again refused permission, arguing that any such interviews would 'present [Annie and Charlotte] with an emotional pressure which is both intolerable and against their welfare'.

There was another hearing, before Dame Elizabeth Butler-Sloss, the highly-respected President of the Family Division. On 8 May 2001, she made an order allowing the CCRC to interview Annie and Charlotte. Nevertheless, Lois continued to resist for many months. She complained about the fact that my case had been prioritised, and brought in her local MP to try to intervene on her behalf. Her solicitors wrote to the CCRC to say that Lois 'believes the children do not want to be interviewed by anybody... and that would extend to being interviewed about being interviewed'. The CCRC naturally asked whether Lois was now refusing to comply with the court order.

There was yet another hearing. Lois tried all she could to prevent the interviews taking place. She said that Annie and Charlotte 'have said to me they do not want to be interviewed, they want to be left alone' and that 'I regret having gone along with the idea of the CCRC interviewing the girls'. She also argued that the CCRC's request was a breach of Article 8 of the Human Rights Convention, the right to family life. At this time, too, she also referred to the *Sun* report, saying that media attention like that was 'pressurising the girls, the pressure being that they have the power to clear their father'.

Another hearing was scheduled for January 2002. Finally, even Lois had to accept that, legally, she didn't have a leg to stand on. The hearing was uncontested. Lois said, 'I do give leave for them to be interviewed formally, if they consent to do so'.

So, after the hearing, the children, finally, were asked directly: did they wish to be interviewed?

Yes, they said. They did want to be interviewed.

As much as for myself, I was relieved for them. There was so much that hadn't been looked at carefully and, whatever was going to happen, it was right that everything came out. I knew that Charlotte, from the very beginning, had wanted to give evidence. Her point was, I was there, I know what happened – why have these other people been called and not me? So I was pleased for them that they would now have the chance to rid themselves of this burden; and that their evidence should at last be heard.

Chapter Thirty-Three

Annie and Charlotte
Re-interviewed

Annie and Charlotte were re-interviewed on Tuesday, 5 February 2002. This time, Annie went first. She asked not to appear in vision and so the camera focused on the main interviewer. Although the interviews were again conducted at Battle police station, this time they were undertaken by officers from an outside force, Kent Police, brought in by the Criminal Cases Review Commission. A representative from CAFCASS sat in on the interviews. The CCRC oversaw the interviews but did not participate or intervene in any way.

Despite the fact that there were three separate organisations involved, the standard of interviewing was as inept as it had been the previous times the girls had been interviewed. Since, as before, those conducting the interviews were fully trained, this merely bears out the point that the fault lies entirely with the abysmal training processes and that blame should not be attached to the interviewers.

Even though the CCRC had provided the interviewing team with 'a volume of material' and also the videos of the original interviews, it was difficult to discern any planned approach to the interviews.

On this occasion, proper preparation was even more of a fundamental requirement than usual. This was because the interviews themselves were a uniquely tricky assignment. The girls might naturally have assumed that officers wanted them to go over their evidence again. That, however, was not the purpose of the interviews.

They had been set up in order to establish whether there had been an abuse of process in the case. The content of the girls' original video interviews was, from the defence point of view, entirely satisfactory. The girls were vital alibi witnesses and, in all normal circumstances, would automatically have been called to give evidence. However, because Lois had subsequently reported changes in the girls' evidence to police, they had not been. She then compounded the difficulty by refusing the defence access to her daughters. Siôn's lawyers had no way of knowing what the girls' evidence actually was; and no barrister can call witnesses blind. So had the defence been unfairly deprived of its key witnesses? Had the course of justice been perverted?

These were the issues that needed to be resolved. Consequently, the purpose of the re-interviews was not to ask the girls to reiterate their evidence about what happened on the day of the murder; the purpose was to establish whether or not they had actually told their mother what the mother had reported to police that they had told her.

However, once the dialogue started, it was obviously going to be impractical to maintain a demarcation line between the latter and the former purpose; obviously, what Lois said the girls told her concerned what had happened on the day of the murder.

So, in these probably unique circumstances, interviewing the girls necessitated a sophisticated and rigorously planned approach. However, nothing in what was to follow could be described either as pre-planned or as sophisticated. The interviewers just tried to muddle through.

Here's what happens as they struggle to explain the exact purpose of the interview to Annie:

We're not going to ask you anything specifically about what happened on the 16th, sorry on the 15th, and… when you were interviewed…

Annie and Charlotte Re-interviewed

The thing we would ask you is that any answers you give us is from what you actually remember, as happening when Billie-Jo died, alright?

Wrong, already. Annie should be casting her mind back not to the day of the murder but to the alleged conversations with her mother over the following months. The interviewers haven't asked a single question yet, and already they themselves are muddling the purpose of the interview.

These are extracts from what follows:

I: When Mum asked you what mood was he in, you said a bit of a funny mood?
A: Do I have to try and remember the conversation, or?
I: I think [what] we're after is whether what your mum has reported back is accurate... what you really need to do is try sort of imagine yourself back there... and just try and think what was going on at that time, who you was talking to and generally what the conversation was about.
All we're trying is to find out from you if you remember saying that. And if what is reported back is right, but likewise if you don't remember saying them, we're not asking you to fill in gaps...
CAFCASS: There's a third alternative, which is that you didn't actually say it.... Do you see, there's three alternatives. You didn't say it, you did say it, and you remember it, or you can't remember... .

I: Do you remember saying that he was in a bit of a funny mood?
A: No.
I: Annie, is it that you don't remember or you didn't say it? Is it that you don't remember the conversation at all?
A: I don't remember saying it at all.

I: This is the next day... you'll have to bear with me a little bit, it's quite a lot I'm just trying to scan.

A: That I said to my Mum again?

I: Yes... All of these are comments that you've made to your Mum.

A: Oh, right.

CAFCASS: Well, you may have made to your Mum or you may not, whether you remember making them or not, isn't it?...

I: We're trying to make this as un-confusing as possible, but actually this is becoming more confusing.

CAFCASS: You just say whether you remember the event and whether you remember telling your Mum about it. Sometimes you might remember the event and you might not remember telling your Mum or you might not remember the event, or, you know, any combination really.

The interviews, which were intended to be un-confusing, turned out to be confusing. It is almost unbelievable that the interviewers appeared to be striving to work out the interviewing format as they go along. As a result, they never are able to establish how they should be framing the questions. If there is uncertainty over what the question is, then how can the answers have the necessary precision? The contributions from the CAFCASS representative make it clear that he is trying to disperse the clouds of confusion, although in the end he too weakly succumbs to nebulousness: '... or, you know, any combination really'.

What should have happened is that, firstly, the interviewers should have set out all of Lois's assertions or allegations separately and in a clear and consistent form. They should then have put each one to the children, and asked these questions in relation to each:

1. *Do you remember saying that to your Mum?*

2. *Whether or not you remember saying it, do you think you might have said it?*

3. *Whether or not you might have said it, is the statement, to the best of your knowledge, true or not true?*

The questioning needed to be as schematic as that, to enable precise answers to be obtained. Instead, the whole thing is chaotic.

Because of the manner of the questioning, the impression is frequently created that the assertions have actually happened. Here's one important passage:

> Q: [Annie] went on to say that after leaving the house to continue washing the car she attempted to get back in, but Siôn wouldn't let her?
> A: I don't remember that.
> CAFCASS: You don't remember the event or you don't remember saying it?
> A: I just don't remember, I don't remember either.
> Q: So you don't remember your Dad not letting you back in?
> A: No.
> Q: And you don't remember telling Mum?
> A: That didn't... that didn't happen though...

Annie's response to this assertion is that she doesn't remember it – one interpretation of which is that it never happened. The questioning, however, leads her down an opposite path – the inference being that it did happen, but that Annie doesn't remember it ('So you don't remember your Dad not letting you back in?'). It is Annie herself, without any assistance from the interviewers, who has to go back to her original point and make it clear: 'that didn't happen though'.

Even aside from the form of the questioning, there are indications that the attitude of the interviewing officers is not right. In Annie's interview, the interviewer commented:

> Q: Where Mum, *quite rightly*, was saying certain things to the police in relation to conversations she'd had with yourself

> [italics added]

Similarly, in the interview with Charlotte that followed, the officer said:

Q: Your mum [has] had a conversation with you and during that conversation you've made certain comments and your Mum has *quite rightly* told the policeman and he's made a note of it

[italics added]

The purpose of these interviews was to find out whether the comments had been made in the first place. In telling the children that Lois had behaved in these instances 'quite rightly', the officers who were supposed to be obtaining the evidence appeared to have already reached their own conclusions.

Nevertheless, out of the chaos and confusion, illumination does emerge. Did Annie actually say what her mother reported her as saying? Time and time again, Annie responds: No, she didn't say that to her mother:

Q:… Annie couldn't remember if she waved to Billie when she said or earlier?…
A: I don't think I did say that actually. I was quite sure when that happened.

Q: Do you remember saying that he was in a bit of a funny mood?
A: No… I don't remember saying it at all.

Q: Annie can remember Billie screaming at her basically they had both argued…
A: I don't remember thinking that, I don't remember that happening

Q: Annie has said Siôn was cross with Billie… You don't remember your Dad being cross with Billie?
A: No.

Q: Annie has stated… Siôn and Billie-Jo had an argument earlier that day.

Annie and Charlotte Re-interviewed

A: I said that on the day?

Q: This is your mum telling the police on the 26th July...

A: No... I know I didn't say that to my Mum.

Q: Annie has tried three times to come back into the house but was refused entry by Siôn. This was when Annie was cleaning the Opel car?

A: I don't remember it.

CAFCASS: Don't remember it as an incident?

A: No, I don't remember it at all.

Q: So you don't remember it as happening?

A: No, and I don't remember discussing it with anyone.

Q: Annie stated that she felt this was because Siôn felt guilty about allowing Billie-Jo to do the painting in preference to herself?

A: Don't remember it at all.

Q: Remember saying anything like that to Mum?

A: No.

Q She stated that Billie-Jo had manipulated Siôn in this way?

A: No, don't remember that at all.

Q: Did you remember feeling that?

A: No.

Q: She also feels that is why Siôn left her alone at home when she went with him to pick up Lottie from the clarinet lesson?

A: Don't remember it at all.

Q: This being a lesson to Billie-Jo and to enable him to spend more time with Annie?

A: Don't remember.

Q: Do you remember saying those things to your mum?

A: No.

Q: She was using the chamois to clean the MG... she stated that Siôn came running down the steps and told both her and Lottie to get into the car.

259

A: I don't remember that happening, I don't actually know what that thing is.

Q: Chamois?… It's one of those leather cloths.

A: Oh, right. I don't remember that at all.

Q: She stated that they drove round the park a couple of times and that neither her nor Lottie were aware of what was happening or why… Do you remember saying that to Mum?

A: No.

Q: Siôn left in such a hurry he didn't have time to close [the door] properly?

A: I don't remember the door being open, I don't remember that at all.

Q: And do you remember saying that to mum?

A: No.

Q: So you don't remember it happening and you don't remember saying it to Mum?

A: No.

Q: Siôn took Annie to the rear of the dining room at the Gaimsters' and said to her, 'We'll be alright, we were together, weren't we, Annie?'… It is actually quoted here: 'We'll be alright, we were together, weren't we, Annie?'

A: I don't remember him, don't remember him saying that.

Q: She discussed the fact with Lois that Siôn preferred Billie-Jo to herself and the fact that Billie-Jo flirted with Siôn?

A: Don't ever remember saying that.

Q: OK, is that something, Annie, that you felt?

A: No, not at all.

Lois told police that Annie had told her of 'an entry in Billie-Jo's Forever Friends diary stating that Siôn has hit her'. Annie was asked about this.

A: I remember her diary but I don't remember ever thinking that there was [such] a thing in there.

Q: Did you ever see that entry?

A: No

CAFCASS: Did you know that entry was in the diary?

A: No

Again, here, the question from the CAFCASS representative is dangerous in that it appears to be predicated on the basis that there was such an entry. In fact, there wasn't.

There is one further passage:

Q: Siôn suddenly came running down with a peculiar look in his eyes and then drove the girls off to Do-It-All after driving round the park in a state of disorientation?

A: Don't remember that.

Q: Don't remember saying that?

A: No.

Q: To Mum?

A: No.

Q: Do you remember Dad running down with a peculiar look in his eyes?

A: No.

Q: Do you remember him driving round the park in a state of disorientation?

A: No.

Towards the end, Annie says, in bewilderment:

A: All these things, my mum, like, reported back to police?

Shortly afterwards, she goes to the toilet and then refuses to return to complete the interview.

Charlotte, who is happy to be in vision for her interview, is then questioned. The outcome is broadly the same, as she says:

I don't remember any of these discussions…

… No, I don't remember telling my Mum these things …

Q: Lottie then said to her mum, then I just knew?
A: I don't remember saying that.
Q: Don't remember saying that?
A: No, I don't remember anything to do with that.

Q: She knew her Dad had killed Billie but knows he didn't do it on purpose…
A: Don't remember saying that.
Q: Is that a thought you had at the time?
A: No, I don't think so, no.
Q: And you don't remember speaking to Mum about that?
A: No.

There were several reasons why Lois's reports should have raised questions. Firstly, her accounts contradicted the girls' own first-hand accounts; yet there was no reason to suppose that their original testimony was flawed or compromised in any way.

Secondly, they contained internal contradictions. According to the 16 July report, Lois said that 'Annie actually witnessed Siôn kick Billie-Jo'; according to the 27 November report, Lois said that Annie herself did not witness this.

Thirdly, Lois's fresh account of what, she claimed, Annie had said contained expressions that did not sound as if they were part of Annie's vocabulary, for example 'manipulated' or 'disorientated', or 'chamois' leather. A particularly interesting aspect of 'chamois' is that it wasn't in Siôn's vocabulary either. He never used the term and had always referred to 'leather'. The defence carried out an analysis of all the family's statements; the only one in the family who used the word 'chamois' was Lois herself.

Fourthly, virtually all of Lois's reports concerned alleged conversations, for which supporting evidence was obviously going to be non-existent. However, there were occasions when it seemed that supporting evidence would be available (for example, in the reference to Billie-Jo's Forever Friends diary); on these occasions, the documents did not support what Lois had said.

Fifthly, the reports contained illogical elements. According to Lois, Charlotte said that when she realised that her father had not taken any money with him – 'then I just knew'. But, whether intuitively or not, Charlotte can't have known anything at that stage; they hadn't found Billie-Jo. The idea that because her father had forgotten to take money with him on a shopping trip, Charlotte 'just knew' that he had murdered her sister (which is the inference) makes no sense at all.

In addition to these questions could now be added the vital one: the children had disowned them. They were nothing to do with us; these remarks may have been attributed to us, but we did not say them.

Yet it was Lois's reports that had not only led directly to the abuse of process and therefore the unfair trial in the first place, but had also been partially responsible for the case being turned down at appeal by Lord Justice Kennedy.

In the judgment, he said that he thought the 4 March report that 'Annie tried to get into the house when cleaning, and the appellant would not let her in' was 'of particular significance'.

The witness herself had now been asked about this. Had it happened? Annie had been perfectly clear: '… that didn't happen though… '

Both the trial and the appeal court judgment had been heard on the basis of seriously incorrect information.

These new interviews also threw an intriguing fresh light on the original ones. Firstly, Annie is adamant that her original account was complete and accurate. She was asked, 'Was there anything else she remembered afterwards?' She responded, 'No, there wasn't'.

Secondly, she objected – and who could blame her? – to the patronising way in which those interviews had been conducted:

> I kind of knew exactly what was going on but... even though I was really young, they were treating us like childs [sic]. I just wanted to say, look, I know what's happening, 'cos at my first interview like, the questions they were asking, I knew what they were getting at.

Thirdly, because the girls' evidence had provided an all but unassailable defence for Siôn, the Crown's only line of attack had been to argue that Siôn had coached or influenced Annie (or as the police had put it, using their own psychobabble: 'Annie has had her own thoughts reconstructed by Siôn').

Now, Annie is asked who she had spoken to about the events of that day:

> A: I think I spoke to my Mum about it too [as well as Charlotte].
> Q: Who was the main person you felt you could talk to [about] it?
> A: My Mum.

There were two important pieces of evidence that Lois claimed came from Annie, but which Annie saw very differently. Lois reported that she, Annie, had seen Siôn kick Billie-Jo during the 1996 holiday in France. Annie commented:

> My Mum used to bring that up quite a lot... I remember my mum bringing that up quite a few times, that, like, event.

Lois also suggested that Annie regarded it as unusual for Billie-Jo to be left in the house on her own. Annie responded:

> A: No, I've never really thought it was unusual.
> Q: Right.
> A: I remember my Mum saying to me once that it was unusual, but I don't remember ever saying it, like, I think I said it was unusual.

So if anyone was likely to be influencing Annie, it was not Siôn; it was her mother.

Charlotte's interview is much briefer, but even so she takes the opportunity to reiterate her main point about the gate from her original interview:

> I remember when we came back, remembering it was open because… I remember seeing the rabbit hutches which were down the end.

Poor Charlotte. She had a gilt-edged piece of evidence. It was wonderfully observant of her to have noticed such a vital piece of evidence; in normal circumstances, she would have been a star witness. She kept mentioning her evidence at every opportunity. But it was inconvenient evidence; so the authorities kept ignoring her.

Both girls had provided robust answers. They proved that when the jury had convicted at trial, and the judges had turned down the appeal, both courts had been seriously misled. At the second and third trials, defence lawyers would take tactical decisions not to introduce arguments about the feeble quality of the interviewing, on the grounds that this might merely confuse the juries. They felt that the girls' responses were sufficiently clear and should stand without being possibly tarnished by other considerations.

In another respect, the interviewing did affect the progress of the case. Had it been conducted rigorously, there would have been no possible room for dispute and, in all probability, no prospect of further trials. Afterwards, however, there remained isolated pockets of ambiguity that the prosecution could retreat to. Had the standard of interviewing been more rigorous, the barrenness of the prosecution's landscape would have been exposed; there would have been no hiding place.

Chapter Thirty-Four
Wakefield

The main enemy for most prisoners is not the bullying or the routine wing violence, as bad as some of those incidents are; or the unrelenting emotional pressure on the prisoner; or the knowledge that the staff are there to undermine you and break your spirit. The real fight is to retain your determination to keep going rather than give up.

In waging this battle in prison, the principle enemy is the corrosive monotony. Unfortunately, it's insidious because many men simply don't realise what's happening to them.

Everything is so institutionalised that you have to fight to keep your mind alert. For a number of men, including myself, it was important to get up before unlock at 8.00am. I'd rise at about 6.30, and then spend some time reading. I had a ritual that I'd also clean my cell – I did the floor with a damp rag and then went through all the surfaces. I didn't do it because I needed to keep the cell clean but because I needed to have some kind of discipline that I imposed on myself, that was nothing to do with the prison. Similarly, there were moments dotted throughout the week when I could create my own routine. I'd go for exercise, or to the library, or listen to radio programmes like Marcel Berlins' *Law in Action*.[32]

Some men steeped themselves in the law and often ended up knowing more about it than some lawyers. They had built their own cardboard shelves and had their Lever Arch files arranged around the cell. So they had walls covered in legal papers – judgments, copies of Archbold, copies of the *Times* law reports, other photocopied articles and reports. Some men specialised in certain areas, like matrimonial matters and the custody of children; other men knew about the forensic science aspects of criminal investigations. Men tended to know where the expert advice was within the prison. Sometimes I could go to someone's cell, sit down and have a coffee, and it would be just like being in the average solicitor's grubby office, except that there would be a toilet at the back of the room.

These men were keeping themselves mentally alert; and the prison didn't like it. They'd think of excuses to disrupt them – telling them, for example, that all their laboriously assembled paperwork had to be removed because it was a fire hazard.

The prison staff encourage dependence on television. On the one hand, it means the staff have something to threaten to take away from them; on the other hand, if men are watching television, they're not thinking, they're not causing trouble, and they're certainly not fighting their case. Television is easily the cheapest way of ensuring that the prison population is sedated.

In a maximum security prison, your letters are censored, your telephone calls are recorded, as is who comes to visit you, and how you interacted with prisoners or staff – there wasn't anything that you could do that wasn't monitored. The books you order from the library are also recorded. If any man ordered pornography (and the staff would have a very broad definition of what constituted pornography) that would be noted.

The psychology department would place certain books in the library specifically to find out who took them out. These would be books about sex or violence. They deliberately put Vladimir Nabokov's *Lolita* in there.

If you took it out, that would be noted down and it would go on your file. So if you knew who Humbert Humbert was, it would reduce your chances of being released.[33]

Sometimes there would be lock-downs, when all prisoners would be locked in their cells, perhaps for up to two to three days while all the cells were searched. Obviously, there was no prison work during that period. Extra staff were drafted in from outside, and men's meals would be delivered to their cells. All prisoners had a prop sheet, which listed their possessions. Prison rules prohibited anything being loaned or borrowed. Anything that a prisoner wasn't allowed to have, or that wasn't on his prop sheet, would be confiscated. Of course, at such times, items would be thrown out of the windows or flushed down the toilets.

The searches would be conducted by the DST (dedicated search team), who arrived in heavy black boots and black reinforced clothing and were regarded as the SS of the prison service. While lock-downs happened only rarely, individual cells were regularly being – to use the prison jargon – 'spun'. The usual aim was to disrupt and dishearten the prisoner. When I went back after searches, the cell would be a complete mess: the mattress would be on the floor, pictures had been taken off the walls, things thrown down, cupboards turned out.

Because my cell was spun so often, I had regular arguments about it with governors. I was worried that the aim was to gain access to my legal papers so that information could be either passed to the police or leaked to the media. After legal correspondence about my CCRC submission had appeared in the *Sun*, I was especially wary.

Eventually, I simply used to take all my legal papers out with me. I'd bundle everything all up, every last piece of paper, and made sure they were all bagged and sealed with security ties. It was all a massive inconvenience, and an extraordinary waste of time, but it occurred on a regular basis.

All prisoners had to suffer moments like this. In theory, they had redress, but if you wanted to go outside the prison staff, to the Board of Visitors or the prison ombudsman, there were so many stages to get through that many men just couldn't be bothered. They couldn't invest that much emotional energy in it; they knew that it simply wasn't worth complaining – you had to keep your eyes on the bigger picture.

I became the wing rep. This meant, for example, that I met with the company who supplied the prison canteen and shop and gave them feedback and offered suggestions. There were also meetings with governors to discuss the needs and requests of prisoners. Men would raise specific concerns – the showers were too cold; there should be more exercise opportunities in the summer; more than twelve books should be allowed in a cell.

Throughout my years at Wakefield the pressure placed on me by the prison psychology staff was constant. My sentence planning boards, which I stopped going to, were just horrendous. There are twelve people sitting at a table facing you, telling you you're never going to be released until you admit guilt.

They have many ways of exerting pressure:

'Jenkins, you'd like more exercise opportunities? Do some offending behaviour courses.'

'Jenkins, you get three visits? You could have five, if you start doing offending behaviour courses.'

I was immovable so, finally, they played what they thought was their ace.

'If you don't accept guilt', they said, 'you'll lose your television.'

'That's fine', I said, 'I don't have one anymore.'

When I gave up my television, the staff refused to take it off me. It just sat there in the cell. Eventually, I took it along to the screws' office and said, 'Here, I don't want this'.

Afterwards, whenever probation or psychology staff came to talk with me, they'd always say:

'Siôn, why don't you take you television back? There's so much you'd enjoy'.

Finally, in the summer of 2004, when I knew I was going to appeal anyway, I did take it back so that I could watch Wimbledon.

The other times when things were often difficult for me in Wakefield were when I was in the press. Often what is reported in the tabloids had a direct effect in prison. The press has a knack of unsettling people. In the summer, when the prison is hot and tempers are frayed, if there were unpleasant allegations in the press, there would be trouble. Prisoners love the notoriety of getting their name in the papers. If they can rediscover the excitement of that transient fame by attacking a fellow prisoner, especially one who's fair game because he's already been castigated by the media, they will.

There were many occasions when I'd be featured in some newspaper. I'd be stopped by a governor who'd say, for example, 'Siôn, you're in the *News of the World* today. Do you want it stopped?'

I'd always let it go out, on the basis that if the staff wanted to stop it, it was probably a positive report. When I was in the press and it was bad (and there was a consequent risk that I would be attacked), they were perfectly happy for it to be distributed; but if there was a favourable article about me, they'd try to persuade me to stop it. All I can say is that although the staff attitudes were perverse, they were consistent in their perversity.

I tried to view it all philosophically. I knew if there was a good article one week, there would be a bad one the following week. So I never became too despondent when there was a bad article or too elated when there was a good one.

Occasionally, you could win over individual members of staff. One day, a senior officer (a man who's now governor grade) spoke to me privately.

'I've just been to visit my parents', he said. 'I was sitting by the fire with my father and he asked if you were here at Wakefield. He said he thought you were innocent.

'I think you're innocent too. I just wanted to wish you all the best.'

Such moments, however, were rare.

Christmas in prison continued to be the saddest time for everyone. A lot of men could only get through Christmas if they were in a stupor –

through drugs or alcohol (the hooch that prisoners made on the wing). Prisoners were not allowed presents under any circumstances. Even men serving twenty- or thirty-year tariffs were not allowed to have anything sent in. This made it very hard for their relatives.

Fortunately, thanks to the continuing publicity and my website informing everyone about the case, I always received hundreds of Christmas cards from loyal supporters. One Christmas Eve, a prisoner named Pat came to the cell to ask if he could borrow just one of mine. Prisoners like Pat received no Christmas cards at all.

I had anticipated a second visit from my daughters before they went abroad, but Lois objected and I did not see them. I was grief-stricken because I thought I might never see them again. Annie wrote to tell me exactly when they were leaving, and on the day they left the country I felt as if my limbs were being amputated.

Gill Ball, Lois's mother, then sent me the cruellest letter I have ever received in my life. She wrote to say that she had seen Lois, Vince and the girls off to Tasmania. They were such a lovely family together, she commented. She asked me, Why didn't I just confess and leave them alone?

No doubt her efforts would have been applauded by the prison psychology service.

Chapter Thirty-Five

Despair, Elation and Tragedy

On 27 May 2002, over the wing landing phone, my father broke the news to me that my grandmother had died. Afterwards, I needed to be by myself. I had spent many happy times with her when I was growing up. After my conviction, and despite her age (she was ninety-two when she died), she had always been an indomitable supporter. She sent in whatever she could – cards, letters and even money – to encourage me to remain resolute. One of my abiding regrets is that I was never able to see her again after my conviction.

The next day I asked one of the governors whether it would be possible for me to attend the funeral at Strata Florida Abbey in mid-Wales.

'You're too high-profile', he replied, 'for that to be allowed'.

I pursued the matter, and I was then told that if the prison did permit me to attend I would have to be chained to two prison officers throughout the service. The governor also took the opportunity to tell me (whether it was true or not, I don't know) that the press had already been enquiring at the prison about whether I would be going to the funeral.

For two days, I deliberated. Eventually, I reached the only possible conclusion: that my attendance in handcuffs would only create more upset and distress, and that the day itself would be marred and overshadowed. My mere attendance would lead to a disruptive press presence. When I finally had to acknowledge to myself that I could not go, I felt renewed anger for those I felt had betrayed me and those whose actions had brought such grief on our family.

At moments of greatest despair like these, I would take out the photographs of my daughters and push myself to stay focused and sane.

Eventually, I was able to see for myself the transcripts of the girls' interviews with Kent police and the CCRC. I shut the door, sat down at the small desk and read through them slowly and carefully. It took me about an hour. By the end, I knew the full extent of what Lois had done. Even though I'd been to some extent prepared for what was to come, the emotional shock was still overwhelming.

Then, on 9 February 2003, Lois launched another public attack on me, this time in the *Sunday Times*. I could discern no overriding reason why the article needed to be published at this juncture but it certainly risked inhibiting my chances of success with the CCRC by smearing me publicly again.

There followed more months of waiting.

At lunchtime on Monday, 12 May, I was in the kitchens when two prison officers came in and said it was important for me to call my solicitor.

I knew there could be only one possible reason why it was important to phone Neil. I asked the other lads to cover for me while I raced to the phone.

Once there, I was too nervous to do it.

After a while, I decided to phone my father. If it was bad news, I wanted him to break it to me. I phoned, and before I could ask anything I heard the news that brought a shiver to my spine and tears to my eyes.

'You've been referred back to appeal', he said.

An hour later, my door was opened. I stepped out to be met by other men coming to congratulate me. There was no jealousy (even though what had happened to me was exactly what many wished would happen to them). They were very gracious in their congratulations. Appeal court, here I come again.

I returned to my afternoon stint in the kitchens with uplifted spirits. Shortly afterwards, I was called for what everyone called a piss test. This was my fourth in a short space of time. I knew that the selection of prisoners for urine drug tests was 'random', and I was aware that this 'random' selection of prisoners routinely included me because the prison knew that the results would be negative. Accordingly, this would help to improve their statistics on prisoners' drug-taking. I gave a sample of urine, and the prison officer winked mischievously at me as I asked how it was that they so rarely tested the actual drug-takers.

When the elation over my referral to appeal had passed, I did wonder whether Lois's *Sunday Times* article had been instrumental in delaying my referral back to the appeal court. After all, I was referred to appeal in May 2003 on the basis of evidence that had been in the CCRC's possession since February 2002. However, I also knew that Dawn Butler, my caseworker at the CCRC, had been diagnosed with cancer and was seriously ill.

Then, in July, I had my second, and final, visit from my daughters. They had flown back from Tasmania for a brief stay. It was a key moment in my life. As I looked forward to their visit, I wondered how they might have changed. Would Maya even remember me? I had last seen her when she was seven. Now, she was thirteen. I had missed half her lifetime.

I can still feel the anxiety I felt as I walked towards the visiting room. I walked in and there they were: Charlotte, Esther and Maya. (But Annie wasn't there, which was so disappointing; I never found out why.) All three were now young women. Charlotte was upset again. She just couldn't stop crying. She didn't stop for the whole visit; she found the experience so very upsetting. Because she was crying so much, and because of what I felt for her, it took me all my willpower not to cry myself.

With the exception of Charlotte's appearance at the appeal court, that was the last time I saw them.

Despair, Elation and Tragedy

As I have explained, it had been impossible for me to have their photographs on display. Once I knew I was going back to the Court of Appeal, however, one of the first things I did was to put their pictures up again.

One of the few comforts I was allowed in prison was *Classic FM* magazine, which my brother had arranged to be sent to me every month. I was especially grateful because it always came with a free CD and so I was able to build up a small music collection. One month, friends wrote in to the station's Saturday request programme and asked if a piece of music could be played for me. The management at Classic FM declined to do so, on the grounds that they didn't play requests for convicted murderers.

After all that had happened to me, this seemed almost an injustice too far for some of my supporters. Over the next few days, they made representations and, to its credit, the station changed its policy. The following Saturday, a request was played for me.

What made this extraordinary, even uncanny, was that on the same programme they also played a request for Dawn Butler from her husband. He referred to all her hard work for the Commission and sent her his best wishes for a speedy recovery.

Tragically, however, she did not recover and she died, at the age of forty-four, in March 2005. I know of many people who believed that this was a great loss to criminal justice processes in this country; I certainly know that I have good reason to be eternally grateful to her.

Chapter Thirty-Six
Lois's Third Statement

Siôn had now been granted what most prisoners long for: a second crack at the appeal court. First appeals are almost invariably futile; at that stage, the Court of Appeal is disinclined to set aside the jury's verdict. A second appeal is altogether a different prospect.

Having carried out a thorough analysis of the evidence and accordingly referred a case back for a second appeal, the CCRC produces what is known as the statement of reasons. The statement in this instance was powerfully argued and made it clear that the case had been referred back primarily because of the re-interviews of the children. In the Commission's view, these constituted:

> ... new evidence, not before the jury, that suggests that Mr Jenkins could not have committed the murder.

The Commission pointed out that the girls were 'crucial alibi witnesses'. Yet, the defence had been unfairly deprived of their evidence at trial because of Lois's reports. The Crown Prosecution Service had deliberately drawn this material to the attention of the defence. The material had then 'mistakenly led the defence to believe that the girls had changed their evidence and were now hostile to Mr Jenkins'. However, the Commission asserted, the information in those reports was 'inaccurate in important respects'.

The new evidence obtained from the re-interviews 'directly called into question what has been said by their mother about [Annie and Charlotte] having changed their accounts'. As a consequence the defence, in reaching its decision not to call the girls at trial, had been 'wrong-footed'.

The CCRC had been impressed by Annie and Charlotte:

Both girls are giving honest responses and are trying their best to say only what they actually remember. Neither girl gives the impression that they are trying to say what they think is required of them. It is clear that they are fully aware of the implications of their answers, not just for their father but also for their mother, in that they are being asked to clarify whether what she told the police was in fact accurate and truthful.

The Commission set aside the prosecution suggestion that Siôn may have 'coached' Annie, saying that this was 'not... as certain as previously implied'. They went on to underline the fact that 'there has never been any suggestion that Lottie had been coached'. Moreover, her evidence was particularly supportive of Siôn with regard to 'the gate being open when they got back'.

They analysed the chain of events that had led to the children being 'debriefed' and criticised the Bentovims' report, pointing out that it 'appears to be based on Mr Jenkins' guilt being a proven and accepted fact'. Despite its lack of objectivity and the fact that it was based on no research whatever, this report had played an important role in the progress of the investigation'.

The CCRC also considered other aspects of the case. At trial, the prosecution case had been based on the presumption that the scientific evidence pointed unquestioningly to Siôn's guilt. The CCRC begged to differ:

The Commission does not consider that the scientific evidence unequivocally establishes that the bloodspots on Mr Jenkins could only be as a result of him being the murderer.

The Commission had also carefully examined the evidence in relation to Mark Lynam. They pointed out that they had had access to all the material on the HOLMES database, and thus were able to perform a much more thorough assessment of all the evidence than the defence had had a chance to do.[34]

This analysis led to two important conclusions. Firstly, it was 'not possible to say with certainty that [Lynam] was alibied, as the analysis shows some time gaps'. Nor, secondly, could it be shown 'that all of the clothes that he was wearing on the day in question have in fact been tested for blood'.

The CCRC's two-year analysis of all the evidence in the case had shown that the jurors at Siôn's 1998 trial had been given disastrously incorrect information. They were told that the scientific evidence proved that he had committed the murder; this was untrue. They were told that Mark Lynam, the alternative suspect, could not have committed the crime, both because he had an alibi and because his clothing was not bloodstained; this was also untrue. They had also been led to believe that the defence could have called Siôn's daughters as defence witnesses but had chosen not to do so; the CCRC had proved that that was not the reality of the situation. In all these important respects, the trial jury had been seriously misinformed.

With a new appeal now in the pipeline, the most important consideration was to bring in new barristers. Neil O'May, whose responsibility it was to select counsel, took soundings. At a meeting in Bindman's offices on 22 May 2003, Bob Woffinden and David Jenkins said that they would like Clare Montgomery, one of the highly-regarded QCs who had set up Matrix Chambers, to do the appeal.[35] Additionally, they wanted Julian Knowles, also of Matrix, to be the junior on the team. Neil then went to Wakefield prison, where Siôn also told him that he wanted Montgomery and Knowles.

Lois's Third Statement

Neil warned that both were in continual demand and would have heavy commitments. After making enquiries, however, he was able to deliver the encouraging news that both were very keen to take on the case.

One of the first priorities for the new legal team was to plan the strategy for the appeal. Would this be argued primarily on the basis of the children's evidence? How much consideration should be given to the scientific evidence? And what weight should be placed on the circumstances surrounding Mark Lynam? Their initial feeling was that the children's evidence was of paramount importance.

Events now took yet another dizzying turn. After the CCRC had referred the case to appeal, WDS Capon went to see Lois. On 23 July 2003, she took a statement from her. This became Lois's third statement in the criminal proceedings. (She had made others for the purposes of proceedings in the family court.) It was massively important. In making it, Lois directly repudiated her daughters' comments in the re-interviews and re-asserted her own version of events.

Lois was shown five police documents, some of them lengthy, which concerned her reports from 1997 of what she claimed the girls had said to her. She was asked to comment on them:

Having read the reports, I can say that all five contain correct information on what the girls have said to me… All the information in the reports was given to me directly by them…

She added:

Although, as previously mentioned, in the days following the murder I had my own feelings as to Siôn's possible guilt, the girls' comments over the years have *formed the foundation for my certainty of his guilt*.

[italics added]

279

Here she was jacking up the girls' purported comments and making them bear an even heavier load than they had before. Bearing in mind what the children actually said during their five recorded interviews, this was an extraordinary thing to say.

The combination of the re-interviews of the children and Lois's statement in response created a breathtaking situation: Lois was going to be a witness for the prosecution; and her daughters were going to be witnesses for the defence.

In fact, the third statement now placed the children in an impossible position. They would not be able to accommodate both their parents' situations. They could get their father out of prison on a murder charge, but only at the cost of potentially putting their mother into prison on a charge of perverting the course of justice.

At this time, all communication between Siôn and his daughters ceased. Their letters to him stopped; and the letters he has written to them have all been unanswered.

Accordingly, the defence found that even contacting their would-be star witnesses was fraught with difficulty. They were on the other side of the world; and, in order to contact them, lawyers had to go through the person who appeared most implacably hostile to the defence: their mother. Lois refused to deliver Neil O'May's original letters to Annie and Charlotte until Annie's school exams were finished; Lois said she did not want her to be distracted. When the letters were finally passed to them, in November 2003, Charlotte wrote back to O'May to say that she would be able to come to court any day except her eighteenth birthday (which was to be 19 March 2004).

The appeal was scheduled for the summer of 2004. The presiding judge was going to be Lord Justice Sir John Kay, who had handled the important appeal of Sally Clark but who, at the time, was probably best-known for being the father of the rugby union player, Ben Kay, a member of England's World Cup-winning team in November 2003. Lord Justice Kay set a clear schedule for the appeal. It was going to be lengthy and complex and so he arranged a number of hearings in order that important aspects could be properly sorted out in advance. He impressed those who attended these hearings with his grasp of the details of the case.

However, relations between defence and prosecution, which were never good, soured significantly over the winter months. Perhaps the main bone of contention was Lois's clear reluctance to make the girls available to the defence. At the end of February 2004, O'May wrote to them for a third time, and enclosed a letter from their father in which Siôn tried to emphasise how important it was for him that they should attend court.

On the morning of 4 March, Charlotte telephoned O'May. He then explained to her the necessity of seeing her prior to the hearing. She said in that case she would return to England before the appeal started in order to go through her evidence with him beforehand.

Coincidentally, there was another preliminary hearing at the appeal court that afternoon. Lord Justice Kay made it clear that he wanted the next full hearing to be the final resolution of the case; he said he did not want further pieces of evidence emerging later on and necessitating further hearings.

With this aim in mind, he instructed the Criminal Cases Review Commission to undertake a fresh inquiry into the case. He was struck by the evidence of the bin-liner pushed through the victim's nose; and the potentially corresponding evidence from the police station which the CCRC had brought to the court's attention (the defence had not previously been aware of it) of Lynam having concealed pieces of plastic in his underpants. Kay felt he needed to know whether there was evidence to indicate an interest in plastic or plastic bags. The CCRC embarked on this new inquiry as a matter of urgency.[36]

At this hearing, Lord Justice Kay was told about the telephone conversation with Charlotte, although the defence created the impression that both girls were now available to give evidence and, in doing so, overplayed its hand.

On 9 March, Vince Ives, Lois Jenkins's partner, wrote directly to Lord Justice Kay. He made a strongly-worded complaint about the efforts the defence team was making to get the girls to court. Ives wrote:

I would respectfully suggest that the approach being made by Mr Jenkins and his lawyer borders on harassment... The girls are effectively being forced by Mr Jenkins to volunteer to give evidence... This manipulation of witnesses by an appellant must be wrong.

At the next hearing, Lord Justice Kay was plainly angry. Ives' letter overstated the position (Charlotte had freely indicated her wish to give evidence), but it was true that Annie had made no contact with the defence. Kay upbraided the defence lawyers for having misled him about the readiness of *both* girls to appear at appeal.

It is of interest that it was Ives, and not Lois herself, who wrote the letter to Lord Justice Kay. After all, Ives himself was in a poor position to raise concern. Annie was already over eighteen, and so should have been allowed to speak for herself, and Charlotte was only a few days away from her eighteenth birthday. In separate courts on separate occasions, two senior judges, Lord Justice Gage and Lady Justice Butler-Sloss, had told Lois that it was in the interests of justice for the children to be properly interviewed.

However, it was as a direct result of Ives' letter having been made public by Lord Justice Kay that the Criminal Cases Review Commission said it would have to put into the public domain correspondence from Lois and Ives in connection with the re-interviews of the girls in February 2002. It now turned out that, immediately afterwards, Lois and her partner had made equally strenuous complaints about those.

The defence had previously known nothing of this.

Lois and Ives had written to Kent police and to CAFCASS. Lois had also sent copies of a lengthy letter of complaint not only to the CCRC, but also to the consultant psychiatrist Dr Clare Lucey[37] and to Lady Justice Butler-Sloss. Additionally, Ives had made an official complaint to their MP, Michael Foster.

Lois complained about having been placed in a position where she had to allow the children to be re-interviewed:

Lois's Third Statement

It is enormously stressful to encourage one's children to do something which you know is wrong for them.

She explained, however, that she had realised at the last court hearing that it was best for 'the girls to concede graciously and [for her to] attempt to lessen the blow for them'. She explained that she had only 'encouraged' the children because she felt that satisfactory arrangements regarding the interviews had been agreed. These had included, or so she thought, the fact that she should be given 'feedback' about the interviews. In the event, she said, she received no feedback, 'simply a goodbye'.

She related what, according to her, had happened in the interviews. She said that, when Annie had come out for a toilet break, 'she was, to me, obviously distressed'; she was 'crying and shaking'. According to Lois, Annie said afterwards that she:

> ... felt she had been hammered with dates and times which no one could possibly remember... [she had] felt like vomiting for the last ten minutes... but no one had realised or offered her a break. She frequently used the word 'tricked'. She [Annie] also became very concerned that Lottie might be being bullied.

With regard to Charlotte, Lois said that she:

> ... was indignant... she was persuaded to give a minute-by-minute account of the day despite being promised this would not happen. There is a feeling that the girls were grilled for almost three hours in total as to whether or not their mother (and another family friend) lied to the police.[38]

Lois asked:

> Is it ethically acceptable to grill children as to whether or not their mother and main carer, and other adults who have helped them to

283

cope, have lied to the police... and simultaneously ask them to recount the specific events of that day, without at least safeguarding the welfare of the family in some way?

She concluded:

I am frequently asked by telephone, in the streets, by the media, by family, and by people I have never met before... 'What is happening?' How can your children be interviewed again after five years?' 'Is there no end?'

In his letter to the family's MP, Vince Ives said that Lois and Annie and Charlotte had left the interviews feeling 'tricked and distressed'. Even though he had to admit that he had not been present at the interviews he was complaining about, Ives made a specific complaint about the professional conduct of the CAFCASS representative:

... not only did he not intervene, he allowed [the] interview to reach a stage where the child felt physically sick before she felt she could leave.

Both girls knew they were being asked about things they hadn't in effect agreed to, but neither felt they could leave once the interviews had begun... I am still shocked that some of our initial fears regarding the nature [of] such an interview... have come to be realised.

Lois added that the children themselves knew nothing of these complaints as she had not told them.

All this created another extraordinary situation. The girls had been interviewed about whether their mother had accurately attributed particular comments and ideas to her daughters. Now, Lois had attributed comments and ideas about those interviews to her daughters. Would a repeat process now need to be undertaken?

Not in this case.

Lois's Third Statement

When they had been directly asked whether they would give fresh interviews, both children had readily consented. There was no reluctance, no 'blow' to be 'lessened'. Charlotte was not asked to give 'a minute-by-minute account of the day'. The idea that the children had been 'grilled' is nonsense; if anything, the interviewing process was too feather-bedded. Annie herself had complained about the patronising tone of the original interviews. The only interview in which the questioning had become in any way insistent and potentially uncomfortable was Annie's second interview, and Lois herself was seated alongside Annie during that.

Although, in the CCRC interview, Annie herself was not in vision, the video record does not suggest that she was on the verge of tears at any point. It was clearly explained to both children that they could stop the interview or have a break whenever they wished – as, indeed, Annie did. There is no suggestion that she is in any distress until after she has spoken to her mother outside.

In response to Lois, the CAFCASS representative said that 'neither Annie nor Lottie showed any outward signs of distress... I was very surprised to see that she [Annie] was clearly upset in the waiting room a few minutes later'. The CCRC bluntly told Lois that many of her points were 'demonstrably wrong'. They did concede that 'it would perhaps have been better had these questions been asked five years ago, but the fact is that they were not'. The Commission members were, of course, much too well-mannered to point out whose fault it was that those questions had not been asked five years earlier.

In its statement of reasons, however, the Commission did acknowledge that the girls' responses in the re-interviews had as many 'implications' for Lois as they did for Siôn, and in view of this it is perhaps not surprising that she was so worked up about them.

The ill-feeling between defence and prosecution rumbled on. It emerged that prior to Lord Justice Kay initiating an inquiry into the psychiatric background of Mark Lynam, the police had, in January 2004, requested a report on Lynam from a psychiatrist at Ashen Hill.

In fact, this was the second occasion on which Sussex police had conducted further inquiries into Lynam's possible involvement in the murder of Billie-Jo even though, with Siôn in prison, the case had theoretically been solved. After Bindman's took over the case in January 2000, one of the matters they were keen to pursue was whether there was bloodstaining on any of Lynam's clothing. (As the CCRC pointed out, hardly anything had actually been tested.) The defence's attempts to initiate further testing were, however, pre-empted by Sussex police who, in August 2000, undertook further tests on Lynam's clothing themselves.

O'May complained to the Crown Prosecution Service:

> You will appreciate that... these actions may well have destroyed material. At the very least, the prosecution appear to have attempted to forestall any defence examination of the exhibits... .
>
> The only other explanation for the actions of Sussex police is that they themselves are not convinced that Mr Jenkins is indeed the murderer of Billie-Jo Jenkins and are consequently carrying out further investigations into the case.

At another preliminary hearing prior to the appeal, issues of confidentiality and privilege were discussed. As has been explained, the legal battle about whether the children were to be re-interviewed had moved into the family court in 2000. Family court proceedings are normally governed by strict confidentiality and can be neither reported nor made known to outside parties. Lord Justice Kay said that he had received the final judgment in proceedings in the family court, but had initially been unsure whether it should even have been disclosed to him and his fellow judges.

However, he said that he had obtained the full consent of Lady Justice Butler-Sloss, the President of the Family Division, and hence could now authorise its disclosure to the criminal court. Obviously, the facts of the case remained the same whether it was being litigated in the criminal or the family courts. Kay re-iterated that it was his intention that, for this new appeal, all of the material should be available to all of the parties.

The other matter concerned legal professional privilege. The defence intended to re-argue the abuse of process point: that, but for Lois's reports, the girls would have been called as witnesses at trial. Richard Camden Pratt, for the Crown, argued that in order for the prosecution to be able to test that evidence it was necessary for them to see the full record of Siôn Jenkins' discussions with his lawyers in the months leading up to trial.

Normally, all this material is covered by legal professional privilege. It is regarded as fundamental to the justice system that someone has the opportunity to discuss all matters with his lawyers knowing that they will remain absolutely confidential. However, in line with his stance that everything should be available to everyone, Kay believed that this material should be handed over.

'When they [the girls] come to give evidence', he explained, 'we're entitled to assess them on the basis of the whole of the background... I see no reason why that material should not be disclosed.'

'This would allow the Crown a forensic advantage to which they're not normally entitled', Montgomery pointed out. She also raised the question of whether the Crown could be entrusted with this material; was there a chance, she asked, that it would leak out any further?

'We believe we can trust people to deal with cases properly', responded Kay.

Although the matter was left to Siôn (only he could actually permit the disclosure of the material), the judge's views were plain; Siôn sanctioned the disclosure to the prosecution of his confidential conferences with lawyers.

Kay recognised that feelings were running high and that there was considerable tension between defence and prosecution. At the end of this hearing, he emphasised to everyone, 'It's helpful if we continue to be told about any problems on either side... It's vitally important we know exactly what the position is.

'We've got to defuse this case, or we will be prevented from doing justice.'

Annie finally responded to Bindmans' repeated requests for her to get in touch by sending a fax from an internet café. She said she did not wish to attend court to give evidence, but hoped her video interviews would suffice.

For the defence, this was perhaps better news than they by now expected, in that she was confirming that the videos accurately represented her views. The judges, however, viewed it as inadequate; Lord Justice Kay still wanted, if possible, the hearing to address all the evidence.

No one had any doubt that the Court was faced with a highly unusual situation that, perhaps, called for highly unusual initiatives. Kay recognised that it was 'an astonishingly difficult situation for any family to face'.

He proposed that he should write a letter to both girls. 'I will say to them', he said, '"you need to help us as much as you can and no more than that. You should not think that the whole of the outcome depends on what you are going to say"'.

'We need to increase the chances that they'll come', he explained, 'and be in a frame of mind where they can help the court.

'I also intend writing to Mrs Jenkins, trying to reassure her that they [the girls] will be dealt with sympathetically and explaining that the Court is in charge and will remain in charge.'

After the Easter break, the Court had the girls' responses. Charlotte, as she had previously said, would come to give evidence. Annie, said Kay, 'courteously, but firmly' refused to attend.

'She will not talk to anyone, even her sister', he said. 'She adamantly says she will not discuss it.'

Kay then said he was prepared to write another letter, asking Annie if she would be prepared to explain her feelings, and whether she would like to discuss the situation. He was not optimistic, however.

'I think I know the answer', he said.

He was right. He did know the answer. Annie didn't wish to discuss the matter further.

'We'll have to make do with what we've got', Lord Justice Kay said.

Lois's Third Statement

The appeal was set to start on Monday, 28 June.

For Siôn, having had to wait more than a year, it was a moment for which he was well prepared.

Chapter Thirty-Seven

PIE

The foundations of the scientific defence against the murder charge were painstakingly laid by Professor David Denison and Professor Robert Schroter.

After the failure of the first appeal, Denison remained so anxious about the case that he continued to work on it in his own time, and in large part at his own expense. He also brought in Schroter, who was professor of biological mechanics at Imperial College, London, to assist with the case.

At a legal conference before the appeal, Clare Montgomery told Denison that in order to demonstrate to even the most sceptical audience that the human body could behave as the defence was asserting, then he would have to use real blood. That, then, is what Denison and Schroter did – using both stored hospital blood that was past its sell-by date and, then, Denison's own blood.

Together, they conducted a number of series of experiments concerning blood expiration that became of increasing importance in demonstrating that the defence explanation of the bloodspots (expiration spray) was not only viable in itself, but was an overwhelmingly more feasible interpretation of the available information than the prosecution theory (impact spatter).

In doing so, they transformed the way in which forensic science work of this nature is conducted. The British forensic sciences services have now accepted that real blood should be used in such experiments.

By this stage, with the case having been the subject of increasing controversy for six years, there was a growing annoyance among some in the scientific community that the post-mortem on Billie-Jo had not been handled differently. Obviously, at the time of a murder, no one can have any idea what course the case is going to take. Nevertheless, someone should have been astute enough to realise that this one was probably going to have some lasting significance; even as the post-mortem was being conducted, the case was featuring prominently in the press and in radio and television news bulletins.

From that perspective, it is unfathomable that so little was done to preserve vital material that may later have enabled the case to be clarified. For example, as John Sinar, the neurosurgeon, commented, 'It is unfortunate that the brain was not removed and preserved for later microscopic examination'.

Remarkably, all that was preserved were four small sections of the lung, one from each lobe, that were taken for histological examination. In the interim, however, nothing had happened to them; they hadn't been examined by anyone. As the years passed, there was even some uncertainty about what had happened to these slides.

Once they had been re-located, Professor Helen Whitwell and Professor Christopher Milroy did initial histology work for the defence, and pointed out that it was clear that the lungs were inflated – so there must have been a blockage.

However, further examination was important. Defence scientists, however, made repeated requests to undertake this. Eventually, permission was granted. The slides had turned up in Guy's hospital, but there wasn't a microscope available there. Professor Denison arranged instead for the slides to be examined at the Royal Brompton hospital.

On Tuesday, 15 June, in the hospital's pathology department, with the appeal due to start in less than two weeks' time, a small group of scientists gathered to examine the slides. Denison was there, together with Schroter and also Andrew Nicholson. Dr Ian Hill, who had conducted the post-mortem, also attended.[39]

It was Professor Nicholson who made the spontaneous observation that would transform the case.

'Did you realise she had interstitial emphysema?' he asked.

Pulmonary interstitial emphysema (PIE) occurs when someone is making violent efforts to breathe, but the main airways are blocked. As a result, the lung is torn; the air cannot get out and will be forced under pressure into the interstitial linings of the lung.

Billie-Jo did not suffer from any respiratory disease; nor do severe head injuries cause interstitial emphysema. It is only seen in healthy people if their lungs have come under pressure in a variety of ways: through being held in an arm-lock; strangled; smothered; drowned; artificially ventilated at too high a pressure; or if they have been rapidly decompressed whilst holding their breath, for example when coming up from a dive. It is the second most common cause of death for divers.

This immediately proved two things. First of all, that Billie-Jo did not die instantly; there had been time for these physiological changes to take place. Indeed, the scientists subsequently also noted signs of atelectasis (a partial collapse of the lung), which also indicated that she had survived for some minutes after her lungs had been obstructed.

Secondly, that she had suffered a blockage of her airways. The first appeal court had rejected Denison's evidence precisely because it was predicated on the basis that there had been an upper-airway blockage and, as Lord Justice Kennedy emphasised in the judgment, there was 'no evidence of any blockage' – Dr Hill having firmly told the court as such.

Hill's evidence had been highly controversial at the time of the first appeal – mainly because he was giving opinions about the post-mortem that he had never expressed before, and he had made no notes that supported his testimony. Nevertheless, in dismissing the appeal, the judges had relied upon Hill. Now, further scientific work had proved him wrong. Indeed, at a stroke, nearly every aspect of the scientific evidence given by the prosecution at both the first trial and the first appeal had been shown to be either wrong or incomplete.

It was remarkable that a chance discovery like that, virtually on the eve of the appeal, should change its entire perspective.

Chapter Thirty-Eight
A Four-leaf Clover and Another Tragedy

My valedictory week at Wakefield started the weekend before I was due to leave. I had known some men for nearly six years and had developed a number of strong friendships.

During those last days, I received a letter wishing me good luck from Sir Ludovic Kennedy. From time to time during my imprisonment, he'd written to me and I was always thankful for his wonderfully encouraging letters. He'd also referred to my case in his book, *Thirty-Six Murders & Two Immoral Earnings*.[40] His letter was just another of those small signs that made me feel that, at last, the judicial winds were set fair for me.

I didn't go to work that week. I told the prison that I'd got so much to do packing up and putting all my paperwork together for the appeal that I wouldn't have time. I looked through everything I had accumulated over the past six years. I had never kept a diary or any letters because they would have been taken and read by prison staff. What I did have were CDs, my small music system, a rug, a bedspread and items of clothing. There were also about thirty books: not many, but at least the staff now turned a blind eye to the notional limit of twelve.

A Four-leaf Clover and Another Tragedy

I decided to leave everything behind – partly because I did not want painful reminders of my imprisonment, and partly because I knew that these items, few as they were, would be appreciated by the other men.

I did have one prized possession: a large wooden board. Prison mattresses are thin and uncomfortable and quickly lose their shape. So by placing the wooden board underneath you could firm up the mattress and get a proper night's sleep. When people knew I was leaving, it was the one thing that everyone wanted.

At about 8.00am on Friday, 25 June, I left. Twelve hours later, I was sitting in a cell in Pentonville prison. There, prison officers passed on some good news, and some bad. The good news was that someone had sent me a four-leaf clover as a good-luck token for the appeal; the bad was that they were unable to pass it on to me – it would contravene prison service regulations.

My appeal was to be held in Court 4, the largest courtroom at the Royal Courts of Justice. This time I was not so green. I understood that many of the judges simply saw their role as to safeguard the integrity of the system. They would want to encourage the perception that the criminal justice system did not make mistakes and would dismiss my appeal if they could. I was well aware, however, that I had four advantages this time: I knew that the presiding judge, Lord Justice Kay, was someone whom we not only felt we could trust but who appeared determined to see justice done – rarely had all the preliminary ground been trodden as thoroughly as it had in my case; I knew that my grounds of appeal were substantial; that we had the last-minute bonus of the discovery of PIE in the microscopic slides; and I knew that I had a very impressive legal team, and that their planning and preparation for this appeal had been meticulous.

There are, however, some things for which there can be no preparation.

Even as everyone was assembling, Neil arrived with a terrible piece of news. Lord Justice Kay had suffered a serious heart attack over the weekend and was in intensive care in hospital.

Sadly, he died later that week.[41]

The appeal would be handled instead by Lord Justice Rose, the vice-president of the criminal division of the Court of Appeal. Not surprisingly, in these circumstances, he was completely unfamiliar with the case and totally unprepared to be hearing an appeal. So the appeal was immediately adjourned until the Wednesday afternoon in order to give him an opportunity to begin to get to grips with the case.

So, finally, the appeal began. In Court 4, the appellant sits in a dock with a steel grill around it.[42] Unfortunately, this is on the prosecution side of the court. As I looked out, I could see Vince Ives and David Mann immediately in front of me, sitting with Sussex police. Later in the appeal, Peter Gaimster put in an appearance. He, too, sat with the police. My lawyers, family and friends were on the further side of the courtroom.

The appeal was most noteworthy, in media terms, for the fact that my ex-wife and daughter had flown over together to give evidence, but for opposite sides. It seemed an unreal situation.

I will never forget watching Charlotte walk to the witness-box. I had never seen her dressed so formally. I was filled with mixed emotions. On the one hand, I was profoundly sad that she had ever been placed in such an invidious position; on the other hand, I was so proud of her for coming all this way in order to speak up for me. Our eyes met; hers seemed full of tenderness; mine, I hope, were filled with a father's love.

Neil did have the meeting with her before the appeal took place. However, Lois had stipulated that she must be accompanied by a social worker. This had not pleased any of us, as we were aware how antagonistic towards me the social workers had been from the outset. However, it was a condition we had no alternative but to accept.

It was accordingly interesting that Neil was very impressed with Charlotte after his meeting with her. He found her clear and articulate. However, just before she gave evidence, we had noted that she was surrounded by police and the social worker and associates of Lois. Then, when she came to give her evidence, she was plainly overwrought. She clearly found the process such a strain that I wanted to cry out and stop the proceedings. Nevertheless, she showed commendable courage in continuing until the end. Neither was she going to leave until important facts that supported my case had been given.

Lois approached the stand. Her hair was darker and she looked at the judges with pained eyes. She would not look me in the eye.

It was at this stage that her allegations of domestic violence were first raised as part of the case. Although everyone in court heard them, they could not be reported at the time. As a result, she wasn't required to give chapter and verse, so her allegations were actually the more insidious for being so nebulous.

Under cross-examination from Clare Montgomery, Lois seemed to find it difficult to keep to the point, but Clare was always quick to change direction and follow. Lois appeared irritable and histrionic. She kept relying on her avowed intention of trying all the way through to protect her children.

When the appeal ended, judgment was reserved. It would be given three days later, on Friday, 16 July. That Thursday evening, I played my last game of chess with my cellmate.

The next day, as I took my seat to hear judgment given, the court was absolutely full.

Chapter Thirty-Nine

Innocence
Regained

Siôn was understandably on tenterhooks as he waited for the judgment, but those who had sat through the appeal knew that prosecution scientists had made three highly significant concessions during the appeal.

Adrian Wain, the forensic scientist, had acknowledged that the bloodspray pattern on Siôn's clothing was not dissimilar to that from exhalation sprays produced experimentally by defence scientists. At the pre-appeal meeting of experts, Dr Hill had agreed with the finding of PIE. He then conceded at the appeal that his original evidence had been in error and there had after all been an upper-airway blockage. At the very end of the appeal, John Widdicombe, emeritus professor of physiology at the University of London, a key member of the prosecution team at the original trial, also conceded this point.

Accordingly, there was a reasonable level of confidence among Siôn's supporters that the three judges – Lord Justice Rose, Mr Justice Curtis and Mr Justice Wakerley – would have no alternative but to quash the conviction.

On 16 July 2004, when they delivered their judgment, that is indeed what happened. However, the judges ordered a retrial, a course of action that has been more or less adopted as appeal court policy since the House of Lords judgment in the Pendleton case.[43]

The judges said:

> It will be for a jury to assess the inter-relationship, weight and conclusions to be drawn from *the whole of the evidence* in this case.
>
> [italics added]

No sooner had the judgment been read out in open court than it virtually disappeared. It became a kind of *samizdat* publication. It was not available on the usual websites. Still today, even legal practices signed up to online subscription services can obtain only an expurgated version.

Appeal court judges do have to give reasons for their decisions (apart from anything else, it is a requirement under Article 6 of the Human Rights Act), but no one seems to have thought through the consequences when a retrial is being ordered. In such cases, it would seem that judicial comment on key areas of the evidence is not merely redundant but positively unhelpful. So it would seem sensible for potentially prejudicial judgments in future to be given in camera.

Two further aspects were of interest. Firstly, the judges alluded to one obvious difficulty in holding a retrial: much of the original scientific evidence had not been adequately preserved and had already disappeared. About 75 per cent of the bloodspots had disappeared from the clothing; the blocks from which the lung tissue samples were taken had also been lost.[44]

The judges decided, however, that this was not an insuperable difficulty.

Secondly, Clare Montgomery made an immediate bail application for Siôn. Although the judges appeared favourably disposed towards this, Lord Justice Rose made one passing observation which appeared to illustrate how susceptible all of us can be to false witness testimony. Pointing out that one reason to withhold bail was the possible influencing of witnesses, Rose said:

We have heard some evidence capable of construction of an attempt to influence Annie… It was the incident during the first week after the murder.

Montgomery responded firmly:

My Lord, there was no incident.

Having deliberated further, the judges decided that they would cede responsibility for the decision about bail to the trial judge.

None of Siôn's supporters would have professed themselves entirely happy with the appeal or its outcome. Nevertheless, the key objective had been achieved. The conviction was quashed. After six years, Siôn was officially restored to a state of innocence.

Chapter Forty
Back in Belmarsh

My appeal having been allowed, Clare Montgomery immediately asked that I should be granted bail. To my disappointment, Lord Justice Rose decided to defer the matter in order to allow it to be dealt with by the judge who would be handling the retrial. There was no doubt that I would get bail. After all, I had previously been on bail for fifteen months without mishap. Clearly, however, the judicial processes were going to take a few days.

I was soon back in Belmarsh, going through the same reception area and the same bureaucratic processes as I had six years earlier.

On my second day there I received a visit from Fiona Haines, a member of the chaplaincy team. She had visited me when I was first convicted and I shall never forget her kindness then, when I was emotionally at my weakest. She would arrange for me to be brought out of the cell so that we could talk near an open window on the landing. It was very good to see her again.

I was there for nearly three weeks, during which time I received a great deal of encouraging mail from people congratulating me on the outcome of the appeal; amongst these letters was a brief message of support from a woman named Tina Ferneyhough.

As had happened on previous occasions, I seemed to be the last to find out about matters concerning my liberty. On Monday, 2 August I was reading in the cell when I heard a news report on the radio that I had been granted bail. Mrs Justice Anne Rafferty had been appointed to hear my retrial, and Clare had successfully applied to her for bail. The sum was fixed at £250,000. I was again to reside in Aberystwyth with my parents and I had to sign on at the local police station every day.

I was, of course, delighted. I went out into the yard for my last period of exercise. A Cypriot businessman approached me. I knew he was intelligent and shrewd, and that he maintained he was being stitched up.

'Make limited phone calls, avoid using your mobile', he said to me. 'The police will monitor you. Yours is a very high-profile case and the police will want to win. They will go for you. Be very, very careful.'

Later on, I would have good cause to remember what he'd said.

I was leaving prison. I packed my bag and was locked into a small cell near the reception area where I waited. And waited.

After some hours, an officer came to say there was a problem. My heart sank. Sussex police had raised a belated objection to bail on administrative grounds. It was, I think, something to do with the fact that my aunt and uncle, Iona and John, had each agreed to be bail guarantors and had, as before, put up £50,000 of the money, but the police argued that as they held a joint bank account they could not be regarded as separate guarantors.

It seemed ridiculous that Sussex police could be so obstructive. Didn't they have anything better to do?

Finally, the cell door was opened. I was led through reception and then into the large tarmacked area where the sweatboxes pulled in. Then I walked through another door. There were still four prison officers around me at this point. Finally, we came to the prison gates. I was then asked my name and number.

'Siôn Jenkins', I replied, deliberately refusing to give them my prison number. After all, I was now an innocent man.

Slowly the doors started to move apart. It resembled a scene from a movie. I saw the crack that was the outside world getting bigger and bigger. On the other side of the gate stood Bob. He'd been there waiting for almost eight hours while the wrangling with Sussex police was ironed out. I walked towards him and shook his hand. Although I certainly didn't realise it at the time, there were lots of cameras focused on us as we drove away from Belmarsh.

We went to my aunt and uncle's house in Bromley, where members of my family had gathered. It was all too much for me. Through the French windows, I could see delicious sights: trees, flowers and grass. I walked into the garden. It was so green, so lush. I felt so light-headed; I couldn't take in the sheer beauty of it all.

In the lounge, there was a bowl of strawberries. I sat there looking at them, not quite believing that they were real. I was given a glass of wine – a *glass* of wine, in a *glass*. My feet were on carpet. I could sit in comfort and look outside and see the gardens and the sky. For the next hours, as my family chatted in the background, I was in wonderland. Later on, I went up to the bedroom where they had prepared a bed for me that was almost too comfortable to sleep on.

The next morning, I left with my parents in their car on the six-hour journey to Aberystwyth.

We were within half-a-mile of home when I suddenly asked if they could drop me off.

I'd had six years of imprisonment and claustrophobia and stale, rank air and now I wanted to walk the last part of the journey just so that I could fill my lungs with fresh air.

Fifteen minutes later, I turned the last corner and saw, outside my parents' home, a large crowd of journalists and cameramen. I was suddenly trapped. There was no hostility, as there had previously been with the media. They were all friendly, and seemed excited on my behalf, and all of them had questions for me.

What do you do in such circumstances? Of course, you are polite. They were only local journalists anyway. I just answered a few routine questions before going on into the house.

Later, after dinner, I went out again for a walk by the sea. I did not allow myself to think about the retrial. I just wanted to savour the moment. Walking on my own, listening to the waves and smelling the sea air were simply magical.

It wasn't until I returned to the house that I began to realise that I'd stirred up a hornets' nest. The day's headlines now seemed to be, 'Siôn Jenkins gives his first interview since his release from prison'. It was the main news for the entire country on the evening bulletins. It was also news to me.

Chapter Forty-One

The Website is Closed Down – by Order

Even if Siôn had not been in prison for the previous six years, he cannot have been expected to be *au courant* with the priorities and production processes of the British media. Had he understood all the current practices, then he would have appreciated the risks of exchanging any pleasantries at all with the reporters congregated outside his parents' house. But of course, like most other citizens, he was not media-savvy.

The small crowd gathered outside the house contained a number of local journalists, who spoke in welcoming Welsh accents. It was hardly surprising that he should speak to them. They were friendly; he was civil. That was all there was to it. He was certainly wary and made sure the talking was kept to a minimum. A complete recording was made of his answers to reporters' questions. It lasts for less than three minutes. Nevertheless, the damage was done.

There were three particular points of which he needed to have been aware. Firstly, if a subject is sufficiently newsworthy, then two or three quotes can soon be turned into a headline-making interview. Secondly, technological advance has transformed the media industry; words and pictures can now be delivered from almost anywhere to newsrooms across the UK (or, indeed, the world) in minutes. Thirdly, local journalists are never going to keep a story to themselves if there's an opportunity to place it with national news organisations.

At that moment, Siôn was at the top of the news agenda, so newsrooms were ready for what they viewed as fresh developments in the story. Those mid-Wales reporters were certainly able to sell this story nationally. Indeed, since the success of his appeal, Siôn had been receiving a much more upbeat press. At this juncture, the newspapers that had spent six years vilifying him began to wonder whether he might be *persona grata* after all.

At the start of the week, Siôn's release on bail had merely produced another burst of positive publicity: 'Siôn Jenkins returns home' announced the *Daily Express*; 'Freed! Now my son can prove his innocence' was the headline in the *Daily Star* (which had obtained a couple of quotes from Siôn's father). The *Daily Mirror*, which in 1999 had registered the nation's 'joy' at the failure of the first appeal, was apparently now on first-name terms:

SIÔN FREED

Now, the brief exchanges with reporters outside the house in Aberystwyth were transmitted to UK newsrooms and within an hour had become a major news story. Further, the terms in which it was being reported were now remarkably favourable.

The BBC, conscious of the potential judicial pitfalls, was guarded and said almost nothing about the case itself. It quoted Siôn as saying, for example: 'The people of Aberystwyth have been wonderful to both my family and myself… and I feel very much at home here'.

Neither other TV and radio organisations nor the national newspapers were similarly cautious. Their reports were not marked by any restraint:

Daily Express: I'M AN INNOCENT MAN

The Website is Closed Down – by Order

Daily Mail: I'LL BE CLEARED NEXT TIME

Daily Mirror: I'M INNOCENT... AND I'LL PROVE THAT AT
MY RETRIAL

There are two background issues involved here: sub judice and bail. The
1981 Contempt of Court Act prohibits the pre-trial publication of
material which creates 'a substantial risk' that justice 'will be seriously
impeded or prejudiced'. The principle underpinning this sub judice
provision is to ensure fair play in advance of the trial. Its practical effect,
however, is rather different. What it tends to do is to freeze the publicity
process at the point of maximum disadvantage for the defendant.

Clearly, the authorities may now have perceived that Siôn was reversing
the process in this instance.

Then there is the question of bail. There are four main reasons why
police always want a man accused of a serious offence to be remanded in
custody. The first is managerial. If the suspect is being held in prison,
everyone knows where he is, it is a safe bet that there will be no matters
arising while he is there, and all potential problems have been sorted. The
ostensible grounds for the remanding of defendants in custody – for
public safety; in order to prevent their committing further crimes; and for
their own protection – all come within this category.

Then there are the other reasons which would (if they were openly
acknowledged) be less publicly acceptable. If a man is in prison, then his
chances of preparing a proper defence are greatly reduced. He cannot
communicate readily with his lawyers. It will prove very difficult to
arrange legal conferences.

The defendant will also, as a direct consequence of his months of
imprisonment, be emotionally stressed from the very outset of the trial.
Getting ready for trial will mean getting up early, being taken down to
reception, and then waiting around; by the time the prisoner arrives at
court, he will already feel drained.

Then there are the media and public relations considerations. Once someone has been remanded into custody, he is already being viewed as a criminal. The defendant will be able to do nothing to counteract that.

So what had now happened after Siôn's off-the-cuff comments to reporters outside his house was, from the prosecution's point of view, the worst-case scenario. Not only had bail been granted, thereby enabling Siôn to prepare his defence properly, but an entirely positive image of him was being projected in the media. Even the reports that took care not to infringe sub judice were helpful to the defence. The BBC had scrupulously avoided any matters concerning the case; yet the quotes they had attributed to Siôn – which were, on one level, banal and uncontroversial – were ideal, in public relations terms, and would help to generate sympathy for him.

It had not necessarily been Siôn's fault that the dialogue with the media had happened. After all, it was the police who'd told reporters exactly where he had been bailed to, thereby giving them the opportunity to waylay him.

However, the construction immediately placed on those cursory exchanges in Aberystwyth was that Siôn had held an impromptu press conference on his return to Wales and that this was deplorable.

The police now had the leverage to impose their wish-list bail conditions. Mrs Justice Rafferty acceded to them. Two principal new conditions were imposed. The first was that neither Siôn nor any member of his family nor anyone from his legal team was allowed to have any communication whatever with any member of the press.

The effect of Mrs Justice Rafferty's order was so sweeping that, until it was marginally varied some weeks later, Bindman's were unable to discuss anything at all relating to the case with members of the press; and Bob Woffinden was prevented from meeting or even talking to Siôn or members of his family, even though he had been in regular contact with them for the previous six years.

Far more serious even than this, however, was Mrs Justice Rafferty's other new condition. The 'Justice for Siôn Jenkins' website must be closed down. On Wednesday, 4 August, the team running the site were simply told that it had to be removed and replaced with a message explaining its disappearance. If this did not happen, then Siôn would go back to prison.

Siôn Jenkins was held effectively under house arrest in Aberystwyth, and told he could not leave the premises until it had been confirmed that the website was gone.

(Two farcical elements arose in relation to this. If Siôn could not leave the house, he could not sign on at the local police station, thereby contravening another of the bail conditions. Secondly, Sussex police at one stage after the taking-down of the website were adamantly claiming that it still existed. It was pointed out to them that they were not looking online; they were just looking at the cache on their own server where they'd downloaded a version of the website.)

Since all this concerned the publication of any details of Siôn's case, a concomitant effect of Mrs Justice Rafferty's ruling was that none of these dramatic developments in the High Court could be made public in any way. Had these matters been reportable at the time, they may well have attracted a storm of protest.

The upshot was that the website disappeared that afternoon.

All this was as outrageous as it was unprecedented.

The criminal justice system is an adversarial process. That is its defining characteristic. Two sides are involved. In this case, a tide of filth about Siôn Jenkins had been flowing from the moment of his conviction. Siôn was, according to that memorable *Times* headline, a 'liar, wife-beater, adulterer and killer'. Other papers had stated bluntly that he 'had flings with schoolchildren of Billie-Jo's age'.

All of this material was intensely prejudicial – could anything be more compromising for a schoolteacher facing trial than the suggestion that he had 'flings' with thirteen-year-old girls? All of it was untrue. All of it, and much more besides, was available to anyone who surfed the internet for it.

The website was set up partly to try to counteract the highly damaging publicity. It was, in comparison, a trickle of truth.

Mrs Justice Rafferty displayed no interest whatever in inhibiting access to material that traduced Siôn Jenkins. She might just as well have been saying: the tide of filth can continue – but we will cut off the trickle of truth!

If changes to the flow of information are going to be made in advance of a criminal trial, then they must apply equally to both sides. That should be axiomatic.

Three additional points, however, should be mentioned. Firstly, there had been no specific complaint to the Court about the website or the material on it; just the broad one relating to its mere existence. It was noted by those in court that not a solitary example was provided by the prosecution or anyone else of anything untrue that had ever appeared on the website. Indeed, its authors firmly believe that nothing untrue ever has been published on it.

Secondly, after Siôn was bailed on 2 August, the solitary addition to the website was a line giving the basic information about the bail application and only that. Ironically, the website that the judge was closing down was – to a far greater extent than any of the traditional news organisations, and to a greater extent even than the BBC – the one media outlet that was adhering strictly to the principle of sub judice.

Thirdly, Siôn Jenkins was not involved in any respect in the production of the website. As the website authors explained:

The website operated then, as it does now, completely independently. Its content has never been produced by Siôn Jenkins, any member of his family or his legal team.

There was no basis in law on which Siôn or his lawyers could have instructed the website team to do anything at all.

Chapter Forty-Two

Tina

I had a £10 note burning a hole in my pocket. After my 'house arrest' was rescinded, I took my first outing into Aberystwyth to buy cards for my daughters. I had not handled money for six years, and I was looking forward to normal life. I went into a local shop and chose four cards. The girl at the till recognised me and said she was so pleased for me. She refused to take anything for the cards and gave me them as a present. I decided that I'd spend the money instead in a local tea-shop. To my embarrassment, I failed there as well. My afternoon tea was on the house. The staff wished me well, saying, 'It's good to have you back'. I returned to my parents' house with the £10 still in my pocket.

When Neil did return, there were important decisions that we knew had to be made quickly. I wanted Clare to continue to represent me at the retrial. There was then a court hearing to work out a schedule. Clare asked the judge to set a trial date that would enable her to take the case. However, Mrs Justice Rafferty insisted on a trial date of April 2005. Clare had other commitments at that time. We would have to choose a new QC.

As before, there was a name at the top of our list: Christopher Sallon

QC; as before, we were delighted when he straightaway agreed to take it on. Fortunately, also, Julian Knowles was able to remain as the junior barrister. I also knew that this now gave us a team who had successfully worked together before on an important case.[45]

This team was augmented by Sara Harrison, another Bindman's solicitor. Meanwhile, Richard Camden Pratt, having dealt with the case for seven years, had now withdrawn as prosecuting counsel. The Crown had a new team led by Nicholas Hilliard, who was the leading Treasury counsel at the Old Bailey and also chairman of the Criminal Bar Association. He was assisted both by Crispin Aylett and also Alan Gardner.

So there were *three* Crown counsel. My lawyers, not wishing to dispirit me, did not let me see how perturbed they were; but afterwards told me it was the first time they'd known a single defendant to be faced with three prosecuting counsel. The Crown would be putting an unprecedented amount of time, money and manpower into convicting me.

Neil said he would need to see me regularly, so we arranged that I would travel up to London on Mondays and return to Aberystwyth on Wednesdays. My bail conditions were changed. When I was in London for legal discussions, I would stay at my aunt and uncle's in Bromley.

Whenever I did go to London, I was always looking over my shoulder. I knew that more than anything the police wanted to have my bail rescinded and to get me back into Belmarsh, so that my chances of preparing a proper defence would be undermined.

Just before leaving Belmarsh, I had replied to the letter from Tina Ferneyhough. However, after I got bail, I realised that she didn't have my address, nor I hers. Before I left, staff at the prison had gone through everything I had and had put some things, including my address book, in a small plastic bag which wasn't handed back to me.

I assumed it was gone for ever, but I phoned the prison and they did send it on to me. So I wrote to Tina again, giving her my new contact details. As one of the few people in the country not to have followed the recent flurry of publicity, she was surprised that I was no longer in prison. I suggested that, one day when I was in London, we could perhaps meet for a cup of tea.

Tina

In late October, I called one Monday evening and suggested that we could meet the following day after the conference had finished. Tina was a nurse and so she worked shifts; after her shift finished, she took her son Oscar to football training. But we agreed that we could fit in a meeting at the Royal Festival Hall after football training was over.

I arrived early and looked round an exhibition. It was a beautiful evening, so afterwards I sat on a bench directly outside on the South Bank and read. I was engrossed in my book when I suddenly heard someone say, 'Hello'.

I looked up and there was Tina. I was surprised by the impact she had on me. For the next hour, we talked. I listened to her while fumbling with sachets of sugar. The hour passed very quickly. I wanted to tell her how lovely she looked, but this was our first meeting. I was surprised by how comfortable I felt with her and, at the same time, how exciting it was to be with her. I definitely wanted to see her again.

We walked over Hungerford Bridge back to Charing Cross. As we walked, I seemed to feel a charge of electricity between our hands, although they never touched. We caught the tube to Victoria, which was where she lived, and I caught the train back to Bromley. I asked if I could take her to dinner the following week.

We went to a Thai restaurant, the Mango Tree, which is on the busy road leading from Victoria up to Hyde Park Corner, opposite Buckingham Palace gardens. It was close to where Tina lived. The meal was excellent, and it was a very memorable evening. I was attracted by her energy, her togetherness and her capableness. She was a woman on her own; I admired her independence. We shared experiences and opinions, we talked quite deeply about the things that moved us, we laughed a great deal. We walked back to Victoria station and, just before leaving, I bent and kissed her on the side of her face. From that evening, I hoped that we would always be together.

She was born in Southampton in May 1950, but from the age of eleven lived with her family in Portsmouth. Stephen, her brother, worked for their parents, but Tina always wanted to be a nurse. In 1968, she started her training in Portsmouth, and in 1971 married Mark Armstrong, her childhood sweetheart. She went on to take higher qualifications and become a medical ward sister.

After eighteen years together, she and Mark divorced. Then in 1992, she married Miles Ferneyhough, an antiques dealer in the Midlands, and had a son, Oscar.

Using the money left by her parents, who died unexpectedly within weeks of each other, the previous year, Tina bought a house in Groom Place, Belgravia. It proved a timely acquisition. With Miles and her brother, she also opened an antiques business in West Halkin Street, Belgravia – so close to home that it enabled her to look after Oscar on a full-time basis. (Whenever she was needed in the shop, Tina simply took Oscar with her.)

From her childhood, she had regularly visited the Isle of Wight, sometimes taking the ferry from Lymington. One day in 2001, the ferry was broken down and there was a three-hour delay. As she passed the time walking round Lymington, she saw a small house near the quay which she thought she'd buy for her retirement. She was able to afford it straightaway merely by raising money on the London property. However, as she had neither the means nor the time to live there immediately, she rented it out.

By this time, however, Tina was struggling. Her marriage had ended, and the three of them recognised that it wasn't viable to keep the antiques business going. That was wound down, and she went back to nursing at the cancer unit of the Charing Cross hospital.

She was exhausted much of the time. She was a single parent, working hard to keep the home together, and was also doing further study and had very little free time. Thankfully, however, she did find time to write to me.

'When I first read about the murder', she said, 'and saw there was hardly any blood on you, I thought, "Well, he didn't do it". I've been a nurse in A & E and I've seen people who have suffered head injuries – there were lots of fights in Portsmouth on a Saturday night – and there was always a lot of blood.'

When I met her, she was doing an advanced diploma in cancer care and was working in the cancer unit of the Royal Marsden, the country's leading cancer hospital. She had been divorced for four years. I had been divorced for five years, but alone for seven, and in many ways I had shut down emotionally.

On my first visit to Tina's, I had met Oscar, who was then twelve. Within minutes of our meeting, he was telling me all about his schoolfriends. From the first moment he realised that Tina and I were together, he has been delighted by the prospect of, amongst other things, having someone to talk to about football.

During November and December, the Crown were inundating us with fresh material, with new statements from ordinary witnesses as well as scientific experts. Tina played a vital role in helping me to keep abreast of it all and not to cave in emotionally. One new report, by Dr Jeremy Skepper, claimed to have found white specks in the microscopic bloodspots on the clothing. The language of the report was highly technical and I could not claim to have understood it all. But before an all-day legal conference, I met Tina for breakfast at the Charing Cross hotel. She brought along several medical reference books with detailed illustrations of skin sections. She explained the anatomy and physiology of skin layers to me, and I was able to leave for my conference with a much better understanding of the issues.

During that first week in January 2005, I thought deeply about my future. Although the case was building up momentum, I was satisfied that progress was being made in all areas.

I thought about that a great deal. We didn't want to be apart, but what did that mean in practical terms? I prayed and reflected for days. Then, on 11 January, I returned to London, saw Tina and asked her to marry me. She smiled for a moment and then accepted.

Our lives were now to change dramatically.

The major issue was whether we should get married before or after my forthcoming trial. Tina said that her wanting to marry me was not dependent on my acquittal; if I were convicted and given a life sentence, she would stand by me for as long as necessary and be there for me when I walked free. Since the trial was an irrelevance as far as our feelings for each other were concerned, we decided that we may as well marry at the earliest possible date.

We both wanted to marry in church so we arranged to meet Tina's minister, Desmond Tillyer of St Peter's Church in Eaton Square. We walked up the winding steps to the vestry to meet him. He is a gentle man, full of inner strength and wisdom. We discussed the responsibilities of marriage; he asked some probing questions; and, together, we set a date for the wedding. We then had a second meeting. Bearing in mind my situation, he asked Tina about the possible pressures that would be put on her. He asked us about our faith. He appeared kindly disposed towards us.

The marriage banns were duly read out over three Sundays and then the day arrived: Monday, 7 February 2005.

Private matters, however, were destined not to stay private. News of our wedding was passed to the newspapers; we do not know by whom. That week, as we walked into Bindman's for a meeting, a concealed photographer was taking photographs. We weren't aware of it at the time, but we soon found out. A front-page headline story appeared in that Sunday's *News of the World*. There were blown-up photographs of our wedding rings. Within hours, there was a crowd of press outside Tina's house. She found it all quite bemusing. Oscar just enjoyed the sudden attention. 'It's like being a famous footballer', he said.

The *News of the World* headline set the tone for what was to follow:

BILLIE-JO DAD IN SECRET WEDDING
Murder-rap Jenkins marries millionairess

The next day nearly every national newspaper carried reports. This was the *Times*:

BILLIE-JO's FOSTER FATHER SECRETLY MARRIES HEIRESS
and the *Daily Mirror*:

SIÔN THE SNEAK

Suddenly I was in the middle of another media hurricane and the timing could not have been worse. My usual advisers were not available: Neil was on holiday with his family in France and Bob was in New York.

Sussex police now wanted to use the wedding as an opportunity to claim I had broken my bail conditions and therefore should be sent back to prison – even though there had, of course, been nothing at all in my bail conditions as to whether or not I was allowed to get married. Indeed, men in prison often get married. I was on bail: I could attend a football match, go to the opera and I could certainly get married.

Police went to see Father Desmond Tillyer. I think they assumed that we must have deceived him in some way in order to persuade him to perform the ceremony. They were disappointed; Desmond explained that we had been completely candid about the circumstances. He gave a thoroughly supportive statement and said that he had married us with his blessing.

However, another emergency hearing in the case was called. As Mrs Justice Rafferty was then overseeing a murder trial in Lewes, we all had to go down there. Before the hearing, Tina and I together went over all the possibilities. Would I have to go back to prison just for the 'crime' of getting married? On the other hand, if I were to keep bail, then we wanted to vary the conditions to allow us to live together.

Everything that day was traumatic. Several journalists were in attendance, but Mrs Justice Raffery suddenly decided that the hearing would be in chambers – even though court officials had told the press the previous day that it would definitely be held in open court. So the journalists had a wasted day. Then Mrs Justice Rafferty ordered that I be taken down to the cells. Having been a free man for eight months, I now found myself back in the same cell I was held in when first convicted.

After further legal discussion, I was brought back up. Chris Sallon argued my case, emphasising that I had broken no bail conditions. Eventually, the judge had to acknowledge that this was the case and there was no reason for me to be sent back to jail, although she did say to me, 'You are a very lucky man, Mr Jenkins'.

The police, who had turned up in some numbers for this hearing, looked crestfallen. They knew that their chances of getting a conviction would have been greatly enhanced had I been sent back to prison.

Having accepted that our marriage was rightful, Mrs Justice Rafferty acceded to Sallon's point that we should be allowed to live together. However, she imposed very strict conditions. I was to live with Tina in Lymington and had to sign on every day there. I was also not able to move more than ten miles outside the town, except for legal meetings in London. Also, in addition to the £300,000 that we had already raised as bail sureties, Tina had to provide an additional £150,000 of her own money as actual security, and that amount had to be lodged at Bindman's. This was a lot of money for Tina. She had to take out an emergency bank loan, with an inevitably high level of interest.

Moreover, there was still a sting in the tail. The police said I should not be allowed to live with Oscar, on the grounds that I was charged with having murdered a child of approximately the same age. The judge accepted this argument. This new situation involved further disruption to Tina's increasingly hectic schedule and meant that, for a period, Oscar was unable to live with his mother and had to be looked after by other family members. It seems remarkable that the authorities, while always emphasising the importance of the family, are quite prepared to break up families when they have other priorities.

Tina and I said farewell to our family and legal team and left Lewes Crown Court in mid-afternoon, by which time it was already dark. There was just one problem which only the two of us were aware of, and which we'd thought it best not to mention – things were tricky enough as it was.

Tina's tenant in the Lymington house had left at Christmas. In one sense, this was fortuitous; the house was empty and available. However, it had been let unfurnished and the tenant had taken everything with him.

We had just been ordered by a judge to go and live in a house that contained not a single piece of furniture.

Tina

It was after five o'clock when we arrived in Lymington. We then had one of the most hectic half-hours I have ever known in my life, as we bought a kettle, bed linen, towels, a few items from the chemist's and a bed – which, amazingly, we persuaded Ford's, a local shop, to deliver for us within the hour. Having arranged those few essentials, Tina then had to drive back to London to sort out arrangements for Oscar.

About a month later, in London, Oscar returned home from school one afternoon. No sooner had he got in than a woman police officer and a social worker knocked at the door. (They'd obviously been outside waiting for him to return.) Tina had told him not to open the door to strangers so Oscar, who was looking out of the window at them, refused to let these strangers in. The police woman then phoned Tina on her mobile and demanded that she tell Oscar to open the door and let them in. Tina asked if they could return later when she had got home. In the circumstances, she did not want Oscar to be with the police and social services on his own, without support or witnesses.

The police then got nasty. Tina was told that if she did not tell Oscar to open the door straightaway that they would break it down, enter the house and possibly take Oscar into care. So Tina spoke to Oscar and explained what they were threatening. She said he had to let them in, but that she would phone him every five minutes to check on his safety.

Once the police woman and the social worker were inside with Oscar, they started aggressively questioning him about me.

'How do you get on with Siôn?'

'What do you call him?'

'Does he have a temper?'

Tina kept calling back until they left the house. When she returned, Oscar told her that their questions about me had irritated him and he felt the answers he gave had not satisfied them; they had wanted different ones. He told her they had gone all over the house as if they were looking for something. He also said – as well as a great football fan, he is a film fanatic – that it was like *The Matrix*, with one playing Mr Nice and one Mr Nasty.

319

Nothing the police or social services do will ever surprise me again.

A few days afterwards, a social worker phoned me in Lymington. She said that she had been contacted by the police because I had a conviction for murder and she needed to discuss Oscar. I told her that she had been misinformed. I was not living with or seeing Oscar; and I did not have a conviction for murder. It had been quashed.

'What does that mean?' she asked.

I assumed she was pleading ignorance as a ploy to obtain further information, so I just repeated the situation. Her responses revealed that she genuinely didn't understand the position. She then asked what other convictions I had. I explained that I had no convictions of any kind for anything, and I suggested that she contact Neil O'May. She began to sound anxious and said she would do that.

The following day she called back to apologise. Clearly, the police had used her and given her false information in order to put more pressure on me.

Tina and I tried our best to have special times because we knew we might not have long together. My bail conditions this time were more restrictive than they had been originally, when I was allowed to go anywhere, except into Sussex, provided that I reported every day. Now, I was restricted to within ten miles of Lymington. I remember several enjoyable visits to the Isle of Wight, parts of which were within the radius (though I would not have able to go to Cowes or Ventnor).

After a few months, the bail conditions were changed. I could now go anywhere in Hampshire – which, ironically, meant that trips to the Isle of Wight were now out of bounds.

The night before the trial started, Tina and I went to bed early. Our clothes had been ironed and were laid out. The alarm clock was set for 5.15am.

Above left: Debbie Wood, Billie-Jo's natural mother, arriving at Lewes Crown Court in July 1998.

Above right: Bill Jenkins, the natural father of Billie-Jo, outside the Old Bailey in February 2006 during Siôn's third trial.

Below left: Jeremy Paine, the Detective Superintendent leading the initial investigations. Paine is now Assistant Chief Constable of Sussex Police.

Below right: Professor David Denison, respiratory expert from the Royal Brompton Hospital, arriving to give evidence at Siôn's second appeal in 2004.

Above left: Siôn's parents, Megan and David Jenkins.

Above right: Anthony Scrivener, QC, defence counsel at the original trial, arriving at the Old Bailey to give evidence at Siôn's second appeal

Below left: Clare Montgomery, QC.

Below right: Christopher Sallon, QC.

Above: Charlotte Jenkins with her mother, Lois, at the appeal in 2004. Whereas Lois had arrived to give evidence for the prosecution, Charlotte gave evidence in support of her father.

Below: Siôn's solicitor, Neil O'May, making a statement outside the Court of Appeal in buoyant mood – the appeal for a retrial had been won.

Above: Siôn's parents arrive at their home in Aberystwyth in August 2004 with Siôn after his release on bail from Belmarsh prison, having secured a retrial.

Below: Siôn speaks to the media outside his parents' home.

Above: Faced by a wall of cameras, Siôn and his wife leave the Old Bailey on the evening of 8 February 2006 after the jury was sent home for another night having failed to reach a verdict.

Below: Arriving back at the Old Bailey on the morning of 9 February 2006 – the day that Siôn saw his conviction finally quashed.

Above: Siôn with his wife Tina and her son Oscar, on holiday in Sardinia in the summer of 2007.

Below: Siôn with investigative journalist and co-author Bob Woffinden, outside Wakefield prison in 2008.

Above: Siôn with Tina at the Nou Camp to watch Barcelona play a league game.

Below: Siôn meeting the Lord Provost of Glasgow at the Miscarriages of Justice Conference, April 2008, at the City Chambers.

The fight to win justice for Billie-Jo goes on.

Chapter Forty-Three

The White Inclusions

In the interval between the end of the appeal and the start of the retrial, the prosecution set about trying to gather further evidence to support its case. The nature of the material that they could draw on was about to expand significantly. Provisions contained in the 2003 Criminal Justice Act would permit the Crown to introduce evidence of bad character – for example, of previous convictions – and also hearsay evidence. Siôn's retrial was scheduled to start on 8 April 2005; conveniently for the prosecution, the new provisions would come into force just seven days earlier.

So the Cypriot businessman whom Siôn met in Belmarsh was proved correct. The police started to make enquiries at Wakefield prison. They wanted to know if Siôn had shown signs of violence or was liable to lose his temper. The primary objection to soliciting evidence of this kind, from within prison, is that it is more than likely to lead to perjured testimony. Many prisoners are only too prepared to bear false witness; they know their reputations cannot sink any further and even vestigial traces of conscience will have long since disappeared. In return for their testimony, they will then be able to extract from the authorities some kind of favour or reward, be it as major as the dropping of serious criminal charges or as minor as being moved to a less insalubrious part of the prison.

Siôn's stock in Wakefield, however, remained high. A number of prisoners were upset at the trawling for evidence against him. One of the more respected prisoners was greatly alarmed at what was going on. He asked his wife to contact Bindman's to alert them – which she did. The upshot was that the prosecution enquiries in this area proved fruitless.

The police had also monitored Siôn's movements while he was on bail in Aberystwyth, presumably in the hope that he would breach his bail conditions. David Jenkins, Siôn's father, was shocked to be told that there had been a video-camera in one of the houses opposite monitoring the family's movements.

Further analysis of the scientific evidence was, from the Crown's point of view, much more productive. The senior Home Office pathologist Dr Nat Cary was recruited to the prosecution team. He developed a new strategy, arguing that the lung tissue slides did not, after all, show evidence of pulmonary interstitial emphysema (PIE). He maintained that the tearings could have been a 'bubble artefact' – that is, a product of the histological process itself, made when slices were taken from the lung sample. Dr Hill now retracted his appeal court evidence and, reverting to his original position, again asserted that there was no evidence of PIE.

A second strand of the Crown case was developed by Dr Jeremy Skepper, from the multi-imaging centre of the department of human anatomy at Cambridge University. He conducted a further examination of surviving bloodspots and, using electron microscopy, detected white spots within them. For the purposes of the case, they were dubbed the white inclusions.

So what were they? Dr Skepper said they could be particles of skin and could have come, for example, from 'damaged tissue on Billie-Jo's scalp'.

So the prosecution's strategy at retrial with regard to the science was two-fold: to knock down the defence theories about PIE and an expirated spray; and to construct its own case, which was that the presence of the

The White Inclusions

white inclusions within the bloodspots proved that Siôn had violently attacked the girl, as particles of skin as well as blood had landed on him as he did so.

At the forthcoming trial, prosecution experts – Adrian Wain, for example – would refer to the white particles as 'flesh'.

'It seems reasonable to assume that that flesh came from Billie-Jo', Wain commented.

Sallon, cross-examining, challenged him. 'You described this as "flesh"', Sallon said, 'it was actually skin.'

'I understood it was flesh', responded Wain.

The term may have been anatomically meaningless, but it was highly emotive.

Neil O'May spent more than two years assembling a team of leading scientists to assess the prosecution case. Nothing was left to chance; no avenue was left unexplored. The scientific background to the case was examined in painstaking detail.

There was no doubt amongst defence scientists that the Crown's new stance on PIE was misconceived. Three of the world authorities in this field of medicine – Professor Denison; Andrew Nicholson; and William Travis from New York – each re-examined the evidence and again concluded that the evidence of PIE in the slides was 'absolutely unequivocal'. Alan Aitkenhead also provided valuable insights, and concluded that Denison's expiration theory was 'entirely plausible'.[46]

The scientists whom the defence consulted also found the 'white inclusions' argument specious. Altogether, the 158 bloodspots found on Siôn's clothing amounted merely to one drop of blood, which was roughly one-twentieth of a millilitre. This was, as Denison pointed out, 'an almost infinitesimally small proportion of the blood [Billie-Jo] lost as a result of the attack'.

To put the 158 microscopic bloodspots into proportion, a vigorous sneeze will normally generate 20,000 tiny droplets of mucus, saliva and phlegm – that is, about 100 times as many as the number found on Siôn's clothing.

In the circumstances of this murder, it was only to be expected that the particles of blood would contain elements of skin and other matter. Moreover, there were two additional considerations: Billie-Jo's airways would have been damaged by the forcible insertion of the plastic bag into her left nostril; further, her cribriform plate – which is at the base of the skull, separating the interior of the nose from the brain – was fractured. It would therefore not be in any way surprising that microscopic fragments of skin, bone and even brain would be contained in her expired blood.

Peter Morgan looked at Skepper's evidence and explained that there was nothing to suggest that the white particles could have come only from Billie-Jo's scalp. Indeed, he thought there was a 'strong possibility' that they could have originated in the lining of the nose ('the lining of the nasal cavity is delicate'), though nor could he exclude the possibility that they came from her mouth.[47]

Having reviewed the evidence, Laurence Watkins determined that 'it is unlikely that death would have been instantaneous and the brainstem reflexes, including breathing and coughing, could have continued to be present at the time when Siôn Jenkins arrived on the scene'. He added that the respiratory function is 'one of the basic brainstem reflexes' and 'one of the last to disappear during the process of dying'; and pointed out that forcible expiration may not always be loud enough to be noticed.[48]

Robert Schroter, who would take over much of the onus of leading the scientific work for the defence at the third trial when David Denison became seriously ill, and Julian Hunt conducted experiments in ambient air currents to establish scientifically how blood droplets would travel in the atmospheric and environmental conditions that would have been expected on the patio. They concluded that droplets expelled by Billie-Jo would have landed on Siôn's clothing.[49]

The evidence was also examined from another angle. Joseph Slemko was an experienced Canadian policeman who was gaining an international reputation as a forensic consultant in the field of bloodstain pattern evidence. He concluded from the documents that the pattern of bloodstaining on the fleece jacket was consistent only 'with blood being expirated from a blood-contaminated airway'. He explained that, in order for the pattern on the clothing to be created, Siôn:

> ... would have to be in a crouching semi-kneeling position, with the right side and right outer lower trouser leg exposed to the blood source and with his torso twisted right and lowered to expose the inner chest area – a position not consistent with being an assailant, but consistent with him positioning himself to examine her.

Slemko added that the prosecution theory – that the pattern had been created by impact spatter – was 'highly improbable'.

Three leading pathologists, Christopher Milroy, Helen Whitwell and Jack Crane, were also consulted by the defence.[50]

With this extraordinary amount of work having been put into the case, the defence was now ready for the second trial.

However, the Crown wasn't. They told the judge they needed more time to consider the scientific submissions from the defence and asked for a fortnight's adjournment, to which the judge readily acceded.

The defence team was exasperated. First of all, it seemed to them that if they ever needed extra time to consider material, it was either very grudgingly allowed or simply refused; whereas such requests from the prosecution were instantly granted.

Secondly, they could not understand the request. All their scientific reports had been handed over to the other side in good time. Did the Crown have an ulterior motive for wishing to postpone the start of the trial?

Indeed they did. Just as the Crown had been disingenuous in its reasons for wishing to delay the first trial (when they had said they needed time to consult a neurosurgeon, although in the event they had called David Southall, a paediatrician), so they were disingenuous this time also. They needed the delay not to deal with the science; but because they were desperately trying to persuade Lois Jenkins to give evidence.

For the moment, however, all the defence knew was that the trial was now scheduled to begin on Wednesday, 22 April.

Chapter Forty-Four

Court No. 1;
Trial No. 2

That first day, we caught the 5.55am train from Brockenhurst. We got used to catching that train. Despite the early hour, it was always full; every morning, there were always the same people sitting in the same seats. I think we very quickly came to be regarded just as other commuters.

The court day didn't start until 10.30 but we had to be there early so that, at about 9.20, we would walk round to the court. As we turned the corner, we could see the small knot of photographers and camera crews waiting for us. So we just kept walking straight ahead until we reached the sanctuary of the Old Bailey. I know that sounds a contradiction in terms but, in these circumstances, it is an apt description of how it felt.

No.1 Court is the famous one. Stories that have become entire chapters in criminal justice history have been written there. Men had occupied that dock only to end up being sentenced to death. We all knew that some of those unfortunate men had been innocent; if hanging had not been abolished thirty years before Billie-Jo was murdered, I too would be dead.

Inside the dock are stairs leading down to the cells. A prisoner who is on bail, as I was, has to be first led down to the cells below so that, after the judge has taken his or her seat, he can be brought back up again. This is in order to create a moment of theatre; performance is an integral part of the judicial process. So I was taken backstage, as it were, before being brought back up to find myself face to face with Mrs Justice Rafferty, who was resplendent in her red robes. I gave my name, pleaded not guilty, and was told to sit.

The first day was taken up with legal arguments about the admissibility of particular areas of evidence. Rafferty said she had serious reservations about Lois's evidence. She noted that Lois had said she had to move as far away as possible to get away from the constant threat of publicity; and yet, when she finally got to Tasmania with the children, one of the first things she did was to sell a lengthy article about herself to the *Sunday Times*. Moreover, she had written to the judge to say that she was an unreliable witness. In view of these considerations, and also other comments she had made, Mrs Justice Rafferty ruled that Lois would not be allowed to mention any of her allegations that I had been violent towards her.

Evidence from Billie-Jo's friends, Holly Prior and Laura-Jane Conway, was also ruled inadmissible.

The jury members were sworn in. It is not possible to describe what it is like to have your fate determined by twelve strangers. Six men and six women. I prayed that they would listen to the evidence with care and understanding.

Nicholas Hilliard then opened the case for the prosecution. He spoke for a day, using words and phrases that were designed to blacken me in almost every possible way. It was difficult to take. He presented me as a caricature of the person I believe I am. Obviously, what he was saying was for the benefit of the jury and the media – though, at this stage of proceedings, probably more for the latter than the former. Another spate of negative headlines about me was hardly going to dispirit the prosecution.

After the opening speech, the prosecution call all their witnesses in turn. This took altogether about six weeks. There was a minor, but telling, moment towards the beginning. One woman gave evidence about having seen me driving in the car with two girls that Saturday afternoon. From her evidence of where the car was at the time she saw me, it was clear that there should actually have been not two, but three girls in the car – we were taking Ellen home. After the witness retired, a juror who had perceptively noticed the anomaly in the evidence asked a question about it.

'We can't go behind what the witness said', Mrs Justice Rafferty commented – before proceeding to do precisely that. She consulted the lawyers and then simply assumed that, as she put it, the witness 'hasn't spotted the other girl'.

What, I wondered, is the point of bringing a witness to court and asking her to give evidence on oath, only for the judge then to tell the jury that her evidence must have been wrong anyway?

I think this very small episode, however, had an effect on the jurors. I think their natural deference to the whole process began to evaporate from that point. They began to understand that even the most serious trials can be prone to error (which is not to blame this particular witness). Afterwards, the jurors were much more inclined to jump in and put questions about the evidence.

From Monday, 25 until Wednesday, 27 April, for three days, Lois gave her video link evidence. She claimed she needed to give evidence from an undisclosed location in order to protect her privacy.

Video link evidence is worse than unsatisfactory. Lois said on occasions that she had not heard the questions; that there was some problem either with sound or vision; that she had lost her place in the files in front of her. She could also claim tiredness and the fact that it was the middle of the night where she was.[51]

In the third week of the trial, on Friday, 6 May (I now know it was the day after the general election; at the time, I had no idea that was going on), the jury visited the scene of the crime. For the purposes of the visit, my old house at 48 Lower Park Road in Hastings was designated part of the court. It was a day's outing for everyone and it was not without an element of drama.

The judge would be travelling with the jury in a coach. Tina and I would be driving there from Lymington. Chris and Julian were travelling by train and the arrangement was that we would meet them in the station car park.

As we drove into the car park, however, an unmarked car with two men inside swerved in behind us. We knew instantly that the men were police. They ordered me to get into their car, saying they had instructions to take me to the crime scene with a blanket over my head; then, when I left the car to go into the house, the blanket would remain over my head.

In criminal cases, a prisoner or suspect will frequently be driven to court or elsewhere with a blanket over his head. He will be told that this is for his own protection, in order to prevent his photograph appearing in the media, which would mean that witnesses would regard him as the culprit and perhaps be influenced to identify him as the criminal or become prejudiced against him.

Of course, this is not the real reason. The real reason is to deprive the person under the blanket of the presumption of innocence; straightaway, that person is perceived by the community as the offender.

If there had actually been a picture of me on the news bulletins arriving at the scene escorted by policemen and with a blanket over my head, it would have been very bad publicity for me and the police would probably have thrown a party in celebration.

However, on this occasion, they couldn't even pretend that what they were seeking was anything other than a publicity stunt. After all, I hardly needed to worry about shifts in witnesses' perceptions; my picture had been in every newspaper in the country on a regular basis for the past eight years.

So I refused point blank to have anything to do with their media games. A huge row ensued – in full view of the public, as Hastings railway station is particularly busy at that time of the morning. While the police were on their mobile phones, fortunately, Chris and Julian arrived. To my relief, they then argued the matter out for me with the police.

Finally, Chris told them that I would be attending the scene with my lawyers, and that I would be driving my own car. If the police had other ideas, then he would call off the visit and they would have to explain themselves to the judge. Faced with this, the police capitulated. I drove up to my old house in Lower Park Road with Chris and Julian and Tina.

Even so, the whole thing had been arranged as a PR exercise. There were police everywhere. You would have thought there was a major terrorist alert in Hastings. The road was closed. Whole sections of the park had been screened off.

Again, this was designed for the benefit of members of the public, and specifically the jurors, to create the illusion that I was a dangerous man. It was just a performance and, as I said, performance is an integral part of the judicial process.

For the first time in eight years, I returned to what had been our family home. Very little had changed apart from some interior decoration. I walked into the garden where I noticed that many of the shrubs I had planted were now fully grown. The house was full of police, which prevented me from talking freely to Chris and Julian. I tried to point things out to them but, even when we walked to the top of the garden, there was no privacy; a policeman stuck closely beside us.

All in all, it had been an emotionally exhausting morning. I was relieved when we were able to get in the car and drive away. We reached Brighton and, I remember, had fish and chips on the pier.

Normal service was resumed on the Monday and we were all back in the Old Bailey. That Thursday, 12 May, Hilliard went through every tiny detail of my CV and my application for headteacher with Sussex education staff. There was considerable tension about this evidence – it was one of the key factors that soured the atmosphere in the courtroom.

This had been inadmissible evidence at my first trial, but could now be introduced because of David Blunkett's 2003 Criminal Justice Act. It was evidence of bad character. Yet thousands of people must have embellished their CVs over the years – did that make them likely to commit murder?

(I would still like to put forward a limited defence: I was appointed headteacher in December 1996 on the basis of my performance as deputy head over the previous five years, my handling of the interviews and my

MSc in education management. But I'm sadly aware that, with all that has happened, this is now an irrelevance.)

Ken Ashmore was listed as one of our witnesses. He had been chairman of the governors and was the man who had telephoned to offer me the job. At the outset of the trial, we were exasperated suddenly to find out that the police had gone to see him at his home. He had already been cited as a defence witness. I understand the protocol in these circumstances is that if one side wishes to see one of the other side's witnesses, then the other side is informed so that they can have someone present and this then prevents any suggestions of witness-nobbling.

On this occasion, this courtesy had not been extended to the defence. So Neil subsequently went to see him again. Then, just as we were about to call him, we found out that the police had again been to see him without informing the defence. Chris was furious, and there was a huge row with the police outside court. Chris complained in forthright terms to the judge, but she wouldn't do anything. The lawyers then decided that we could not call him, just because we did not know whether he had been placed under any pressure about what to say.

All this was indicative of the number of people working for the prosecution. If they wanted to draft in extra people to go and interview witnesses, they could do so. Tina and I used to say that this was the state's concept of even-handed adversarial combat in the courts: four hard-pressed people working for the defence and about twenty-four working for the prosecution (though they could always have more if they needed them).

There were always police in court and around the courtroom. They were up and down and in and out all the time. There were police officers in court who seemed to do nothing for weeks. There were police accompanying Lois's parents, there were police accompanying Billie-Jo's natural family, there were police officers on the other side of the world accompanying Lois. Tina, much of whose life has been spent working in the NHS, found it almost incredible that public funds were being so extravagantly frittered away in the courts.

My first trial had been over inside a month. This one was different.

331

Being constantly vilified, day after day, for six weeks is very emotionally draining – by the end of it, I was reeling. Nor was it just emotionally exhausting; there was also the travelling. We caught the 6.00am train in to London, and generally got back home over twelve hours later. If we could get seats, I'd look through paperwork for the next day's hearing on the train; if not, I had to do it at home. There was just time for some quickly-cooked dinner before we had to go to bed to get up the next morning. In the circumstances, I felt it was an onerous schedule. Rafferty was sympathetic, so she said she was prepared to vary the bail conditions to allow us to stay in London during the week.

The prosecution immediately objected: what about Oscar? They had insisted upon it being a bail condition that I did not reside with him. On this occasion the judge simply dismissed the objections.

How marvellous it is when bureaucracy and spite are brusquely swept aside and common sense and compassion are allowed to reign. At last, Tina, Oscar and I could now begin to live together. The actions of certain people to prevent us living as a family had caused real emotional hardship, not least on Oscar. All that he gained from the experience was some insight into how shabbily the authorities in this country can sometimes behave, even towards thirteen-year-old children.

On the day that I was originally convicted in 1998, the Forensic Science Service put out a press release, claiming the credit for my conviction. It said that the 'expert analysis' of the bloodstain patterns had 'proved crucial' in identifying me as the murderer.

The chief executive of the FSS, Dr Janet Thompson, said, 'This case illustrates perfectly the power of forensic science in uncovering the truth'.

Adrian Wain, the main forensic scientist for the Crown, then gave a television interview in which he boasted that it was his work that had led to my conviction. 'It was essential', he said of his bloodstain analysis. 'Without my evidence there wouldn't have been a case.'

Together with Russell Stockdale, who had by now retired and wasn't giving evidence, Wain had carried out the pig's head experiment.

Now, cross-examining him in 2005, Sallon asked him what had happened to the pig's ears.

'We cut the ears off', Wain replied, 'so that they wouldn't flap about.'

Some jurors may have thought to themselves that the level of sophistication of some work conducted by the Forensic Science Services was not quite what they had expected.

There were obvious problems with the Wain–Stockdale experiment: to give just two examples, there was no circulation of blood in their pig's head; and the attacker had remained static. In these respects, the experiment certainly did not replicate the attack on Billie-Jo. Moreover, every time that Wain and Stockdale ran their experiment, the results showed that there was more blood on the striking than the non-striking arm of the assailant. That's inevitable, or so you would have thought. But that didn't stop the Crown Prosecution Service from turning common sense on its head. I am right-handed. The majority of bloodspots on my clothing were on my left arm (21 on the left arm; 3 on the right).

Under cross-examination, however, Wain conceded that he had formed the mistaken impression, from talking to police officers, that Billie-Jo was already dead when I found her. He was unaware that there was any possibility that she had still been alive. Nor had he been given any information about my interactions with Billie-Jo, or what I'd said to police and put in my witness statements about pulling her up towards me.

'Was anything said to you by the police about what the defendant said about contact he had had with the body?' asked Sallon.

'No', admitted Wain.

'Was it not good practice in 1997 to find out what contact he had said he had?'

'I agree it was important', responded Wain.

Sallon continued by reading out extracts from the statement I'd been making in that first week, between 18 and 21 of February.

'This is what he says in his statement', said Sallon, 'and you didn't know any of it?'

'No', replied Wain.

Wain went on to concede that he'd never even known what had been said in the 999 emergency calls until the appeal in 2004. He had therefore formulated his initial opinion in total ignorance of highly relevant information about the circumstances. His tentative and uninformed opinion nevertheless became the foundation stone of the prosecution case.

Sallon pointed out that Wain, in arriving at his provisional opinion, had not adhered to the procedures set out in the Forensic Science Services manual. Wain said he was well aware of those provisions because he had helped to draw them up, but explained that the manual was only published in 2002, four years after I had been convicted.

Had the manual been in existence at the time, it would have been very instructive because it says that a forensic scientist:

… should take into account not merely injuries, and the manner of the assault but also contact after the injuries occurred.

These were logical safeguards which were not in place when the case against me was being pursued. Indeed, it was partly as a result of my case that new guidelines had to be drawn up. Yet, although the prosecution knew that the central evidence in my case would now have had to be assessed differently, they nevertheless continued to try to uphold the conviction.

Sallon pressed Wain on the key scientific point in the case, which was the possible confusion between expiration spray and impact spatter. He told him that three highly-respected professors – Denison, Schroter and Lord Hunt – had all concluded that the blood pattern on my clothing was attributable to expiration spray. Wain instantly discounted their views. 'They are not trained forensic scientists', he responded.

Sallon asked:

Sallon: Expirated blood can mimic high velocity spatter?
Wain: I accept that, yes.

Sallon: Did you draw the attention of the police to the potential for confusion between impact spatter and expiration spray?

Wain: I've never denied that the two can be similar.

Sallon: You have never said it, though?

Wain: No.

Finally, Sallon got the concession he wanted, as Wain admitted:

I cannot tell in this instance [whether the bloodstaining was caused by expiration spray or impact spatter].

Dr Ian Hill, the pathologist, had now retired. He had conceded at the Court of Appeal that there was interstitial emphysema in Billie-Jo's lungs. This was the key moment in the appeal – once Hill had said that, there was a feeling that we were bound to win – but the Crown was not happy. So they had recruited a higher-profile pathologist, Dr Nat Cary, effectively to replace him. Hill said that it was 'very unkind' to suggest that he'd been replaced. He asserted that Cary had been brought in 'at my suggestion' to provide 'a second opinion'.[52]

What we wanted to cross-examine him about was his examination, if any, of Billie-Jo's nostrils. Because of Dr Skepper's evidence, this had now assumed a real importance. Skepper was arguing that the tiny white specks he had seen within the bloodspots were 'consistent with damaged tissue from Billie-Jo's scalp'. We argued that they were also consistent with tissue from inside Billie-Jo's nostril, as the skin at the nostrils' entrance is the same as outer skin over the rest of the body.

Hill insisted that he had examined Billie-Jo's nose. 'It's part of routine procedure', he explained. He said he had not seen signs of injury. Sallon then pointed out to him that in all his pages of notes and in his post-mortem report, there was no reference whatever to his having examined the nostrils.

'You don't normally put [it] in', he explained. 'It's one of the convention or methods that were used over the years'.

Sallon pointed out that there were references to all other areas of the body in his notes; but nothing at all about an examination of the nose. Hill emphasised that it was normal for pathologists to do nasal examinations, but not to mention them in their notes. It was, he said, a form of 'shorthand'. Asked if he had used any instruments, Hill relied, 'No – I just looked inside'. He emphasised that an examination of the nostrils would have been 'part of my routine practice'. However, the photographs of Billie's nose at post-mortem showed one nostril blocked with crusted dried blood. Any examination would have required a nasal speculum and a torch, to view the interior of the nostril. One nostril had also had a plastic bin liner inserted into it under force.

Martyn Ismail, who at the time of the murder was employed at the forensic science laboratory in Lambeth, south London, gave evidence about the crime scene. He had been called in twenty-four hours after the murder, late on Sunday afternoon, by which time, he acknowledged, 'a lot had been disturbed' at the scene.

For Ismail's evidence, Neil had had the inspired idea of providing the jury with magnifying glasses so that they could in effect become forensic scientists themselves and find vital evidence that the professionals had missed. Even Mrs Justice Rafferty was given a magnifying glass and she went through the scene-of-crime photographs with keen interest.

By taking the court carefully through the photographs Chris was able to show that that the scene-of-crime work had not been thorough. Many bloodspots over the patio area, and indeed inside the house too, had never been taken into consideration by the prosecution. For example, there were two trellises outside; one had not been removed. So not only had that not been carefully examined for bloodspots, but the wall behind had not been examined either. Many spots at some greater distance from the body than the main concentration of spots had never been examined. The location and size of these indicated a dynamic attack, meaning that there was a high possibility that the attacker would intercept a lot of blood spatter. There was no evidence of this on my clothing. The decision to consult Joseph Slemko had paid dividends because the scene-of-crime work here fell a long way short of the professional standards he was used to in Canada.

'Did anybody order more photographs?' asked Sallon.

'No', replied Ismail, 'I just asked for the usual range'.

'Were any DNA checks done to see whether these further-away spots were those of Billie-Jo or of the assailant?'

'Not as far as I know', replied Ismail.

So potentially vital evidence had just been ignored. We knew that Billie-Jo had defended herself, because there were defensive injuries on her body. We could tell that the attacker had been in different positions when he struck her. He could well have shed blood himself. However the evidence was presumably lost forever because of poor preservation and examination of the crime scene.

As well as the magnifying glasses, the defence had had a second brainwave. Julian Knowles came up with a sheet of white paper, in the middle of which was a near-invisible black spot. This, we were able to explain to the jury with a theatrical flourish, was the total area of all the white inclusions that the Crown claimed to have discovered in the bloodspots and was now relying on as proof that I was guilty. The all-but-blank sheet of white paper made our point very impressively.

There was an odd conclusion to the Crown case. The prosecution's final witness was Fred Robinson, the south-east regional secretary of the MG owners' club. Immediately after the murder, with the ambulance crew tending to Billie-Jo, I had got into my MG car. Having got in, I couldn't understand what I was doing there and straightaway got out again. I suppose the logical conclusion is that I was in shock and not thinking or reacting normally. However, when questioned about it by police, when they were encouraging me to fill in the blanks in my account, I'd said I must have got into the car in order to put the roof up in case it rained.

When this was mentioned at this trial, a member of the jury passed a note to the judge pointing out that this explanation didn't make sense. You didn't need to get in to the car to close the roof; you did it from outside.

It was perceptive of the juror to have noticed, but I still thought the whole issue was explicable precisely because it was inexplicable. At the first trial, my defence had called Professor Michael Trimble to talk about the level of shock that I would have been in at the time; Trimble explained that, in those moments, I could not have been expected to account for every incidental action.

However, the Crown enthusiastically took up the juror's point. Gratefully clutching at whatever straws were tossed in their direction, they overlooked the fact that in the eight years that the CPS had been prosecuting this case, no one had noticed this point. They called Robinson who, looking only marginally more startled by his presence in court than everyone else, gave evidence at an Old Bailey murder trial about how to close the roof of an MGB roadster.

The defence started on Thursday, 26 May. In a criminal trial, the defence has the advantage of going second. In a long trial, however, this may not be an advantage at all. The jurors are ordinary people who have been uprooted from their everyday lives. After six weeks, the excitement of taking part in a major Old Bailey trial will have worn off and the whole experience may well have become as mentally gruelling for them as it is for the rest of us. So the awareness that this is only half-time and there are still untold weeks to go is almost certainly demoralising for them. Will their concentration levels remain as high throughout the coming days as they were for the first six weeks?

With such considerations in mind, defence lawyers can sometimes feel that jurors are becoming overloaded with information and may opt to curtail their own case. However, although it was a dilemma, I was keen to present as much evidence as possible.

This time, I did have the opportunity to go into the witness-box and explain everything from my point of view. The witness-box is adjacent to the jury benches, so I could speak to the jurors directly, almost as if I were having a personal tête-à-tête with them.

However, when I first stepped into the witness-box, I found it more distressing than I had ever imagined. I tried to explain to the jury what had happened, what a state of shock I had been in and how emotionally overwhelming it was to find Billie. But the years of struggle and grief enveloped me. I became distraught and never recovered.

In retrospect, I feel that because I had not given evidence at my first trial, I was not prepared for this moment. For six years I had sat in a prison cell and thought about what I wanted to say, should I ever be given the opportunity. Now it was here, I was submerged by the enormity of it all.

When it was over, I was numb.

Then we played the girls' videos – there were five in all: the three interviews from February 1997 and the CCRC interviews conducted five years later, in February 2002. However, the sound quality on the CCRC interviews was poor. When we played them on the large LCD screens in court, they were barely audible. We couldn't understand why this was because all the interviews had been conducted in the same interview suite at Battle.

There had been constant technical problems throughout the trial. Now, the sound quality of these tapes was a problem that no one could effectively solve. The court took a break while technicians tried to sort out the problem. Eventually, an old analogue television set was brought into court and all the jury members had to come down from their benches and huddle in front of that. No one else in court was able to watch.

In this respect, even more than in others, I felt that the court failed me as a citizen. A key component of my defence was not presented properly in court because of technical problems. Millions of pounds had been spent bringing me to trial, and yet a central part of the evidence demonstrating my innocence couldn't be heard properly. At the time, I was very angry. In my admittedly paranoid state, I believed that the court was complicit with the prosecution in deliberately disadvantaging my defence. I felt sure that, if this evidence had been essential for the Crown's case, then all available assistance and technological back-up would have been at hand to make sure the equipment functioned properly.

Then the long and complex scientific evidence was heard. I worried about this evidence. The science had confused me at times, and I had thrashed the arguments out with the legal and scientific experts for the past six years – so what on earth would the jury, hearing the arguments cold, make of them? Nor was I the only one who was concerned.

'I'm very perturbed about what the jury is making of this', said Mrs Justice Rafferty at one stage. 'We may be asking the jury to referee at a very high level'.

After that, we brought forward evidence from some of those who'd seen Mark Lynam, the first suspect, in the vicinity of my home that Saturday afternoon. These included Brian Kent, the guest-house owner who'd seen him, possibly about ten minutes earlier, but turned him away and had directed him back towards town, which was also towards my house.

This had been an extraordinary case in almost every way and we added another layer of improbability to it by calling as a key part of the defence case a group of Sussex police officers. These were the ones who had arrested Lynam on the Monday afternoon, and then noticed him holding a piece of plastic up to his nose in the police station cell.[53]

By this stage, I'd done a lot of jury-gazing. I felt as if I knew all twelve of them. They and I had shared this ordeal together. All of us on the defence side had looked closely for any indication of their feelings. I'd been dissatisfied with the way I gave my own evidence, but my lawyers were less dismayed. They had noticed that while I talked about how distressing it was to have lost contact with my daughters, two of the female jurors had wiped away tears.

Throughout, the jurors had seemed to show an intelligent interest in the evidence. I thought they were all fully attentive during the closing speeches, which I took to be a good sign. By the end of the trial, one development was absolutely clear: the prosecution case had changed completely. At my original trial, the jury had been told that the scientific evidence proved my guilt. Now, I could tell we'd won the scientific arguments, because in his closing speech, Hilliard told the jury, 'Do not worry too much about the science... it is a compelling case without any science at all'.

At 2.30pm on Thursday 30 June, the jurors were sent out to consider their verdict. To be a defendant at that moment is an extraordinary feeling. My fate was now entirely in their hands.

That first day of waiting was an unbearable strain. My family spent all day on the wooden benches on the ground floor in the old part of the building. In the afternoon, we were quickly called back into court. When that happens, you have no idea whether the jury is delivering its verdict, or asking a question, or whether some other matter has arisen. Tina and I looked at each other and realised that, even after everything we had said and how much we had tried to prepare, we were still not ready. I held her briefly; our hearts were pounding. I went back into the dock. It was a jury question.

On that first day, we'd noticed the police officers were all wearing their smartest suits, clearly anticipating a verdict in their favour with television appearances to follow. Thankfully, their hopes were dashed. Afterwards, they left off their best suits and looked a little more dishevelled as each day passed.

When the jury goes out, the press suddenly get excited again. They hadn't been interested in reporting the evidence in the case; they're only really interested in the denouement. So, from now on, the press filled out the first floor of the Old Bailey and the canteen.

Outside, the cameramen started following us again. Who was to know whether or not that would be my last walk to court, my last journey home, my last hours of freedom?

Even during this very tense period, however, the petty tricks of the prosecution continued. The police said they didn't want me walking around or using the canteen, and so the defence was given a small room on the ground floor, in a part of the building away from the courtrooms, which few people apart from occasional members of staff passed through. I would sometimes stretch my legs by walking on the landing. A Sussex police officer then made a fresh complaint about me 'wandering the precincts', so the judge then confined me to the room. It was not large enough for all of us to squeeze into. I could consult with my lawyers or talk to my family, but not do both at the same time.

Still the jury continued to debate the case. Tina and I suffered a little more every day.

That week, London made world headlines three times for three entirely different reasons – something that had never happened to any city before. On 2 July, there was the Live 8 concert in Hyde Park to 'make poverty history' – or, at least, to get world leaders gathering for the G8 summit at Gleneagles in Scotland to address the issue; on 6 July London was chosen to host the 2012 Olympics (all the others saw the fly-past of the Red Arrows across central London in celebration; Tina and I didn't because I wasn't allowed to leave the court during the day); and – how quickly triumph can turn to tragedy – the next day there were the suicide bomber attacks on three tube trains and a London bus.

With all this was going on around us, we thought, how are these jurors expected to concentrate, let alone to remember evidence they heard in April?

The jurors said that they would not be able to reach a unanimous decision, so at 11.22am on Friday 8 July, Mrs Justice Rafferty gave what is known as the majority direction, meaning that she would be able to accept the verdict of just ten jurors as the final verdict. By that afternoon, we were ready to assume that the whole process was deadlocked. However, the judge kept explaining to the jurors that time was not a factor. Would they like more time to consider? To our complete surprise, they said, yes, they would.

Another nerve-wracked weekend followed. Then, finally, we learned that the jury was returning at 2.50pm on Monday afternoon, 11 July. The foreman stood up.

'Have you been able to reach a verdict on which at least ten of you are agreed?' the clerk of the court asked.

'No', he replied.

My heart sang.

Mrs Justice Rafferty then discharged them. She thanked them for their weeks of attendance and their attentiveness throughout. She then asked Hilliard what course of action he proposed to take. He indicated immediately that the prosecution would seek a retrial.

We left the court. I embraced my aunts and uncles, who were emotionally drained. Back in Wales, my parents, too, were relieved but exhausted. Tina and I went home to Oscar. The feeling among the lawyers was that any new trial would be set for the spring of 2006.

Despite the enormous strain, despite the fact that – as I perceived it – my chances of getting a fair trial diminished each time we went though this process, I was still a free man.

Chapter Forty-Five

Inadmissible Evidence

A new judge, the Honourable Mr Justice David Clarke, was appointed.
There was a hearing before him to arrange the next trial date, which
was then was set down for October – in a mere eight weeks' time.

Siôn's situation was, to some extent, unique. There were very few
examples in criminal justice history of defendants in England and Wales
having to face three trials on the same charge. Questions were already
being asked about the appropriateness of a third trial and whether the
matter should be taken to the European Court of Human Rights. Some
members of the defence team believed that the Crown wanted to rush
ahead partly to forestall the possibility of avenues like these being
pursued. In the end, after further representations, the judge gave an
extension of a mere three weeks.[54]

Meanwhile, in brief moments of respite from the relentlessness of the
legal juggernaut, Siôn and Tina sold Groom Place and moved to a
Victorian property near the sea in Lymington.

Relations between prosecution and defence became increasingly
Arctic. One of the reasons for the sharp deterioration was that the defence

had learned that an extraordinary meeting had taken place. On 4 August 2005, within a month of the end of the second trial, WDS Capon and DC Hilton had met the Gaimsters and Denise Lancaster at the White Hart pub in Fairlight, Hastings.

The police forcibly argued that the occasion had been merely a social one. Their lack of appreciation of its improbity only heightened defence concerns. The case was already bedevilled by the close and regular contact between police and the key participants, which had led to a mutual reinforcing of mindsets about the case. Renewed intimacy between officers and the key witnesses would only lead to further infection of the core evidence.

Moreover the Crown strategy for a trial is not supposed to be orchestrated by the police and the main witnesses. At the meeting, Gaimster stressed that the 'personal touch' of Lois would be better for the prosecution. So, for this trial, she would be flying back to give evidence in person.

For the new trial, the defence team would stay more or less the same. However, Sara Harrison had left Bindman's to have a baby. This time, Neil O'May was assisted by Jessica Skinns and Ezra Nathan. Even so, there was an extraordinary amount of work for such a small team.

The courts' administrators having lurched from one extreme to the other, this trial had been allocated to Court No.7. This was at the opposite end of the first floor from Court No.1 and also at the opposite end of the spectrum of courtroom design. It was panelled in beech, giving it a calmer and more modern ambience. There was no natural light, but there was also no complaint about the technical facilities. For a trial of this significance, however, it was absurdly small.

Mr Justice Clarke inspired confidence from the beginning. A former recorder of Liverpool, he was new to the combative traditions of the Old Bailey. It is here that the adversarial process in England and Wales reaches its zenith (or, depending on your point of view, nadir).

There was a major dispute on the opening day. Dr Jeremy Skepper, on behalf of the Crown, had been carrying out further laboratory tests on the bloodspots on Siôn's clothing. A fresh statement from him was delivered on Thursday, 27 October, just before the trial was due to start. Two days later, at 4.15pm that Saturday, a second statement was e-mailed to Neil O'May.

When the trial began, on Monday, 31 October, Hilliard told the judge that a fuller report from Dr Skepper's report on this fresh scientific work was expected to be served by four o'clock that afternoon, with another to follow at the same time the following day.

What the Crown had purported to discover in these latest tests was that the bloodspots on Siôn's clothing contained not just Billie-Jo's blood but also particles of skin, tissue and bone, as well as specks of paint and fragments of metal. It seemed that the Crown would be seeking to establish that minute traces of the murder weapon itself had been found on Siôn's clothing.

The Crown was hyping this as dramatic new evidence. In context, of course, the situation was rather different. The first trial had been argued on the basis that invisible bloodspots were compelling enough to prove Siôn's guilt; the second trial had been launched on the basis that it was the white inclusions within the bloodspots that provided the scientific underpinning to the Crown's case; at this stage, the third trial looked set to be brought on the basis that guilt could be proved not by the invisible bloodspots themselves, nor by the white inclusions at the heart of some of them, but by even more microscopic fragments contained within the particles within the invisible spots.

At this stage, however, the judge had no interest in what the tests might have showed; he was concerned merely that they were being carried out at all. He asked how it could be that this work was now in progress, over fifteen months after the quashing of Siôn's original conviction and more than eight-and-a-half years after the murder of Billie-Jo. The prosecution lawyers had only one excuse – unspecified family illness – which sounded desperately feeble. They are used to getting their own way with many Old Bailey judges; Clarke was not prepared to be rolled over.

For the defence, Sallon argued that if the new work were to be admitted as evidence, then he would be asking for 'a substantial adjournment' – of, he indicated, at least three months – in order for the defence to be able to find and brief fresh experts, and for them to have the time to carry out their own work and to assess both the prosecution's claimed results and their impact on the case as whole.

On Tuesday morning, Mr Justice Clarke told the court that, 'Until yesterday I had had no indication from any source that there was any possibility of fresh evidence being served'. He said that in his view all this new evidence could have been gathered in time for the previous retrial; it was now being presented far too late in the day. Accordingly, he did not allow the prosecution to bring it forward. That was his final decision.

Ironically, it was the Crown which, to the consternation of the defence, had been rushing to expedite the trial; it had now been hoist with its own petard.

In other rulings about the admissibility of evidence, the judge concurred with Mrs Justice Rafferty and ruled that Lois's claims of domestic violence were inadmissible. On the other hand, he allowed the evidence of Peter Gaimster, although he harboured reservations about it.

'There is clearly substantial material for cross-examination', he told the defence.

He also allowed in witness evidence from Holly Prior and Laura-Jane Conway, schoolfriends of Billie-Jo. Their evidence was hearsay. When Siôn had originally been tried, hearsay evidence was inadmissible, as it had been throughout the entire 900-year history of the criminal justice system. However, it could now be presented because of the changes brought in by the new Criminal Justice Act 2003. Even so, the Act leaves the admissibility of the evidence to the judge's discretion, and in this respect Mr Justice Clarke was departing from the previous ruling of Mrs Justice Rafferty, who had disallowed this evidence.

Mr Justice Clarke ruled in favour of the evidence on the understanding that both women would give evidence and be available for cross-examination.

It soon turned out, however, that this was not necessarily the case. The Crown was having difficulties with Laura-Jane, who was a most reluctant witness. She spoke of 'the mental strain' and sent in a note from her doctor.

Eventually it was agreed that, being apparently both too stressed and too inconvenienced to be able to appear in court in London, she would give her evidence from Hastings via the wretched video link system.

This was bad enough, but Siôn would have been even more dismayed had he fully appreciated the antipathy towards him at court. One afternoon just before Christmas, with only a few in the courtroom, Nicholas Hilliard was setting out his papers prior to beginning his cross-examination of Siôn.

'Good luck, Mr Hilliard', a member of the court staff said to him deferentially, 'I hope you get him this time.'

Hilliard looked up. 'I hope you enjoy the show', he replied.

Chapter Forty-Six

Wonderful Witnesses

The third trial got under way.

By this stage, a number of points in the Crown's presentation had been dropped. They had acknowledged that their use of the word 'flesh' in describing the white inclusions was unjustifiable and they had withdrawn it.

Secondly, they had amended the scene-of-crime video. At the first trial, this had freeze-framed at the end on a picture of Billie-Jo, as if it were a film cut by a Hollywood studio for maximum emotional impact. This had now been dropped.

Thirdly, they had originally maintained that my note-taking was indicative of a guilty man trying to get his story straight. However, Hutt had not given evidence at the first trial. Once they did call him to give evidence, at the second trial, he acknowledged that he had recommended the note-taking course of action. So obviously this point too had to be dropped.

Finally, they had more or less conceded the 'white spirit' point. At the first trial, they claimed that the trip to Do-It-All was unnecessary. We didn't need white spirit, they had said, there was some in a container already in the house. They had tried to convince the jury of this by showing a picture of the container clearly displayed in a cupboard. All the items obscuring it had been moved aside. We pointed out that this was doctored evidence. They were forced to agree that it was very misleading and that, as the white spirit had been at the back of the cupboard, it was understandable that anyone would have forgotten it was there.

However, as soon as I heard Nicholas Hilliard's new opening speech, I knew that this trial was going to be presented differently. The emphasis was going to be less on fact and more on innuendo. The Crown was distancing itself from the forensic science and the medical evidence and relying more on presenting me as a bad and devious character who, almost regardless of the evidence, deserved to be convicted.

So long-forgotten family incidents were now being aired, ripped out of context and blown out of all proportion. One of the age-old sayings we all learn as we grow up is, 'that's the exception that proves the rule'. Yet with both the law and the media today, uncharacteristic incidents are reported as if they're characteristic – the very opposite of what they actually are. In that way, the exception becomes the rule; and what has been common sense for hundreds of years is turned on its head.

'Jenkins slapped Billie-Jo?' Yes, on one occasion, I did. Billie was attacking and scratching Esther, who was about six at the time. I had to get Billie off to prevent real harm to Esther, and I slapped Billie – not hard – to try to control her. I'm not proud of it, but it did the trick and she calmed down.

And why is that information in the public domain at all? Because I told the police about it. I was trying to assist their investigation and was under the misapprehension that they would assess it carefully rather than simply distorting the circumstances and using it as ammunition against me.

There was even a story that I had punched Annie. I can also remember exactly what happened on that occasion. It was when she was about ten years old. She was being bullied at school; she'd put on a little weight and was beginning to lose confidence in herself. Her shoulders were slumped forward; she was hiding behind her hair.

'Annie, there's no need for this', I said. 'Don't feel you have to look timid – perhaps one reason you're getting bullied is that your body language has identified you as a target.'

So she made great efforts to start doing something about her posture. Then one day, she mentioned again that she was getting some stick at school and she had her shoulders slumped again. I prodded her in the tummy – 'Think about your posture', I reminded her. Lois was there; and later reported this as a punch.

The police will leak such things to the media, so that the reports then become further decontextualised. They can be set alongside wholly fictitious incidents, so that the target – frequently, like me, a defendant – is left deeply compromised. If you're on trial for murder, it's not what you want to read.

As I listened to Hilliard's new speech, I was surprised to find out that the 'MG point' – that I would not have got into my MG to put the roof up as that could only be done from outside the car – had now been incorporated into the prosecution opening. Hilliard, however, did not tell this jury that no one on the prosecution side had ever realised this and the idea had been supplied to the Crown by the previous jury.

As he skated over the science, I noticed that a number of new points had emerged to replace it. 'Jenkins never even looked outside to establish the alleged attacker had gone', he said. The innuendo was that I hadn't looked for an attacker because I knew there wasn't one. Obviously, the real reason was that it had never occurred to me to do that. Had I been asked to post-rationalise it, I suppose I'd have said that I was preoccupied with Billie-Jo and in any event would have assumed the attacker had fled the scene.

Then Hilliard mentioned the black bucket, one of the two that were used to wash the cars that afternoon. How, Hilliard asked rhetorically, had the black bucket ended upon the patio?

I don't know what everyone else made of all this, but it was baffling me. Because the black bucket was in a certain place on the patio, therefore I had murdered Billie-Jo? I could hardly believe my ears.

After that, there was another jury visit to the crime scene at 48 Lower

Park Road but this time it went ahead without me. The judge looked surprised, but I could not face going through all that again.

When Peter Gaimster gave evidence, he started off by saying that, at the social occasion with police officers at the White Hart pub, they discussed 'nothing of relevance' to the case. He then admitted that he had suggested that it would be 'helpful' if Lois gave courtroom evidence.

So Lois did give evidence in person for the first time. She became a vital witness for the Crown even though she had nothing to say about the murder. (She had already told police, 'I wasn't even there at the time – remember that.') The prosecution's purpose for Lois being there was to damage me in whatever way she could. I still have difficulty in accepting that, even though I'm the father of her four daughters, she wanted me put in prison for life.

If I hadn't known her, I would have thought she was a police officer. She was dressed in dark colours and her hair was even shorter. She took the stand on Thursday, 10 November and finally finished her evidence a week later, on the afternoon of Thursday, 17 November.

She was like flint; she was so hard against me. She said I had 'rages', another new concept the prosecution had developed for this trial. How was I expected to counter that? It could only be my word against hers. In my opinion, the prosecution thought they would benefit by introducing fresh areas of disagreement and clouding what should have been the simple issue at the heart of the case.

When Lois went into the witness-box, the press benches, which had been sparsely populated since Hilliard's opening, had immediately filled up again.

One of her allegations was that when I had taken Billie-Jo on a trip to London to look round drama schools, I had allowed, or perhaps encouraged, her to over-dress. She said she thought Billie-Jo was wearing stiletto heels and told Hilliard:

She was dressed too old for her age – she had a large leather and fur jacket. I asked her to take it off, it didn't seem appropriate. It was borrowed from somewhere, I don't remember where it came from…

The next day, there was a report in the *Times* about Lois's evidence. It was headlined:

BILLIE-JO 'PARADED HER SEXUALITY'

As the phrase was in quotes, the *Times'* readers would have understood it to be a direct quote from what Lois had said in court. In a case where the prosecution had, from the very start, been trying a nudge-nudge wink-wink approach to suggest that there might have been some sort of sexual tension between Billie-Jo and myself, headlines like this were extremely damaging.

The following morning, in the absence of the jury, Sallon immediately drew it to the judge's attention. Mr Justice Clarke and all the lawyers then carefully went through their records of the previous day's proceedings. The words attributed to Lois had never been said by her (or, indeed, by anyone else). Nor was the purported quote even in the actual news report; it seemed to have been invented in the *Times'* newsroom.

The judge expressed his 'considerable concern'. He said he wanted his concern forwarded 'to the press generally and in particular to the editor of that newspaper' and emphasised that any repetition would not be tolerated. Then, when they came back into court, the jurors were warned about being influenced by media reports.

Throughout the history of my case, there was persistent anxiety about the way it was being reported; but the *Times* was the only newspaper ever singled out for a judicial reprimand.

When Lois was cross-examined about what Billie-Jo was wearing when I had taken Billie-Jo to drama schools, she had to concede that she had come with me to London. So that in itself put an entirely different complexion on this allegation. And those clothes that had become so retrospectively controversial? Where had the jacket come from?

Lois: I think she borrowed it.
Sallon: It came from Julia Gaimster.
Lois: Oh, yes, she quite often lent us clothes...

Julia, who was a designer and lecturer in fashion, had often kindly lent her and the older girls clothing. Meanwhile, when Billie's friends later gave evidence about her boots, Holly Prior said, 'They had a heel, a normal heel, they weren't stilettos'; and Ruth Bristow said, 'they were black leather ankle boots with a heel, like a platform heel'.

So, when this episode was properly examined, there was nothing suspicious about it at all. The papers could then have reported the reality of the situation to correct the misleading impression that had been created during Lois's evidence-in-chief. But they didn't. No national newspaper reported any part of this or, indeed, any of Lois's cross-examination.

At one point she began to stare at Vince Ives and David Mann, who were seated together in the public gallery. She asked for a break and then demanded that Tina who, she said, was looking at her too intently, be removed from the court. Tina certainly wasn't going to move and so, on this occasion, Lois did not get her own way.

Lois had suggested that Billie-Jo and I had had a row on the day she died.

'There had been no argument earlier that day, I suggest', Sallon said to her.

She didn't respond.

'The only argument,' he continued, 'was an argument that *you* had with Billie-Jo. Siôn never had an argument with Billie-Jo, did he?'

'I'm really sorry,' said Lois, 'I'm losing my concentration. Could I have a five-minute break?'

Chris concluded his cross-examination by explaining to the jury that the defence had discovered that she had taken on a literary agent who specialised in non-fiction accounts of true crime. When this was put to her, she said she no longer had any intention of writing a book, but didn't deny that the agent was acting for her. So she had a financial interest in the outcome of the trial; she'd make money in any event, but it stood to reason she'd make more if I were convicted.

Holly Prior was the first of three compelling witnesses. Until she appeared, I hadn't realised how grey and stuffy and full of cant the trial process had become – with various witnesses being afraid either of attracting criticism or of losing their jobs and so being circumscribed in what they said. Holly was different. She lit up the courtroom. She was blonde and bubbly and full of youthful exuberance. She did not have to worry about being professionally compromised; she simply told the truth, clearly and matter-of-factly.

Holly had been a good friend to Billie. I remembered the happy times the two girls had spent together and was pleased to see her looking so well. Yes, she was a prosecution witness, but that didn't matter. Because she told the truth, her evidence didn't harm me in any way. Indeed, I believe it benefited me considerably.

Laura-Jane Conway was altogether different. She said that I'd punched Billie in the face and so Billie had turned up at school one morning with blood all over her shirt. She said she saw Billie with bruises all over her arms and legs and that she'd been chased through a pub by a man. Very little of her evidence dovetailed with anyone else's. No one else had seen Billie-Jo at school with blood all over her shirt (something they would have been expected to remember). No one, indeed, could even recall Laura-Jane as having been a close friend of Billie's. Ruth Bristow, who was Billie's closest friend, agreed that 'Holly was one of her best friends', but when asked about Laura-Jane responded, 'I don't remember her... I wasn't aware Billie-Jo was close to her'.

Laura-Jane finished by saying, 'Why would I exaggerate? Why would I lie? I've no reason to make it up.'

Later, an issue arose about a part of her evidence and Mr Justice Clarke commented, 'I would be extremely reluctant to have her brought back'.

It was Ruth Bristow who was the second excellent witness. She, too, was bright and open, and clear and compelling. She said that she had always assumed that Lois and I were Billie's natural parents – 'when she told me [that she was fostered], I didn't believe her'.

Ruth had often been to our house, and had had sleepovers there. She described it as 'a very normal, loving family home'. It was of interest that the only violence she knew about in connection with Billie was the time when Billie had hit her. She said, however, that 'I just left it. I didn't want to make a scene about it.'

Ruth pointed out that she and Billie frequently changed together for P.E. classes and that she never saw any marks or scratches on her, other than on the one occasion mentioned by Holly.[55]

In the interval between the second and third trials, Neil had worked exhaustively on the scene-of-crime photographs, getting as many enlargements as possible. He then went through them all, examining each in minute detail, and copied all the bloodspots he could see on to acetates attached to each photograph, in order to show how many had been ignored in the Crown's scene-of-crime analysis. Once the full picture was taken into consideration, Sallon was to argue, a very different scenario emerged.

So, once again we gave the judge and the jury the magnifying glasses and allowed them to be Sherlock Holmes for a morning. They could find for themselves bloodspots that the Crown had neglected to take into consideration when the case against me was being constructed.

In fact, one jury member proved particularly observant. Examining the police bundles of scene-of-crime photographs, this juror noticed that a bloodspot that appeared on one enlargement had disappeared from another showing the same area of patio. The judge and all the assembled lawyers studied the two photographs and confirmed the correctness of the juror's observation. The judge commended the juror for having spotted something that all the expert witnesses had missed. It was another example of the fact that the evidence, which is presented in court as being of unimpeachable quality, is often nothing of the kind.

Under cross-examination, Adrian Wain did concede that bloodspots at the scene had been missed.

Once again, there was the utmost friction between the defence and Dr Hill in what was virtually a continuation of the dispute from the previous trial (not that this jury knew that, of course). Chris argued that, in order for Hill to have conducted a proper examination, he would have needed a nasal speculum and a small torch.

'We don't have those in mortuaries', Hill responded.

Asked how, in that case, he had examined the nose, he replied, 'I just looked'.

Chris pointed out to him that post-mortem photographs clearly showed dried blood blocking Billie's nose. Any injuries to the nose would therefore have been concealed; it was unrealistic that Hill could have examined it merely by looking. Nor had Hill made any note of having examined the nostrils.

'We don't record everything that we do', he said.

However, I thought the most telling exchange occurred when Chris asked Hill about his notes from the time of the original post-mortem.

Sallon: Was anything said to you concerning the black plastic bag?
Hill: No.
Sallon: So it is very unlikely that you were told about the bag being inserted and pulled out?
Hill: Yes.
Sallon: So [as far as you were concerned] this was a murder case without exceptional features?
Hill: Yes.

Under re-examination, Hill said that he'd been 'quite upset' by the cross-examination, which he'd thought 'most unkind'.

'I think I probably would have examined the nose when I could clean it properly', he told Hilliard, 'that would have been my normal practice'.

The Crown also called Fred Robinson again. As before, he looked startled to be there and so the eccentricity of this evidence being called at all provided some light relief.

On Monday, 12 December, a more extended moment of light relief was provided by a fire drill. The alarm sounded and everyone had to evacuate the building. Barristers, ushers, stenographers, security staff, jurors and everyone else were all congregated outside. Standing there in the road, Tina and I found ourselves very close to the jurors in my own case. They were astonished, just goggle-eyed. I could tell they were trying – but failing – to suppress looks of shock and amazement. Clearly, it had not crossed their minds that I was on bail.

The jurors were getting a totally different perspective from merely having seen me in the dock. The fire drill allowed all the players to be presented differently. It was as if we were actors, breaking off for the afternoon tea-break, but still in our costumes.

I went into the witness-box on 19 December. This time, although many aspects of the evidence continued to distress me, I felt stronger and more in control. I thought my replies to Hilliard were more confident and more to the point. I responded not to him but deliberately looked straight at the jury and tried to explain what it had been like actually to find Billie.

I left the witness-box satisfied that this time I had explained everything properly and clearly.

Some readers may point out that I was bound to do better a second time, having already had a full rehearsal. I would agree, but I'd point out that that factor applies to all retrials. Since many witnesses, whether prosecution or defence, will have done it all before, then the repeated process becomes even more artificial than it was the first time. Those responsible for the criminal justice system should not be encouraging retrials but working out how to avoid them.

Then the court recessed for the Christmas holidays. It was a peculiar time. It was my first Christmas with Tina and Oscar. Despite the fact that it was a strange intermission, we engaged in the rituals of Christmas just as any other family did. We had already bought Oscar some presents and that weekend we got a Christmas tree. We ordered a turkey. We decked our halls with holly and mistletoe from the garden. We decorated the tree and arranged the presents beneath. When I went to collect the turkey, I'd forgotten my ticket. Well, that's one advantage of being infamous. Everyone knew who I was. 'Turkey for Mr Jenkins? Right here.'

It was very memorable, but it was impossible to overlook that it could be our first and last Christmas together. I was due back in court on 3 January. I took some pictures of Tina, just in case I would need them for my cell wall.

After Christmas, Chris Sallon told the court that we had decided not to call Professor Denison. He had been a wonderful servant to the defence cause and was essentially irreplaceable; but by the end of his time in the witness-box at the second trial he had looked exhausted. Neil decided that his health was such that he should not be asked to take the stand again, even though no one doubted that he would have been more than willing. Instead, different areas of his testimony were dealt with by Professors Schroter, Nicholson and Aitkenhead.

One of the great advantages of having Tina as a member of the team was that, with her medical background, she had a good understanding of pathology and physiology, as well as a good memory for the medical evidence. She suggested that we should call Shelley Dolan as a witness. The jurors may have found the experts too theoretical; Shelley was someone who had dealt with real-life situations.

So she became the third compelling witness. She was the head of nursing at the Royal Marsden, the country's leading cancer care hospital in South Kensington, London. She explained that she worked with seriously ill cancer patients, a percentage of whom were obviously going to die. She would be involved with those patients at the end. As they were dying, she said, they would often emit a gasp of air, especially if their body was moved. She said there would not necessarily be a sound accompanying the gasp. If there was, it could be almost inaudible, although she would hear it as, at such times, she would be working in a totally quiet environment. This was the phenomenon of the last sigh, and she said it could occur up to several minutes after death. At that point, a nasal spray could be emitted by the dying patient.

'It is not unusual', she said, 'for bodily fluids of all types – blood, saliva, urine, faeces – to escape from the body.'

Patients with head injuries, she pointed out, are more likely to emit a bloody spray.

'So if we're doing emergency resuscitation', she continued, 'or we're preparing a body for the mortuary, we have to take unusual precautions and wear protective goggles, or sometimes a full-face visor. It's become more essential as health and safety legislation has become more stringent.

'There have been times when I've been dealing with bodies when I've thought everything was clean, but afterwards I've noticed blood on me – so you may not realise it has happened until afterwards.

'In my clinical experience, it is more common than uncommon, and it is part of my job to explain to less experienced staff and to the bereaved family members that that is what may happen.'

In my original witness statement, I had described pulling Billie up towards me so, in the light of this evidence, there was a strong possibility that I would have had a blood-spray on my clothing. Hilliard barely cross-examined her; there was nothing he could say. Shelley Dolan's straightforward evidence about her professional experiences had destroyed what Lord Justice Kennedy had described (when turning down my first appeal) as 'the crux of the prosecution case'.

After that, we again called witnesses to speak about Mark Lynam's movements and behaviour around the time of the murder.

In his closing speech, Hilliard told the jury that they could set the scientific evidence to one side and still comfortably convict me. By the end, the Crown was trying hard to dissociate itself from the claims it had once put forward as established fact – that the scientific evidence itself proved that I had killed Billie-Jo – and to obtain a conviction on the basis of character assassination.

Obviously, I thought of it as an immoral prosecution from the outset; but, as it had gone on, it really had become a lowest-common-denominator case. The Crown had ditched the evidence; all they had left was prejudice. I was an unsavoury character and therefore, although there was no evidence, I must have done it. By the time Chris had finished his closing speech, once again I found it hard to understand just what I was doing in the dock at all.

Nevertheless, as the jurors retired to consider their verdict, we were very apprehensive.

The case now over, the press began to appear. As before, reporters waiting for the verdict congregated outside the courtroom and filled the upstairs canteen.

I don't know how we all coped with the strain. Every hour seemed to last for days. There were several jury questions, at which time we all had to go back into court, not knowing whether or not it was the verdict.

I did know I would have one indication of how things stood.

'If it's a guilty verdict', the dock officer had said to me, 'I'll have other staff with me'.

Then, as if the strain of waiting for the verdict was not enough, there was another bolt from the blue. On Thursday, 26 January Mr Justice Clarke announced in open court that he was placing a restraining order on Tina's assets.

It appeared that the Legal Services Commission (LSC), the body that administers legal aid, had deemed our case sufficiently serious that they had passed it over to its special investigations unit (SIU). They were now claiming that because Tina and I were a married couple, Tina's assets were mine and therefore she was liable for all the defence costs of the trial. Before we'd untangled this mess, it suddenly seemed as if my going to prison for life would not be enough for the state; they were also going to deprive Tina and Oscar of their home.

The SIU claimed that it was necessary to take out the restraining order because Tina had not responded to a letter dated 17 January, which required her to respond within seven days.

Because it came as such a shock, we didn't initially understand what had happened. It was only as a result of frantic efforts by our lawyers that we managed to defer it all until after the trial. Once we had a chance to sort it out, we did so.

Firstly, Tina had not received any letter from the SIU. Secondly, even if she had received it, it would in any event have been impractical for her to have responded within seven days. In order to answer all the questions, there had to be disclosure of information by third parties, such as banks and building societies, which would inevitably have taken more than seven days.

Thirdly, the SIU was acting on entirely incorrect information, which was hardly surprising as its sole source appeared to be the *News of the World*.

So, oblivious of their own incompetence, they had contacted the judge to say that Tina owned three properties. The judge then placed the restraining order on them, preventing them from being sold.

Afterwards, we sorted out the actual position, which was this: as I had no assets, then, should the court make an order, the LSC would have to go through normal civil proceedings to recover the money and, if necessary, bankrupt me. As Tina could prove that all her assets were in existence before our marriage, they could not recover the debt from any of her personally-owned assets.

In all the ten-year history of the case, this was just another shocking episode. The SIU is supposed to be an investigations unit, but they obviously hadn't bothered to do any investigating at all. They'd just been gullible enough to believe what they read in the *News of the World*. Then they had deceived the judge. They had not simply placed the incorrect information before him, but had made Tina and I appear so devious and undeserving of sympathy that they had goaded him into acting on the misinformation in open court. He had placed a restraining order on three properties – the most expensive of which, the Belgravia house, was no longer Tina's. Had its new owners wanted to sell the property during this time, they would have been dumbfounded to learn that there was a High Court order preventing its sale.

On Thursday, 2 February, the jury said they would not be able to reach a unanimous verdict. Therefore they were given the majority direction (that a 10–2 verdict would suffice). We went through another tense weekend. My nerves were in shreds.

There was, however, one piece of good news during that awful time: we learned that, should the jury be divided again, nothing further would happen. The Crown would not be seeking a fourth trial.

However – good news usually was accompanied by bad – it then emerged that Crown counsel wanted the jury to be given what is known as the Watson direction. We objected, but lost the argument. So the jury was brought back in to court to be given the direction by the judge:

Each of you has taken an oath to return a true verdict according to the evidence. No one must be false to that oath, but you have a duty not only as individuals but also collectively. That is the strength of the jury system. Each of you takes into the jury-box with you your individual experience and wisdom. Your task is to pool that experience and wisdom. You do that by giving your views and listening to the views of others. There must necessarily be discussion, argument and give-and-take within the scope of your oath. That is the way in which agreement is reached.

If you cannot reach agreement, then you must say so.

Defence lawyers believe that the giving of the Watson direction is like the judge cracking his whip to coax reluctant (acquitting) jurors into line with the (convicting) majority. I was told – afterwards – that there is always a conviction after the Watson direction has been given.

It seems to me that it may have been appropriate in the days when verdicts had to be unanimous, and perhaps one stubborn juror could be thwarting justice – although, in fact, it wasn't used then. Now, when the minority must constitute at least twenty-five per cent of the jury, its use seems questionable.[56]

Of course, the direction is delivered in a kind of legal code, so jurors will not appreciate that what they are being told has just been the subject of fierce legal argument. Despite all our fears, it didn't seem to make any difference.[57]

At the start on Thursday, 9 February, there was another bombshell. The jury asked questions about the position of the peat-bag in the side pathway and whether they could have the black bucket with them in the jury-room. They were provided with the bucket, and the crime scene video was re-run for them, with the frame being frozen when the peat-bag could be seen on the drive.

As far as Tina and I were concerned, the mental turmoil at this point could not have been greater. If, after such a lengthy retirement, they were asking questions like these – because we regarded both the peat-bag and the black bucket as complete red herrings – then the outlook could not be blacker.

During that week, Tina and I made all necessary arrangements. I had to get ready for a possible conviction. It was like preparing for your own death. I'd packed a prison bag and Tina had a list of all the things she needed to do. Writing out that list was just terrifying, but I did want her to be as ready as possible. In the event of a catastrophic outcome, it would be better if there were a prepared list of tasks.

Then we were called back into court. At first we thought it was another jury question. But then I realised it seemed to be more important than that. There was a lot of commotion. Was it a result? I looked through the glass door with some trepidation.

The dock officer was on his own.

I didn't know what was going to happen. I went into the dock and spoke to Neil through the glass.

'The jury's hung', he said.

I knew that every police officer, every journalist was watching. I could see the public gallery and knew that all eyes there were on me. So I heard what Neil said and didn't show any emotion.

I returned outside to the dock officer who smiled broadly.

'You're going home', he said.

That brief wait outside was one of the most momentous periods of my life. It had been nine years, but now it was over. I gave a prayer of thanks that the ordeal had ended. After what seemed like ages, the judge re-entered the courtroom and I was summoned back in. The jury foreman then told the court that they were not in agreement and that 'further debate will not change this'. The judge then dismissed the jury.

'You have failed to reach a verdict', he said, 'but that is not a failure because it is part of the essence of the jury system that sometimes trials end in this way.'

The court was then cleared while we all awaited the formalities of the end of the case. As I was sitting with Tina in the hall outside, two women – Margaret Coster, Billie-Jo's aunt, and Bev Williams, a family friend – stormed through the hall and attacked me.

'It ain't over yet, you fucking child-killer!' they screamed, 'It ain't over!'

They scratched at my face and drew blood before any of us had a chance to react, and then Ezra Nathan and other Bindman's staff intervened to pull them away. I thought the whole incident was stage-managed. The two women had been in the public gallery, which can only be accessed through a separate entrance. They should not even have been allowed through to this central area. The Old Bailey is – hardly surprisingly – chock-full of police and security guards, all of whom appeared to be doing nothing whatever to prevent this attack on me.[58]

Because my lawyers complained strenuously, the two women were briefly held downstairs but, of course, I said we would not be pressing charges.

We then all went back into court. Six jurors had voluntarily returned for the denouement. After the fracas outside, the judge sternly emphasised that there must be no interruption to proceedings. The prosecution formally offered no further evidence and the judge directed that Not Guilty should be entered against my name on the indictment.

Those were the two words I had so longed to hear.

He then said that there was no longer any reason for reporting restrictions to remain in force. 'Proper reporting is now permitted', he said, 'including proceedings in the absence of the jury.'

The case had finished, but there was still more theatre. The landing was totally cleared in preparation for our exit. I walked to the toilet because I needed to spend just five minutes by myself. I splashed cold water on my face and looked in the mirror. I could see the strain in my eyes but, I thought, no longer the fear. Then I went back and sat down. We checked through the statement I would be reading outside. Bob and I had originally drawn it up for the appeal in July 2004, but it needed few adjustments.

Then, with family and close friends beside us, Tina and I walked down that wide staircase for the last time.

We went outside. Tina was holding my arm. The media had been cordoned off so there was a small area where we stood and I could finally read my statement to the cameras. I knew that both the BBC and Sky television were broadcasting live. I really couldn't believe it was all happening.

We went back to Bindman's. A few of us had lunch together and then Tina and I went to Waterloo. I saw the newspaper placards; the station concourse seemed to be filled with pictures of me. It momentarily registered that the press were taking an antagonistic line. I felt I'd been through so much and yet people who didn't know me were still writing hostile material. I couldn't understand why they would want to do that, although I'm not really sure how much of that I did take in at the time. All I knew was that I would not be going back to court again.

We walked through to the platform and caught the train to Brockenhurst. We were going home.

Part III
The Invariable Clue

Chapter Forty-Seven

The Fourth Trial by the Fourth Estate

The unfriendly publicity that Siôn momentarily registered as he and Tina made their way through Waterloo station proved a mild foretaste of what was to follow.

The press has famously been described by Thomas Carlyle, the nineteenth-century historian, as:

> The Fourth Estate [which is] more important far than [the first three]. It is not a figure of speech, or a witty saying, it is a literal fact.[59]

Now, it appeared as though the Fourth Estate, having been cheated of its hoped-for outcome in Siôn's third trial, had set up a fourth trial of its own in order to declare him guilty, either of what he was charged with or – well, anything sufficiently serious would do:

The Sun: 'You're a child killer… everyone knows it'

Daily Express: You murderer! Billie-Jo's aunt punches teacher as jury fails to reach verdict and he walks free

The Guardian: Jenkins: the allegations of violence the jury never heard

Daily Mirror: The Lost Evidence: Judge banned 'key forensic clue'; Freed dad Siôn 'battered his wife'

Daily Mail: Billie-Jo: What The Jury Was Not Told
The missing evidence included:
Allegations by Jenkins's first wife Lois that he was violent towards her and the children
His daughter Annie's statement that he once punched her in the stomach in a fit of temper
Details of his alleged adulterous sexual encounters with teenage girls

Daily Telegraph: Still No Justice for Billie-Jo

The Independent: What now for Jenkins, with a new life but a reputation left in tatters?

Never before had a man newly acquitted of murder been confronted with such a tirade. There even seemed to be broad approval of the two women's physical attack on Siôn. The themes of the headline reports were that these gut reactions of Billie-Jo's natural family were understandable; that justice had been thwarted; and that Siôn would have been found guilty if the jury had been allowed to hear further evidence.

Though a free man, one legally absolved of the charge that he had killed Billie-Jo, Siôn would be deeply stigmatised by this coverage. In conducting its own fourth trial, the media appeared to be saying: the law may have proved unequal to the task of bringing Siôn Jenkins to book – but we will remedy that failing. The Fourth Estate was now representing itself as a higher authority not only than the first three, but also than the law.

What this outburst of media hostility betrayed, firstly, was a collective abrogation of journalistic responsibilities.

Journalism should be straightforward enough; the reporter asks questions and reports the responses. In an adversarial criminal trial, there are two sides of whom the journalist can ask questions. It is inevitable (or so one would have thought) that in the event of a conviction that process is skewed in favour of the prosecution; and, in the event of an acquittal, it is skewed in favour of the defence.

After Siôn's acquittal, therefore, one would have assumed that reporters, before filing their copy, would be bombarding Neil O'May, Siôn's solicitor, with questions about the case – especially as, in this instance, contacting the defence presented no difficulties whatever. Bindman's, where O'May is head of the criminal division, is one of the most media-friendly law practices in the country.

In the wake of Siôn's acquittal, however, O'May was not bombarded with questions. The number of reporters ringing to ask about the case was precisely zero.

A handful did, indeed, contact him, but these journalists had no questions about the case; rather, they wanted to know how much money Siôn was likely to make as a result of his acquittal.

So not only were the reporters uninformed, but they made damned sure they stayed uninformed. Newsrooms had prejudged the outcome of the case; they were going to write what they were going to write. The inviolable tradition of gutter journalism – never let the facts get in the way of a good story – would prevail.

It is, probably, common knowledge that journalists will prepare both 'guilty' and 'innocent' accounts in advance of a high-profile trial verdict. In this instance, one reporter commented that he'd never before written alternative versions that differed so little.

This raises two questions: firstly, why were the press so oblivious of the evidence in the case? Secondly, why, given that they knew so little, were they all so antagonistic?

The most obvious explanation for their ignorance is that they hadn't attended the trial.

With the third trial about to start, there were arguments about seating arrangements in court, one of which concerned the small size of the press box (which was hardly surprising, given the small size of the court itself). A month beforehand, the department of constitutional affairs (DCA) had gone to the trouble of inviting applications from news organisations for special passes to attend the trial. Although a number of newspapers did not respond, expressions of interest nevertheless comfortably outnumbered the available seats. The DCA accordingly distributed the passes amongst those news organisations that it considered most significant.

It immediately became clear, however, that the protests from the media at the poor press facilities were hypocritical. The media had little interest in covering the trial. The sole concern of most organisations was to make sure they weren't excluded from the grand finale – the jury's verdict. One television news service, for example, was given two passes by the DCA for places in court but never used either. Reporters from other organisations who were assigned to cover the trial left after the prosecution opening and only returned three months later, after the jury had retired.

This is not quite as remarkable as it may appear. When the press excitedly covered the great mid-twentieth-century criminal trials in their entirety, they could do so because the trials were packed with concentrated drama and lasted less time than a cricket test match: the John Straffen trial (1952) took three days; the Ruth Ellis trial (1956) was over in a day-and-a-half. By contrast, the third Jenkins trial began on 31 October 2005 and ended on 9 February 2006.

Today, papers simply can't afford to have news reporters tied up on one story for that length of time. So, in such circumstances, they rely on the Press Association (PA), the country's main news agency that supplies news to all media outlets. Yet PA has two reporters at the Old Bailey.

Superbly professional though they are, their task of covering its eighteen courts simultaneously is occasionally beyond them.

If a newspaper were to say to its readers: sorry, we can't afford to send reporters to cover football matches, but instead we'll rely on PA reporters, two of whom will be covering eighteen games – then that paper's sports coverage would have zero credibility. So why should anyone expect its trial coverage, operating under exactly these conditions, to be even vaguely informed, let alone authoritative?

What then happens, at the end of a high-profile trial like this, is pure farce. Once the jury has retired, reporters who are ostensibly covering the trial, but who have not previously set foot in the courtroom, assemble in ever-increasing numbers at the Old Bailey to await the verdict.

In this instance, the verdict was a long time coming. The press therefore spent almost two weeks milling around the Old Bailey corridors, drinking coffee in the canteen and catching up on gossip with colleagues. Then, at times when a rumour started that a verdict was imminent, they began queuing at the door of the courtroom.

It wasn't only the lawyers who observed that if, instead of spending all that time hanging around, the reporters had actually attended at least some of the trial to find out what was going on, they'd have better served their public.[60]

Of course, the press is always ready to change its tune and had done so in the summer of 2004 when Siôn's second appeal was successful. At that point, he was being treated sympathetically. However, Mrs Justice Rafferty then prohibited all dialogue between the media and the defence, and that put the situation into reverse.

Tina Jenkins, whom Siôn married in February 2005, fell foul of the media from the moment she entered the story. She'd been moved to write to Siôn because, in view of her personal experience as a nurse, she disbelieved the prosecution case. From the papers' perspective, there were two problems with this explanation of how they first got into contact: it reflected favourably on Siôn; and it was infuriatingly mundane. However, this was easily overcome; some papers simply invented an alternative version, telling their readers that the couple had met through 'an internet dating site'.

They also followed the lead of the *News of the World* in reporting that Tina was an art-dealer and a millionairess. Yes, she had worked for a time in art and antiques, albeit without ever making much money from it. She also owned a London property worth more than a million pounds; of course, in a buoyant property market, so did a significant number of senior journalists who would never have sanctioned references to themselves as 'millionaires'. So the initial reports about her were entirely misleading. Again, the papers could have reported the humdrum truth – that Tina was a cancer nurse who had made a shrewd investment when the property market bottomed out in 1992; but they didn't.

Some might argue that the dissemination of these false reports does no real damage, as there is in any event a widespread public scepticism about the media. The evidence here suggests otherwise. The people who were certainly influenced by these reports, and indeed fell for the *News of the World* story hook, line and sinker, were the special investigations unit of the Legal Services Commission. Their misconceived actions led directly to further unnecessary heartache for Siôn and Tina.[61]

At one of the police briefings near the end of the trial, officers were asked about Siôn's alleged relationship with a seventeen-year-old girl. The police responded that they had no information about that. In this instance, therefore, the press received no encouragement to publish untruths – but they didn't need any. The rumours were enticing enough. They decided to allow the gossip to become the basis for assertions that Siôn was an 'adulterer' and had had affairs with teenagers or even schoolgirls. As the reporters who wrote them almost certainly realised, all these suggestions were completely untrue.

Perhaps, some people might have argued, the media antipathy could be excused by the fact that the trial had not culminated in a triumphal acquittal, but in a divided jury (two divided juries, in fact).

Yet this would have misconstrued the legal position. In respect of the second Old Bailey jury, its indecision was final. The case against Siôn was now closed, and Not Guilty had been entered on the indictment sheet. Siôn was not a partly-guilty, partly-innocent man. In accordance with the basic principles of English law, he was a wholly innocent man.

Some of the mis-reporting can indeed be accounted for by the frisson of being able to report the supposedly esoteric, 'the evidence the jury never heard'. Why this should preclude the *defence* evidence the jury never heard is initially puzzling.

One suspects, however, that the default approach of newspapers is one of pure malice; after all, it makes 'better' copy. In this respect, the most dispiriting aspect of gutter journalism in Britain today is that it is no longer confined to the gutter press. It appears to have defied gravity to seep up out of the gutter and into more elevated sections of the media.

Only the BBC made an effort to cover the whole trial; no one else did. Some newspapers, having reported the outcome with a feigned authority, did not have the honesty to admit to their readers that, far from having objectively assessed all the trial evidence for themselves, they hadn't even bothered to apply for press passes.

The headlines produced at the end of the trial revealed that the media had constructed its own image of Siôn. When he woke up on Saturday morning, 15 February 1997, he was a deputy headteacher with no criminal record and against whom there wasn't a shred of suspicion of misconduct. By the time of the acquittal, the media had turned this family man into an unsavoury and deeply dislikeable bully. It was a picture that had no basis in reality and existed only in the media's imagination; nevertheless, it was one that seeped into the public's collective consciousness.

The media had based their characterisation, whether directly or indirectly, on the evidence of Lois Jenkins and Peter Gaimster, since virtually all the damaging allegations originated with them; so we need to examine the strength of this evidence, almost all of which was – as the media could have trumpeted – evidence that the jury didn't hear.

Chapter Forty-Eight

The Reliability
of Lois

On 14 February 1997, the evening before the murder, Lois and Siôn were in a pub together in Hastings when Peter and Julia Gaimster asked them to go with them to a music concert. Lois wanted to go, and so she telephoned Regine, the au pair, to ask if she could babysit for longer than they had originally agreed. Regine refused. Lois became angry, and there was a flare-up between them that still rankled the next morning.

In Lois's first statement, she related that the matter was smoothed over on the Saturday morning because Regine explained to her that she had:

… wanted to go out with Ardie, her boyfriend, as it was Valentine's night. I hadn't realised this…

Twelve days later, in her second statement, Lois explained the dispute differently:

I telephoned Regine and was left in no doubt that things were not well with her, as it was Valentine's night and she wanted to go out…

Subsequently, when Lois is told that her husband has murdered Billie-Jo, she responds by telling the police three things: that there was a last-ditch attempt by his family on the evening before their 1982 wedding to persuade him not to marry her; that Siôn has a mysterious leg injury; and that his parents have been unsupportive since the murder. All the assertions could have been easily checked. Medical records would have revealed the true state of Siôn's leg. Interviews with Siôn's friends and family would have ascertained the reliability of Lois's assertions.

In the wake of receiving the traumatising news that her husband had killed her daughter, it would be natural for Lois to experience deep shock that might impact on her perception of events. She told police that Annie couldn't understand 'why Dad needed white spirit because he had bought some the day before'. But Siôn hadn't bought white spirit the day before. He had indeed gone shopping at Do-It-All, but the police recovered the receipt and Siôn had not purchased white spirit. Nor did Annie think he had.

On 10 March 1997, Lois told WDC Julie Gregory that on the afternoon of the murder (as the latter reported):

> ... [Siôn] had insisted Lois go out with the younger two, which was unusual. She mulled over whether the murder could have been premeditated...

Siôn had not 'insisted Lois go out with [Esther and Maya]'. Siôn had actually suggested that the family stay together for the afternoon. In fact, Lois was taking the younger children to town because Esther wanted to spend some of her birthday money at Debenham's. They were then going on to the beach. Dealing with these events subsequently in an article for the *Sunday Times*, Lois wrote:

> The two younger girls... wanted to come out with me to walk the dog on the beach and to shop in the town.[62]

On 13 March, Lois reported Annie as having told her that Siôn 'didn't phone the ambulance for a long time'. The relevant time period that afternoon is established by Charlotte's call to her mother's phone (when she was trying to find out where her father was) and by the first call to the ambulance services (3.38pm). There was a great deal to be fitted in to that half-hour period. Siôn had not neglected to phone the ambulance 'for a long time'. Nor, on the evidence of the girl's interviews, would Annie have said that.

That same day, 13 March, DC Hutt reported that Lois said to him:

Siôn has got a criminal record for damage to and theft of a vehicle and asked me whether we had actually found that out.

What the police found out, in fact, was precisely the opposite: that Siôn hadn't got a criminal record for anything.

After Siôn's conviction, the defence was naturally keen to know what exactly the children's evidence was. There followed a struggle that lasted almost two years to force Lois to allow the children to be interviewed. Even after Dame Elizabeth Butler-Sloss, the president of the family division, had said on 8 May 2001, 'the mother must make the girls available because I am giving leave [for them to be interviewed]', Lois still managed to hold out for another nine months.

On 6 December 2001, in a lengthy statement drawn up because she was applying to the Court to get the 8 May order set aside, Lois said that Siôn 'has consistently maintained he was with the girls... I assume to elevate them to the position of alibis'. She then stated:

When [Siôn] and I went for a walk on Tuesday, 18 February, he gave me a version of events inconsistent with what he later told the police.

Lois made many statements and reports to police against her ex-husband. So it is remarkable that nothing more was ever heard about this alleged inconsistent version either before or since.

It was not until the children were allowed to speak for themselves that the full truth about the case began to emerge. Siôn was finally on the starting-grid of the long road to justice.

In the wake of the girls' interviews, Lois and her partner, Vince Ives, made strenuous complaints to all and sundry about the way they had been handled – which all concerned immediately refuted.[63] Then, with the CCRC on the point of referring the case back to appeal, Lois wrote a full-page account of her involvement in the case for the *Sunday Times*, in which she railed against 'the endless appeal system' and what she termed the justice industry:

> The justice industry thrives, Billie-Jo's death having fuelled and fed the many facets of this grinding wheel. Of course, there must be an opportunity for review of convictions and safeguards against miscarriages of justice, but at what cost to the victims, and to what extent in terms of the manipulation of the public?[64]

It was an interesting observation.

After the case was referred back to appeal, Lois made her third statement in the criminal case. This was her decisive statement in which she re-affirmed that her reports to police 'correctly' reflected what Annie and Charlotte had told her.

When she was giving evidence at the third trial Crown counsel Nicholas Hilliard asked her about this third statement:

> *Hilliard*: In that statement were you asked to deal with your discussions with the police… and reports that had been made to officers about what the girls were saying?
> *Lois*: (Nodded)
> *Q*: I don't know whether you can confirm that the contents of this statement are true… [or] if there is anything you want to alter in it or change?
> *Lois*: No, I have read it through.
> *Q*: It is correct?
> *Lois*: Yes.

Lois was holding fast to her position. It became a recurring theme of her evidence: I am right, and if my daughters' recollections now differ, they are wrong.

Also in her third statement, Lois explained the circumstances in which she said she'd originally come to believe the worst:

> Three or four days following the murder, and in the middle of the night, it suddenly dawned on me that Siôn was, quite possibly, responsible for Billie's murder. I think these thoughts may have resulted from the way that Siôn handled a press conference earlier in the day...

What then is to be made of the fact that the day after the press conference, Lois and Peter Gaimster spent some time telling police why they thought Felix Simmons was the most likely suspect? As a result, the police arrested and questioned him and held him in custody overnight. When Simmons was released, Gaimster went to Hastings police station to complain and to express his fears that his family, and also Lois and Siôn and their family, were now in danger. As a result, the police went to his house the next day to install a new security alarm system linked directly with the police station. In the event, Gaimster's fears were not realised.

A further feature of this extremely significant statement was that Lois made references to the violence which, she said, she had suffered from Siôn.

Apart from her allegations, however, there was no evidence of this whatever.

Regine, the au pair, the one independent outsider who was actually living in the household, had not witnessed any violence. Billie-Jo herself had regular private meetings with social workers and never mentioned any violence in the household.

Lois herself was, professionally, a social worker. She was also in constant contact with social services over the five-year period from 1992 to 1997, from when they started to foster Billie-Jo. During that time she was interviewed privately on several occasions about all aspects of her family life. She made statements in court, especially in the proceedings leading up to Lois and Siôn obtaining a Residency Order for Billie-Jo. At no time had she suggested that there was anything at all wrong with her marriage, let alone that she was suffering any violence.

When informed that her mother had told police that her father had been violent to her, Charlotte shouted out, 'That's not true'.

After making her highly damaging third statement, Lois and her partner, Vince Ives, continued to try to forestall the possibility of the children giving evidence at the Court of Appeal. On 9 March 2004 Ives wrote to Lord Justice Kay insisting that the defence was putting unacceptable pressure on the girls to attend.

In the event, Charlotte did give evidence, although not Annie. Asked at the appeal why Annie was not testifying, Lois responded, 'She does not want to come back' (from Tasmania, presumably). Clare Montgomery then commented, 'I suspect the reason is that she knows she would have to tell this Court she told the police that you were a liar.'

Montgomery continued:

Montgomery: You knew, didn't you, that Annie had told the police that many of the things you reported her as saying, she hadn't said.

Lois: I have never discussed ever the contents of the interviews in 2002…

Montgomery: You had no idea Annie had been saying, 'I didn't say those things my Mum reported me as saying' and indeed, 'It was my mum who was saying those things'?

Lois: No, I didn't know she'd said that. In fact, I discovered that she had said that in the media on Saturday for the first time.

Why did the prosecution want Lois to make her third statement unless it was in order for her to rebut what her daughters had said in their re-interviews – as she had confirmed in her sworn testimony only a few hours earlier?

Lois went on to tell the Court of Appeal judges that the children had insisted they would not do interviews:

> *Lois*: The girls were quite adamant that they did not want to be interviewed… They are quite phobic about not wanting to speak to anyone.
> *Montgomery*: No, Mrs Jenkins, you say they are quite phobic about not wanting to speak to anyone. When the CCRC said, 'Will you speak to us?', they said, 'Yes'.

Lois then gave an entirely fresh version of what had happened at the end of Annie's interview:

> *Lois*: Annie went totally hysterical when she came out of her interview.
> *Montgomery*: Annie 'went hysterical' because she realised that you had consistently lied to the police about what she was saying in 1997.
> *Lois*: That is your interpretation… Annie came out… and she was extremely distressed. They had someone from [CAFCASS] looking after them… and she tried to explain to that person that she was distressed and needed to leave the interview. That person did not seem to understand…
> *Montgomery*: Mrs Jenkins, the Court has the video, they can see what happened.

As a result of her time in the witness-box at the Court of Appeal, Lois developed an intense dislike for Clare Montgomery, describing her as 'appallingly rude and just awful'.

She resolved to avoid giving evidence at the retrial.

Nevertheless, the prosecution needed her in place. DCI Steve Dennis, who was now in charge of the case, told her, 'You are our Number 1 witness'.

On 9 September, the police sent her an e-mail:

The Reliability of Lois

Mr Dennis would like you to know that the whole team are
motivated and are pushing towards strengthening the evidence both
around forensic science and true motive, but we do need your help.

The police needed to meet her to go through the case. Lois did not want
a meeting to take place anywhere in Australia, and so the police paid for
her and Ives to fly to England. Lois was then interviewed at Littlehampton
police station on 4 and 5 October. At the end of the week, with her
statement having been drawn up ready for her to sign, she told police that
'she believed there was an occasion at William Parker School when seven
female teachers made a complaint about Siôn'.

This information was important – if true. It wasn't.

Lois now complained about the family liaison officer, and so was
assigned a fresh one, WDC Debbie Upton. She then asked for a copy of
Siôn's bail conditions, which the police passed on to her.

On 7 January 2005, Lois learned to her consternation that the
prosecution did intend to call her as a witness at the retrial. She told them
(according to police records):

> ... that she would be staying in Australia. She said they [the family]
> couldn't deal with it any more, physically or emotionally.... . Lois
> was adamant that she would not be returning to give evidence. She
> stated that she would not set foot in England all the while Siôn was
> on bail and walking around.

The police did not take 'No' for an answer. Further, Lois learned that
because she was listed as a witness, the police would no longer discuss
aspects of the case with her.

'I told her', reported Upton, 'it would not be right to discuss the
forensic evidence with her.'

Lois complained about this to officers whom she knew from earlier
stages of the inquiry, but her approaches were rebuffed:

Lois stated that she didn't understand why she was not able to speak to certain officers... she expressed her dismay at not being able to speak to officers whom she has previously had contact with.

After news of Siôn's wedding to Tina had been in all the papers, Lois again contacted Sussex police:

Lois informed me that Siôn's picture has appeared in the *Daily Telegraph*, showing him going up the steps of his wife's house in Belgravia. In her [Lois's] opinion, this is proof that he is breaching his bail conditions and she specifically requested that I pass this information on.

On 23 February Siôn's bail conditions were varied to allow him to live with Tina. Lois immediately requested a copy of the new conditions. The prosecution consulted Mrs Justice Rafferty, who said she wasn't allowed to have them. Lois complained again to police:

She thought bail conditions were meant to protect the public, and she feels the revised bail conditions fail to do this, particularly in view of the fact that Siôn is now living close to her parents. She believes her parents are obvious targets as he knows that they have access to her girls.

By this point, with the trial date looming, the judge ordered the Crown Prosecution Service to audio-record all contacts with her.

The defence had found out that Lois had a literary agent who specialised in accounts of true crime acting for her. The agent wrote to police asking for case exhibits which, he said, were needed within thirty minutes of the jury's verdict. It appeared that Lois was planning to maximise any financial benefit she could gain from the trial.

At that stage, if she would be dropped from the list of witnesses, the police might well be able to speak to her more freely, as they had done in the past. However, the police were still trying to persuade her to give evidence. DCI Dennis told her it was her 'civic duty' to do so. In the face of the mounting pressure, Lois wrote to the trial judge, Mrs Justice Rafferty. 'I've written a letter which I've read over and over again', she told police, 'and I hope it's completely honest and fair and thorough. I've decided that that's my final decision'.

In this letter to the judge, Lois said that she would not give evidence and explained her reasons:

> I have become confused and disorientated in terms of memory... When giving yet another statement in October last year, I found myself totally confused and doubting my own memory to a disturbing degree... I have great difficulty remembering whether I saw, said or thought something... In short, I no longer trust my memory.

She concluded by saying that she hoped the Court would be able to make reference to her statements and that it would 'accept my apologies for my absence'.

That was the point that had been reached by 8 April, when the trial was due to start. The last-minute two-week delay secured by the prosecution, ostensibly to deal with the scientific evidence, was actually needed to persuade Lois to reconsider her decision not to give evidence.

On 9 April, a prepared note was read out to her over the phone and the following points were set out:

> 1. It has become clear that if Ms Ball [Lois Jenkins] does not come, not only will the jury not hear her evidence from the witness-box but her absence will also affect some of the other evidence that the prosecution are allowed to call and may mean that the prosecution are not allowed to call some evidence at all.

> 2. It has been suggested in open court that she lied to the police about what the children were telling her in the months after the murder.

3. It has been claimed that she persuaded other witnesses to lie to the police.

4. By perverting the course of justice in this way, it has been suggested that she hoped to ensure that the defendant was convicted of murder and that she kept custody of the children.

Prosecution counsel have said that it would not be right for the police to go into further details of any allegations that might be made. Prosecution counsel has asked that Lois be informed that if she comes to give evidence she will be able to look at all relevant documents and to meet prosecution counsel to discuss any concerns with him before giving evidence.

WDC Upton commented in her report that, as she read this out to Lois, 'I got the impression that, throughout this conversation, Lois was close to tears, if not crying.'

Lois afterwards said that 'Someone used the words "criminal offences", which freaked me out'. She asked:

Can the defence say to the prosecution or judge we want you to charge this woman with lying or perverting the course of justice, or would it be the police who had to charge the person?

... I know I haven't lied so I can't see who they're thinking that they're going to get to say I lied. I mean, even if someone did say I lied, I can't imagine what's the problem with it, because I haven't lied to anyone.

She knew, however, that the prosecution were in earnest and she began to give ground:

I mean one thing is absolutely sure, I'm quite categoric... that I'm not coming to the UK to give evidence... Neither will I give evidence from Australia.

So the idea of her giving evidence by video link from the southern hemisphere was developed. The police pointed out that the time difference would be a logistical problem.

'It's going to make it a bit restricted', said WDC Upton, 'as to how many hours a day they can really sit and talk to you.'

'Well, how many days do you think – I mean, surely a day would be enough, won't it?' replied Lois.

'Given the amount of time and hassle I'm going through to do it in the first place, it would be courteous if they could try and arrange it in one day.… I can't imagine why anyone would want to sit there and listen to me for two whole days.

'I wasn't even there at the time – remember that.'

Nevertheless, the video link arrangements were made. WDC Upton and DI Phil Mays were to fly out to be with her. Upton asked Lois if she would like to read through all her statements as preparation for giving evidence.

In the context of the case, Lois's response is of incalculable significance:

I looked at it all last time and I just got completely confused. I didn't have a clue whether I was coming or going, so I don't think there's much point. I can't see the point of reading through previous things because I know for a fact that… the recorded thing last October [the Littlehampton interview]… that will completely not tie up, I know it doesn't, with bits and pieces from the appeal and previous notes…

In the appeal, saying to me you said such and such in a statement and such and such in the Family Court and it didn't tie up and such and such in some other 1998 statement and, *to be honest, with you, I haven't got a clue…* which of those things are absolutely 100% accurate. So I don't really know if it will make any difference me reading anything…

The jury will have to accept that I'm going to tell what I can remember and *half the time it might not be true…* because I don't have a very accurate memory of a lot of things.

[italics added]

The most important witness would indeed appear in the witness-box and give evidence before the jury, despite the facts that 'to be honest with you, I haven't got a clue' and that *half of what she would say might not be true.*

This was the witness whom the Crown Prosecution Service was so desperate to recruit to its cause and, indeed, without whom the retrials could not have taken place.

Chapter Forty-Nine

The Evidence of
Peter Gaimster

Peter and Julia Gaimster moved into St Helen's Road, on the other side of Alexandra Park from the Jenkins family, in July 1994. At the time of Billie-Jo's murder in 1997, they had a ten-year-old daughter, Natalie, and a six-year-old son. Julia lectured in fashion at Croydon College. Gaimster owned a traditional seaside gift shop in Hastings old town.

While Julia was at work, Peter would take over responsibility for the children. He employed an assistant to look after the shop while he ferried the children between home and nursery school. It was through taking them to Hilltop nursery that he met Lois Jenkins, and she soon became firm friends with both Peter and Julia. Their children also got to know each other. Siôn, being regularly preoccupied with work, was little more than an occasional member of this small social network.

In February 1996, Lois asked Siôn if he would mind if the Gaimsters came with them on their annual summer holiday to France, and he agreed. For two weeks in August, they all went to Brittany, renting a cottage near Quimper from a British couple, Mr and Mrs Maddison.

On the day of the murder, Gaimster closed his shop at about 5.00pm.

At almost exactly that time, Siôn telephoned Julia and asked her and Peter to come round, without the children, to see them at Denise Lancaster's. Peter was still out, so Julia drove straight there on her own and saw Siôn on the pavement outside. He told her what had happened. Julia returned home immediately to make arrangements for her own children. She didn't know where Peter was, but drove to the Anchor pub and found him there. They then returned together to Denise's. 'I can't really remember if me and Julia had a conversation on the way', recalled Gaimster. 'I was in total shock.'

Shortly after 10.00pm, the police drove Siôn and Lois to the Gaimsters'. 'Julia and I dealt with the children', explained Gaimster, 'getting the sleeping arrangements sorted... Both Siôn and Lois were in a state. Lois was crying; Siôn was ashen-faced. He couldn't speak... He just sat there staring. He eventually went up to bed at about 11.00pm. He wanted to be on his own. Lois stayed up with us until about 1.00am.'

Four days later, on the Wednesday, Gaimster and Lois indicated to police that Felix Simmons was a strong suspect for the murder. Simmons was then arrested and held in custody overnight. Hearing of his release the next day, Gaimster and two friends went to Hastings police station to make strenuous protests. Gaimster said he would now need police protection.[65]

The following Sunday, 23 February, he went to Hastings police station to make his first statement. He explained how he had got to know Siôn and Lois, adding, 'I know Lois better than Siôn due to his heavy work commitments as headmaster at William Parker School. He is not at home much when I visit'.

His statement concluded by saying that they expected the Jenkins family to remain with them 'for another two weeks'. DC Paul Hilton, the officer taking the statement, reported that Simmons remained Gaimster's 'main area of concern'.

The day after Gaimster made this statement, Siôn was arrested from his (Gaimster's) home at eight o'clock in the morning and was questioned over two days. On the second day, Gaimster went with Lois when they took Annie to the Old Courthouse for her second interview. Police officers had just 'fed into Mum' by telling Lois that Siôn had murdered Billie-Jo. Over those hours, as Gaimster himself put it, 'We, that's me and Lois, talked a lot'.

Gaimster spoke again to DC Hilton. The information that he now began to provide was in sharp contrast to that he had given a mere two days earlier. After Annie's interview was finished, everyone was taken back to Hastings police station. Siôn, meanwhile, had been released. He went to the Gaimsters' house, but only Rita, the young au pair, was at home. She did not allow him inside. After he'd left, she telephoned Gaimster who, it seemed, was now concerned for her safety. So WDS Capon drove Gaimster back home. On the way, he divulged some concerns about Siôn. So it was that a 'French farmhouse kick' began to feature in the case. According to Capon's record:

> [Gaimster said to me], Would I promise him that I would never tell Lois what he was about to say. I made that promise to him.
>
> He went on to tell me that during the summer last year he holidayed in France with Siôn, Lois and the children. He then told me that Siôn had 'kicked the living daylights out of Billie'. I asked him how Billie had reacted and was told that she stayed in her room all night and didn't come out. It was following this that everybody was made to swear on the Bible that nothing would ever be mentioned about this. [I do not know who 'everybody' is.]
>
> I did not go into further detail with him at that time, as we were arriving at his house.

As Capon herself acknowledged, Gaimster had 'totally dismissed the fact that Siôn could be responsible; it was *only after he was arrested that everything seemed to fit into place.*'

Over the following days, Gaimster became closer to Lois. 'He was around Lois's house a lot more', explained Natalie in her witness interview with the police. Referring to the weeks after the murder, she said, 'We just lived round there [at Lower Park Road]. Lois was like a second Mum to me, I probably saw her more than I saw my own Mum.'

On 26 February, Gaimster told Capon that Siôn was planning to flee the country and go to South Africa. He followed this revelation with his second account of the 'French farmhouse kick'. He now claimed that, while the children 'were at the bottom of the stairs crying', he went into the bedroom and 'witnessed Siôn kicking Billie-Jo'. He added that 'Lois then went upstairs' and that the three of them 'were in the bedroom for approximately an hour-and-a-half'.

He also brought up the idea that Siôn might have been violent towards Lois. 'He can give no facts about this', Capon writes, 'but states that at some stage Siôn tried to strangle Lois in bed'.

Her record continued:

[He] states that Lois in her heart knows that Siôn murdered Billie, but she is now so confused with the fact that Siôn has told her that he is being framed and the fact that she has received a phone call from Siôn's parents… On the Sunday prior to Siôn being arrested, Lois was made to swear on the Bible that she would not divulge any past history or information in respect of her relationship with Siôn…

So Gaimster was now providing Capon, one of the main investigating officers in the case, with material that, for Siôn, could not have been more damaging. One of her more significant notes is: 'Although there has been no conversation to this effect, Gaimster believes that Siôn will believe he can get away with this [murder]'.

Capon's report is fascinating. Read again her note: '*Siôn will believe he can get away with this [murder]*'. Opinion, masquerading as established fact, appears to be being fed in both directions.

In his first account, Gaimster stated that, after being kicked, Billie-Jo stayed in her room all night and didn't come out; by the next day, this had changed: 'Lois went upstairs and all three of them were in the bedroom for approximately an hour-and-a-half'.

The Evidence of Peter Gaimster

Gaimster mentioned swearing on the Bible. This would have been a highly-charged and memorable occurrence. Yet the first time he recalled it, Gaimster stated that it had happened in front of several witnesses, himself included, six months earlier in France; the next day he said it had happened to Lois alone, just three days beforehand in Hastings.

His second statement, made on 3 March, was primarily concerned with the French farmhouse kick. Gaimster said that 'as I walked up the final flight of stairs, I could hear raised voices... of Siôn and Billie-Jo', although 'I could not hear any speech'. He explained that as he got to Billie-Jo's room, 'the door was open... Billie-Jo was laying across the bed... Siôn's right leg was back away from his body'. It looked 'as though he had just kicked something... It looked to me as if Siôn had kicked her'.

On 15 April, he made another statement. He now said that, 'As I got to the open door, I saw Siôn throw Billie-Jo violently across the bed. She landed on the bed crying... Siôn then violently kicked Billie-Jo using his right leg with full force.'

The following year, just before the first trial, he made a fourth statement. More than six years were to pass before he made a further, fifth statement, on 5 November 2004. Gaimster now said that he also had specific memories about Siôn reluctantly surrendering his clothing for forensic examination; about Siôn spending a lot of time writing notes, and also secluding himself with Annie; about Siôn declining to wear his fleece jacket soon after the murder; about alleged conversations with Siôn about the blood at the murder scene; and also about Siôn's concerns over his job promotion.

It was an ideal statement for prosecution purposes, because of its overall picture of Siôn behaving in a guilty fashion after the murder; because of the way it ostensibly buttressed every part of the Crown case; and also because of the help it specifically gave to the prosecution in the area of motive.

The statement again revisited the 'French farmhouse kick':

As I went up I could hear the noise increasing in volume and I could

tell that a serious argument was taking place… I heard Siôn…
shouting, it was loud, it certainly wasn't a gentle chat. I could hear
Billie-Jo, she was crying and she screamed, 'Get off, leave me alone,
it's not my fault'.

The background to all this was well-established. On that August evening
in France, Siôn and Lois had gone out for a meal together. (The next
night they would stay in and allow Peter and Julia to go out). While they
were away, the children played outside in a cornfield, and Billie-Jo
twisted her ankle. The children all ran back in, with Billie-Jo crying and
hobbling. Peter and Julia consoled her, and Lois and Siôn tended to her
when they returned.

By this stage, Gaimster had given five separate accounts of what he said
had subsequently occurred.

In the second statement, he said, 'Siôn and Lois seemed to take over in
respect of the children and started getting them off to bed. I stayed
downstairs with Julia.' In the final one, he states: 'the children then started
to get ready for bed by having a bath and getting into their pyjamas. Lois
and I were involved in helping them.'

Initially, he said that, on going upstairs, 'I could not hear any speech'.
He later stated that he had heard Billie-Jo screaming, 'Get off, leave me
alone, it's not my fault'.

Having told WDS Capon that Siôn had 'kicked the living daylights'
out of Billie-Jo, he then said 'it looked to me as if Siôn had kicked her'.
Later, he said that Siôn had 'violently kicked Billie using his right leg with
full force'.

When the 'French farmhouse kick' allegedly happened, there were
altogether thirteen people in the farmhouse. It was not only the families
who were there. Mary Maddison and her husband owned the property
and lived in an adjacent cottage. That evening they had come in to meet
their guests socially. There is no evidence that the Maddisons were aware
of anything untoward. There is also no evidence that Billie-Jo ever
mentioned it.

The Evidence of Peter Gaimster

Natalie Gaimster had said that Billie-Jo 'was really open, she just talked about everything'. Holly Prior, another friend, who was a prosecution witness, was asked:

> Q: Would she suffer in silence?
> *Holly*: No…
> Q: Did she ever tell you about being kicked by her dad?
> *Holly*: No

Lois described what happened that evening after she and Siôn arrived back, as follows:

> I wanted to take her to the hospital as her ankle was going blue, but in the end I bandaged it and put her to bed. Peter was there. I then sat up with Peter and Julia talking until about three o'clock in the morning. Siôn went to bed earlier, which was not unusual. Siôn does not like small talk.

This is what Gaimster says about the following morning:

> It was *immediately* obvious that morning that the atmosphere in the house had changed. Siôn was very quiet and *everyone* seemed *subdued and shocked* after what had happened the night before…

But why would 'everyone' have been 'subdued and shocked'? By Gaimster's own account, no one knew anything about it. Certainly, both Peter and Julia said they said nothing about this to Lois; *that's their evidence*. How could she possibly have been 'subdued and shocked' when she didn't know anything had occurred?

Natalie Gaimster was also interviewed about the alleged incident, albeit not until October 2004.

She explained that she and Charlotte were in the bathroom cleaning their teeth. Siôn and Billie-Jo were coming up the stairs when they heard that she described as a 'one-off yelp'. She went on to say that Siôn took Billie-Jo across the landing into his and Lois's bedroom.

> *Natalie*: Then we heard her crying out. We looked towards the door, it was basically shut, I think, slightly open… We couldn't see what was going on, that's why we went downstairs. She just sounded as though she was crying, in pain.
>
> *Q*: Did you hear Siôn's voice?
>
> *Natalie*: No.

Natalie's account makes it clear that she and Charlotte could not see what was going on because the door was pushed to; no one could see into the room from the stairs.

They went downstairs, and Charlotte told her mother, Lois, and Natalie told her father that something had happened with Billie-Jo. Peter Gaimster then went upstairs, and so did Lois.

Subsequently, Natalie said, Billie-Jo came into their bedroom (the four older children were all sharing the same one) and Lois followed to speak to Billie-Jo. According to Natalie, Lois said to Billie-Jo, 'Peter and Julia said you were fine earlier, it can't be that bad'. Natalie went on:

> So at that point I didn't think it had anything to do with Siôn, I thought it must just have been her ankle… I didn't find out for years until, I think, Dad had to give evidence about it and Dad said, I saw him hit Billie, and I thought, 'What!', I didn't realise.

In fact, Siôn's explanation of what happened is that he was behind Billie-Jo as she went up the stairs. Her sprained ankle had eased and so she had forgotten about it until she accidentally put her weight on it and cried out in pain. Siôn took Billie-Jo to the nearest room and as she was crying naturally gave her some privacy by pushing the door to.

Everything that Natalie Gaimster says is entirely consistent with that.

Furthermore, in relation to the moment when Julia broke the news of Billie-Jo's death to him, this was what Peter Gaimster originally stated:

At about 5.40pm I saw *Julia drive up to the pub* in her car. *She came in* and said, 'There's been a terrible accident, Billie-Jo is dead.'

And this is what Julia said:

I went home, sorted the children out and then *drove to the Anchor* public house believing that Peter would be having a drink. I found him, told him what had happened...

As the years passed, they remembered it differently. In her second statement, in October 2004, Julia said:

I had to go and sort my kids out and go down to the shop and collect my husband and the very first thing I said to my husband...

Giving evidence on oath at the second trial, Gaimster said:

Q: So, after you have learned that Billie-Jo is dead and you have learned that the Jenkins's are at 70 Lower Park Road, do you go to No.70?
A: That's right, yes. I was clearing out *my shop* and *my wife called* me and told me that there's been an accident and that Billie-Jo was dead and she came to pick me up.

In Gaimster's fifth statement, seven years after the incident he gave for the first time an account of the moment, later on the evening of the murder, when Siôn briefly declined to put his fleece jacket on.

This is what he said:

One other thing I would like to mention is that on the day of the murder, we were at Denise's, Siôn was in the living room, with the girls and Lois. We spent an hour or so at Denise's. We arranged to get everyone back to our house. As we were all leaving Denise's, she came out and said to Siôn, 'You've forgotten your fleece', and it was really cold. It was in February. Siôn was not that keen to take the fleece. We waited whilst he went back up the stairs to get it and he said, 'Oh, alright' and he took it.

This is what Gaimster said in his original statement:

We got to Denise's, walked in and I saw that Siôn and Lois were there...

I didn't really know what was going on but I knew that Billie-Jo was dead. I had to do something. Buster, the Jenkins' family dog, was playing up, so I said I would take him. Lois gave me an address in Ore (in Firle Close) of some friends. I left with Buster to drop him off.

I had problems finding the address so *eventually* went *home* to see what was going on and to see Julia.

As I got *home*, Julia was there and she told me Siôn and Lois were going to stay at our house with the children. I was told at this point by Julia that Denise had told her it didn't look like an accident. I felt physically sick and *gagged in the kitchen*. I could not believe what was happening. I then *rang* [Connell Vickers – Gaimster's friend] who explained to me where Firle Close was because I still had the dog.

I *eventually* drove to Firle Close, dropped the dog off and returned *home*. Siôn and Lois were at my house by this time...

I would like to say that I went to Safeway's after dropping off the dog. I returned *home* and Julia had told me to go to get milk and wine. It was after I returned from Safeway that Siôn and Lois were there.

[italics added]

The Evidence of Peter Gaimster

He took the dog from Denise Lancaster's house to be looked after elsewhere; he had problems finding the address and eventually returned home; there, he 'gagged' in the kitchen and made a telephone call to find out where the address was; took the dog a second time, this time finding the address; called in at Safeway's to purchase milk and wine; and then returned home to discover that Siôn and Lois had by then arrived from Denise's.

All that is perfectly straightforward. All the other evidence dovetails with that, including the evidence about the children needing to be driven to the Gaimsters' by Denise Lancaster's brother (because Julia had not got the car; Peter had taken it); and the evidence of the police who took Siôn and Lois to the Gaimsters. But he does not mention the fleece incident, because he wasn't there at the time.

Another incident Gaimster recalls for the first time seven years after the incident was a conversation with Siôn about his job:

> I said to him, 'Congratulations about the job', and he said, 'Well, it's not definite yet'. I said, 'Well, you've got the job, haven't you?' and he said something like, 'Well, you never know, you never know'. I said, 'But, you've got the job', and he said, 'Well, they've got to take up the references'. I said, 'You'll be fine', and he said, 'Well, you never know'...
> I got the impression from Siôn from that conversation that the job was not in the bag...

This was exactly the kind of thing the prosecution wanted to hear, as they would be suggesting at the second trial that Siôn murdered Billie-Jo partly because of stress as a result of his promotion not having been rubber-stamped.

In his first statement on 23 February 1997, this is what he stated then:

> I know Lois better than Siôn due to his heavy work commitments as *headmaster* at William Parker School, a local boys school.

[italics added]

399

Gaimster later recalled Siôn's reluctance to hand over clothing for forensic examination:

> The day after the murder, Steve Hutt came round... and said he needed to get the clothes that the Jenkins's had been wearing the day before.... Lois said, 'That's fine' and she shouted up the stairs to Siôn but there was no answer. Lois went and got her clothes and the children's clothes and they were bagged. This took quite a while. There were more calls to Siôn to come down with his clothes and we were hanging around in the hallway probably for a good 15 minutes.

There were several witnesses to this, including the police officer, DC Hutt. No one else who was there reported that Siôn kept them all 'hanging around for a good 15 minutes'.

Gaimster's testimony was heard at two trials. In retrospect, we are now able to judge the strength of Gaimster's evidence.

Chapter Fifty

The Footprint on the Patio

One of the incriminating aspects of Siôn's conduct was held to be the way he behaved and both what he said and what he did not say in the aftermath of the murder, and during the rest of that day (Saturday) and the next (Sunday). He gave confused and sometimes incomplete or incorrect answers to some police questions. He had also got into his MG for no discernible reason.

Meanwhile, PC Christopher Bruce, one of the first officers to arrive at the house, witnessed the brutality of the murder scene and described what he saw as 'horrific'. He said that afterwards he and his colleague were both 'in a terrible state'. They were straightaway sent for counselling (or, to use the contemporary jargon, 'welfare debriefs').

Bruce made a statement, but there were significant omissions from it. He subsequently found that, 'I was remembering things that I hadn't put in my statement'. He had forgotten, for example, some exchanges with Siôn. He put these into his pocket-book when, after speaking to a colleague, he remembered them three days later.

When Denise Lancaster was summoned to help, she had responded immediately. As she rushed straight into the Jenkins's house, she pushed past a somewhat startled Dr Robert Megit, who was standing on the doorstep.

Mrs Lancaster then made a statement about what happened that afternoon. It contained no mention of Megit.

This puzzled the police. At the end of the week, they went back to her and asked her for an explanation. Her memory refreshed, she did recall what had happened. She made a fresh statement incorporating the detail about Dr Megit. As far as the police were concerned, this satisfactorily resolved an anomaly in the evidence.

So there were unexplained aspects of parts of the original testimony of Denise Lancaster and of PC Bruce and of Siôn himself. Logically, all were due to the effects of shock. Allowances were made for the effects of shock on the police themselves or on important witnesses like Denise Lancaster; the kinks in the prosecution's evidence were smoothed out.

Any effects of shock would inevitably register to a much greater extent with Siôn, as the foster father of the murdered girl; yet, far from greater allowances being made for him, he was treated very differently. In his case, no allowances at all were made for the effects of shock; any kinks in his evidence were presented as evidence of guilt.

Once the police suspected Siôn, they should have tested the evidence properly. They should have reconstructed all that he was meant to have done in that period and timed it. In fact, they did recreate the journeys, but only in two parts with different drivers in different vehicles on different occasions. There was never a single reconstruction.

According to these separate reconstructions, the first journey took ten minutes thirty seconds; the second, fifteen minutes twenty-one seconds: roughly twenty-six minutes in total. There is no video record of the first journey. There is of the second, and from that it could be seen that the police car had a smooth journey, with no hold-ups at traffic lights and no queue of Saturday afternoon traffic waiting to turn into the Sainsbury's and Do-It-All car-park. Siôn's evidence was that his own journey was not as unimpeded.

Because they were undertaken separately, the police reconstructions did not allow for the time spent getting out of the car at the roadside, and climbing the steps up to the house; and then leaving the house and getting in the car again. A minute for each seems the least amount of time it would have taken. In all, that's twenty-eight minutes of the time period used up.

Only five minutes remain unaccounted for. That's not five minutes for Siôn to batter Billie-Jo to death; that's *five minutes altogether* for him and the children to spend inside the house. So the time available for Siôn to complete a remarkable double transformation and (a) lose his rag and murder Billie-Jo and (b) recover his equilibrium and return to normal? Even on the prosecution's own scenario, it must be a maximum of two minutes.

Not only was this wholly unlikely, but there was no background evidence to suggest that anything like this would have been in Siôn's character. There was no evidence to suggest that he could turn violent with children or, indeed, at all. Naturally, the police exhaustively examined all available records from the education department. Over the course of his career, Siôn had not been violent or lost his temper in situations at school. This was what one former colleague from the McKentee school in Walthamstow recalled:

> Siôn was calm, well-organised, good-natured and good-humoured in class. It was a very challenging school but he had tremendous patience... If he had to discipline kids, he would appeal to their better nature and encourage their self-esteem. Of all the people I worked with, Siôn was one whom I never saw lose his temper. He was remarkably controlled and not confrontational at all.

A former pupil at William Parker said:

He was a good teacher and a very likeable person. He had a good relationship with everyone in the class and seemed popular with everyone. He dealt with disobedience in class fairly and in a calm manner. He was not one to raise his voice excessively or snap. I do not remember him ever losing control with students.

There were many other testimonials along similar lines. Naturally, the prosecution consigned all these to the cutting-room floor, as they did not support its case. However, they must have been accurate observations; otherwise, of course, Siôn would not have been appointed to the posts of deputy headteacher and then headteacher. He may have exaggerated his academic background in his CV, but in order to obtain these posts he needed – and got – good references from those he had worked alongside.

The police also carefully examined the social services records. Again, there was nothing to suggest that he had ever been violent in domestic situations, let alone lost control in such an extraordinary way. Indeed, the records suggested precisely the opposite: that he didn't lose control at all, let alone with children.

Nor was there any evidence that Siôn was unhappy or tense or stressed that day. It was, in fact, Lois who had had her tetchy moments during the twenty-four hours before the murder. On the Friday evening, she had had an argument with Regine. Then, on the Saturday, she had had run-ins with Billie-Jo, with Annie, and then with Regine again. It was Lois who'd been stranded at the supermarket with three children and a trolley of shopping she couldn't pay for.

When they rejected his first appeal, the judges discerned something unusual in Siôn's behaviour that afternoon. They said he:

went without money by a circuitous route to buy an item that he did not need.

Judges are often accused of not living in the real world. Though the criticism is generally misplaced, this is one of those rare occasions where it would be amply justified.

Siôn took the car the long way round the park because he always drove off in the direction the car was facing for safety reasons; he did not want to make a dangerous turn on a busy road. Then he momentarily thought about abandoning the journey, but was persuaded by Annie to continue.

As for buying 'an item that he did not need', the defence made some enquiries. Had any surveys been conducted by retail research organisations to discover the propensity of people to purchase items they did not need? No such surveys, it seems, have ever been conducted – for the obvious reason that the retail sector hardly wants to run the risk of giving the public reasons not to shop.

If such a survey were to be conducted, however, one could reasonably suppose that it would show that a high percentage of people do regularly buy items they do not actually need; and that, chief among these redundant items, would be articles like white spirit, when half-filled bottles have been languishing forgotten for years in the furthest reaches of disordered cupboards.

There was, however, another aspect of that first appeal court judgment that was much more dangerously misguided. Lord Justice Kennedy blandly said that:

'They [the police] were *entitled to seek to persuade* Mrs Jenkins that her husband was the killer'.

One of the greatest dangers for the integrity of crime investigations is the inadvertent influencing of key witnesses. If the influencing is not inadvertent but *advertent*, then this will completely undermine the integrity of an investigation. It was bewildering that senior judges lacked all comprehension of that.

One professor of psychology reflected that their entitled-to-seek-to-persuade comment demonstrated 'total ignorance of psychological processes that have been understood by, and indeed taught to, first year undergraduates for over fifty years'.

Because of a growing perception that victims and the bereaved were not being treated with sufficient consideration, a new police post was created – that of family liaison officer (FLO), whose job it was to support the next-of-kin in the aftermath of tragedy.

However, the FLOs' primary duty was not, in fact, to the victims but to the police. They very much remained part of the police team and indeed regarded it as part of their function to gather evidence to assist the inquiry. In the Billie-Jo investigation, the officers designated as the FLOs were the ones who were told to 'feed into Mum' – and thus (although they could not personally be blamed) contaminate the inquiry.

At the second appeal, Lois Jenkins gave evidence about how much the presence of the officers meant to her in that period and, indeed, how WDC Gregory had helped her to begin re-living her life:

Lois: My understanding of police officers being there at the house, and they were there – they weren't at night, but during the day they were there most of the time – was that we couldn't function without them being there.

We really couldn't. The first – I mean, we had a problem getting – buying bread and milk and food and Julie Gregory took me shopping for the first time.

Q: Julie Gregory?

Lois: One of the family liaison officers. She actually taught me how to shop again. I had forgotten. Took me round the supermarket and, you know, said, 'Hold your head high, take your food, put it in the trolley'. It is unbelievable to remember how scary it was.

The children testified to the closeness of the relationships with the officers. Asked if she could remember their names, Annie replied, 'Anne Capon and Steve Hutt'. At one of the arranged meetings for Siôn with the children, Maya had referred to WDS Capon as 'Auntie Annie'. Charlotte was also asked in interview which officers she knew well:

The Footprint on the Patio

Charlotte: Yeah, there was one. Well, they were all involved, but then one called Steve Hutt, we're still friends with him, he sends us cards all the time, for birthdays and things.

However, the intimacy between investigating police officers and the key witnesses meant that their shared perceptions were constantly recycled and thereby reinforced and entrenched. It is no wonder that, as the case unfolded, the perceptions of key witnesses changed to fit in with what they imagined the case to be.

Even more disastrously, the misinformation was then circulated beyond the immediate participants in three distinct ways. Firstly, the town of Hastings was an almost perfect environment in which to spread these rumours. Siôn was headteacher-designate of the town's well-established boys' secondary school. He had also stood for the local council. While only a few knew him, many would have *known of* him. He was therefore exactly the kind of semi-prominent person about whom rumours will spread through a community like wildfire.

Generally, the more unexpected and shocking the rumours, the more efficiently they will be circulated; and, in the process, they are inevitably embellished. The rumour-mongering will only have been intensified by the fact that Siôn's school was closely associated with the town's rugby club – which used the school's playing fields for its matches. A number of police officers were leading members of the rugby club. It can reasonably be assumed that officers, whether engaged on the murder inquiry or not, would have passed on something of what they'd heard about the case.

Meanwhile, officers actually engaged on the inquiry would, when interviewing witnesses, pass comments along the lines of, 'If you knew about him half of what we know about him... '

This creates a double-edged problem. On the one hand, the malicious rumours are widely accepted as fact; on the other, many of those who know better and privately reject them are nevertheless inhibited from speaking out – and even appearing as witnesses – because of the poisoned atmosphere.

The misinformation was passed directly to specific people – for example, to Arnon and Marianne Bentovim. Everything they were told by the police, it seems, they credulously accepted. They then turned the misinformation into a quasi-authoritative report. This then became a supposedly secure platform from which others could launch further untruths.

So, right through the case, misinformation was being circulated by supposedly unimpeachable sources. This continued up until virtually the last day, when the Legal Services Commission passed misunderstandings to the judge. Mr Justice Clarke, naturally believing what he'd been officially told, then acted on the information in open court, which only fuelled further antipathy to Siôn and Tina.[66]

The whole process of public vilification being used as a substitute for actual evidence reached its disastrous conclusion when David Blunkett, then home secretary, introduced the Criminal Justice Act 2003. Hearsay and evidence of general bad character had, throughout the entire history of the legal system, been locked firmly outside the courtroom. Now, Blunkett ushered in the scurrilous tittle-tattle and elevated it to the status of admissible evidence.

The rocks on which the criminal justice system was founded – that the evidence must be direct and should relate solely to the specific charge – were swept away. The Jenkins case would be the first major trial in which they applied. The impact of the new atmosphere of legal licentiousness was extraordinary.

From the defence point of view, the task of clearing Siôn was made immeasurably more difficult. Having failed to unearth a single piece of cogent evidence against Siôn, the prosecution now had a perfect fall-back position. They could say: he must be guilty, just look at what a nasty piece of work he is.

So, in the second and third trials, much testimony that was heard in court had only emerged *after* witnesses were told that Siôn had committed the murder.

Part of the prosecution case concerned injuries supposedly inflicted on

Billie-Jo by Siôn. This was to illustrate perfectly why such testimony should never be allowed in the courtroom.

Holly Prior, undoubtedly a truthful witness, said that one morning at school she'd noticed scratches on Billie-Jo's face and shoulders. Billie-Jo told her that the injuries were caused by her father; she asked Holly to swear not to tell anyone.

When Ruth Bristow gave evidence, she confirmed that she recalled these injuries – 'they were sort of grazes', she said, 'not deep scratches' – and said that Billie-Jo had told her that she had got them in a fight with another girl at school; and that some of the scratches were probably caused as a result of Billie-Jo's schoolbag, which she wore over her shoulder, having been pulled.

'She wouldn't go looking for a fight', explained Ruth, 'but if someone confronted her, she would lash out.

'I was going home with her that day. She said that if Lois asked how she got them, to say she'd been scratched by bushes. She didn't want her to know she'd been in a fight.'

What seems to have happened is that Billie-Jo had had some aggro at school, had come off worse and didn't want anyone to know. Holly confirmed that Billie-Jo could get 'picked on… she just didn't get on with everybody'.

Accordingly, Billie-Jo explained the scratches by inventing different versions for different people who questioned her. However, to Ruth, her closest friend, Billie-Jo had confided the truth – along with the plea to collude in inventing another version for her mother (Lois).

Those who argue that it was right to hear this evidence, and that no harm was done as the truth emerged from the testimony, have overlooked two vital matters. Firstly, the Crown called Laura-Jane Conway. Although her evidence was strongly attacked in the courtroom, her remarks were broadcast to the world outside by the media. Accordingly, they became added grist to the mill in the vilification of Siôn.

Secondly, Siôn was fortunate indeed that Billie-Jo had chosen a friend of such integrity as Ruth Bristow. Another friend might well have been afraid of appearing in court on behalf of such a publicly-reviled figure, and the untruths may then have prevailed by default.

While the fantasies were being disseminated, the actual evidence was being overlooked. On finding Billie badly injured on the patio, Siôn had described his touching and movement of Billie, long before he was told of the invisible blood spray on his clothes. It was the police who did not relay this information to the forensic scientist before he wrote his initial reports. Today this would be against their Code of Practice.

There was, indeed, another stark piece of evidence: a footprint on the patio. It was clearly observable.

There is bad evidence in a case (and impressionable witness evidence falls squarely into that category) and there is good. As crime investigators worldwide would instantly recognise, this evidence was way beyond 'good'. It was gold standard.

Billie-Jo had swept the patio that afternoon so the footprint could not have been there earlier. It appeared to be the print of a male wearing boots with patterned soles. It would have been straightforward to match the print to a particular boot.

However, the footprint did not match Siôn. Nor did it match any member of the family. Nor did it match any member of the emergency services who had been at the scene.

The print must have belonged to the murderer.

Amazingly, one of the ambulance crew had noticed muddy footprints on Billie-Jo's leggings. He mentioned these in his statement, and gave evidence about them. When the body was moved, however, the prints were lost. Yet this was further very persuasive evidence to the effect both that the murderer's footwear was likely to leave impressions; and that – in apparently standing on the body of his victim – the culprit was behaving in a deranged way.

However, while the investigators were ignoring the extraordinarily powerful evidence at the crime scene – like the footprint, like the bin-liner – they were instead squandering vast amounts of public money in the futile task of trying to prop up their disastrous theory and link Siôn Jenkins to the crime. With the third trial about to start, they commissioned further scientific work.

The aim of the work was to detect microscopic fragments of human material inside the 'white inclusions' that themselves were within invisible bloodspots. As it happened, however, fragments of human material – whether bone, brain matter or anything else – were not present. What the Crown discovered instead were fragments of metal. Could this have come from the murder weapon, the bloodied tent peg? The research continued (without the knowledge of the judge who had, of course, disallowed the evidence).

The results became known towards the end of the trial. Again, the Crown's tests had drawn a blank. There was no connection between this piece of metal and the murder weapon. Wherever it came from (and, one would assume, it was just standard atmospheric debris), it was not the tent peg. This was the 'evidence' the jury did not hear.

The facility with which, in English courtrooms, prosecution lawyers can make bricks without straw has long been understood.[67]

The CPS was set up in the full knowledge that some unmeritorious cases will be won in the courtroom and was established specifically to prevent unwarranted cases from going to trial in the first place.

One of the CPS's key precepts is that it must prosecute cases 'fairly'. Additionally, there is an obvious duty on its staff, as servants of the Crown, to behave ethically. Against this background, it is interesting to consider what happened in this case, which was taken to court by Sussex CPS.

On 21 April 1998, with the Lewes trial about to start, the defence presented an expert report from John Sinar, consultant neurosurgeon at Middlesbrough general hospital. He delivered a second report just over a week later on 29 April.

In these reports, he emphasised a number of striking points:

- that patients with open head wounds will often survive for a period of time (about twenty minutes was certainly feasible). Indeed, he stressed that, 'it is not the norm for patients to die immediately'.

- that the pooling of blood on the patio strongly supported the idea that she had not died instantly.

- that unconscious patients will exhale mucus or blood either when being moved or spontaneously.

- that this exhaled blood (or mucus) will spray medical staff.

All this, therefore, suggested that Siôn could have been sprayed with blood as he tended to Billie-Jo. Sinar pointed to all the circumstances suggesting that this is indeed what may have happened: 'Mr Jenkins tried to lift her by her right shoulder and whilst doing so was in a crouched position. He then heard a squelching sound... This could well represent exhalation of air from bloodstained air-passages. It is also possible that when he turned her, she may have exhaled... certainly the act of turning her would have resulted in some mechanical stimulation to her chest and this could result in exhalation...'

Sinar added two further points:

- that Siôn had no brain matter on his clothing and this would have been anticipated [had he been the attacker]: 'brain is clearly seen in [Billie-Jo's] hair and... it is my experience from dealing with patients... that contused brain... could well have been transferred to the assailant'.

- that there was no bloodstaining on Siôn's thighs, which suggested that he was in a crouching position when the spray landed on him. This obviously supported the idea that he was tending to her rather than attacking her.

The prosecution having received this material, the judge, Mr Justice Gage, then granted them a six-week adjournment so that they could find a neurosurgeon of their own to comment on Sinar's reports.

They did find a retired consultant neurosurgeon, who submitted a report which broadly endorsed Sinar's findings. What, therefore, did the prosecution do?

They dropped him like a hot potato.

They then drafted in David Southall, professor of paediatrics at Keele University, to deal with this area of evidence. He told the jury that Billie-Jo, in her condition, could not have expelled the 2.3 litres of air necessary to create the bloodspray on Siôn's clothing.

Q: In your considered opinion is [the defence thesis] a viable explanation for the bloodspots found on Siôn Jenkins?
Southall: I have no doubt at all in my mind that I regard that as impossible.

This answer by itself demolished the defence case and paved the way for Siôn's conviction and sentence of life imprisonment.

However, Southall was a paediatrician and, behind the scenes, there was great controversy about his involvement in the case. First of all, the Crown had been granted a six-week adjournment to bring in a neurosurgeon, not a paediatrician; and secondly, just what were Southall's credentials for claiming expertise in the field of neurosurgery?

Having learned of his involvement, Sinar commented: 'I must confess to being surprised that a specialist paediatrician… feels competent to deal with matters so clearly within the neurological speciality… I have never come across a paediatrician dealing with young patients in an intensive care unit suffering from head injuries.'

Donald Campbell, a Harley Street neurosurgeon who also provided a report for the defence, knew Southall well. 'Southall and I were in the same hospital [North Staffordshire] for three-and-a-half years', he wrote. 'Over that period, he did not attend the treatment of acute penetrating

head injuries in children or adults in the Accident Department...
paediatricians played no part in the management of major head injuries.'

With regard to Southall's testimony that Billie-Jo would not have been
able to expel 2.3 litres of air, Campbell commented bluntly that his
evidence was 'simply incorrect'.[68]

In December 2007, Southall was struck off the medical register on the
grounds of serious professional misconduct relating to a 'deep-seated
attitudinal problem'. Without justification, he had in two instances
accused a parent of murdering a child (according to the General Medical
Council, as reported by the BBC at the time).

In these circumstances, was the CPS adhering to its legal duty to
prosecute cases 'fairly'?

The jury at Lewes were kept in the dark about the fact that the
prosecution's own expert agreed with the defence. That evidence, all of
which was provided in 1998, before the first trial, has stood the test of
time. If the CPS had acted as they should have done and abandoned the
prosecution, then Siôn would not have been wrongly convicted, millions
of pounds of public money would not have been wasted and the
murderer of Billie-Jo may by now have been caught.

Chapter Fifty-One

The Man in
the Hall

Over the last ten years I have often reflected on what happened on Saturday, February 15th, 1997. I have often been asked who I believe is responsible and whether future legal action is likely following a new police investigation. I don't know what the current state of police activity is in relation to Sussex police, but after sifting through reams of legal papers and piecing together the jigsaw of events on that dark day, I now believe I do know who murdered Billie-Jo. I have stood face to face with him. I have spoken with him. I know what he looks like and remember his mannerisms. So why has it taken until now for me to realise all this? And what does the holding of this information mean in terms of finally apprehending Billie's killer? Let me now try to explain for the first time what I believe happened.

Prior to Billie's murder we had been plagued with prowlers and people using our back garden as a shortcut. I had organised for security lighting to be fitted and this seemed to work. We then went through a period of time where such concerns were not so prevalent. Billie had not seemed concerned with prowlers generally anyway; her primary concern had been over a man with dark hair that she'd seen wearing a smart leather jacket, and who she'd noticed watching our house from the park. She had noticed this man a number of times and was concerned that he might be watching her. Billie didn't mention this particular man again until later in 1996 when she said that she was becoming uneasy again. We talked about it and Lois, I know, told Billie always to close her bedroom curtains when she got undressed at night. It hadn't dawned on her that although she couldn't see anything outside, when her light was on someone else could see inside, if they were standing at the back of our house. But as I said, my family's general concern with prowlers seemed to decrease after I'd fitted the security lighting. We got on with living at Lower Park Road; we didn't want to change our usual family routines, but became more conscious of our security during the evenings. It was only a matter of weeks prior to Billie's murder that I had visited a local estate agent with a view to putting our house on the market. I didn't want anyone in the household to feel anxious for their safety.

I've obviously given thought to the possibility of someone taking a shortcut through my garden, finding Billie and then, through a succession of circumstances, ending up attacking her. But somehow this possibility lacks credibility. I'm sure there are circumstances when a loner trespasses, and on coming across a householder commits an act of violence, but in this case I am not convinced. My reasons have been formulated because of other relevant evidence.

At my appeal in 2004 and at subsequent trials the evidence relating to other suspects was presented and argued over by the defence and prosecution. I know myself from bitter experience that it is so easy for circumstantial evidence to be presented in such a way that an innocent man may be wrongly convicted. But it was important, bearing in mind the Commission's view on the police investigation regarding other suspects, that the evidence was again reviewed by the Court of Appeal, and then by the two juries designated to hear the evidence in my case.

When I was acquitted my first weeks and months of freedom were difficult. It is only relatively recently that I have felt ready to start the process of dealing with the feelings of hurt and betrayal that erupted within me when I was first arrested. But the process of recovery has had other benefits. During the preparation for this book I have analysed and re-read hundreds of statements in order to understand what really happened to Billie. I have attempted to look for the missing key that might open up the case and point me towards the person who murdered my daughter. What was to follow surprised me and was to lead to a journey of discovery. I was also left with the realization that I had probably found the person who had murdered Billie. The answer was to be found in my witness statement and in a collection of witness statements taken from those individuals who first attended the scene of crime after I had phoned for an ambulance. The answer to this murder has always been there.

It was a matter of days after Billie's murder that I was first asked to give a witness statement. That statement was a long and detailed account of what had taken place on the day of the murder. I was unprepared for everything that was going to unfold over the next week. Billie's murder devastated us all and we found ourselves as a family simply responding to events around us. But I wanted to do everything I could to help the police and so I made sure that my witness statement was as thorough and as accurate as I could give.

The statement went to 42 pages and included all the details that I could remember. The police said they needed the statement to help them find Billie's killer and so I painstakingly provided everything I could. When I had finished giving the statement I rested and tried to make sense of everything with Lois. We got through the weekend and then on Monday, 24th February 1997 I was arrested. The reason I'm explaining this part of the story to you again is because despite the fact that I have been interviewed, examined and cross-examined over the details in my witness statement and other related matters, I have rarely read my original statement. I have known the events of the day so well that I have never felt the need to read my account again. When I was preparing for my second trial I did read my account before taking the witness stand and at the time nothing stood out to me. Both my defence and the prosecution made good use of the statement to represent their positions. But it was after my second trial and particularly following my acquittal that I studied my witness statement again and saw something that led me to reinvestigate part of this case.

Following my own instincts, I found evidence that led me to question the assumed facts of the day. My findings were to leave me with feelings of dread, anger and sadness. Had I, at last, found Billie's killer? I want to describe what I first told the police and how this account might always have held the answer. I don't want to repeat things that have already been written about or to cover the whole statement, but I do want to take you back to the first minutes following the discovery of Billie's body.

When I returned to the house after the trip to Do-It-All we found poor Billie's body lying in a pool of blood. I phoned for the ambulance first and then phoned Denise Lancaster. Denise came around immediately and we shared the responsibility of looking after Annie and Lottie, who had always been with me, and caring for Billie while waiting for the arrival of the ambulance and police. Those first minutes after finding Billie were cataclysmic. I can remember them very well. I was with Billie before Denise arrived. When Denise entered the dining room she went to the patio and tried to help Billie. We were both shocked and didn't know what to do, as her injuries were so severe. At one point Denise left Billie and remained with Annie and Lottie whilst I comforted Billie. My daughters then started to become more distressed and so Denise and I crossed paths; I went to Annie and Lottie in the front playroom and Denise returned to Billie. The door to the dining room was now shut. The girls calmed down when they saw me and I told them everything would be all right. In a moment of quiet desperation I stood with my girls and prayed that Billie would live.

It wasn't long before the ambulance arrived, although at the time it felt like an eternity. I led one of the ambulance crew in to the hall. At the point that he went to Billie, a plain-clothes police officer spoke from behind me. In my witness statement I said the following to the police (and I quote from my witness statement verbatim):

> The very next thing that I can recall is being in the hall and talking to a dark-haired officer who was standing near me, he was not in uniform but I was aware that he was a Police Officer so I assume that he must have told me. I don't know what the conversation was about but we did talk.

This man was standing in the hall. I turned around and looked at him. He said, 'She's going to be OK.' I couldn't respond. By then I was beginning to close down emotionally. I needed help and this man's words offered some comfort. We spoke and he offered more reassurances. He then left me staring at the door to the dining room.

The next thing I knew was that another police officer was coming in to the hall. My statement continues:

> The next thing that I can recall is seeing a uniformed police officer come into the house, through the front door. He was also dark haired and I think he had a small beard. I think that he came over to me but I can't recall what he said. I think he then went into the dining room. I don't know where the other policeman had gone.

The second police officer was PC Bruce. When he approached me I said in my witness statement that:

> I can recall telling the uniformed officer that I needed to be with Billie...

I specifically said that he was a uniformed officer because at the time I didn't know his name and therefore wanted to make a distinction between him and the first, plain-clothes, officer that I had spoken to.

When I spoke with PC Bruce I told him that I needed to go back to Billie. He placed his arm on me and said, 'You can't go in there.'

After the events of this day I was to see PC Bruce again, and my description of Bruce was accurate. He did have a small goatee beard and I was to recognise him again at Hastings Police Station. I was also to see him in Court over the course of three trials.

The next officer I described was Sergeant Anne Capon who was to take a leading role in the investigation. In my witness statement I said that,

> The other thing is I can recall seeing a lady police officer, who was quite tall with swept back greying hair… I remember her because she spoke with care and authority.

I was to be interviewed by Capon at Hastings Police Station. She was tall and did have greying hair. She also spoke with care and authority. I had described her accurately. I was also to see her again at three trials and at a hearing in Lewes Crown Court.

Suffice it to say that I described the relevant details of all the people who first entered my home to help Billie and my family. Those first police officers were important figures in the events of the day as were the two ambulance crew who tried to save Billie's life. They were also to appear in court for the prosecution over the course of three trials.

From the moment I was charged I rarely picked up my statement again. I was soon being questioned about it and was to be finally charged with murder. My trial was often a blur. I was physically there but much of what took place didn't register because of the strain and trauma that filled me. From the day of my conviction much has been said and written about Billie's murder. Although many believed me to be guilty I never stopped believing that one day I would be free and that my acquittal would enable me to track down her killer.

It was after my second trial and whilst preparing for my third that I decided to start the process. I laid out all the witness statements in my study and re-read my own again. I needed to know that I hadn't missed something. As I read the statements nothing sprang to light, but I noticed when I read my own statement again that I didn't have the first police officer's statement. I had the two statements written by the ambulance crew and also other police statements concerning those who had at some point attended the scene of crime. I had the statements written by Bruce and Capon but to my surprise I couldn't find the statement of the first man, the plain-clothes police officer.

I asked my solicitor to find and send me the statement. Unfortunately he couldn't find it and was unsure whether he'd ever seen it. I asked him to write to the police and to request it. Wider events then took over and my third trial began. It was a bruising affair but finally I was acquitted on 7th February, 2006. After a period of recovery I then restarted the process of studying the evidence again and I returned to the 'lost' witness statement.

I had now read all the other statements but I needed to know what the first man had written in evidence. The second police officer to arrive had been PC Bruce and his statement had been useful to me in understanding those first minutes of police activity. As I said in my witness statement after speaking with Bruce, 'I don't know where the other policeman had gone.' I forget the exact moment I was told, but the statement by the plain-clothes police officer did not exist. There was no record of there having been a plain-clothes police officer at the scene of crime before PC Bruce walked into my home.

I thought about this for a few days and discussed the matter with Tina. I needed to know that I wasn't going mad. I had seen this police officer; he had spoken to me. He clearly knew that someone was hurt because he tried to comfort me before leaving the house. Soon after that my home was full of professionals trying to help. Over the next eight years I did not give a minute's thought to this first 'police officer'. As far as I was concerned he was one of them and the police knew who he was. At the time of finding Billie he had also been helpful so I had nothing to say against him. The police took my witness statement over three days and I explained to the interviewing police officer that I had spoken to a plain-clothed police officer before PC Bruce. He accepted what I said and on no occasion followed the details of this up with me. I was questioned by two other police officers concerning my witness statement and at no time did the police ever question my description of events regarding this man. As I have already said, I have been through three long trials and the Crown has never questioned my analysis on this point. In fact the prosecution were often at pains to point out that my witness statement was a very detailed affair and that it demonstrated I could remember events very well at the time of Billie's murder. But after my three trials I started to question why this man, who I believed to be a police officer, had never given evidence for the Crown despite him apparently being the first police officer to attend the scene of crime.

So who was this man? The police say they have no record of him and that no police witness statement exists. If this is the case then surely it begs the question why I was never questioned about him. When I first mentioned him to Sussex police they accepted what I said and so I assumed that he was just another police officer attending a scene of murder. If they had no record of this police officer attending the crime scene before Bruce, then why didn't they say something?

Some might argue that I must have been mistaken. I would argue this is not the case. I remembered the faces of all those who attended the scene of crime in those first minutes and in my witness statement described them and some of their features. Others might suggest I've made him up; that he was a phantom plain-clothes officer, created to enable me to suggest that this man was the murderer. But if this were the case it would be somewhat strange if having created a defence, I then chose not to use it for the duration of three murder trials. I went to these trials knowing that I faced a life sentence if convicted.

I did speak to this man. He stood before me in my hall and I remember him clearly. I would estimate he was approximately 5 feet 10 inches tall and about 40 years old. He wore a dark navy or possibly dark olive overcoat and was smartly dressed. I could see that he was wearing a tie under his coat. He had highly polished shoes. It was this fact that reassured me that he was a police officer. He had dark hair and had flecks of grey running through it – almost as if the grey in his hair were highlights. His face was pockmarked and had a shine to it. His skin was also quite pale. When he said that Billie was going to be alright I believed him. He seemed unfazed by what was happening around him. At that moment if he had asked me to do anything, within reason, I would have done it. As far as I was concerned this man was an experienced police officer who appeared before me after I had called the police. He hadn't needed to ring the doorbell as the side door was wide open and had been since Denise's arrival.

I honestly believe that this man is responsible for my daughter's murder. I believe he killed her in cold blood for reasons that I can only speculate and surmise. Over the past year I have again tried to fathom what happened in the minutes leading up to Billie's death and how it was that I probably faced Billie's killer only for him to walk out of my home and to a life devoid of justice.

It is my belief that he knew Billie and that this was the man she feared. She had spotted a smartly dressed man watching our house from the park. On that occasion he had worn a leather jacket. But her anxiety was to fade over the coming months and life seemed to then go on as normal. However, on the day of the murder I believe he entered my home from the side-gate and that he walked around the back and found Billie. I don't know why he murdered her or what motive led him to do so with such brutality. But I believe that having done so he panicked when he heard the family return and, believing that we were all going to come round the back way, he'd entered my home with the intention of leaving undetected via the front entrance.

When I arrived home with Annie and Lottie one of the girls exclaimed that the side-gate was open. I had shut it before we set off for Do-It-All. Billie's killer knew that he'd opened the side-gate and, hearing the girls running up the sideway, decided that we'd all enter the house not by the front door but by the side passageway, where we'd expect to find Billie painting the patio doors. I believe his response was to enter the house hoping to make his exit via the front of the house. But we didn't walk round the back. I put the key in the front door and went in. I suspect that it was just before this that he'd shut the dining room door. But now he was faced with a dilemma. He couldn't leave by the main door as people were coming in, but likewise he couldn't be sure that someone might not come round from the back. I believe at that moment he went into the lounge and hid behind the open door. Whilst I frantically made phone calls from the hall he remained where he was, waiting for the right moment. Denise was to arrive but all through the frenetic activity of comforting Billie and Annie and Lottie he continued to remain silent and still. It was when I was in the hall outside the dining room, with one of the ambulance crew tending to Billie, that he appeared. Denise had by now taken Annie and Lottie upstairs. He chose this moment to present himself to me with cold precision, as he now realised he had to make his move to get out.

The reason I believe he hid in the lounge is because if he'd been in the ground floor toilet I would have seen him when I went in there before the ambulance crew arrived. He could not have hidden under the stairs, as I would have noticed him coming out. The girls were in the playroom so that only leaves the lounge. My back was to the lounge when he came out, so for that moment I assumed that he had come in through the side door and simply walked up to me. I now believe that he had been hiding behind the partially opened lounge door.

Having now considered the likelihood of these events in some detail I have had to face the real possibility that this man, dressed in an overcoat and saying he was a plain-clothes police officer, was in fact Billie's killer. I asked myself why I didn't notice any blood on his clothing, but his overcoat was dark and I now suspect that any blood spatters on him would have been disguised. This interpretation might sound fanciful to some and shocking to others, but the question I keep asking myself is, if he was not responsible then what was he doing in my house at that time? He knew that Billie was hurt because he said that she was going to be alright. So how did he know that she had been attacked? If some argue that he must have been a police officer then why has a statement never been produced? The police would not willingly and knowingly obstruct the course of justice and withhold a witness statement: what possible motive would there be for such an action? Another point that finally dawned on me when I thought about my three trials was that this police officer has never given evidence at any of my trials despite the fact that he was ostensibly the first police officer to attend the scene of crime and the first officer to speak with me.

The answer, of course, is that he never was a police officer. I think he was the murderer and he had deceived me to get out of the house. So what does this realisation now mean? What am I now to do? I cannot investigate Billie's murder and bring a prosecution but I can work with the police to reopen this case and to try to find this man. I have a clear picture of him in my mind's eye but now need to help the police create a photo-fit picture so that the process of tracking him down can now begin. Eleven years might have passed but I am convinced that if I were to see him again I would recognise him. There are other memories concerning his smell and accent that I am able to provide. If I had been questioned about this man in 1997 things might have been different. I want and need the police to help me find him.

I have often thought of returning to Hastings since my acquittal in the hope of finding him. But my face is well known in Hastings and my perceived notoriety would make it virtually impossible for me to look for him without drawing attention to myself. And looking for him might be worthwhile emotionally and psychologically but the chances of finding him in such circumstances would be like finding a tiny needle in a large haystack. I do believe that one day he will be found and that one day he will have to answer as to why he was in my home at the time of Billie's murder.

The next step for me will be to arrange a meeting with Sussex police to discuss this aspect of my witness statement. The idea that at last the process of finding Billie's real killer can begin is thought-provoking and humbling. I feel that, at last, I am able to start the journey to get justice for the daughter I loved and cared for. The fact remains that this man was in my house at the time of Billie's murder and no one has an answer as to his identity. Have I looked into her killer's eyes? How long will it be before I face him again?

Chapter Fifty-Two

Epilogue

As I sit in my study reflecting on the last eleven years it is sometimes difficult to comprehend and take in all that has happened to my family, and to a host of other people whose lives have been affected to varying degrees following Billie's murder. How does one attempt to sum up the actions, behaviour and the emotional turmoil of all the players that have, in some way, touched this case?

My first thoughts are with Billie who lost her life. She would have been twenty-five in March of this year. I often recall conversations with her and wonder what she would have made of these past eleven years. Would she now be married, with children of her own? How would her life have touched and influenced those around her? As it was, her short life was to change the lives of many close to her but clearly not in the way she would have expected.

My own life since the acquittal has been a difficult journey. It was only after I'd left the Old Bailey following my third trial that I was able to start the process of facing the past. The process has been a hard one. For the first six months I found myself moving from and between a range of conflicting feelings. One day I felt at peace and the next I would be filled with anger and melancholy. It was hard for Tina to keep track of my emotional well-being.

I think one of the hardest things I've had to cope with has been the number of loose ends that continue to float around me. When I was arrested back in1997 I was suddenly taken from my wife, children, friends, job and work colleagues. I didn't go through a process where my life gradually changed and where I was able to prepare psychologically and emotionally for change. I woke one Monday morning and was arrested for a murder that I didn't commit. It was from that moment that my life was dismantled and everything I'd known and which identified me as the person I am was unceremoniously removed. Today I'm beginning to feel that the process of tying up some of those loose ends has begun.

Recently I began a series of counselling sessions to work through some of the feelings that have left me emotionally bruised. Strangely when I first came out of prison I was unable to engage in any kind of therapy and wrongly believed that I could heal myself with the passing of time. This was a misguided thought brought on, in part, by years of having to work through things alone in a prison cell. Thankfully those days have past and I'm now able to engage with the idea of needing others more easily.

For the past year I have been doing a Masters degree in Criminology and Criminal Justice at the University of Portsmouth. I decided to do the course because I wanted to understand more objectively what had happened to me and what continues to take place every day in our courts and prisons. I wanted to understand miscarriage of justice and why so many people continue to be wrongly convicted every year. The common view is that it is only a small number who are wrongly convicted in our courts, but unfortunately this assumption is far from the truth.

One of the problems is that the focus is generally on high-profile cases of justice in error and so ignores the wider picture. Rather than considering only high profile cases that are referred to the Court of Appeal Criminal Division by the Criminal Cases Review Commission (CCRC), I believe we should also reflect on other lesser-known cases.

Epilogue

There are those that are sent to the Court of Appeal from the Crown Court and those cases that are heard in the Crown Court following a conviction in the magistrates' court. A review of the statistics given by the CCRC for 1998 (the year I was convicted) indicated that seven convictions were quashed by the Court of Appeal. The numbers every year remain low. But if we include all quashed convictions from the Crown and magistrates' court then this number jumps dramatically to an annual average in excess of 4000 cases. By focusing only on high profile cases we are led to believe that the criminal justice system works and that when it occasionally goes wrong we have the Appeal Courts to put it right. What this does is disguise the extent of miscarriage of justice and conceals the systemic error that pervades much of the current system.

One argument might be that the cost of a conviction in the Crown Court, particularly if it leads to a custodial sentence, is higher than most sentences handed out in the magistrates' court. The argument might be that if an error occurs in the lower court then at least the punishment won't be as harsh as those in high-profile cases. Unfortunately this analysis rarely sits easily with anyone who knows what it is like to be accused of something they have not done.

The media play their part too in how miscarriage of justice is conceptualised and understood. It is sometimes argued that the language of the legal system differs with how the media portray and communicate miscarriage of justice and that this miscommunication creates problems for us all in being able to discern what it is that is actually happening in our courts. Whilst it is also the case that some investigative journalists choose to take a campaigning role in those cases where there is general disquiet with the safety of a conviction, there are many other members of the press who seem to prefer the status quo being upheld. One could easily be led to think that the media actually rejoice in conviction, not because they necessarily believe that justice has been done, but a conviction permits the press more latitude in what they are able to report following a guilty verdict, and this, of course, sells newspapers.

I attended the Miscarriages of Justice Organisation conference in April

2008 in Glasgow and spoke with some of the key figures in miscarriages discourse. The organisation was set up by Paddy Hill, one of the Birmingham Six, who was charged with murder and conspiracy to cause explosions after twenty-one people were killed following blasts at the Mulberry Bush Pub and Tavern in 1975. The Six, including Paddy, were finally released in1991 having unjustly spent sixteen years in prison.

I first met Paddy while I was serving a life sentence in Wakefield. He was visiting Michael Stone and I was with my family. Paddy walked across the visiting room to wish me well in my fight for justice. It was good to see him again in different circumstances. The organisation that he's now involved in seeks to support men and women who are suffering from post-traumatic stress following wrongful conviction. As I walked around the conference hall and chatted with journalists, legal and medical practitioners and others concerned with miscarriage of justice, the scale of the problem seemed overwhelming.

It is when you enter real life family situations that the tragedy of miscarriage of justice feels even more poignant. I was invited to attend a meeting of the campaigning group London Against Injustice recently. The group meets opposite the Court of Appeal every month to campaign for men and women who they believe have been wrongly convicted. It is truly heart-rending to hear the stories of mothers, fathers, sons and daughters campaigning for those they love.

When I was sent to Wakefield Prison I always believed that eventually my conviction would be quashed. The years inside were long and painful, as each day seemed long and tortuous. I never settled. I never experienced any respite. Each day involved a battle to stay focused, as the only waking thought of many victims of miscarriages of justice is, of course, the pursuit of justice and truth. Despite my unhappiness during the years in Wakefield I felt able to return this year to visit a prisoner I had known for five years. I first met Victor Nealon on A wing in 1999. We soon chatted with each other and it quickly became apparent that he too was fighting his conviction. Over the years, and after reading much of the legal paperwork against him, I believe that this man has been wrongly convicted.

It was a strange experience arriving at Wakefield Station and then walking to the prison. For the first time I was able to apprehend the commitment of my parents, brother and extended family who had visited every month for six years. I approached the prison gate and walked in with my visiting order. My fingerprints were checked and I was given a rub-down before progressing to the next stage. I saw a prison officer who had known me on A wing. The last time we had spoken I had been Jenkins AW4265. The language used now was different.

All the visitors went through another security door and I was asked with others to stand on some rubber mats whilst the drug dogs checked for concealed drugs. After being checked we then entered the visits room. I walked over to my designated table and sat on one of the chairs. The last time I had been in this room I had sat in the red chair, the one set aside for the prisoner. As I waited for Victor to come into the room I noticed another prison officer, who came over to chat. I had known John for two years, as he had worked in the kitchen whilst I was there. He now worked in the security department. In the time I had known him he was always a fair and just man. I respected him because he'd done his job professionally and did it with humanity and grace. After talking for ten minutes, Victor then came in and John left. I then spent just over an hour with Victor and caught up with what was happening in his life. The time went quickly and all the visitors were soon asked to say their goodbyes. The act of standing up and walking to the exit door was a strange experience. I looked back and saw Victor and other men who I'd known on the wings. Some of the men I thought were innocent. Others I knew were guilty, yet some of their faces expressed the remorse of men who knew they had made poor choices in their lives.

For the last six months Tina, Oscar and I have been living in Southsea. During my second trial at the Old Bailey we sold our home in London and moved to Lymington. We lived there for two years and enjoyed the tranquillity the house offered after my acquittal, but then we decided to move to Southsea so that I could be near the University. I'm currently working on a research proposal for a doctorate and hope to begin research later this year into a range of issues that affect women and miscarriage of justice.

As a family we love the city and think of it as our home, certainly for the foreseeable future anyway. Tina grew up in Portsmouth so it's been enjoyable listening to her stories of what the town was like in the Sixties.

My family life has been an important factor in me being able to rebuild my life. When I now go to the theatre or out for a meal I never forget my past and the love and encouragement I received whilst fighting my conviction. Tina and I will celebrate four years of marriage next year. She has become my closest friend and soul mate. She stood by me in my hour of greatest need and this has strengthened the bond between us. Even when celebrating our first wedding anniversary in February 2006, we did so whilst standing outside an Old Bailey courtroom, waiting for the jury to give their verdict. Such experiences are hard to describe and fully comprehend. To know that another human being is standing with you and that come what may, they will always be there for you, is surely one of the greatest gifts that God can give a man.

Both Tina and I have a mutual interest in fighting against injustice and in helping those caught by the system. Tina has done this for many years so my desire to challenge aspects of the criminal justice system and to help those who need and want help will be a shared goal and enterprise. But it is my desire to find Billie's killer that will be my prominent thought. To this end, I will return to Hastings and initiate those actions that I believe are necessary to apprehend the man I saw in my hall minutes after Billie's murder.

I will have other important priorities this year, too. It has been four years since I last saw and spoke with my daughters. I saw Lottie, Esther and Maya in Wakefield prison just before the CCRC released their Statement of Reasons referring my case back to the Court of Appeal. I saw Annie last on my daughters' previous visit to Wakefield. For Annie and Lottie the results of the CCRC investigation into their mother's comments to the police must have placed them in an impossible position. The dilemma they faced when confronted by the Commission's report, coupled with their parents' acrimonious divorce, must have weighed heavily upon them.

I am now in the position of not knowing where my daughters are living, other than believing that some of them are still in Tasmania. About a year ago I contacted the Salvation Army Family Tracing Service to help me make contact with them. Unfortunately hopes of finding them and resuming contact never came about. I still do not know where they are living. Throughout my years in prison and when fighting various murder trials my daughters have always been my Achilles' heel. While in prison I could face most things that were thrown at me, but the loss of my daughters would often crush me. I faced three murder trials and at one time while on bail had to deal with three police forces; this too I could cope with. The media too have played their part in causing both my family and me profound sadness. However, we coped. But nothing has been comparable to the sense of loss I've experienced from being estranged from Annie, Lottie, Esther and Maya.

For much of the time since my incarceration, including the time after my acquittal, I have been unable to talk about my feelings over their absence from my life. I have struggled to understand why and how this situation has come about and when I did think about it, inevitably I would soon close down and become introspective and unsettled. To lose one's children in such circumstances is like having part of you wrenched from your side. The seriousness of it means that for much of my waking day I think about them. I remember conversations and asides that we enjoyed together; I remember their individual dispositions and characters and am locked in to worrying about them – whether they're happy, fulfilled, safe and at peace with themselves; the feelings, in short, of any parent who is separated from their child.

I have been asked why I don't fly out to Tasmania to find them. This is something that one day, if contact does not happen in the near future, I will have to consider. The situation is, however, complex. I have wanted to give them time to heal and recover from their feelings of loss and bereavement. One day they were in a loving family and preparing to return to school after a half term holiday. The next day they'd lost their sister and a week later their father was taken from them. The situation was then to deteriorate to such an extent that I think it is a miracle that they have had the strength and fortitude to come through it. I did not willingly leave my children. I did not walk out on them, and they have always been my primary concern. I have always loved them. Our separation was not their fault or mine.

For their sakes and for mine I hope that when they feel the time is right we will come together. I simply want to be their father again and to restore the years that have been taken from us. I know that their childhoods have finished and that those years of separation cannot literally be given back. But there are other dimensions, which are more spiritual in nature, and these are forever lasting.

As I prepare for a new future I do so with Tina and with the belief that these years have a purpose. I am not seeking to forget my sadness or to pretend that Billie didn't lose her life or that I wasn't wrongly convicted for it. I have always wanted to live in the real world and that hasn't changed. But in apprehending the magnitude of personal events I also want to step out from being constrained by my past and to use whatever experiences God has handed me for the good of others.

My hopes for the future are neither sentimental nor shallow. Identifying systemic error in the criminal justice system and working with others to challenge identifiable failures has to be grounded in the realms of what is possible and practicable. As well as challenging the system there are also others who have found themselves caught in a world that they never thought possible. I have visited several prisoners fighting their convictions over the last year and this commitment to helping the wrongly convicted will, I know, become a way of life.

Epilogue

This story has involved a case that you may or may not have been familiar with. What is important – and what I would like to leave with you – is that being arrested, charged and convicted for a serious crime and then being sent to prison for it, despite being innocent of the charge, isn't something that just happens to other people. It can happen to anyone and at any time. When I speak with families going through this experience they talk of a veil being lifted; of seeing a side of life that they never believed existed. They thought that such things would never happen to them because they've always been a law-abiding family. They think, 'If we were ever arrested we'd just tell the truth and then everything would be fine. It's only the guilty that have something to be worried about, isn't it?' Unfortunately this is not always the case.

Life is often unpredictable and uncertain, yet when reviewing the efficacy of the criminal justice system, we prefer to think in terms of certainties: that the guilty are convicted and that the innocent are acquitted. We accept that mistakes might occasionally be made but that we have the Court of Appeal to correct any failures in justice. But those who have been there, who have experienced wrongful conviction, they know that success following this route is fraught with difficulties. When someone is convicted of a serious offence, despite being innocent, it is nothing short of a miracle if they persuade the Court of Appeal that their conviction is unsafe. For many who have experienced the Court of Appeal, the court appears to be no more than a body whose function is simply to uphold and rubber-stamp the decision of the first tribunal. Some would argue that justice, in this context, is more about protecting the system and those individuals who work within it, rather than correcting injustice. The unpalatable truth is that too many men and women, through no fault of their own, are serving long sentences for crimes they did not commit. They have been failed by a system they probably once believed in. It is this system we all share as fellow citizens.

Acknowledgements

Many, many people were involved in Siôn's long struggle to overturn his conviction. We further prevailed upon the generosity of most of them by asking for their assistance in the preparation of this book.

Foremost among these were Siôn's immediate family – his parents, David and Megan; his brother, David Llewellyn; and his aunts and uncles, John and Iona, and Sue and Alwyn, all of whom have, with good humour but beating hearts, unflinchingly stood by him every single day.

Double thanks are similarly due to Siôn's lawyers – both for what they did in the course of their professional duties, and for going far beyond those parameters in order to help us put this material together. The legal team was headed by Neil O'May, and thanks are due particularly to him, as well as to others at Bindman and Partners, especially including Sara Harrison, Jessica Skinns and Ezra Nathan.

Anthony Scrivener QC and John Haines began the courtroom defence all those years ago; and they continued to be committed to the case long after their professional association with it had ended.

The subsequent legal team ultimately comprised Clare Montgomery

QC, Chris Sallon QC and Julian Knowles, who all burnt every candle at every end in the pursuit of justice, and were then equally generous with their time and their insights afterwards. Special thanks are due to Julian for reading the draft manuscript so carefully and making such astute observations. All of his suggestions, we hope, have been incorporated into the final manuscript.

Some of the scientists who became involved in the case and gave much valuable time and energy towards it became so committed that they ended up as friends rather than professional experts. We would like to thank them all, but in particular Professor David Denison, for whose dedication everyone was deeply grateful, and Professor Robert Schroter, who was equally determined to see the case through to a satisfactory conclusion.

Adrienne Page QC and Adam Speker were kind enough to read the draft manuscript and make valuable comments, and so also Angela and Tim Devlin.

Of course, none of those who have read and commented upon the manuscript bear any responsibility for mistakes or oversights that remain.

Siôn is especially grateful to all those who stood unhesitatingly beside him, even in the darkest times – including Roger Mitchell and his wife Margaret.

The Canon Rev Stuart Bell and his wife Prudence were the first 'outsiders' to hear Siôn's whole story from start to finish. Ever since, their commitment to his cause has never wavered, even though they both had to endure uncomfortable moments along the way. Indeed, they also befriended and assisted many other supporters. We are both very grateful to them.

There are many others whom it would be invidious to name, including those who launched, persevered with and developed the website. They are private people, who wish to remain anonymous. But they know who they are. They have spent years working behind the scenes to fulfil the objective of seeing a terrible wrong righted, and their work has been enormously appreciated. There are many, many more, both in Hastings and throughout the country who have been similarly inspired by a sense

Acknowledgements

of grievous injustice, and have provided continuing support and encouragement to both Siôn and myself.

After the struggle to overturn the conviction, there followed – seamlessly, as it seemed to us – the struggle to get this book published, as one publisher after another exercised commercial caution and declined to risk a potentially controversial title. But when friends were really needed, friends were there; and David and Heather Godwin gave far, far more of their time, emotional energies and professional expertise than we had any right to expect. Our deepest thanks to both of them.

Finally, Siôn would like to thank Tina and Oscar for their endless support.

Notes

1   Stephen Fry – the humorist, author, actor, film director, etc. etc. – has made the same point in television interviews.

2   Not his real name.

3   From Lois Jenkins' second statement, 7 March 1997.

4   Michael Stone was subsequently convicted of the murders. A long legal process ensued: his conviction was quashed, but Stone was then re-convicted at a retrial. Nevertheless, the doubts surrounding his case are Himalayan. Siôn, who knew Stone in Wakefield prison, is among those who believe him to be innocent.

5   Not his real name.

6   This only became an issue because the *Daily Mirror* carried a front-page story headlined, Nobody told us our Billie-Jo was dead (18 February 1997), according to which Debbie Woods said that she had been left to find out for herself what had happened from the newspapers. As far as Siôn is concerned, that story was untrue.

7   Not her real name.

8   It is important to emphasise that the material about Felix Simmons is taken from police records of what Lois Jenkins and Peter Gaimster told

441

them on Wednesday 19 February. There is no independent confirmation for much of it.

9   The Criminal Cases Review Commission were later to report, regarding this second interview, that 'the style of questioning appears... to be more pressing.'

10   Former Chairman of Kwik Fit.

11   As this small episode showed, Sir Brian Smedley, who died on 6 April 2007, was one of the most independently-minded members of the judiciary. The most famous demonstration of his independence occurred with his handling of the trial of four directors of the Matrix Churchill company in 1992. They were accused of selling arms to Saddam Hussein's Iraq; their defence was that they had acted with the support of the Ministry of Defence. Mr Justice Smedley caused considerable embarrassment to John Major's government by ruling that the accused had no case to answer. See obituary, The *Times*, 10 May 2007.

12   Considering this point, the CCRC was later to say, '... the Commission does not consider that there are *significant* changes...'

13   See page 204.

14   After his release, Siôn made a formal complaint about Dr Arnon Bentovim to the General Medical Council.

15   Billie's body had not yet been discovered, so there was 'nothing' to know.

16   The judges' rules governing disclosure of evidence were superseded by the Criminal Procedure and Investigations Act from 1 April 1997.

17   See pages 107 and 406.

18   In fact, the Bentovims' report was never in evidence before the jury; however, it was, as the CCRC noted, 'extensively referred to in the trial judge's rulings and in the Court of Appeal judgment', and the police had also relied on their advice.

19   At his court appearance when he was wrongly convicted of murder in Paris in 1931, Henri Charrière, whose adventures are famously related in *Papillon* (Harper Perennial, 2005), was told, 'You're too well dressed: you ought to have come in something very modest indeed. That was a huge tactical error of yours.'

Notes

20 See pages 413-4.

21 Michael Trimble is professor of behavioural neurology at the Institute of Neurology in London.

22 A request for a pillow may suggest that a prisoner is asking to be featherbedded; but, of course, that isn't the case. If people need to sleep with their heads raised up, then depriving prisoners of pillows is only one step away from depriving them of sleep. The conditions of imprisonment could not have been more harsh than those endured by Henri Charrière (Papillon) in the French penal colonies in the 1930s, yet he too lamented being deprived of a pillow.

23 Susan May was convicted of the murder of her elderly aunt Hilda Marchbank in Royton, Greater Manchester, in May 1993. The conviction, on the basis of much-disputed scientific evidence, was highly controversial from the start. May's original solicitors were subsequently criticised for 'glaring deficiencies' in the preparation of the case for trial. Since May had cared for her aunt for some years, she seemed an unlikely suspect; a local burglar who seemed a likely suspect was himself murdered while May was still in prison. She lost her first appeal in February 1997. The CCRC then referred the case to appeal in November 1999, but the Court of Appeal rejected her case again in December 2001. May, who was released in April 2005, remains determined to prove her innocence.

24 *Anybody's Nightmare* (Taverner, 1998). Shelia Bowler was wrongly convicted of the murder of her aunt, Florence Jackson. Tim and Angela Devlin are the son and daughter-in-law of Lord Devlin, one of the outstanding judges of the second half of the twentieth century.

25 See, for example, *Hastings Observer*, 30 July 1999, 'Jenkins TV Prog Pulled'.

26 *Daily Mirror*, 22 December 1999.

27 *Sun*, 22 December 1999.

28 See page 169.

29 Historically, judges in England have regarded themselves as being so far above the fray that conflicts of interest couldn't possibly apply to them. However, they were given a huge awakening over the issue in November

1998 when a House of Lords judgment in the extradition case of General Augusto Pinochet was successfully challenged on the grounds that one of the judges had associations with Amnesty International, one of the parties to the case. At a fresh hearing before a new panel of judges, Lord Browne-Wilkinson acknowledged that the burden was on the judge to disclose the facts. 'Otherwise', he remarked, 'we're ditching the first thing I ever learned about English law – justice must not only be done but be seen to be done.'

30   Child and Family Court Advisory and Support Service.

31   The *Sun*'s story was followed up by the local press in Hastings and Brighton.

32   BBC Radio 4.

33   In 2007, leading writers voted *Lolita* the fourth greatest work of literature of all time, behind *Anna Karenina*, *Madame Bovary* and *War and Peace*; see the *Observer*, 4 March 2007.

34   In response to the policing failures of the Yorkshire Ripper investigation during the 1970s, the computerised HOLMES system (Home Office Large Major Enquiry System) was introduced in 1986 to assist police forces in the investigation of major crimes. It was replaced by the updated HOLMES2 from July 1999.

35   At a hearing before Lord Justice Kay in January 2003, Montgomery had successfully argued the appeal of Sally Clark, the commercial lawyer who was wrongly imprisoned, on the basis of flawed medical opinions, for the murders of her two small children.

36   See page 67.

37   Dr Lucey, consultant child and adolescent psychiatrist, had seen the children in February 2001.

38   The 'family friend' referred to is obviously Peter Gaimster.

39   Robert Schroter is professor of biological mechanics at Imperial College, London. Andrew Nicholson is professor of thoracic histopathology at the National Heart and Lung Institute in London; and also professor of respiratory pathology at Imperial College school of medicine, London.

Notes

40   Profile Books, 2002.

41   Ironically, Kay was replaced at the Court of Appeal by Lord Justice Gage, the judge for Siôn's first trial.

42   Stricter security measures were put into force at the Royal Courts of Justice after an incident in October 2002 when Mr Justice Pitchford was attacked by a disappointed appellant who leapt from the dock and punched him several times in the face.

43   Donald Pendleton had been questioned regarding a murder in Bradford, West Yorkshire, in 1971, but was then eliminated from inquiries. In 1985, the murder having remained unsolved, Pendleton was re-arrested, charged, convicted and sentenced to life imprisonment. He always protested his innocence. He lost an appeal and in 1999 the Criminal Cases Review Commission referred the case for a second appeal, which was also lost. His lawyers, solicitor Jim Nichol and barrister Michael Mansfield QC, then took the case to the House of Lords.

In December 2001, the law lords, headed by Lord Bingham of Cornhill, the former Lord Chief Justice, determined that, in turning down the second Pendleton appeal, the Court of Appeal had exercised its responsibilities wrongly. They quashed the conviction (and so Pendleton became the second person to be released as a result of a Lords judgment - see note 45, page 312). In giving judgment, the lords emphasised that the appeal court 'is not and should never become the primary decision-maker' and that it 'has an imperfect and incomplete understanding of the full processes which led the jury to convict'. The court was told not to substitute its own opinion for that of the jury.

In the light of that, sending cases back for retrial, a power which appeal court judges had hitherto used sparingly, became the norm rather than the exception.

44   Dr Hill himself described the loss of the blocks as 'regrettable'. He said that the blocks and the slides had been stored at St Thomas's hospital, but then were moved when the forensic medicine department was closed. He accepted that, 'Had the blocks been available, then further sections could have been cut, thus allowing further sampling of the lungs.'

45   In 1996, Bob Woffinden took the case of Phillip English to Bindman's. With Christopher Sallon QC and Julian Knowles as the barristers, the case went to the House of Lords where it achieved, in terms of legal significance, a double first: English was acquitted of the murder of a policeman in Gateshead, thus becoming the first person to be released from prison directly as a result of a Lords judgment; and the law of joint enterprise in murder cases was re-defined.

46   William Travis is thoracic pathologist in the pathology department of the Memorial Sloan Kettering cancer centre in New York, and professor of pathology at Weill Cornell medical college, also in New York. His expertise is regularly called upon by the World Health Organisation. Alan Aitkenhead is professor of anaesthesia at Nottingham University.

47   Peter Morgan is professor of oral pathology at King's College, London and consultant in oral medicine and pathology at Guy's and St Thomas's hospitals, London.

48   Laurence Watkins is consultant neurosurgeon at the National Hospital for Neurology, London.

49   Schroter is professor of biological mechanics at Imperial College, London. Hunt is professor of climate modelling at University College, London. In May 2000, he was created Lord Hunt of Chesterton.

50   Milroy is professor of forensic pathology at Sheffield University; Whitwell is professor of forensic pathology at Birmingham University; and Crane is professor of forensic medicine at Queen's University, Belfast and the state pathologist for Northern Ireland.

51   For an analysis of Lois's evidence, see Chapter 48.

52   These comments were actually made by Hill at the third trial.

53   See page 67.

54   Here are four examples of multiple trials on the same charge:

(1) In July 1923 Henry Griffin was tried at the Old Bailey for the murder of Ada Kerr in Twickenham, south-west London. The jury were unable to agree and were discharged. A second jury was also unable to agree. With the prosecution considering whether to press ahead with a third trial, Griffin died of a heart attack in Brixton prison.

Notes

(2) In March 1963, Robert Reid was tried, again at the Old Bailey, for the murder of Annie O'Donnell, a bookseller in Clerkenwell. The jury could not agree and he was re-tried. The second trial, like the first, lasted a week, and again the jury could not agree. Two days later, he was put on trial for a third time, but this time the prosecution offered no evidence and he was acquitted.

(3) In May 1974, at Birmingham crown court, Donat Gomez, a thirty-three-year-old Jamaican man, was acquitted of the murder of the prostitute Mary Armstrong in Stoke on Trent. Remarkably, Gomez, who was convicted of grievous bodily harm and living off immoral earnings, had faced four trials (the earlier ones having been held at Stafford crown court) – although the total period he was on trial was only sixty-three days.

(4) At the Old Bailey, in September 2006, Dwayne Vincent, leader of the garage music artists' collective So Solid Crew, was acquitted of the murder of Colin Scarlett after three trials. However, the second trial had not gone the distance as it was stopped after a prosecution witness retracted his evidence. Bindman's were also the solicitors in that case.

55   For an analysis of this area of evidence, see page 409.

56   Majority verdicts of 10-2 were allowed after the 1967 Criminal Justice Act; the Watson direction was first used in 1988.

57   In fact, there doesn't seem any consistency among judges about the approach to be used. Mrs Justice Rafferty had said virtually the opposite to the jury at the second trial (albeit, again, in a kind of legal code). When giving the majority direction to the jurors, she said firmly, 'Do not be tempted to compromise your conscience'.

58   See the *Daily Mail*, 10 February 2006: 'Incredibly the fracas was initially broken up not by police or security guards but by Ezra Nathan, a slightly-built grey-haired adviser from Bindman's solicitors. Moments later Sussex police officers involved in the case ran over to intervene'. The report was written by Paul Harris, who was a witness.

59   Thomas Carlyle, *On Heroes and Hero Worship* (1841). A century earlier, Henry Fielding, the Bow Street magistrate and author of *Tom Jones*, had

depicted the first three estates as the Monarchy and the two Houses of Parliament – the Lords and the Commons.

60   Behaviour such as this exposes the hollowness of media claims to want to televise trials in the public interest. Actually, the media have no interest whatever in informing the public about criminal law issues or in examining the finer points of the trial process; all they are interested in are the commercial possibilities of being able to televise high-profile criminal trials – as, among others, Louise Woodward, herself the victim of a televised criminal trial, has pointed out (see the *Guardian*, 27 November 2006).

61   See pages 361-2.

62   *Sunday Times*, 9 February 2003.

63   See pages 282-5.

64   *Sunday Times*, 9 February 2003.

65   See Chapter 14.

66   See page 362.

67   See, for example, Julian Barnes, *Arthur & George*, about the 1907 case of George Edalji and the subsequent campaign of Sir Arthur Conan Doyle to establish his innocence:

> Litchfield Meek [defence solicitor] gave George [Edalji] a worldly smile. 'In my years in the courts, Mr Edalji, I've seen bricks made from all sorts of materials. Some you didn't even know existed. Lack of straw will be no hardship to Mr Disturnal [Crown prosecutor]'.
>   Having been convicted, Edalji reflected: 'Yes, Mr Meek had been correct about the fellow's skill at making bricks despite the unavailability of straw.' (Jonathan Cape, 2005).

68   See 'Billie-Jo expert "grossly misled" murder trial', The *Times*, 10 July 2004.

Index

(The initials BJJ, LJ, SJ and TJ refer to Billie-Jo Jenkins, Lois Jenkins,
Siôn Jenkins and Tina Jenkins, respectively)

Index

Index

Index

Index